Small Business Management

An Active-Learning Approach

D.R. Stokes

*David Stokes is a Senior Lecturer in the Business School at
South Bank University. Educated at Oriel College, Oxford and
the City University Business School, his career in management
has involved both larger and smaller businesses.*

DP Publications Ltd
Aldine Place
LONDON W12 8AW
1992

Acknowledgements

This book is dedicated with all my love to my 'innovators',
Charles and Florence Stokes.

*A CIP catalogue record for this book is available from the
British Library*

ISBN 1 873981 12 0
Copyright D.R. Stokes © 1992

First edition 1992

Typeset by
    DP Publications Ltd

Printed in Great Britain by
    Ashford Colour Press, Gosport, Hants

Preface

Purpose of this book

The principal aim of this book is to provide a course of study in the management of the small enterprise, or business.

It is intended to be used in the classroom on a variety of business and management courses at undergraduate, and post graduate level. It can also be used by those who wish to study the subject on their own. The material in the book has been developed from the teaching of, and feedback from, small business components in HND, BA (Business Studies), Certificate in Management, Diploma in Management Studies, and MBA courses, as well as workshops for intending or practising small business managers.

Need

This book aims to fill a gap. There are many publications targeted at would-be entrepreneurs and existing small business owners, which give general and detailed advice on how to set up and run a small enterprise. There are also many articles and books of a more academic nature which survey the small business scene, investigating crucial topics such as the role of the small business in the economy and society, or detailing the common experiences of small businesses in a wide variety of management contexts and situations.

This book is intended to give the student one main source of reference on small business management. Firstly, it aims to help the student understand more about the specific management issues involved in setting up and running a small enterprise. Secondly, it aims to provide the student with a summary of some of the research studies and debate on the small business sector, in order to develop an individual perspective in a wider context.

Approach

The book is structured around an active learning approach. Although a considerable amount of information is given in the book, the aim is to impart skills and knowledge by engaging the reader in interesting tasks and activities which build on existing understanding.

There are three main sections:

Section I: Activities and scenarios

This section is designed so that the reader can develop what they already know through activities of several types:

Quick answer questions: These are intended to provoke thoughts around the subject matter without further reference to other text as answers are suggested in each unit.

Scenarios: A specific small enterprise situation is described, and issues and problems specified as tasks for the reader to undertake. (Guidance is given to the lecturer in the lecturer's supplement where activities may also be suitable for group work.) References are given to Section III, the Information Bank, to help students where they need it. However, students with some knowledge and experience of the subject under discussion can attempt the tasks without reading through sections they already understand.

Extended tasks: An activity is suggested at the end of each Unit which is designed to develop understanding of the subject of the Unit through observation of small enterprises in action.

Section I is divided into 15 Units, which link directly to tasks in Section II, the Ongoing Assignments and the 15 Units in Section III, the Information Bank, which has more detailed information around each topic covered.

Section II: Ongoing assignments

To build on understandings developed in Section I, there are ongoing assignments which the student is asked to undertake unsupervised. This can form the basis of assessed work if required. The ongoing assignment is based around the choice of an enterprise or business idea by the student, and the development of that idea in three main assignments.

Assignment 1: The feasibility study

This is divided into a series of sequential tasks in which the student chooses and evaluates an area of opportunity to a preliminary level which indicates the likelihood of success or failure.

Assignment 2: The route to market entry

The student is asked to evaluate the alternative methods for developing their selected opportunity. This involves looking at franchising, buying existing businesses, as well as starting up from scratch. The alternative legal forms are also considered.

Assignment 3: The business plan

The student is asked to complete the detailed planning for their idea as a business plan. A suggested format and stages are identified to help the reader draw up this important document.

Section III: The information bank

This section gives the reader necessary information to understand the relevance of the small business sector in a wider economic and social context, and the management aspects which particularly affect the success or failure of a small enterprise. It is sub-divided into 15 Units which link directly to the 15 Units in Section 1, and also relate to specific tasks in the *Ongoing assignments* (see Overview of Layout below).

Lecturer's supplement

A guide based on the experiences of using this material in the classroom is available *free of charge* for lecturers adopting the book as a course text.

How to use this book

This book can be used as a work book in the classroom, as a guide for less supervised study, or a mixture of both.

However used, the first two sections of Activities and Scenarios, and Ongoing Assignments, are the basis for the learning process. The student should work through these in the order indicated, with support where necessary from the Information Bank and other recommended works of reference.

Overview of layout

1. The feasibility study

Unit no	Section I Activities and scenarios		Section II Ongoing assignments		Section III Information bank
1	Small business and the national economy	1.1	Know thyself	1	Small business and the national economy
2	The entrepreneur and the owner-manager	1.2	Identifying the opportunity area	2	The entrepreneur and the owner-manager
3	Small business and innovation	1.3	Selecting the idea	3	Small business and innovation
4	The customer	1.4	Knowing the customer	4	The customer
5	Market research	1.5	Researching the idea	5	Market research
6	The small business environment	1.6	Assessing the risk	6	The small business environment
		1.7	Summary of the feasibility study		

2. The route to market entry

	Section I		Section II		Section III
7	Routes to market entry	2.1	Choosing the method	7	Routes to market entry
8	Franchising	2.2	Looking at franchising	8	Franchising
9	Buying an existing business	2.3	Buying an existing business	9	Buying an existing business
10	Forms of small business organisation	2.4	Selecting the appropriate form	10	Forms of small business organisation
		2.5	Summary of the route to market entry		

3. The business plan

	Section I		Section II		Section III
11	The business plan	3.1	Outlining the plan	11	The business plan
12	Successful and unsuccessful small business strategies	3.2	Deciding the strategy	12	Successful and unsuccessful small business strategies
13	Management of resources	3.3	Managing the resources	13	Management of resources
14	Marketing	3.4	Planning the marketing	14	Marketing
15	Money	3.5	Forecasting the money	15	Money
		3.6	Summary of the business plan		

Contents

Section II: The ongoing assignments

Section III: The information bank

Section I

ACTIVITIES AND SCENARIOS

How to use this section

1. This section is organised into 15 units, which are best worked through in sequence. Each unit contains Quick Answer Questions, Scenarios, Tasks and an Extended Task.

2. *Quick Answer Questions* are designed to stimulate your thoughts and experiences of the topic under discussion. Understanding and retention of information is more likely if it is related to what you already know and have experience of, so it is important to attempt to answer these questions. As you are working through the text have pen and paper to hand and formulate your answers, before reading on.

   Answers, or suggested responses, to the Quick Answer Questions are to be found nearby in the text, indicated by headings which correspond to those of the Quick Answer Questions.

3. *Scenarios* are used to describe a situation illustrating some of the topic areas under consideration. Whilst they are fictional situations, and fictional characters, they are drawn from real-life examples of small business and enterprises.

4. A number of *Tasks* are listed at the end of each scenario. Attempt each task in order, referring where necessary to the relevant part of the Information Bank which is signposted in the Tasks.

5. At the end of each Unit in Section I there is an *Extended Task.* This is a general activity, designed to provide more understanding of the subject of the Unit through observation of small enterprises in action. The Extended Task should not be attempted until the reader is familiar with all the contents of the corresponding Unit of the Information Bank. Where the reader is undertaking the Ongoing Assignments relevant to each Unit it may not be necessary to undertake every Extended Task.

6. The corresponding Unit of *Section III, The Information Bank* should be read completely before moving on to the next Unit. At the end of each Unit, it is important to consolidate the learning of the Unit by tackling the relevant task of the *Ongoing Assignment.*

Unit 1: Small business and the national economy

This unit looks at the place of the small business in the national economy, attempting to define its scope and importance in the health of the nation.

The small business revival

There has been a resurgence of interest in the small business as an important factor in the national economy.

Quick answer question: What is a small business?

How would you define a small business? Attempt to write your own definition of a small business, compared to a medium sized or large one.

Until the 1970s there was a widespread belief that business would become increasingly concentrated in large units. It was thought that economic growth depended on mass production techniques. The economies of scale created by new technologies and global marketing would inevitably confine small firms to a peripheral role in support of larger units. Business research and education overlooked small business management which was regarded in an inferior light.

Today there is great interest in the fortunes of the small business sector with all party support for policies promoting the growth of small enterprises, in recognition of their importance to the health of the economy.

What is a small business?

The 1971 Bolton Report (the report of the "Committee of Inquiry on Small Firms") defined a small business by three essential characteristics:

1. Personalised management by its owner
2. Small share of its market
3. Independent ownership

It also used some specific measures depending on the industry, such as:

☐ Manufacturing: 200 employees or less

☐ Retailing and miscellaneous services: £50,000 turnover per annum or less (£500,000 at today's prices)

It is generally accepted that there is no uniform 'small firm sector' designated by some simple size criteria. Small enterprises are involved in such a huge range of activities, in widely differing environments that they do not lend themselves to generalised descriptions and suppositions.

Quick answer question: Why are small businesses important to the economy?

What contributions to the health of the economy do small businesses make? Write down as many factors as you can think of.

The Bolton Report represented a turning point in perceptions of the small business. The committee thought that the small business sector would inevitably decline further and that it needed deliberate support. Its principle recommendation, that a Small Firms Division should be established under a Minister for Small Firms, was implemented.

Why are small businesses important to the economy?

The Bolton Report advocated support for the small business sector on the grounds that small firms have several special contributions to make as:

❏ an outlet for enterprising individuals who would not necessarily flourish in larger environments;

❏ the most efficient size of unit in some markets;

❏ specialist suppliers, or sub-contractors to larger companies;

❏ suppliers to specialised markets, too small for larger companies;

❏ competition to prevent monopolies;

❏ innovators of products and services;

❏ a breeding ground for new industries;

❏ the 'seedbed' for tomorrow's large companies and their leaders.

Quick answer question: Inevitable decline?

Do you agree with Bolton's view that the small business sector is subject to long term decline?

A striking feature of the statistics produced at the time of the Bolton Report (1971) was that the decline of the small business sector had gone further in the UK than in other developed nations. Britain's industry was, and still is, more concentrated than in the USA, Japan and Germany, which begged the question: why wasn't the UK economy doing better if convergence of industrial resources was the way forward?

Inevitable decline?

The small business sector has shown a remarkable revival. It has grown more numerous, employing more people and responsible for more output in the developed world since the mid 1970s. In the UK the number of firms employing under 200 people grew from 1.8 million in 1979 to 2.5 million by 1986, providing over half of all private sector employment. The total number of self-employed people has also risen rapidly from 1.9 million in 1979 to 3.4 million by 1990.

Scenario: Andrea goes green

Andrea had made up her mind to leave the large company where she worked. She had been unhappy there for some time, disliking its impersonal, bureaucratic methods. When she had started in the accounts department, five years before, she had been impressed by the efficiency of its production techniques and encouraged by its profitability. Now she despised its lack of concern for the environment in favour of short term gain.

She had been approached by a friend to set up a health food shop, and had readily agreed. She wasn't quite so enthusiastic about breaking the news to her husband John, however, as she would be exchanging the security of employment for the risky world of small business.

"Just tell him that 'small is beautiful'," encouraged her friend. "It's more important to contribute to a healthier, more natural world than earning money that you'll just waste on trashy consumer goods."

To Andrea's surprise, she did not need to use these arguments on her husband. When she discussed the idea with him he was supportive of it immediately.

"It's about time you got out of the rut you're in at work. If I can get a big enough redundancy package I'll join you myself. It's about time these big companies had a spot of competition. Entrepreneurs who can put new ideas into action and create jobs are what's needed now. Not those dinosaurs of nationalised industries and multinational corporations," John said.

"Well that's not quite why I want to do it," Andrea had started to explain when her father came in to see them.

After Andrea explained her idea to him, he took a less sympathetic line. "It's out of the frying pan into the fire. You'll end up working for big business whether you like it or not. Who do you think is going to supply your stock? Large companies of course. They still control everything, small business or not. The only difference working in a small firm is that you'll get paid less for it, and have to work harder. No unions; no negotiating power if your suppliers want to put up their prices. Big business will have you where they want you."

Andrea had not realised that small business could lead to such big issues.

Tasks

1. *Who do you think is right?*

   a) *Andrea and her friend, believing that running a small business will be 'beautiful' in the sense of promoting the quality of life?*

   b) *John for putting his faith in entrepreneurs to reform the economy?*

   c) *Dad who believes that big business will still call the shots?*

   Comment on the merits and misconceptions of each of their views.

> See the information bank in **Section III: Unit 1, 3.1,** page 164.

2. *Why do you think small business has revived, reversing its previous decline and tempting people like Andrea to set up their own business? Try to give some reasons why small may be a more 'beautiful' form of business organisation in today's environment.*

> See the information bank in **Section III: Unit 1, 3.2,** page 166.

In conclusion

Now complete your reading of the Information Bank, Unit 1, 'Small Business and the National Economy'.

When you have done this you are ready to tackle the Ongoing Assignment 1, Task 1.1, 'Know Thyself', and/or the Extended Task below.

Extended task: Food and drink

Consider the local community with which you are most familiar. Draw up a list of the types of businesses which provide food and drink to this community. This should include food and drink taken away to be consumed in the home or elsewhere, as well as food and drink consumed on the premises. For example, your list should include such categories as supermarkets, fast food restaurants, off-licences, and other business types.

In each of the categories you have listed, write down some of the businesses actually operating in this category.

Now try to divide them into 'small' or 'large' enterprises (you may also need a 'medium-sized' category).

This data can be used in subsequent Extended Tasks, so try to include as many local businesses as possible. Now try to answer the following questions:

1. In each of your categories, which is the predominant business size – small or large? What are the trends in terms of size – towards smaller or larger enterprises?

2. What are the particular contributions which those small businesses make to the local economy? Are these contributions increasing or decreasing in importance in your experience?

Unit 2: The entrepreneur and the owner-manager

This Unit considers the differences between an 'entrepreneur' and an 'owner-manager' of a small business. It looks at their characteristics, backgrounds and motivations for starting a small business.

Quick answer questions: Entrepreneur or owner-manager?

What do you think are the meanings of the terms 'entrepreneur' and 'owner-manager'? What do you consider the similarities and differences between the terms are in practice in small business?

There is great diversity among those involved in small enterprises, just as there is diversity among the types of small businesses. The term 'entrepreneur' is often used to describe anyone involved in managing a small business.

Entrepreneur or owner-manager?

'Entrepreneurs' take existing resources and redeploy them, often in a creative way, to give them greater economic value. This original meaning of the word implies that they are agents of change, innovators of new products, methods, or markets. They are less concerned with managing what exists in the most efficient manner, and more involved in looking for and exploiting new opportunities. They can work in small and large companies.

'Owner-managers' may or may not be entrepreneurs. They own and manage a small enterprise, in a way which fits with their personal motivations. They may therefore be opportunist, entrepreneurial-type owners, or they may be conservative, artisan-type managers more intent on survival than seeking innovative change and growth.

Quick answer question: Entrepreneurial traits

What personality traits do you think are most likely to be found in the successful entrepreneur?

There are many different types of entrepreneurs and owner-managers, from the 'soloist' who prefers to go it alone, to the 'grouper' or team builder who thrives on shared decision making; from the 'high-tech' engineer to the 'alternative life-style' craftsman.

Entrepreneurial traits

The successful entrepreneur can have a number of traits which single them out:

☐ *Need for achievement:* their social backgrounds may give them an overriding need to achieve. This can come from childhood deprivations, or competitive urges born of self-confidence.

☐ *Self-determination:* they probably have great faith in their ability to control their personal environment, rejecting too high an influence of chance or fate.

☐ *Desire for independence:* they wish for autonomy believing that independence of action is the only sure way to get what they need.

☐ *Innovation:* they constantly seek opportunities to be innovative in meeting market demands.

Whilst entrepreneurs may share some of these characteristics, no one single trait can be said to be the secret of entrepreneurial success.

Quick answer question: Motivations

Think of some situations in which people consider setting up their own business. What are their main motivations?

The diversity of types of entrepreneurs and owner-managers means that their personalities and backgrounds will differ widely. There will be many exceptions that break any suggested 'rules' of entrepreneurial types.

This is in part dictated by the different reasons for setting up in business in the first place.

Motivations

Some people *'pull'* themselves in small enterprises, others are *'pushed'*. Some common motives in both cases include:

'Pull' influences:

☐ desire for independence;

☐ desire to exploit an opportunity;

☐ turning a hobby or previous work experience into a business;

☐ financial incentive.

'Push' influences:

☐ redundancy;

☐ unemployment (or threat of);

☐ disagreement with previous employer

Scenario: Peter, Paul and Mary prepare to take the plunge

PETER BLAIR works for a large engineering company as a Senior Buyer. Since leaving school ten years ago with very few qualifications, he has been employed by the same company, working his way up from the shop floor to production management. He is now responsible for purchasing for several production units, handling a total budget of several million pounds. The schedules are tight and he is renowned for keeping to them.

He has become increasingly bored and restless in his company, frustrated by what he considers to be an over bureaucratic approach to business. No-one listens to the new ideas he puts forward, he claims. He feels he needs a change.

Now he is seriously considering leaving his job, and setting up on his own. His company is operating a voluntary redundancy scheme, which would give him the equivalent of about one year's pay.

PAUL BARLEY teaches mathematics at a large comprehensive school. Although he found education a rewarding career for many years, he now feels hemmed in by the routines and policies of a large institution. He wants more control over his own destiny in an environment where extra effort is directly rewarded.

Paul enjoys the challenge of analytical problem solving, an ability he employs to the full when he regularly plays chess for a local club. He believes he has discovered a market opportunity related to this hobby and has already begun to investigate it.

Well educated to degree level, he has had no real commercial experience or training and he is therefore hesitant to change career in his early 40s. He has very little capital to invest, although his wife has offered to support them in the first year or so by working full time.

MARY BARTLETT is a housewife with two children in primary school. After gaining a diploma at Art College she worked for a while for a graphic art publisher; she found the most enjoyable aspect of her work there was working with a project team to meet defined objectives. She stopped work to raise her family, but now her children have started school she is looking for a stimulating job, that will permit flexible working hours.

She has always thrived on having plenty to do and values her independence very highly. Mary feels her best option is to become self-employed, starting a business which will allow her to work the hours that suit her whilst providing her with a real challenge. She is looking for an opportunity which she considers will fit her art background and experience.

Tasks

1. *Summarise the strengths and weaknesses of Peter, Paul and Mary, in relation to their desire to become entrepreneurs, running their own business.*

HELP **?** See the information bank in *Section III: Unit 2, 3.1–6.1,* pages 177–182.

2. *What would you suggest that Peter, Paul and Mary do next?*

HELP **?** See the information bank in *Section III: Unit 2, 6.1–6.2,* pages 181–182.

In conclusion

Now complete your reading of the Information Bank, Unit 2, 'The Entrepreneur and the Owner-Manager'.

When you have done this you are ready to tackle the Ongoing Assignment 1, Task 1.2, 'Identifying the Opportunity Area', and/or the Extended Task below.

Extended task: Local entrepreneurs and owner-managers

Consider some small businesses with which you are familiar, and their owners and managers. (If you completed the Extended Task in Unit 1 you can use the list of small businesses you drew up for that.)

1. *Which do you consider to be 'entrepreneurial'? What sets them apart from other small businesses in respect to their entrepreneurship?*

2. *Considering the owners, can you list their ages, gender, marital status, social backgrounds, likely education and ethnicity? How do these compare to the information given in Section III, Unit 2, 5. 'Owner-manager backgrounds'?*

3. *What do you consider were the main influences which 'pushed' or 'pulled' these owners to set up their own business?*

To answer these questions in detail it is preferable to interview some owner-managers. Where this is not possible, observation and previous knowledge can reveal a considerable amount of information.

Unit 3: Small business and innovation

In a competitive environment, innovation is a key activity in both small and large organisations. This Unit explores the strengths and weaknesses of small firms in the context of innovation. It also considers some likely sources for innovative opportunities.

Quick answer question: Small versus large

What advantages and disadvantages do small firms have compared to large firms when it comes to innovating new products, services or processes?

Small firms are often considered as more innovative than larger companies. Large firms have recognised this notion to some extent by decentralising their activities, particularly those involved in creative work.

Small versus large

In fact there are advantages and disadvantages for both small and large firms undertaking innovative activities.

Small firms tend to have the *advantages* of:

❑ entrepreneurial, opportunistic management;

❑ fast internal communications able to react quickly to new problems or opportunities; and

❑ closeness to the market place to understand needs.

But they have the *disadvantages* of:

❑ insufficient resources to finance high costs of R&D and growth if ideas are successful;

❑ low resources of technical personnel;

❑ management problems in coping with complex issues, patent protection and legislative requirements.

Large firms have the *advantages* of:

☐ financial resources to cope with high fixed costs of research and development;

☐ the marketing and financial muscle to take advantage of high growth opportunities; and

☐ the management to administer and control legal requirements and complicated issues.

However they can have the *disadvantages* of:

☐ inflexible, bureaucratic structures;

☐ risk-averse management; and

☐ remoteness from the market place which causes opportunity areas to be overlooked.

Q Quick answer question: Innovative entrepreneurs

Can you name some innovators? Write down some entrepreneurs who have been noted for their innovative abilities.

One reason why small firms are linked so closely to innovation, is the role played by a few key entrepreneurial individuals. Some creative talents do not fit into larger organisations and need the independence of a smaller unit to fully develop.

Innovative entrepreneurs

Some examples of innovators who have only thrived by setting up their own business include:

☐ Clive Sinclair, who developed electronic goods such as calculators, digital watches and home computers for mass consumption.

☐ Anita Roddick, founder of the Body Shop, one of the UK's most successful franchise chains with over 600 outlets world wide.

☐ Stephen Jobs, and Stephen Wozniak, who began making Apple computers in their garage when larger organisations turned down their idea.

> ### Quick answer questions: What is an innovation?
>
> *Consider the following business concepts:*
>
> | | | |
> |---|---|---|
> | McDonalds | The Body Shop | Laura Ashley |
> | Amstrad | 1st Direct (banking services) | Disneyland |
>
> 1. *In what ways were they innovative? Specify for each one what differentiates them from other businesses.*
>
> 2. *Give some other examples of business innovation, identifying what sets them apart.*

Many successes have been born of relatively small changes to existing products or services, or they have drawn together existing, but hitherto unrelated practices. Innovation is more than invention in that it puts good ideas into practice. It is not confined to new products or services; it can relate to new markets, marketing methods and ways of doing things. Nor do innovations have to be that original – they are rarely the result of one-off inspiration.

> ### What is an innovation?
>
> *The following business concepts have achieved world wide success through innovations which rely heavily on developments which preceded them. They have succeeded by recognising trends and by using existing knowledge to exploit them.*
>
> **McDonalds:** *Standardisation of speed of service and quality of product (beefburgers existed well before McDonalds believe it or not!)*
>
> **The Body Shop:** *Environmentally-friendly beauty products, originating from 'native' recipes.*
>
> **Laura Ashley:** *Turned the clock back, recreating fabric and clothing styles reminiscent of English country life in Victorian times.*
>
> **Amstrad:** *Packaging of technology goods to meet consumer preferences – usually developed and manufactured by subcontractors.*
>
> **1st Direct:** *Banking services by direct mail or telephone, eliminating the need for a High street presence.*
>
> **Disneyland:** *A fun fair taken to extravagant lengths and scale.*

Scenario: Sheila and Richard discuss the first 12 months

Sheila met Richard, an old friend, for lunch. They had plenty to talk about as both had set up in business by themselves recently. Sheila had opened an aerobics dance school and Richard an American-style restaurant.

"So how have you managed in your first year?" Richard asked.

"I can't say it's been easy, but then I didn't really expect it to be," replied Sheila. "But I have found it much more competitive than I imagined. As you know I've been doing aerobics to keep fit for years, but I had no idea how many people were involved in it as a business. I have struggled to break into the regular keep fit market in any big way. However I have found my classes for Mums who have just had a baby, and want to get back into shape, very popular. Also I run some sessions for the over 60s who don't want to come and compete with 20 year olds in leotards, but who are increasingly interested in keeping fit. How about your restaurant – it's been open for about 12 months now as well hasn't it?"

"Yes, although it seems like 12 years," laughed Richard. "Having worked for an American chain for several years, I thought I knew all there was to know about restaurants like mine. But I've found that I need to adapt to local circumstances. I have to admit when I opened my restaurant I virtually copied the company I worked for – style, menu everything. Why change a winning formula? There was nothing like it around here, and the chain told me that this area was not a target for development by them. So I thought I would try it myself – a proven concept in a new area. Worked brilliantly for the first six months – very popular all the time, especially with younger people. Then summer came, and a lot of my regulars went on holiday, or just needed a rest from us I suppose – they'd been in so many times!"

"It's the problem of operating in a town this size," Sheila interrupted. "There just aren't enough young people to go round – that's why I've had to branch out. Now I'm even taking my services to the business park, and running sessions for managers in their lunch hour – it's easier than getting them out in the evening, and a lot of them don't live around here anyway."

"Yes, you're right," said Richard, "there aren't enough young people – which is why my previous employers were only interested in opening up in cities, not towns this size. So I'm having to adapt their formula to appeal to a wider audience. I'm running a special promotion for families with younger children during the holidays – seems to be very popular with mums, tearing their hair out with children at home all day, who want a break from cooking. For the same reason I've also started a take-away service."

"I wonder if we'll survive to talk about it in another years time" smiled Sheila.

Tasks

1. *In what ways have Sheila and Richard been imitative in just following existing methods? In what ways have they been innovative?*

See the information bank in **Section III: Unit 3, 3.1– 3.4,** pages 191–193.

2. *Innovation can take place not only in the origination of a product or service, but also in new markets, to which it is made available, or new ways in which it is distributed to customers. How would you classify the types of innovation developed by Sheila and Richard?*

See the information bank in **Section III: Unit 3, 3.2,** page 191.

3. *Can you think, from your own experience, of other ways in which their services could be innovative?*

See the information bank in **Section III: Unit 3, 4.,** pages 193–197.

In conclusion

Now complete your reading of the Information Bank, Unit 3, 'Small Business and Innovation'.

When you have done this you are ready to tackle the Ongoing Assignment 1, Task 1.3, 'Selecting the Idea', and/or the Extended Task below.

Extended task: Innovation and local business

Consider the list of local businesses you drew up for the Extended Task in Unit 1. (If you did not complete this task draw up a list of businesses, large and small, involved in the food and drink industry which operate in a local community with which you are familiar).

1. Which ones do you consider to have been innovative, and in what way(s)?

2. Is there a noticeable correlation between the likelihood of innovation and the size of the business in the sample you have considered?

3. Consider the changing age profile of the UK population. (For example, the numbers of young people are declining; in 1987 there were 3.8 million 15–19 year olds, compared to 3.2 million by 1991. The numbers of older people are increasing. By 2030, deaths are expected to exceed births, and the population will actually shrink. By then, there will be a projected 3.4 million people over 80, 60% more than in 1992.) What innovative opportunities for the food and drink industry of your local area could come from such changes? Looking at one of the small businesses in particular, how can it exploit these changes to its advantage?

Unit 4: The customer

This Unit focuses on the market place in which a small firm operates and, more particularly, the customers that it seeks to serve. Every business, large or small needs customers if it is to survive. Many enterprises, which may not at first sight seem like a business, also need customers.

Quick answer question: Who will be my customers?

Consider the following enterprises. Identify the most likely customers for their products or services. Be as specific as you can about which customers the enterprise will depend on most.

1. *A jeans boutique*
2. *A furniture restorer*
3. *A local firm of accountants*
4. *An instant printer*
5. *A real ale brewery*
6. *A copying equipment dealer*
7. *A health studio*
8. *A library*
9. *A secondary school*
10. *A refuse collection service*

The marketing philosophy of putting the needs of customers at the centre of business operations seems only common-sense. Certainly it is not a new concept; its origins are as old as commerce itself. In practice however customers are not always easy to identify.

Who will be my customers?

1. *15–25 year olds, male and female in catchment area of shops*

2. *Hotels, restaurants or private householders in limited geographic area*

3. *Small business in local area*

4. *Small business, clubs and societies, in local area*

5. *Free houses, public houses and bars*

6. *Offices, in their area*

7. *25–40 year olds, upper socio-economic groups largely female*

8. *Local residents, heavy users under 20 and over 60 years old*

9. *Parents of children between 11–16 years old in catchment area and the children themselves*

10. *Local residents*

Customers may not be the ultimate users of a product. A small firm often markets its products or services through a chain of distribution which keeps the producer removed from the consumer.

The limited resources of a small enterprise make it particularly important to identify target customers precisely. To meet customer requirements more closely than competitors, a small business needs to concentrate those resources on specific targeted groups – to use the rifle rather than the blunderbus.

Quick answer questions: Customer focus

How can a business grow away from its customers and lose touch with them?

What advantages and disadvantages do small businesses have in staying close to their customers?

Specific groups of customers are often referred to as 'segments'; segments can be further sub-divided into specialised groups or 'niches'. The more precisely a customer grouping is defined, the more precise the definition of their requirements can be.

Customer focus

Businesses grow away from their customers in a number of ways:

☐ As firms get bigger, and require more levels of management, the key decision makers can become remote and out-of-touch with customers. This is often where small business scores over larger companies.

☐ Business has become very complex with a variety of forces such as banks, suppliers, employees, competition, legislation and other partners demanding attention, as well as customers. The owner-manager of a small firm can be at a disadvantage as, in trying to cope with all these forces, they sometimes take their eye off the most important influence of all – the customer.

☐ Management of growing firms requires efficiency, which usually comes from policies and rules. As companies grow the need for systems increase which can limit their flexibility in dealing with customers.

☐ Technology often makes possible new products for which there is no real lasting demand. Small as well as large companies have fallen into this trap.

Scenario 1: Bryony Hannam's picture framing idea

Bryony Hannam decided she was particularly suited to a picture framing business, and she was sure there was a need for the service in her home town. There were other picture framers but Bryony reckoned they fell into one of three categories:

a) small back street traders, often working part time with long delivery times and poor choice of framing materials, although usually inexpensive;

b) art galleries offering a framing service. She was personally intimidated by the rarefied atmosphere of these, and she knew others who were similarly put off. They also offered limited choice and long delivery times as they normally sub-contracted the work to other framers.

c) high street poster shops, which targeted a young market primarily interested in posters. Although they offered other types of framing, their main business was the ready made, clip frame.

Bryony was convinced there was a need for a different type of framer – one who focused on the home owner. She felt they wanted good quality framing which would coordinate with their interior decor. They also wanted convenience, in terms of where to shop, and a quick delivery time, with friendly helpful service from staff who related to their needs. She planned to set up in a position near to the main shopping centre, serving the local community. She also felt a location near to car parking was important as framed pictures were often bulky and awkward to carry any distance.

Tasks

1. *Who will be Bryony's customers? Identify clearly the niche she sees in the market place.*

HELP **?** | See the information bank in *Section III: Unit 4, 2.1– 2.4,* pages 202–203.

2. *Why does she think they will buy from her? What are the benefits she plans to offer her target market?*

HELP **?** | See the information bank in *Section III: Unit 4, 3.1– 3.5,* pages 204–206.

Q

Quick answer question: The competitive edge

The benefits offered by a small firm can be summarised as its 'competitive edge'. To truly represent a competitive advantage these benefits need two main characteristics. What are they?

Small firms usually operate in a very competitive world. Some are so specialised that they have no direct competition. But for highly specialised firms, substitutes can often be just around the corner. A restaurant offering an unusual oriental cuisine may have no direct competition, but alternative ways of eating out, or of spending disposable income on other leisure activities, form the real competition.

The competitive edge

The competitive edge of a small business answers the question: "What benefit(s) do I offer this group of customers that will influence them to buy from me rather than anyone else?"

The two key characteristics of these benefits are that:

☐ the benefits are relevant and important to the target customer group; and

☐ the benefits on offer amount to a significantly better package than those offered by competitors.

Scenario 2: Bryony tries it out

Bryony was feeling frustrated. She had decided to test out her picture framing idea before incurring significant overhead costs but the results so far had been discouraging. After setting up a small workshop at home, she had tried to find some customers. First she distributed a simple leaflet to local homeowners, outlining the service that she was offering. She followed this up with some personal sales calls on the houses she had leafleted. She had also introduced herself to local art clubs and made presentations on picture framing. As this failed to generate any substantial business, she had called on local offices, shops and hotels to see if they could give her any business. This approach had not generated any worthwhile orders either.

Bryony decided to talk over her problem with a sales training manager to see what she was doing wrong.

"People seem very interested at first," she told him, "but that's as far as it goes – no-one is prepared to give me an order."

"What exactly are you saying to these people?" asked the manager.

"Well I explain in some detail the service I'm offering. I tell them about pictures and framing and how they should be matched together and blended to an interior design style, so that they are in harmony with their surroundings. I describe how I frame the pictures and the types of material I use so that they know they will be getting individually produced craftsmanship, not mass-produced inferior quality goods." Bryony was getting quite enthusiastic just describing her presentation, but then her voice trailed off as she concluded, "they nod seeming to agree, and then say, 'we'll let you know'. They never do of course. I'm beginning to believe that no one is really interested after all."

The training manager had a fair idea of her problem, from what she had told him. "Your experience reminds me of a story that we often use on our sales training courses," he said. "It's about a father and his small son. They were out Christmas shopping together in a large department store packed with every kind of toy and game imaginable. To begin with the boy seemed to be having a great time, not to mention the dad. Then the son lost his enthusiasm and began to whine that he wanted to go home. The father was disappointed and scolded the boy, who began to cry. The father relented and bent down to comfort his son. When his eyes were on the same level as his son's, the dad looked up as someone knocked into him. For the first time, he saw the store through his son's eyes. There were no decorations, train sets or other toys. No robots or games. Just legs and shopping bags; big feet, trousers, skirts, and sharp edged bags. Rather than fun, the scene was terrifying. The father made up his mind to choose a quieter day to take his son out for a treat."

"A very touching story," said Bryony, "but I don't really see what it's got to do with my customer's reactions!"

Task

What message is the training manager trying to convey to Bryony through his story? What advice would you give Bryony to improve her presentations to prospective customers?

HELP **?**

See the information bank in *Section III: Unit 4, 3.5,* page 206.

In conclusion

Now complete your reading of the Information Bank, Unit 4, 'The Customer'.

When you have done this you are ready to tackle the Ongoing Assignment 1, Task 1.4, 'Knowing the Customer', and/or the Extended Task below.

Extended task: Local customers

Consider the list of small local businesses you drew up as part of the Extended Task in Unit 1 or Unit 3. (If you did not complete either of these tasks then draw up a list of small businesses involved in the food and drink industry, which operate in a local community with which you are familiar.)

1. *Who is the target customer for each business? (If you have a long list, you can restrict your answer to five or six businesses.)*

2. *What 'benefits' are offered this target group?*

3. *How do these benefits differ from those offered by competitive businesses? Which businesses have what you would consider to be a Unique Selling Point?*

Unit 5: Market research

This Unit considers the importance of market research for a small firm, and the methods available to owner-managers for gathering information about their market place.

A common image of an entrepreneur is of someone taking decisions based on intuitive feelings about the market place, a 'gut-feel' rather than statistical, researched evidence.

Investigations into how small firms are set up, and operate, partly confirm this view, as owner-managers seem reluctant to carry out formalised market research. However, successful entrepreneurs do have a good understanding and knowledge of the markets they are serving and the environment in which they exist.

Quick answer question: Inexpensive research

In what ways could a small business owner find out about the market place without elaborate or expensive research?

It is not just having a general feel for the market place. Successful owner-managers will be constantly updating their information about what is happening out there. They will also know there are particularly critical moments for a small enterprise, when specific information is required for an important decision.

Quick answer question: When to research

When is it particularly important for a small firm to carry out market research?

The timing of research is important to make sure that relevant and up to date information is available before key decisions are made. The value of such research will depend not just on the answers, but on the questions. Good research involves asking the key questions.

Quick answer question: Asking the right questions

Take the situation of:

1. *A new business start-up.*

2. *A small business about to expand by opening a second retail outlet.*

3. *A small manufacturing company considering a new product line.*

What key questions do you think should be asked in each situation?

Inexpensive research

Small business owners can find out about the market place in a variety of inexpensive ways:

☐ *Desk, or secondary research:* using published information from government sources (e.g. population and trade statistics), directories (e.g. Kompass, Kelly's, Yellow pages), trade associations, trade magazines, bank reports, published surveys (e.g. Financial Times, Economist reviews), Chamber of Commerce and local government information (e.g. town or regional plans), competitive leaflets and published information.

☐ *Informal networks:* talking to people directly or indirectly involved in the business area, e.g. customers, suppliers, competitors, bank managers, members of the trade association or Chamber of Commerce.

☐ *Observation:* watching what happens in the market place e.g. counting shoppers in a high street or visitors to an existing supplier, visiting trade shows and exhibitions, observing customer behaviour in their own business (if already set up).

When to research

It is particularly important for a small firm to carry out research in the following situations:

☐ *Before start up:* Any study of the feasibility of a venture has to have input from research in the market place.

☐ *Before major decisions:* Significant decisions that could affect the survival of an enterprise deserve as much research as possible. These include: specific expansion plans; opening new outlets; setting up new production facilities; launching new products or services; significant capital expenditure on plant and equipment; and large increases in staff and overheads.

☐ *Before marketing campaigns:* Information on customer preferences and the effects of previous sales and marketing campaigns should be analysed and used to determine the next marketing campaign, and can be used to decide the level and mixes of resources to be used.

❑ *When things are going wrong:* Before any frantic activity is undertaken to put things right, it is always wise to find out exactly what is wrong. The symptoms may be visible, for example, sales are in decline. But what is the underlying cause, the root problem? Research is often needed to find out.

Asking the right questions

The key questions to be asked are actually the same in most situations:

❑ Who will be the customers?

❑ Why will they buy from me, and not somebody else?

❑ How much will they buy, and when?

❑ What are the opportunities and threats that will be brought about by this change?

❑ What are my strengths and weaknesses in dealing with them?

Although the basic questions are the same, the detailed questions will be different, depending on the situation and the existing level of information.

Scenario 1: The case of the disappearing sales – episode 1

Peter was worried. The sales achieved by his small design firm were showing clear signs of levelling off. For the first time since he started the business three years ago, his invoiced sales were showing no increase over the previous year. Before, he had always achieved substantial growth, sometimes doubling his previous year's sales.

At first he had put the problem down to the recession – customers just not buying as much as before. But then he had noticed other patterns which were less dependent on the national economy. He had built up a reasonable customer base in the first two years of doing business, and these original customers were the ones he relied on today.

The recession had not affected them at first, and it was only now, when the economic forecasters were saying that the worst was over, that his sales had turned down.

His strategy had not changed since he set up. He specialised in computer-aided designs to overcome specific problems encountered by manufacturers of technical products. He had concentrated on the market local to him, as he was providing a very personal service. Those companies were primarily involved in the military market i.e. manufacturing products for use by the armed forces.

Peter decided that he needed to investigate his problem more thoroughly by researching his market place. He consulted an old friend, an experienced market researcher.

"My first problem is that I don't know what my problem is!" he explained to his friend, Katrina. 'So I don't really know what sort of questions to ask, nor to whom."

"That's not so unusual," she explained, "but if you try to establish some objectives for your research then it should become clearer. What is the fundamental issue that you wish to research? Once you can answer that, then the rest follows. The main issue can be broken down into some possible solutions, and each one researched to test their validity, for example."

"How will I research these issues? I have no market research budget like your clients, you know. This is something I will have to do myself," said Peter.

"I am sure that there is plenty of secondary information that already exists which can help you," replied Katrina, "and you can learn a lot by talking to customers and other people in the trade – even your competitors."

Tasks

1. *Establish some market research objectives for Peter. What is the fundamental issue he needs to research?*

See the information bank in *Section III: Unit 5, 2.1, 2.2 and 3.*, pages 211–212.

2. *Expand on the objectives you have established by listing some questions you would like answered to help Peter better understand his problem.*

See the information bank in *Section III: Unit 5, 2.1 and 2.2*, page 211.

3. *Suggest how these questions could be answered. What research methods would you propose using?*

See the information bank in *Section III: Unit 5, 4., 5. and 6.*, pages 213–218.

Scenario 2: The case of the disappearing sales – episode 2

From his research, Peter found out some very interesting information. His customers were not unhappy with the service he was offering. It was their own business that had changed. Military expenditure by the UK government, and most western countries, was being cut to benefit from the reduced threat from the old Warsaw pact countries. His customers were therefore looking at their own business strategies in light of the reduced expenditure on their existing product lines for military use. He reported back to his market research friend.

"All the customers I talked to are having a long hard think about their own strategies. It's not just the military market that's affecting them. There are technological changes too. Until recently everyone wanted technical components to be as small as possible. Making the end product smaller was the name of the game, but now its gone far enough. There are few extra benefits to be had from making anything still smaller."

"What are they looking for now?" asked Katrina.

"Power," replied Peter. "More power from the same sized unit that is. Instead of making it smaller, make it the same size, but more powerful."

"It seems you need to find out more about what your customers intend to do next, doesn't it?" asked Katrina. "And what else you could do if they all decide to stop buying your designs."

"Don't tempt fate," smiled Peter, "although you're right – I do need a contingency plan."

Tasks

1.   *What information does Peter require next?*

HELP **?**   See the information bank in *Section III: Unit 5, 2.1 and 2.2*, page 211.

2.   *How do you suggest he obtains it?*

HELP **?**   See the information bank in *Section III: Unit 5, 5., 6. and 7.*, pages 214–220.

In conclusion

Now complete your reading of the Information Bank, Unit 5 'Market Research'.

When you have done this you are ready to tackle the Ongoing Assignment 1, Task 1.5 'Researching the Idea', and/or the Extended Task below.

Extended task: A research proposal

You have been asked by someone who is considering opening a fast-food restaurant in the town where you live to design and undertake some market research, to give them more idea of the feasibility of their project. They have asked you to present them with a proposal for market research which has a budget of only £500, plus your own time. Write down the outline of your proposal to them, including your research objectives and methods.

Unit 6: The small business environment

What sets the small business apart from larger business? This unit argues that industries or market sectors play a major role in determining the environmental conditions of a small firm. Government policy in the UK is also reviewed as an important influence in the environment.

The Bolton Committee felt that the general environment of small firms was so hostile that they needed protection to guarantee their survival.

Quick answer question: Endangered species?

*Can you name some industries or market sectors where small firms are hardly found at all and others where they seem to be the **most** common form of business unit?*

In practice, the environment of a small business is determined by the industry or market sector in which it operates. In some sectors small enterprises thrive, in others it is a rare business form. This is not by chance.

Endangered species?

Small firms are less numerous in manufacturing industries (especially in more mature sectors such as car manufacturers, tobacco companies) and more common in the services and construction sectors, where they account for 90% or more of the total. Areas where small businesses are common include:

❑ restaurants and wine bars;

❑ business services (such as secretarial and recruitment agencies);

❑ transport (such as taxis, driving instruction);

❑ retail distribution, especially book shops and newsagents and franchised outlets;

❑ professional services (for example architects, design companies, accounting and physiotherapy practices); and

❑ building companies and household services (such as plumbing).

Quick answer question: Barriers to entry

What barriers do you think exist that might deter a small firm from entering a specific market?

The extent of competition and fragmentation within an industry will be governed by more than the force of the existing rivalry between competing companies. Other forces – the potential for entry into the market by others, the potential for substitute products, the power of buyers, and the power of suppliers – will also have a bearing. These competitive forces will determine how suitable a given market place is to the small business form.

Barriers to entry

Barriers that may deter entry into the market by small firms include:

☐ *Economies of scale* by existing companies that give lower unit prices for higher levels of output (e.g. in production).

☐ *Product differentiation* by existing companies which have built up some form of loyalty to their product or service (e.g. brand loyalty).

☐ *Capital requirements* to set up and effectively compete in the industry (e.g. plant and equipment or premises).

☐ *Switching costs* to a customer; there are often hidden costs involved in changing from one supplier to another, for example, the costs of retraining operators if a new type of equipment is purchased, or the costs of obsolete stock once new items have been substituted.

☐ *Access to distribution channels* which are the accepted economic means of presenting and delivering goods to the customer (e.g. shelf space in a supermarket).

☐ *Other cost disadvantages* which a new supplier to the market place will suffer (e.g. from lack of experience, lack of suitable premises).

☐ *Government policy* and legislation which may place specific requirements on entry (e.g. licensing laws for restaurants, pubs and wine bars.).

Quick answer questions: Powerful buyers

Can you think of an industry in which the buyers or customers exercise a very high degree of control over their suppliers?

Why do you think they have achieved that power?

Buyers influence the environment of the small firm by the extent of the power they have in negotiating with their potential suppliers. Some buyers have little power over their suppliers because they have little choice (for example over monopoly suppliers or where alternative suppliers cannot be conveniently accessed), or because they have little inclination to negotiate (for example, if the purchase is relatively insignificant to them).

Powerful buyers

Some buyers or customers are extremely powerful. For example, the food supermarket chains such as Sainsbury and Tesco dictate terms to their suppliers. These conditions exist where the buying in a particular market becomes concentrated in the hands of a relatively small number of customers and the supply is from a numerous, fragmented group. Thus the small number of supermarket companies exert considerable influence over small, fragmented food producers, and this power has developed along with the concentration of food retailing.

Scenario 1: Christopher surveys the scene

Christopher Hugo was setting up a new business. He had worked as a design and production engineer in larger companies for several years. Now his belief in his own abilities, and a desire for independence, was taking him along the path towards small business ownership.

He was confident of the technology he was dealing with. His background was ideally suited to the 'design and build' type of operation in specialised electronic circuits that he had in mind.

What he was less sure about was the environment in which he would be operating, compared to his previous employment. He considered that there would be two fundamental differences: as a small firm his power in the market place would be negligible to begin with; he would also lack the resources to carry out any longer term research into new products compared to the larger company he currently worked for.

In considering a strategy to overcome these two problem areas, he decided to use the services of the 'Enterprise Initiative', partly funded by the Department of Trade and Industry. This provided him with a business consultant to help him think through his problems.

At their first meeting, the consultant had begun by asking him about the customers for his product and services.

"Well, this is where I have to make a careful choice to begin with, I think," Christopher replied. "The particular design service with limited manufacturing that I am offering will have appeal to two distinct types of customers. First there are the large manufacturers who are producing products with electronic components, which can be anything from household items, such as washing machines and fridges, to military weaponry – tanks, rockets and the like. These companies are turning more and more to smaller companies to do specialised work for them. The company I worked for was doing this for example: rather than employ our own design department to actually build prototypes, we sub-contracted out many aspects of new product development. We may have conceived the idea of the end product, but we would go to more specialised firms and ask them how they would make a certain part of it. If we liked their ideas, then we would give them the order to design a prototype and, if that worked, manufacture the actual component. I know that I could pick up quite a lot of that work from my existing contacts among the big electronic companies."

"How many of this kind of customers are there?" asked the consultant.

"Well not too many these days," said Christopher, "as they are all merging and taking over each other. But it depends as well how many market sectors I go for, or whether I just restrict myself to, say, the military market. That way I build up an expertise in what they want."

"But with your eggs all in one basket," interrupted the consultant.

"Yes but isn't that the problem with a small firm?" Christopher carried on," I just won't have the resources to develop lots of markets, and different products. I am going to be very restricted in what I can do. My eggs are going to have to be concentrated in one place – I will just have to hope that no one sits on the basket."

He smiled, hoping for some words of wisdom from the consultant which would dispel his feeling of helplessness.

"That's right," said the consultant, adding to his gloom, "you certainly will be very restricted in what you can do, which makes it even more important to be in the right market place in the first place. Some baskets are safer than others, although they might be harder to get into. You said you had a choice of two types of customers; who are the second group?"

"My only alternative to the big boys is to go for the smaller ones. There are plenty of small electronics companies around, mainly towards the service end of the business, providing design and product development, but not much manufacturing volume. They may be providing a design service – again possibly to larger companies – but lack the relevant expertise in a specific technology such as mine. Or they will be providing products in specialised niche markets with low volumes and usually plenty of design features; it could be an area of education for example where the market is limited to a few products per college or university."

"And how many of this group are there?" asked the consultant.

"Oh, hundreds, if not thousands. That's the problem. How could I possibly sell to enough of them to achieve a realistic turnover? They will each have very limited buying requirements, although as a total it will undoubtedly add up to quite a lot," said Christopher.

"A very different environment to operate in" summarised the consultant. "Your choice will fundamentally affect the type of business you will become, and the resources you will need."

Tasks

1. Is Christopher right in thinking that the environment of a small firm has only two fundamental differences to the large firm – lack of power in the market place, and lack of resources to develop new products? What other influences do you think the smallness of his business will have?

HELP **?** See the information bank in *Section III: Unit 6, 5.1 and 5.2,* pages 237–238.

2. Christopher has sought help from the Enterprise Initiative. Where else might he turn for inexpensive advice and information?

HELP **?** See the information bank in *Section III: Unit 6, 4.4,* pages 234–235.

3. If you were the consultant, how would you advise Christopher in terms of the relative merits of the two environments he is considering? What will be the barriers to entry into each market segment?

HELP **?** See the information bank in *Section III: Unit 6, 2.,* pages 224–229.

Quick answer question: Justification for policy

What justifications are there for government policies which deliberately encourage and favour small firms?

The UK government has introduced many measures to encourage and support the small firms sector. This has come in three main ways:

☐ financial assistance;

☐ lightening the tax and administrative burdens; and

☐ information and advice.

Generally this assistance has been available to all types of small firms, regardless of geographic area or business sector.

Q | **Quick answer question: Criticisms of policy**

What criticisms do you think could be made of policies which are nationally applicable to all types of small business?

Justification for policy

The support of the small business sector by government initiatives has been justified on the grounds of:

☐ creation of jobs;

☐ competition to larger firms;

☐ innovation of new products and services;

☐ to "level the playing field" with larger companies which otherwise might derive unfair advantage in coping with government regulations and paperwork.

Criticisms of policy

The impact of supportive policies is unknown in detail and there is no hard evidence that the small business sector could not have developed strongly without government assistance. There is evidence however which suggest some defects:

☐ *regional bias:* financial incentives have particularly benefited the richer Southern areas of Britain, whilst areas in the North of England and Scotland have had relatively less support despite higher levels of unemployment;

☐ *no selectivity for winners:* those small firms which can demonstrate a higher potential to create employment have received no better treatment than very small firms, or even the self-employed one-man band;

☐ *confusion:* the availability of help from many different sources, and several government departments, has caused some confusion and inefficiencies.

Scenario 2: One year later

A year after he had started his business, Christopher was quietly pleased with the progress he was making. Following advice from the business consultant, he had developed a strategy which avoided over-dependence on any one large customer. Although it had been hard work to begin with, he had achieved considerable success working with smaller companies. He had used a one-off sub-contract order from a larger firm to get things moving, but he had invested considerable time and effort in developing relationships with a variety of specialist electronic producers. He had limited his activities geographically by concentrating on a group of customers trading locally. Because he was near-by, and providing the sales and technical effort himself, he had impressed many customers with his customised products, so that his designs were unique to each customer. The prototypes he developed with customers required considerable creativity, which he was able to provide.

His problem now was lack of funds to expand and invest in some new equipment. His confidence had grown with his order book, and he realised that he needed another £50,000 to develop the business fully. His bank was supportive but required personal guarantees which Christopher was unhappy to give. He was advised to seek outside investment, but he was so disappointed with the response he received from a venture capital company, that he complained bitterly about it to a friend.

"I couldn't believe it", said Christopher. "This investment analyst actually told me that I needed too little money! He wasn't prepared to consider investments of less than £100,000. I don't need that amount, but I don't want to put my house on the line with the bank for a smaller amount either. What am I supposed to do?"

Tasks

1. *Christopher has found some advantages in his 'smallness'. Specify what you think these are from the information given. What other advantages do you think small firms might enjoy over larger ones in other markets?*

| HELP | ? | See the information bank in *Section III: Unit 6, 3.*, pages 229–231. |

2. *The venture capitalist did not want to invest only £50,000 in Christopher's company. Can you explain the logic behind their lower limit of £100,000 investments?*

   What do you suggest Christopher does next to try and secure his £50,000 funds without giving personal guarantees?

 See the information bank in *Section III: Unit 6, 4.2,* pages 231–232.

In conclusion

Now complete your reading of the Information Bank, Unit 6 'The Small Business Environment'.

When you have done this you are ready to tackle the Ongoing Assignment 1, Task 1.6 'Assessing the Risk', and/or the Extended Task below.

Extended task: Local support

Find out what organisations exist in your local area to support small enterprises. Contact as many as you can and obtain literature and information on their services. A good starting point may be your local TEC. Your local borough or district council may also have details on what services are available in the area.

If you were about to start up a small business, how useful do you think you would find the services on offer?

Ongoing assignment 1: The feasibility study

If you have completed Units 1 to 6 inclusive in Sections I and III, and Tasks 1.1 to 1.6 inclusive in Section II, you should now conclude the Ongoing Assignment 1: 'The Feasibility Study' by completing Task 1.7 'Summary of the Feasibility Study'.

Unit 7: Routes to market entry

This Unit considers the alternative routes for market entry as a small business, and looks at the advantages and disadvantages of a business start-up.

Quick answer question: Possible routes

As well as starting-up a brand new business what other possibilities are there for involvement in a small enterprise as an owner-manager?

Give some examples of actual businesses that have developed from each category.

In identifying how to pursue a given business opportunity, the basic choice is between beginning a new business or buying an existing one.

Possible routes

Beginning a new business: This can be achieved either as:

❏ a start-up (e.g. forming a new manufacturing firm); or

❏ a franchise (e.g. Body Shop, Burger King).

Buying an existing business: This can be done as:

❏ an outright purchase (e.g. buy a public house);

❏ a 'buy-in' (e.g. join a firm of solicitors as a partner); or

❏ a 'buy-out' (e.g. the management buyout of Video Arts).

Quick answer question: The start-up

What do you think are the advantages and disadvantages of a business start-up compared with the other possible routes to market entry?

The choice of route to market entry will depend on two key factors:

❏ the personal motivations and aspirations of the prospective owner-manager; and

❏ the situation and context of the business opportunity and the industry it is in.

The start-up

Each route will have some general advantages and disadvantages.

Advantages include:	Disadvantages include:

Advantages include:

- ❏ *Creation of the owner-manager*
  –freedom of choice;
- ❏ *Control of owner-manager*
  –personal decisions count;
- ❏ *Satisfaction of owner-manager*
  – 'all my own work';
- ❏ *Clean sheet*
  –the only problems are new ones;
- ❏ *Match between business and owner-manager*
  –tailor-made opportunity;
- ❏ *Help from various agencies*
  –public and private sector assistance.

Disadvantages include:

- ❏ *Unproven idea*
  –will it work?;
- ❏ *High failure rate*
  –low odds of success;
- ❏ *Hard, lonely work*
  –doing it alone;
- ❏ *No market share*
  –no existing goodwill;
- ❏ *Barriers to entry*
  –many obstacles to overcome;
- ❏ *Difficult to finance*
  –not a proven concept.

Scenario: Shallow or deep end?

With all their children now grown up and no longer living at home, Janet and Mike Bloomfield were reconsidering their futures. He had long wanted to work for himself, rather than the large leisure group that currently employed him. Janet worked in a hospital as a physiotherapist, but also had ambitions of working for herself. They were discussing the possibilities one evening.

"It sounds very attractive to start a new business," said Mike, "but its security that holds me back; my current job gives me a guaranteed salary, and a good pension in 15 years time. I like the thought of the independence of my own business, but the insecurity worries me. What if I didn't make enough to cover our mortgage?"

"Well you're not going to get independence *and* security from your own business, that's for sure," said his wife. "You've really got to decide what is more important. You could look at franchising. Isn't there a lower failure rate for franchises?"

"Yes, if they're any good," replied Mike, "but it would be just like working for someone else. I don't want to swap one head office for another, and be taking some risk. No I think we should consider buying an existing business. At least it's got a track record that can give us an idea of its success."

"Or we could start on a part-time basis," suggested Janet. "If I kept my job, and you found something you could dip your toe into rather than jump in at the deep-end, then we might keep our security whilst we're finding out about the risks involved."

"That would be a good idea if I could think of a business that suits my background, that I could do on a part-time basis. As you know, I would ideally like to run a small hotel, similar to the ones in the chain I work for now. But I can't see how I can do that on a part-time basis," said Mike, his resigned expression indicating that he had been over this dilemma in his mind before.

"OK, why don't we buy a hotel then?" suggested Janet. "We could sell up our house and live in your hotel. At least we would be buying an asset."

"Well that's a thought," said Mike more cheerfully. "But what would you do? Perhaps we could set you up in your own practice first, whilst I carry on with my job, until we're both ready."

"I'm not sure we're ever both going to be ready," said Janet.

Tasks

1. *There is a wide scope of risk-taking possibilities for Janet and Mike, starting with minimal commitment to higher risk options. List all the options that you think they should consider as a spectrum, starting with low, and ending with higher risk alternatives.*

> HELP **?** See the information bank in *Section III: Unit 7, 2.1,* pages 242–244.

2. *What do you think they should do? Evaluate the alternatives you have suggested and recommend a route of entry into small business owner-management for them.*

> HELP **?** See the information bank in *Section III: Unit 7, 2.2,* pages 244–245.

In conclusion

Now complete your reading of Information Bank, Unit 7 'Routes to Market Entry'.

When you have done this, you are ready to tackle the Ongoing Assignment 2, Task 2.1 'Choosing the Method', and/or the Extended Task below.

Extended task: Business routes

Consider either a well known company that was a business start-up within living memory or a small local firm with which you are familiar (e.g. restaurant, a free house, a shop, a garage etc). Write an analysis of why the owner-manager(s) of your chosen business selected the route to market entry that they did.

Unit 8: Franchising

This Unit considers the definition and scope of franchising, as well as examining its advantages and disadvantages as a small business type.

Quick answer question: Types of franchise

In fact there are several forms of franchising. Can you describe how the different types work?

Although franchising is regarded as an American phenomenon, it has its roots in the British brewing trade. In the late 18th and early 19th centuries British brewers developed a system of tied house agreements which still operates today.

Types of franchise

These early forms of franchising were simply product and trademark agreements, in which manufacturers distribute products through licensed dealers. Today franchising includes:

- ❑ *Manufacturer-retailer franchises,* in which the manufacturer appoints an agent or dealer who sells direct to the public. Car dealerships and petrol station outlets are common examples.

- ❑ *Manufacturer-wholesaler franchises,* in which the originators franchise independent middle-men who distribute to retailers. The soft drinks industry (e.g. Coca-Cola, Pepsi-Cola) operates largely this way.

A more recent and comprehensive type is:

- ❑ *'Business format franchising'.* This represents a more in depth relationship in which the franchisor provides a complete business concept as a package to the franchisee. It covers such aspects as trade name, logo, support in setting up and financing the business, design of premises and other equipment, operating and information systems, national and local marketing, training and research and development.

Quick answer questions: Famous franchises

Which different franchises can you name? Which seem to be the most common industry types?

Franchising is big business in the USA. It is estimated that about one-third of all retail sales, and 10% of the gross national product is involved in franchising.

Although less well developed in the UK and Europe, it is growing fast especially as a business format. Retail sales in the UK are over £5 billion, through 18,000 outlets.

Famous franchises

Some well known franchises in the UK include:

Apollo Window Blinds, Budget Rent-a-Car, Burger King, Dyno-Rod, Fast-Frame Instant Picture Framing, Kall Kwik Printing, Knobs and Knockers, Pizza Express, Prontaprint, Sketchleys, Spud-U-Like, Thorntons, Tie Rack, Wimpy, McDonalds, Body Shop.

The most common types of franchises are involved in food and drink (especially fast food). Business services and home improvements are also common.

Scenario: Franchised framing

Bryony was convinced she had discovered a market gap for picture framing in her home town (as we have previously described in Unit 4, 'Scenario: Bryony Hannam's Picture Framing Idea'). However, she felt constrained to go ahead because she had very little business experience and, although she was familiar with the art world, she had never framed any pictures herself.

In her investigations of the market place, she had discovered that she could get help from various quarters. There was no shortage of part time business courses in the area; there were picture framing courses available from a weekend introduction to more extensive practical training. The manufacturers of framing equipment and the suppliers of materials all offered her training and advice in setting up.

She also discovered a nationally operated franchise which initially sounded very attractive. The franchise offered her a complete package for setting up as a picture framer: from the design of the retail premises and workshop, the purchasing of supplies, the craft and techniques of framing itself, through to the marketing of the business, and the management of its cash flow and other financial aspects. They could promote her outlet as part of a national operation and help her keep up to date with the latest developments in the framing world.

When Bryony read through the franchise agreement, she had second thoughts however. The financial implications were considerable. As well as an up front fee of £10,000 she would have to pay them an ongoing royalty of 10% of her total sales revenue. In addition, she would still have to pay for the fitting of the premises, to their exact requirements, and find the finance for equipment and working capital which they estimated at a further £25,000. Despite assurances that finance would be readily available, Bryony wondered if she would ever be truly independent with such heavy liabilities and constraints on how she could operate the business. She discussed the idea with her accountant. "I've looked up this particular franchise," he commented, "they are members of the British Franchise Association, so that gives you some guarantee of their authenticity. They have proven the business by running a pilot unit, and they are now quite well established."

"If it's such a good deal for me, as they claim, why do they give so much away. What's in it for them?" asked Bryony.

Tasks

1. *How would you answer Bryony's question? In other words what are the advantages, and disadvantages for franchisors?*

> **See the information bank in *Section III: Unit 8, 6.3 and 6.4,* page 252.**

2. *Identify the advantages and disadvantages of Bryony proceeding with the franchise.*

> **See the information bank in *Section III: Unit 8, 6.1 and 6.2,* pages 251-252.**

> **Quick answer questions: Is it a small business?**
>
> *What characteristics do franchises have in common with other small firms? How do they differ?*

The Bolton Committee did not include franchising in the scope of their report on small businesses in the UK, as franchisees did not fully conform to their definition of an 'independent business'.

Is it a small business?

Franchisees operate legally separate businesses which they own, just like other small businesses. They control their day to day activities and their staff just like other small businesses. However they do not have full control over important marketing decisions, such as products and services offered, pricing, presentation and distribution.

These are important constraints that make franchisees into little more than managed outlets according to some observers. Most franchisors and their franchised outlets would in total amount to a medium or large size business.

However many small firms have controls on their activities which are as significant as those imposed by franchisors on franchisees. Buyers and financial backers can effectively reduce the independence of a small firm. Franchisees share many of the management and environmental issues that concern any small firm owner-manager, such as the employment and management of staff, bookkeeping and quality assurance.

In conclusion

Now complete your reading of Information Bank, Unit 8 'Franchising'.

When you have done this, you are ready to tackle the Ongoing Assignment 2, Task 2.2 'Looking At Franchising', and/or the Extended Task below.

Extended task: A local franchise

Consider a franchised outlet or business in your local area.

Write an analysis of that franchise, with details of the format that is provided, i.e. the products, the logo, trademarks, and image. How successful do you believe this enterprise has been compared to similar non-franchised businesses?

(If you are able to talk to the owner-manager of a franchised outlet to understand their views on the fors and againsts of franchising, so much the better.)

Unit 9: Buying an existing business

This Unit looks at the possibility of buying an existing business as a route to market entry. Although small businesses are not quoted on stock exchanges, there is an active market involved in the buying and selling of small firms. 'Business Transfer Agents' act as intermediaries between sellers and potential buyers, in much the same way as estate agents deal with property transactions. A key question for a buyer to ask is: "Why is this business for sale?"

Quick answer questions: Why is the business for sale?

Can you give some examples of:

1. *Different types of sellers of small businesses?*

2. *Their motives for sale?*

The types and motives of buyers also differ.

Quick answer questions: Who is the buyer?

Can you give some examples of:

1. *Different types of buyers of small businesses?*

2. *Their motives for buying?*

Why is the business for sale?

Sellers and their motives include:

Small business owners:

❏ cashing in on success or cutting losses;

❏ retirement;

❏ break up of partnership;

❏ wish to expand with a new partner;

❏ re-investment elsewhere.

Larger companies:

☐ small business unit not meeting targets;

☐ return to core activities;

☐ take-over by new owner, who sells off some smaller units.

Franchise:

☐ sale of owned outlets to franchisees;

☐ franchisees selling up.

Forced sale:

☐ sale of assets or on-going business of an unsuccessful small firm.

Who is the buyer?

Buyers and their motives include:

Outright buyer:

☐ wish to purchase complete business, rather than use resources in start up;

☐ barriers to market entry prevent start-up;

☐ sufficient cash for purchase from redundancy/inheritance/savings;

☐ existing small firm wishes to buy competitor.

Buy-in:

☐ desire to join existing business as a new partner, necessary in many professions e.g. accountants, doctors ;

☐ wish to invest in existing management of small firm.

Buy-out:

☐ existing management buy-out of small part of larger firm.

Buying an existing business can have advantages as a route to market entry for a small business. A potential buyer may be new to business ownership, an existing small business owner wishing to expand, or the manager of a small business unit which is for sale.

> ### Quick answer questions: What are the advantages and disadvantages?
>
> *What are the advantages of buying an existing business compared to a new business start up, or franchise? What are the disadvantages of buying an existing business?*

Most of the literature on purchasing an existing business contains the warning: "Beware: buying someone-else's business can be damaging to the buyer", or words to that effect. Certainly there are many commercial, legal and taxation issues involved in buying a business.

What are the advantages and disadvantages?

Some of the *advantages* of buying an existing business include:

- overcomes barriers to entry;
- immediate turnover and income;
- immediate market share;
- existing assets – premises, equipment, employees;
- existing goodwill with customers;
- track record – may be easier to finance;
- possible 'insider' knowledge if management involved.

Some of the *disadvantages* of buying an existing business include:

- possible liabilities;
- uncertainty over records;
- risk in goodwill – will it remain after the owner leaves?;
- historical problems in the business;
- not 'all my own work'.

Scenario 1: Bryony Hannam considers buying an existing business

Whilst investigating her idea of a picture framing business, Bryony Hannam discovered that a framer and picture gallery was for sale, located not far from her home town. She decided to investigate further, and asked the business transfer agent handling the sale to send her the particulars. These are summarised below:

SOUTHGATE AND CO.

Business agents and valuers

On the instructions of the shareholders,
FOR SALE
ART ENTERPRISES LTD trading as GRAY'S FRAMING STUDIOS

IMPORTANT: These particulars are confidential:
Staff are unaware of the impending sale.

GENERAL: Established by our client some five years ago, we are now pleased to offer for sale 3 picture shops well situated in market towns, and a framing workshop, giving combined sales of £300,000 gross per annum.

PRICE: We are instructed to seek offers in the region of: £150,000 (one hundred and fifty thousand pounds) for the entire issued shares of the company.
Stock to be transferred at an additional valuation (approx. £50,000)

THE RETAIL PREMISES: There are 3 shops, all in good positions next to busy High Streets in sizeable market towns.
The premises are leasehold, with terms left to run of 12, 17 and 22 years. Rent review patterns are 5 yearly, with reviews due in 2 years time.
Each shop is staffed by a Manager and an assistant.
Each shop is furnished and fitted to a high standard, with picture and frame moulding displays, carpeting and other furnishings, a desk and an electronic cash register. Sales areas in the 3 shops vary at 700, 900 and 1200 sq.ft.

THE WORKSHOP: The workshop of 2000 sq. feet is situated in a small industrial estate. The lease has 16 years to run, with a rent review due next year.

The premises are comprehensively equipped with all the machinery and tools needed for the provision of a successful and efficient framing service.

Equipment includes: Mitre saws and guillotines
Pneumatic under pinner
Glass cutting table
Dry mounting press
Mountboard cutter and trimmer
Worktables, racks and shelving
Assorted small tools
Large capacity air compressor

Staff: The workshop employs 1 manager and 2 framers.

THE BUSINESS: The business was established by our client 5 years ago. Since that date, the business has expanded from a single unit to the current three unit operation.

The principle activities are those of:

1. Bespoke framing
2. Framed and unframed pictures.

1. **Bespoke framing.** The company offers a high quality framing service for customers which accounts for approximately 60% of turnover. Production, according to the customer's specification, is carried out centrally and delivered back to the retail premises within a 7 day period. Particular strengths of this service are:

   * wide choice of frames and mounts
   * quality of production
   * level of service provided by retail staff.

2. **Pictures.** The company retails a range of pictures from reproduction prints and posters, limited editions, to original oils and watercolours. The majority of stock retails for between £10-£150. Particular strengths are:

   * wide range of images available
   * affordable prices.

FINANCIAL INFORMATION

Past trading results:

£'000s	Current Year	Prior Year	Next Year Forecast
Sales (net of VAT)	260	180	325
Cost of materials	85	60	105
Gross profit	175	120	220
Overheads:			
Salaries & wages	90	75	100
Rent and Rates	45	28	50
Other	10	7	15
Total overheads	145	110	165
Net profit	30	10	55

Net profit is before depreciation, interest and directors salaries and fees.

THE PURCHASE PRICE

The business is for sale at £150,000 comprising:

Value of leases remaining:	£35,000
Value of equipment and machinery:	£15,000
Value of fixtures and fittings:	£10,000
Goodwill:	£90,000
	────────
Total	£150,000

In addition stock will be charged at valuation – estimated at £50,000.

Liabilities, including creditors, borrowings and hire purchase agreements will be discharged prior to completion of the sale.

FUTURE DEVELOPMENTS

The sales forecast for next year includes a full years trading by the third shop which opened part way through the current year. Overheads are based on actual costs plus inflation so that the forecast result is considered most realistic by our clients.

Bryony's reaction

Bryony was excited after she had done some initial calculations: "It's just what I'm looking for, " she told her husband. "And I won't have to go through all the trauma of starting up from nothing. The business is obviously successful judging by the sales figures. I know one of the shops – it's very similar to the idea I was working on – just not in this town, that's all. But of course, I could always open up another outlet here as I had planned to do – except that I will have a ready made workshop and existing sales to keep me going from day one."

"What about the price?" her husband asked. "Your mother only left you £75,000. Where will you get the rest from?"

"I'm going to talk to my accountant about the price, but the bank manager has already said I can borrow the rest – with the house as guarantee of course. If the stock is £50,000, I will have to borrow £125,000 at interest of £16,000 per year. The profits more than cover that," replied Bryony.

"What about your salary? You will need something for your efforts, not to mention return on the money you're putting in," her husband persisted.

"If it makes the forecast profits next year, the business will still have profits of nearly £40,000 after interest, which sounds a good enough return to me," argued Bryony.

The accountants caution

The next day Bryony saw her accountant, who had been studying the particulars and the finances in more detail.

"I'm concerned about this forecast," he said. "If the business makes the projected figures for next year it may be worth what they're asking. But part of that result will be down to you; if you buy it, you will be running it by then. Why should you pay for future profits? It's what the business earns now that they're selling, not what you can do with it tomorrow. If it is so sure to improve next year, why are they selling it now?"

"The agents told me on the phone that the shareholders were a husband and wife team who are getting divorced and want to sell the business as a result," Bryony replied.

"Well that may, or may not, be a genuine reason for sale. You will need to find out more. Can you talk to the managers?"

"No, no-one in the organisation knows it's for sale," said Bryony.

"What about the assets, and this stock you will be buying? Do you know anything about them? How new is the equipment? Is it what you want? Is the stock right for the business when you will be running it? If not it might be better to start from scratch, and even compete with them, as it sounds from what you've said that they've lost interest in the business," suggested the accountant.

"Yes, I know I will have to check these things. The agents say I can have a tour tomorrow – I'll be introduced as a customer." said Bryony.

"The other worry I have is buying the shares. It would be better to buy only the assets, and not the company itself," continued the accountant. "Unless there are tax losses we can use, that is."

"I thought the particulars state that they will pay off any liabilities outside the sale." said Bryony.

"They do," replied the accountant, "but that only applies to liabilities we know about. When you buy the shares of a company, you may be buying liabilities we don't know about – disputes with suppliers, employees, past tax claims, VAT problems – there are a lot of possibilities."

Tasks

1. *Bryony has thought of some of the advantages of buying an existing business. What others might there be for her in this proposition?*

> See the information bank in **Section III: Unit 9, 8.1,** pages 275–276.

2. *What will be some of the problems? The accountant has mentioned several, but list some other potential pitfalls.*

> See the information bank in **Section III: Unit 9, 8.2,** page 276.

3. *How can Bryony find out more information as suggested by the accountant? What else does she need to know about, and how can she go about getting the information? What other advice does she need?*

> See the information bank in **Section III: Unit 9, 4. and 5.,** pages 262–270.

4. *Do you consider the price for the business a fair one? Make an alternative valuation, and suggestions for justifying this to the owners.*

> See the information bank in **Section III: Unit 9, 6.,** pages 270–273.

Basis of valuation

Businesses for sale are usually given a price based on their tangible assets, and intangible assets or goodwill, as was the case for Bryony Hannam's company for sale.

Quick answer questions: Tangible and intangible assets – to have or not to have?

1. *What types of tangible assets might a small business have? Give some examples of business types which will have mainly tangible assets.*

2. *What types of intangible assets might a small business have? Give examples of businesses with predominantly intangible assets, which can only really be valued on profits.*

3. *Give examples of small business with a reasonable mixture of the two.*

Assets are valued at either a market price for individual assets, or often a multiple of profits where a market price is less obvious.

Tangible and intangible assets – to have or not to have?

Tangible assets include:

☐ freehold and leasehold property;

☐ plant, machinery and equipment;

☐ fixtures, fittings and furnishings;

☐ debtors ;

☐ stocks.

Intangible assets include:

☐ goodwill;

☐ image and reputation;

☐ employees;

☐ 'intellectual property' (e.g. patents, trademarks and licences);

☐ customers.

Business types with predominantly tangible assets include:

- ❏ agricultural small holdings and farms;
- ❏ property development companies;
- ❏ unsuccessful freehold shops.

Businesses with predominantly intangible assets include:

- ❏ consultancies;
- ❏ training companies;
- ❏ estate agents;
- ❏ landscape gardeners;
- ❏ insurance brokers;
- ❏ accountants and solicitors;
- ❏ import/export agents.

Businesses with a reasonable mix of tangibles and intangibles if they are successful include:

- ❏ hotels and restaurants;
- ❏ small manufacturing firms;
- ❏ picture framers;
- ❏ medical practices;
- ❏ wholesalers;
- ❏ transport companies;
- ❏ leisure companies such as squash clubs or health centres.

Scenario 2: Bryony looks at a BIMBO

Bryony Hannam pursued her investigations into Gray's Framing Studios with such tenacity that she discovered some very interesting facts. Talking to one of the suppliers helped her to find out the reason why the business had been put onto the market.

"It's immoral," she complained to her husband, "all this work I've done, only to find that the workshop manager is going to buy out the couple owning the business. It seems that they have put the business on the market just to find out what sort of price it might fetch. They intended all along to sell it to the workshop manager, not an outside buyer."

"Did the agent know?" asked the husband.

"Evidently not, I got this from a supplier who is out of favour with the manager, but who knows what he's up to," answered Bryony.

Well you've found out quite a lot about their business, that can't be wasted effort. But there's not much else you can do now is there?" Her husband tried to console her, knowing she had grown keen on the idea.

"Well there is something. Maybe I should talk to the manager. I don't suppose he's got all the money necessary himself; it could work to my advantage if he needed a partner. After all he's got all the inside information on the business. It would be a safer bet to buy it with him," said Bryony thoughtfully.

A week later Bryony was with her accountant again.

"That's right," she explained, "he's only raising £20,000 from his own pocket. He's been offered the rest of the money from a finance company who would buy loan stock, with the balance as an overdraft from the bank."

"This workshop manager seems to be quite smart," mused the accountant, "by offering loan stock, he plans to retain a majority of the ordinary shares for himself no doubt. How much does he plan to offer did you say?"

"£100,000 plus the value of the stock," answered Bryony. "He's putting up £20,000 for shares and the finance company will buy £20,000 worth of shares, but also put in £60,000 of loan stock, which has no voting rights, but qualifies for profits at a preferential rate. He plans to raise the £50,000 or so for the stock as an overdraft. He says it's not all necessary and can be soon reduced, especially with credit from the suppliers. So he's effectively planning on buying half the company for £20,000," Bryony summed up.

"You've certainly found out a lot. Why did he tell you all this?" asked the accountant.

"I was introduced to him by this supplier as you know, and it was soon obvious he still has two problems. First he doesn't have any experience in running anything other than the workshop, and the shop managers aren't interested. Secondly the finance company are making lots of demands with seats on the Board and monthly reports. He's beginning to think it will be rather like being part of a larger company, even though he will own half of it," said Bryony.

"So what is his solution?" asked the accountant.

"I suggested he might be better off with a working partner who will put up money in a similar way to the finance company, but help him run the business and expand it – open new outlets, look after the marketing. In other words me! And he's accepted in principle," Bryony beamed her pleasure.

"Ah, you're talking of a BIMBO," said the accountant, quickly adding before he was misunderstood, "a 'Buy-In, Management Buy-Out', they're becoming more common, and do seem to have some advantages."

Tasks

1. *What do you consider to be the advantage of this approach? What are the potential problems?*

HELP **?** See the information bank in *Section III: Unit 9, 3.3 and 3.4,* pages 261–262.

2. *What finance package made it possible for the workshop manager to realise 50% of the equity, for less than 15% of the total consideration? What deal do you think Bryony should strike with him?*

HELP **?** See the information bank in *Section III: Unit 9, 6.3,* pages 272–273.

In conclusion

Now complete your reading of the Information Bank, Unit 9 'Buying an Existing Business'.

When you have done this, you are ready to tackle the Ongoing Assignment 2, Task 2.3 'Buying An Existing Business', and/or the Extended Task below.

Extended task: Garage for sale

You work for a business transfer agent as a negotiator responsible for finding buyers for small businesses for sale. The owners of a local garage have instructed you to sell their business. It is profitable, with a good base of customers for repairs and maintenance. It also has the agency for a Japanese car manufacturer, specialising in four-wheel drive vehicles. You have interviewed the owners, and gathered the information you require about the business.

Your task now is to write up the particulars of the business for sale in a form which will be given to prospective purchasers. It will outline the nature of the business, and give basic financial information to justify the purchase price that you have put on the business.

Unit 10: Forms of small business organisation

This Unit looks at the choices of legal identity for small firms. The legal structure under which it is most appropriate for a small business to operate depends on the situation and objectives of the business and its owner(s).

The first decision, which restricts the choices of legal format available, is ownership. Owner-managers can choose to 'go-it-alone', or elect to team up with someone else with whom they share ownership of the business.

The four basic forms of small business organisation are:

☐ limited company;

☐ sole trader;

☐ partnership; and

☐ co-operative.

A sole trader is self descriptive. Partnership and co-operatives have more than one owner. Only the limited company can be either solely or jointly owned.

Quick answer question: Different company

In what other important respect is a limited company significantly different to a sole trader or partnership?

Each form of business organisation has advantages and disadvantages which will be more, or less relevant, to the business in question.

Different company

A limited company is a separate legal entity; it takes on a life and status of its own which is not dependent on its owners, who can thus limit their liability for its obligations and debts. As a distinct legal body, the company employs its directors who thus become employees for tax and other purposes.

Sole traders or partnerships are inseparable from their owners, who thus accept full liability for all the problems and indebtedness of the enterprise, even if this affects other assets they may own outside of the business. As the business has no separate status to employ them, they become self-employed. This does not mean however that a company is always the best form for starting up.

Scenario 1: Janet and Mike take the plunge

Janet and Mike Bloomfield had come to a momentous decision. Mike had often talked of giving up his job with a large leisure group and running a small hotel in their favourite seaside town; Janet had been working as a physiotherapist for many years and wanted to set up a practice of her own. Now that the children had all left home, they were preparing to take the plunge. Mike had found the ideal hotel for sale, with under-used space on the ground floor, which would make an ideal area for Janet's physiotherapy practice.

Now that they had found a buyer for their home and their offer on the hotel was accepted their move into small business was becoming a reality.

Raising the money

The hotel was for sale freehold, and they planned to live in it themselves. They had calculated that the proceeds of the sale of their house, plus a mortgage, would pay for the hotel, but not their estimate of the necessary refurbishments Mike planned, nor the investment in fittings and equipment for Janet's practice.

☐ Estimated start-up costs were: (£'000s)

cost of hotel	250
refurbishment	20
physiotherapy practice – conversion and equipment	20
working capital	10
Total	300

☐ Funds available were: (£'000s)

net proceeds of sale of house	200
mortgage on hotel	50
other funds required	50
Total	300

Mike and Janet had talked to their bank manager about funding the difference. He had asked for a second mortgage on the property plus a business plan he could approve, before he would commit to an overdraft.

Then Janet's father had offered to invest in the business. He had some spare capital which he was happy to put into their venture, provided he received a reasonable income from it.

Discussing the form

Janet had been discussing the alternative legal forms of business organisation with their solicitor and she asked Mike for his views.

"We will need to make a decision soon," she urged, "as it will affect how we buy the hotel and start to trade. Do you think we should form a company or operate as a sole trader or in partnership?"

"Well, I assume we cannot be a sole trader as there are two of us," replied Mike.

"Not necessarily," said Janet. "We could run our businesses totally separately, and therefore each operate as a sole trader."

"What's the point in that, when we're both under the same roof, sharing in some of the costs?" asked Mike.

"Well," said Janet, "I think we should know how each business is doing, and therefore keep separate records of sales and costs. If not, one might be keeping the other going without us realising it - I'm not going to subsidise you for ever you know!"

Before Mike could respond, Janet continued, "Seriously, if one business does not do well, we don't want it to pull down everything else with it. Suppose one business did fail. If it isn't quite separate, all our assets could be liable."

"Then we need a company to limit our liability," suggested Mike.

"I don't think so," said Janet. "Talking to our solicitor, she says that we can operate as sole traders, with you responsible for the hotel and me for the practice. That way there are less formalities and records to keep and we can be self-employed which delays our tax payments."

"Yes but if we own the property jointly," Mike interrupted, "this means that if one of us fails, our main asset is still on the line. What happens if you are sued by one of your patients?"

"I'm covered by professional indemnity insurance for any mishaps," Janet answered.

"What about your Dad, then?" Mike continued. "If he is going to invest in our businesses, how can he put money into a sole trader?"

"Well I think he can make us a loan, but it may be complicated to split it between us." replied Janet. "Look I'm getting rather confused. Why don't we go through this summary checklist that the solicitor gave me, and make our assessment against each category so that we make a structured decision?"

Checklist for choosing the appropriate form

Categories	Company	Sole trader	Partnership
Liabilities	Liability limited, but personal guarantees and directors' obligations can reduce limitations.	All assets liable including those not involved in the business.	Liability extends to business debts of other partners.
Records & accounts	Legal accounting and audit requirements. Accounts filed open to inspection.	No strict accounting or audit requirements. Records not available for public inspection.	
Setting up	Formalities of registration, although can buy 'off-the-peg'.	No formalities except registering as self-employed.	As for sole trader, except partnership agreement strongly advised to prevent problems, especially of dissolution.
Raising money	Wide choice, including further equity investments.	Options limited to overdraft or loan.	Overdraft, loans or new partners with money.
Selling up	Flexible, as can sell part or all of shares.	Can only sell assets – difficult if only selling part of the business.	
Status	Possibly higher perceived status.	Possibly lower perceived status.	
Tax, National Insurance & pensions	Employee status – PAYE, high National Insurance, but full benefits. Unlimited company contributions to pension. Corporation tax on company profits. Losses retained in company.	Self-employed status: all profits , drawn or not are taxable as income, possibly at higher rates. National Insurance cheaper but less benefits. Tax deductible pension contributions restricted. Losses can be offset against tax on other income.	

Tasks

1. Assess whether or not you agree with Janet, that they should operate two separate businesses. If they were not married, would you advise differently?

> See the information bank in *Section III: Unit 10, 1. and 5.*, page 279 and 287–289.

2. Consider the 'Checklist for Choosing the Appropriate Form' that Janet referred to. In each category decide which would be the most appropriate form for Janet and Mike.

> See the information bank in *Section III: Unit 10, 2., 3. and 4.*, pages 283–287.

3. Decide which form(s) you would recommend they choose.

The co-operative

In recent years, the fourth type of business organisation, the co-operative, has been making something of a comeback.

> **Quick answer questions : What is a co-operative?**
>
> *What do you think a co-operative is? How does it differ from other legal forms?*

With a history rooted in the beginnings of the co-operative movement in the 18th century, co-operatives declined in popularity in the 20th century. Since the 1970s, however they have been growing rapidly from a small base.

> **Quick answer questions : Why co-operative?**
>
> *Can you think of different circumstances in which co-operatives are formed? What are the principle motives of the founders?*

What is a co-operative?

A co-operative is an enterprise owned and controlled by all those who work in it. It can register and have limited liability for its members, but has to adopt the following principles:

❐ members have an equal vote in decisions;

❐ membership is open to everyone who fulfils specified conditions (e.g. number of hours worked);

❐ assets controlled, and usually owned jointly by members;

❐ profits shared equally between members with limited interest payable on loans made by members;

❐ share capital remains at its original value – members benefit from participation, not investment.

Why co-operatives?

The main types of co-operatives are:

❐ endowed co-operatives; workers 'given' the business by philanthropic owner;

❐ defensive co-operatives: workforce take over the business to prevent its closure;

❐ job-creation co-operatives: the unemployed are encouraged to pool resources to create new jobs for themselves;

❐ alternative co-operatives: members seek new lifestyle with alternative social and environmental ideals.

Scenario 2: Janet thinks co-operative

Two years on, Janet and Mike Bloomfield's move to an alternative lifestyle, running their own businesses, was proving to be a success. The hotel had flourished under Mike's experienced management, and was more than repaying the mortgage, loans and overheads.

Janet's business was also developing well, but in a way she had not expected. The demand for physiotherapy in their new location proved fickle. At times Janet had more patients than she could handle but there were lulls in which she had insufficient custom for her services. During one of these slacker periods she decided to try a diversification for her business. She had for some time been interested in alternative forms of healing, and had several contacts practising various types of treatment and therapy, outside of the main stream of conventional medicine. She also knew there was a growing demand for these services. What some of her practising friends lacked was proper business premises from which to operate.

The solution to her problem of fluctuating demand and their lack of accommodation seemed obvious. She invited an acupuncturist, an aromatherapist, a reflexologist, a shiatsu masseuse, a herbalist, and a homeopath to use the facilities she had developed within the hotel.

The centralisation of these services on one site proved a great success, generating sufficient business to provide all the practitioners with a living. Janet was now concerned to devise a working structure in which everyone could happily operate, and be fairly rewarded for their efforts.

"It's not the sort of business that we will ever be able to sell at a capital profit," she explained to her husband Mike. "It's far too dependent on our individual skills to be able to sell it on. But we can make a reasonable income from it, and we all share a common interest."

"You mean healing," said Mike.

"Not just healing," replied Janet, "we want to promote 'natural healing'. We don't need to be pumped full of chemicals to get over the slightest ailment. We can offer a complete range of alternatives which work and have no harmful side-effects. Nor do they need testing on animals. We've really a common cause, that we all believe strongly in, as well as a business."

"Don't get too carried away with the cause," warned Mike, "we still have the bills to pay."

"Exactly," responded Janet, "that's why I want to make it into a co-operative."

There was a silence whilst Mike digested this news and tried to mentally distinguish this business form from the grocery store up the road.

"How exactly would a co-operative work here?" he eventually asked.

"Well, I've asked the local Co-operative Development Agency about it. They're very helpful and keen to support us, and I think it would fulfil our needs as an organisation. We'd all have an equal vote in how things are done, and equal pay, depending on how much profit we make and how many hours we work. Of course we will need to pay you a fair rent for the use of the premises," she added.

"Of course," said Mike.

Tasks

What would be the advantage of Janet's proposed course of action? What could be the disadvantages?

| HELP | ? | See the information bank in **Section III: Unit 10, 6.,** pages 289–291. |

In conclusion

Now complete your reading of the Information Bank, Unit 10 'Forms of Small Business Organisation'.

When you have done this you are ready to tackle the Ongoing Assignment Task 2, 2.4 'Selecting the Appropriate Form' and/or the Extended Task below.

Extended task: A local survey

Look at a copy of your local Yellow Pages (or equivalent business directory if this is not available).

First, consider the listings of two professional services, one involved in a profession (such as 'accountants' or 'solicitors') and one offering a creative service (such as 'advertising agencies' or 'designers').

Compare and contrast the incidence of sole traders and partnerships to limited companies in these categories where this is evident from the listing. What do you think are the major reasons for any differences in the pattern which emerges?

Conduct a similar survey between two manufacturing or distribution sections, one in high technology areas (such as 'electronics components' or 'electronic equipment') and one in a more artisan or craft field (such as 'furniture manufacturers' or 'woodturners').

Ongoing assignment 2: Summary of the route to market entry

If you have completed Units 7 to 10 inclusive in Sections I and III and Tasks 2.1 to 2.4 inclusive in Section II, you should now conclude the Ongoing Assignment 2: 'The Route to Market Entry' by completing Task 2.5 'Summary of the Route to Market Entry'.

1: The business plan

This Unit looks at the when, who, why and what of business planning for the small enterprise.

Entrepreneurship and business planning are often uncomfortable partners. A common representation of an entrepreneur is of a 'wheeler-dealer', who seizes opportunities by gut feel; their instinct for the right deal is thought to make formalised strategies (beyond a few scribbled notes) unnecessary. Lack of planning is seen as something of a virtue; it allows for flexibility and creativity, as well as speed and decisiveness compared to larger organisations which miss opportunities because of the handicap of their structured planning processes.

Yet there are times when a business plan benefits even the most opportunistic entrepreneur.

Quick answer question: When?

Can you think of particular times in the life of an enterprise when business plans are beneficial?

It is not just entrepreneurs who may need to formalise their strategies into business plans. Other groups of people make decisions based upon the business plan of a small enterprise.

When?

Business plans are produced:

☐ at the start-up of a new business;

☐ when a business changes owners;

☐ at a time of major decisions, an investment or diversification proposal to expand, or crisis measures to survive

☐ As an ongoing review of business activities in a constantly changing environment.

Quick answer question: Who?

Who will be interested in a small business's plan, and make decisions based upon it?

Planning is not just for larger organisations with specialised resources; even the smallest business can benefit.

The need for a business plan is often linked to finance. An enterprise seeking funds from external sources will often be required to produce a business plan to justify its request.

Who?

The following groups may base decisions on a business plan:

☐ managers who are responsible for the day to day running of the enterprise;

☐ owners who either already have an equity stake, or are prospective investors in equity, or are interested in becoming a new partner in an enterprise;

☐ lenders who have been asked to provide funds for the business as overdrafts, loans, or loan stock, e.g. banks, venture capital companies, private investors.

However there are benefits other than those associated with raising money in producing a business plan.

Scenario: The entrepreneur versus the planner

A small business owner, Richard Rodrigues, met a corporate planner, Kevin Watkins, for a social drink. The two were old friends, but as they had not met up for some time, they were anxious to catch up on each others news.

Kevin was still working for a large utility company, as he had been when they last met. His work was to assist the line managers in his organisation to produce regular business plans which reflected corporate goals.

Richard's business, by comparison, was small and changing. He had owned a publishing company, which specialised in producing magazines for the medical profession paid for by advertising from drug companies.

"Yes I think I was doing rather nicely in publishing when we last met," Richard commented to Kevin.

"That's all changed now of course. Generic prescribing came along and wiped out that business. Doctors have to prescribe non-branded drugs where possible now, so there's little point in the drug companies advertising their branded products to them. My publications were dependent on that advertising, so the day that generic prescribing came in, I went out – of the business that is."

"You mean you've stopped publishing altogether?" asked Kevin. "Didn't you see it coming and move into some other form of publishing?"

"Well, I heard about it of course, as it was being talked about well before it became policy," Richard replied. "But I didn't think it would affect me the way it did. My advertising revenue dropped by 25%, which was enough to make the publication unprofitable. I had hoped I could ride the storm, but there didn't seem much point once I was losing money. If I'd had more time to develop new products, I probably could have stayed in the same business. There's still plenty of money to be made in medical publishing. But once the cash is flowing out of a business, it's like taking the plug out of a bath of water; its hard to put it back in the hole and keep what you've got. I decided to cut my losses and do something else."

"What did you do then?" Kevin questioned.

"I decided to do something completely different. I bought a toy company, making dolls and childrens' games," announced Richard. "Want to buy it? It keeps me awake at nights with its cash flow problems."

"No thanks. Very seasonal business, I imagine. Still you would have known that before you bought it. What's been the problem?" asked Kevin.

"You're right," said Richard, "I did know it was a seasonal business, but I actually did a very good deal in buying it. The price was rock bottom. I didn't even have to take out any loans. It's just that so much depends on Christmas – it's impossible to plan anything. My accountant checked out the reported profits and balance sheet before I bought the business, so I knew what I was getting. And the profits are there, as the previous owner said they would be. He just forgot to tell me about the cash flow. I nearly went bankrupt in the first year waiting for Christmas."

"Didn't your business plan predict that, or at least indicate there would be some serious troughs in your cash flow?" asked Kevin.

"Like I said, I didn't need any loans, so I didn't need a business plan. I don't have a corporate planning department like yours, you know," said Richard.

"Well I don't want to push my own profession, but I think a business plan would have told you about these troubles in advance. But then I am biased," laughed Kevin.

Richard did not seem to appreciate the joke.

"If I had to put together the sort of five year plan you produce every time I make a decision, I'd get nowhere fast. As a matter of fact, when I found out about this toy company for sale, there was another larger organisation interested. It was only by going down there the next day and making an offer on the spot that I clinched the deal. I expect your equivalent in this other company is still working on the business plans!" he retorted.

"I don't think that's fair at all," responded Kevin. "How can you know what you're doing without some sort of plan? It doesn't have to be complicated or time consuming. And it can show how sensitive a business is to seasonal factors – or more permanent changes like your last business. You know, a business plan may have helped you there too."

"I don't think so at all," Richard said indignantly. "What I needed then was creativity and innovation to change my business, not the straight jacket of some plan. Anyway they are only financial forecasts – crystal ball gazing. What's the point of that when you're going bust?"

"OK, OK, so you don't believe in planning. How about objectives? Do you believe in setting those?" asked Kevin.

"Of course I do," said Richard, "I just don't want to spend my time writing them down, that's all. You sound like the sales manager of my toy company. He's always sending me endless statistics of how he's doing compared to last year. I tell him to get out and see the customers. Don't worry about the targets, I can set those, and I'll tell you if you're not doing well. Just get out there and sell, that's all I ask."

"Well you obviously like centralised control – at least that's something you have in common with us planners, "smiled Kevin.

Tasks

1. *Kevin may well be right to claim that business plans could have helped Richard. In what ways do you think Richard could have benefited from a business plan – in both of his businesses?*

HELP **?** See the information bank in *Section III: Unit 11, 1.,* pages 292–296.

2. *Richard may be right to be sceptical about planning. What are the problems – perceived and real – in writing a business plan?*

HELP **?** See the information bank in *Section III: Unit 11, 1.,* pages 292–296.

3. *Richard claims that plans "are only financial forecasts – crystal ball gazing".*

   What would you want to put into a business plan to make it a more meaningful document? Suggest some outline headings for a business plan for Richard's toy company.

HELP **?** See the information bank in *Section III: Unit 11, 2.,* page 296–301.

In conclusion

Now complete your reading of the Information Bank, Unit 11 'The Business Plan'.

When you have done this you are ready to tackle the Ongoing Assignment 3, Task 3.1 'Outlining the Plan' and/or the Extended Task below.

Extended task: A bank's plan

Most high street banks offer information on business plans with a suggested outline

Obtain an outline business plan from a local bank, and study its contents.

How appropriate do you think the outline plan is for most small businesses?

How would you improve on the structure for your own business plan?

Unit 12: Successful and unsuccessful small business strategies

This Unit looks at the meaning of 'success' for small businesses, and the major influences which determine strategy. 'Strategy' is a word more commonly associated with large organisations. Small businesses are often thought to be run more on 'tactical' lines, with the focus on day to day activities. Strategy, however, is as significant in the success of small as it is in large enterprises.

Quick answer questions: What is strategy?

What do you think is meant by strategy in the small business context? What would be the main ingredients in a small business strategy?

Much of the discussion on 'successful' small business strategies assume that success equates to growth.

What is strategy?

The strategy of a small business integrates its objectives and policies into a cohesive whole, that give activities longer term direction. The main ingredients are:

☐ *Objectives:* broad or narrow targets to be achieved.

☐ *Policies:* rules or guidelines, defining the limits for activities.

☐ *Activities:* sequence of actions, sometimes specified as 'action plans'.

However, the objectives of a small business may not necessarily include growth.

Quick answer questions: Objectives of a small business

What strategic objectives may a small business have? Why is growth sometimes not an objective?

Small enterprise objectives and policies are inextricably linked to the motives of the founders in setting up in business by themselves. These motives can vary greatly, and so the objectives of small enterprises are equally diverse.

Objectives of a small business

The only objective common to all small enterprises is survival. A frequent motive of small business ownership is independence, so retention of independence is also a common objective.

Other objectives include:

❏ growth in value to eventually secure a capital gain;

❏ to provide high income to owner(s);

❏ to ensure the status of the owner(s) in the community;

❏ to ensure a secure future for the heirs of the owner(s);

❏ to provide a satisfying place to work;

❏ to represent a democratic and fair system of employment;

❏ to support 'artisan' methods of production;

❏ to promote environmentally sound business policies.

Some of these goals do not fit well with an objective of growth. Growth could mean loss of independence as the business becomes bigger. It might run counter to aims for an alternative life style through a small business. Growth may pose a threat to 'democratic' business, as in co-operatives, or 'environmentally-friendly' enterprises.

It is difficult to formulate generally applicable 'successful' strategies. The criteria for success, represented by the objectives of the small enterprise, are highly diverse.

Quick answer questions: Unsuccessful strategies

What do you think are the principal internal causes of small business failure? Why do so many go out of business? Try to classify the reasons into some general categories.

'Unsuccessful strategies' are easier to recognise as survival is a common objective. The failure rate among small businesses is high; statistics indicate that one quarter fail in the first two years, and half in the first five years. This may be an over pessimistic view, although the 1990s have seen a considerable rise in failures in the UK.

Unsuccessful strategies

The principal causes of failure within the controllable environment of the small business can be categorised as:

Management: lack of competence in choosing and running the business.

Marketing: lack of demand in the market place, and insufficient or inappropriate, efforts to stimulate it.

Money: not enough capital funds to sustain the business, or misuse of funds that are available.

Scenario 1: Life cycles at Alpha Circuits

Christopher Hugo's electronics company, Alpha Circuits, was at another critical phase in its development. In fact, recently, every year seemed to be a critical one. It had taken him the first three years after start up to grow to a viable size of around £400,000 sales, with some element of profitability. Then in the fourth year sales had levelled off, caused, as Chris discovered, by some fundamental changes in the market place around him.

Chris's timely investigation into the market place had provided him with the clues to refocus his business. His initial orders had come from industries dependent on military expenditure. Determined to reduce his reliance on this vulnerable sector, he had turned his attention to developing commercial-sector customers, where his technology base might be in demand. He had found them in the automotive industry, which was rapidly expanding the number of electronic components in domestic and commercial vehicles.

"Whereas a car today might have 25% of its equipment containing electronic components, tomorrow it will be 60%," one manufacturer had told him.

Focusing on this particular opportunity had required extra money to buy new equipment for his factory, and, as it turned out, to finance a new surge in growth of his business as well. His market strategy paid off, as sales climbed to over £500,000 by the end of his fifth year. Unfortunately, he then almost ran out of money. The growth put increasing strains on his financial resources and systems. Debtors grew as a percentage of sales, and up to date, reliable accounting information was very hard to find. It took Chris some time to re-establish control of his cash flow, and put in some systems to cope with a business that was no longer very small.

With a full order book, Chris was content to spend most of the sixth year working on the efficiency of his company – first the financial aspects, and then the operating systems. Quality control was something he found particularly in need of attention, as customers were becoming more and more demanding in that area. He had little time for marketing, but sales stayed buoyant, rising to over £600,000 by the end of year 6.

The improvements made meant that when he did turn his attention once again to sales in year 7, he could seek out new customers with increased confidence that he could provide an excellent service.

The trouble was that the time between arousing a customer's interest and receiving and fulfilling orders was a long one in his business of electronic design. The amount of time he had spent internally and not externally began to show through in the seventh year, when his order book had a distinctly thin look about it. Shipments flattened off, and annual sales showed no real increase over the prior year. He redoubled his marketing efforts, spending long hours travelling to see customers.

After a year in which turnover had levelled off, and his business had a definite 'mature' look about it, sales began to grow healthily in year 8. It was at this stage that Chris sat down to review where he was going. He talked to an old friend about it one day.

"The trouble is," Chris explained, "that I seem to stagger from one extreme to the other. Every year is crucial – for different reasons. When will I have a normal business that is not in some kind of crisis?"

"What exactly has been the pattern of these crises?" asked the friend.

"Stop-start-stop-start would be the best way to describe it," replied Chris. "The order book looks thin, so I spend my time out selling. I fill up my order book, then the supervisor in the factory yells that she can't cope unless I spend time with her, to sort out production schedules and the ordering of components. Then my accountant tells me that debtors are a bit high, and I should spend some time chasing money. So I take time out to sort out these problems. What happens? You've guessed it. The order book weakens, and I have to dash off and drum up some more business. I'm not sure if I can cope with this up and down existence much longer."

"Have you thought of getting anyone else in to help – at a senior level I mean," suggested the friend.

"Sure I'd love to, but the business can't afford two of us right now. A good man at director level is going to cost the company at least £40,000 all in. That's all the profit we make right now. I need to grow the business by another £100,000 sales to afford someone. But I'm not sure I can do it on my own."

Tasks

1. *Map out the stages which Chris's business has been through so far. Try to draw this as a life cycle graph indicating the key category of problem(s) experienced in each stage.*

HELP ? | See the information bank in **Section III: Unit 12, 1.2,** pages 304–305.

2. *What is the principal category of problem that faces Chris right now?*
   What do you think he should do about it? Outline the strategy you
   would recommend that he adopt, with some specific activities.

See the information bank in **Section III: Unit 12, 3.3
and 3.4,** pages 312–314.

Plans, or just patterns?

Strategy is not just a deliberate planning process, where actions are either
consciously thought through in advance, or form a deliberate reaction to events.

Quick answer questions: Emergent strategies

*Can you give some small business examples where strategy emerges as
a pattern of activity, not deliberately conceived in advance?*

*Consider also how these might then be converted into 'intended'
strategies.*

Strategy is formulated by human activity, as well as human design. Where a
deliberate, intended strategy does exist, it will inevitably become modified
through the experiences of implementation.

Small business is sometimes typified as unplanned, and unstructured, where
owners react to events with no clear strategy to direct them. But even when there
is no purposeful intended strategy, a pattern of activities emerges which have an
element of consistency that amounts to a strategy. When recognised, these are
often then 'converted' to an intended strategy by a deliberate decision.

Emergent strategies

Examples of strategies that 'emerge' as patterns, before conversion to 'intended'
strategies, include:

☐ *Marketing approaches which are often on a reactive basis until a pattern
emerges.*

A small firm had no intended strategy about the size of its customer base. But
one customer liked their products so much that they ordered more and more.
There was no time to find other customers, as this one demanded so much
attention. Anyway why bother, when producing enough is the problem? A
strategy of concentrating 80% of production capacity on one customer
emerged. After a while, the owner realised the dangers in this and
deliberately decided to follow a strategy of broadening their customer base.

❏ *Management strategies, especially those involving people, often emerge as unplanned reactions to factors previously unknown.*

A small retailer employed mainly part-time staff, as they found that the best applicants for advertised vacancies were invariably those only able to work on a part-time basis. When this pattern was recognised, the owner consciously adopted a policy of seeking part-time staff.

❏ *Money strategies are perhaps the most difficult to deliberately plan, except in the short to medium term.*

A small manufacturer did not intend a strategy of long term bank borrowing. But when the owner reviewed the bank statements over a two year period, the overdraft never fell below £30,000. A pattern of borrowing had emerged, and the bank manager advised recognition of this strategy by converting the fixed element of the overdraft into a 10 year loan.

Scenario 2: End of a decade at Alpha Circuits

Christopher Hugo was celebrating 10 years in business with his bank manager.

"It's quite an achievement to survive a decade in your own business. Most small businesses don't make it this far, only about one third some say. How does it feel?" asked the bank manager.

"Oh, I obviously feel very pleased to have made it so far. But right now I also feel quite sad. It's rather like watching one of your own children grow up, knowing that one day they have to leave you," replied Chris

"Surely you're not retiring?" asked the bank manager.

"No, not exactly," explained Chris, "but I have to change something. Young managers these days don't seem to have the same approach as our generation. Take my operations director; he's just decided to give all the shop floor workers Friday afternoon off from 3pm. He says that its modern working practice, but I'd like to know how he's going to make up the lost time, *and* hit his production targets.

Oh and talking of targets, my new accountant is target-mad! We joke that if anything moves, she gives it a budget, but its almost true. Everything we do is allocated somewhere and costed against targets. It can be useful, but it's made the whole place so bureaucratic – forms for everything," complained Chris.

"You don't have to tell me about forms," said the bank manager, "but doesn't the business need this type of organisation now?"

"Well it didn't before I hired all these managers. I sometimes think they are just making a job for themselves. Now they want to bring in consultants to introduce 'total quality management'. Why we need an outsider to come in and teach us the latest jargon I'm not sure," said Chris. "I'm beginning to think I've got the wrong team – these MBAs don't seem very practical people for a small business."

"You're not so small anymore," commented the bank manager. "Your turnover has certainly jumped up since you enlarged your management team. What do you think it will be this year?"

"Well we might even make £2 million. I suppose this is my biggest problem. We're selling more than ever, and growing by 30 to 40% per annum, but I'm not getting any benefits personally. There's no more cash for me to pay myself, and I'm not getting the same satisfaction from my work. I feel they resent my interference – except in technical matters where they're always asking for help. What do you think I should do?" Chris asked.

"Well 48 is a bit young for retirement," joked the bank manager. "Ever thought of selling the business?"

"My accountant tells me to wait a few more years. Although we've grown fast, the profits will not materialise for a while. We've grown the overhead very quickly and it can cope with quite a lot more volume. Just at the moment though our ratios wouldn't look too good in any sale prospectus," answered Chris.

"I'm going to have to put up with them, or put them out, I can't decide which."

Tasks

1. Why do you think Chris is facing the problems he describes? Do you think these issues are caused more by Chris's personality, or by the situation of the company?

See the information bank in *Section III: Unit 12, 2.2*, pages 309–310.

2. What do you think Chris should do about his problems? If you were Chris, what questions would you be asking yourself?

See the information bank in *Section III: Unit 12, 3.*, pages 310–315.

In conclusion

Now complete your reading of the Information Bank, Unit 12 'Successful and Unsuccessful Small Business Strategies'.

When you have done this you are ready to tackle the Ongoing Assignment 3, Task 3.2 'Deciding the Strategy' and/or the Extended Task below.

Extended task: Food and drinks strategy

Consider a small business (preferably involved in the food and drinks industry) with which you are familiar. (See the Extended Task in Unit 1 and subsequently.)

How would you summarise its overall business strategy? Try to do this by reference to the '4 Ms' of management, marketing, money and motives (or objectives of the business).

Which of its strategies would you say were 'intended', and which have 'emerged' as a pattern of activities over some time?

Unit 13: Management of resources

This Unit looks at the management of resources – impersonal and human resources – in the small firm. Small business management may take place in an environment which is different to large business, but this, in itself, does not make it a different skill to other forms of management. To some extent, all businesses, large or small, exist in differing environments.

> ### Quick answer question: What is the difference?
>
> *Do you think that small business management requires any skills that are less needed in larger organisations? If so, which?*

Management is concerned with the efficient use of resources in support of the objectives of the organisation. In a small, as in a large, organisation some of these resources are impersonal, such as premises, materials, machinery, equipment and management systems. However, the key resource will inevitably be people, even though they may not be within the organisation.

What is the difference?

In larger organisations, management is organised into specialist areas, such as production, marketing and finance. The chief executive acts rather like the conductor of an orchestra, who keeps the different instruments in time and in harmony.

In a small enterprise, there are no specialist departments to co-ordinate. Owner-managers have to be generalists, not only conducting, but playing many of the instruments as well. It is this diversity of activities which makes small business management different. In contrast to the conductor of an orchestra, who can walk away for a while without the players stopping, the owner-manager is involved in many functions which require their constant attention. For this reason, they have been likened to the entertainer who attempts to keep plates spinning on top of poles; one lapse of attention and they all come down.

Information is often the key to managing this difficult juggling act.

Unfortunately information only comes from records, which involve administration and 'paperwork'. A problem often referred to by the small business manager is the amount of paperwork they have to do. This complaint focuses on some of the administrative burdens of government regulations, rather than the benefits of having the internal data necessary to run the business.

What information does the small business manager need?

Areas where records are necessary, or desirable, are:

Sales: records of enquiries, follow up and conversion rates; analysis of invoiced sales by products and customers; mailing lists, and results of promotional campaigns.

Production: productivity measures; rejects and wastage; work in progress.

Purchasing: stock value and movement; costs of direct materials.

Personnel: employee records; wages; absenteeism; holidays.

Finance: cash book; sales and purchase ledgers; banking; VAT/PAYE/NIC; management accounts; debtor analysis.

Premises often represent a fundamental resource for a small firm.

The availability of premises, suited to the needs of a new business, has been an important public issue since it was discovered that there was a shortage of small units with flexible leases and facilities in some areas.

Government pressure has lead to the increased provision of suitable property in developments by public bodies, business centres and science parks.

Where is the best location?

Location considerations include:

- ❑ communications by road, rail etc;
- ❑ availability of any necessary skilled labour;
- ❑ nearness to centres of population (and their shopping areas for retail outlets):
- ❑ costs of rent and rates;
- ❑ government and local authority assistance available;
- ❑ proximity to the home of the founder.

In practice, the home of the founder will be the key influence; very few move home to set up a new business.

Premises are only a start to developing the infrastructure of a small firm. Material and equipment resources are another important management consideration.

Q | ### Quick answer questions: What equipment and materials are needed?
What are the main categories of equipment and materials that a small business might need?

List some of the benefits of sound purchasing procedures in buying them.

The identification, sourcing and purchasing of equipment and materials essential to the operation of business is a specialist function in larger firms. Purchasing is just one of the owner-managers many responsibilities, and one that can be easily neglected in the pressure of day to day activities.

What equipment and materials are needed?

Categories of *equipment* that may be needed by a small firm include:

- ❑ production machinery;
- ❑ communication equipment – telephone, fax etc;
- ❑ office or retail furniture;
- ❑ systems equipment – computers and software;
- ❑ personal equipment – cars and mobile phones;

Materials purchased are:

- ❑ goods to be sold on, for example, a retailers stock, or raw materials for a manufacturer;

☐   consumables for office, publicity and canteen use.

Sound purchasing procedures should ensure:

☐   the right items of the appropriate quality for the job;

☐   lowest possible costs;

☐   minimum stocks levels;

☐   maximum stock availability.

Scenario 1: Kimberley runs into conflict

Kimberley Lawson was feeling disillusioned. Her vision of running her own happy business, removed from the hierarchy and restrictive rules of her previous employer, was rapidly crumbling. When she had bought her own restaurant a year earlier, her main aim was to get away from the politics of big business and concentrate on making her own enterprise work, with a group of like-minded people. Her background seemed ideal to make the venture successful. She had trained with a large hotel group, and gained experience in almost every aspect of catering management, from kitchen hygiene to cost accounting. She felt, after her five years employment there, that she knew how to manage all the various functions that were needed to run a restaurant.

She had soon found, however, that this was not enough. She just didn't seem able to cope with all the demands on her when she had first acquired the restaurant.

"It's not that I don't know what to do," she had explained to her husband Philip, when he had enquired after noticing that Kimberley seemed particularly harassed. "It's just that I don't know what to do first. When I worked for the Milton group, everything was organised for you. When I was managing the coffee shop, for example, the menu had already been worked out between the marketing and the finance departments, the staff were employed by personnel, and the food ordered through purchasing. Now I have to do all that myself and manage everything on a daily basis as well. I don't have time to think, let alone plan ahead, and there is no one I can ask to help. Everyone else is far too busy serving customers".

These normal problems of a small business manager were no longer her big worry however. She had eventually learned how to put priorities on her activities, and to distinguish between the most important, and the most immediate jobs, which were not always the same thing.

The real issue now was that she didn't enjoy her work any more. She was trying to explain this to her ever-attentive husband.

"I thought running my own business would be fun – not just for me, but for everyone else involved. I used to dream of working in a small firm where everyone would have the same aims, we would all know what was going on, and we wouldn't have to put up with any of the bureaucratic nonsense that we had at the Milton. What do I get instead? Hassle from him, each and every day."

Philip nodded. He had heard similar complaints before, so he knew that the source of the trouble was one Raymond Bogaerts, master chef. He had been with the restaurant when Kimberley had bought it, and seemed like a major asset at the time. His high standards of innovative cuisine made the restaurant different to its more traditional neighbours, and had helped it to a position of high popularity.

"What's he done this time?" asked Philip.

"This time he has gone too far," raged Kimberley. "He has refused to do what I asked, and demanded a written statement of his terms and conditions of employment. He's driving me back to the old bureaucracy just because he doesn't agree with my methods. As you know, I've suspected for some time that our waste levels in the kitchen are too high. Well now I can prove it. I've spent a lot of time analysing our food costs in relation to our prices. In theory they should be no more than a third of the menu price. They're actually over 40%, simply because we are using too much food. The portions are too big; customers just cannot eat all we give them. You should see what we throw away."

"But aren't your generous portions part of the attraction of the place?" asked Philip.

"You sound like Raymond," said Kimberley. "He believes that we can't reduce portion sizes without losing customers. I told him that was my affair, and nothing to do with him. All he has to do is to cook what I ask. That's when he asked for a written description of his responsibilities. He says he's entitled to one, and that he doesn't like the way I've changed his job. He claims that he was always involved in any menu changes before I took over."

"Isn't it wise to consult him anyway? He does have to run the kitchen after all," suggested Philip.

"I don't mind consulting him," said Kimberley, "as long as he doesn't just refuse to do anything he doesn't agree with. The previous owner didn't understand menus. I do. Besides he doesn't 'run' the kitchen. He may think he does, but I can't trust him to hire the staff anymore. He fills the kitchen with part-timers that he can shout at and give work to on a favour basis as he pleases. I want professionals in my kitchen."

Philip had heard of the chef's slave-driving tactics in the kitchen, but nevertheless tried one last effort to support him. "Yes, but what about the costs? Aren't your staff costs a lot higher than they used to be?" he asked.

Kimberley let out a long breath before replying. "Yes. Which is why the food costs have to come down. His way of making money is to employ inexperienced part timers – female of course – for a pittance. My way is to pay a proper wage for trained people, who will save their extra costs by reducing waste, and generally being more professional in their work. If Raymond isn't going to accept it, he will

have to go. I will make him redundant and work in the kitchen myself for a while.
As I've employed him under two years, I don't think he is even entitled to
redundancy money."

Tasks

1. *Many people would share Kimberley's original vision that a small
   business could provide a happier working environment than a larger
   organisation. Is this a realistic view, or is there as much conflict in
   small as in large organisations? Try and support your conclusions
   with practical evidence.*

HELP ? See the information bank in *Section III: Unit 13, 4.2,*
pages 329–331.

2. *Kimberley's management style is evidently different to her
   predecessors. How do you think Raymond likes to be managed? What
   do you think Kimberley should do? Assess her current management
   style, and the appropriateness of her decision to make Raymond
   redundant.*

HELP ? See the information bank in *Section III: Unit 13, 4.3,*
pages 331–333.

3. *Raymond's method of running the kitchen, with low pay and poor
   conditions, could be likened to the 'Sweatshop'. In what
   circumstances do you think these conditions can prevail in a small
   business?*

HELP ? See the information bank in *Section III: Unit 13, 4.3,*
pages 331–333.

4. *Two points of employment law were raised by this case:*

   i) *Is the chef correct in his demand for a written statement of terms
      and conditions?*

   ii) *Is Kimberley right in thinking she will not have to pay him any
       redundancy money?*

HELP ? See the information bank in *Section III: Unit 13, 4.1,*
pages 328–329.

A small firm with limited resources is particularly vulnerable if any of those resources are affected by misfortune and disaster.

Some insurances are a legal requirement, others desirable, some questionable. Insurance can cover all types of resources, impersonal and people.

Types of insurance

☐ Employer's liability, against illness or injury at work. A legal requirement.

☐ Property insurance for the buildings is normally required by a lease.

☐ Fire, theft and other perils – for premises and contents.

☐ Breakdown or damage – manufacturers, for example, can insure machinery against damage or breakdown.

☐ Loss of profits – insurance to compensate for the full effects of disruption on the trading position of a small firm.

☐ Public and product liability – in case of claims from members of the public.

☐ Professional indemnity – in case of claims of misconduct or negligence in performing a professional service.

☐ Key man insurance – a policy on the life of a key person to the business, usually an owner-manager.

Scenario 2: Leading to problems

Kimberley had made progress in resolving the management problems in her restaurant. Raymond Bogaerts, the chef, had not appeared for work one day, and later telephoned to say he would not be back. Conflicts in small firms are often resolved by one person leaving the organisation.

After a moment of panic, Kimberley had breathed a sigh of relief. "At least I can make a fresh start now that he is gone," she had thought. After a period working in the kitchen herself, she had decided that the only way to develop the business was to recruit another person to manage the kitchen. Kimberley followed the personnel practices of her previous large employer, and carefully drew up a job description and a person specification before advertising the new job. The good response enabled her to select someone she felt was the ideal candidate – experienced and motivated by the thought of working in a small firm. Laura, the new head chef, was given wider responsibilities than just preparing food, so

Kimberley was not too surprised when she asked to see her one morning. But the meeting was not routine; Laura had problems.

"I'm sorry to burst in on you like this, but I don't think I can manage on my own any longer," she blurted out.

"On your own?" queried Kimberley. "I thought we had agreed to work as a team. What's the problem?"

"In a word, communications – or lack of them," said Laura, I need you to tell me more about what is going on. I know we agreed that team work is important, but I feel as though I'm working alone most of the time – until something happens I don't know about, that is, like the meat delivery changing from Friday to Thursday."

"Yes, we've been over that, and I have apologised," interrupted Kimberley, checking her watch as she was due to visit a customer that morning.

"Look I'm not sure what you're getting at exactly, but if this business is to develop the way I thought we both agreed we wanted, then I will have to leave you to manage your area. I don't have time to do my job now that we've taken on these commercial catering contracts, let alone help you with yours. You know what to do, and you have staff of your own, can't we just get on and do it?"

"I know you're busy," said Laura, "but I need your help now and again, and I need you to tell me what you're doing, as it does affect my work you know. I can't just 'get on and do it', unless I get feedback from you. Besides it's nice to talk to someone other than the wash-up now and again."

Kimberley smiled, "OK, I get the message, but not today. I have appointments to keep. I'll make a point of looking in tomorrow."

Task

What is your assessment now of Kimberley's management. Do you think that:

i) *She has made a mistake in her choice of kitchen manager, who does not seem very independent?*

ii) *She is right to insist that, now they have agreed their responsibilities, they should 'get on and do it'?*

iii) *There is anything missing in her leadership of the business?*

> HELP ? | See the information bank in *Section III: Unit 13, 4.4 and 4.5,* pages 333–335.

In conclusion

Now complete your reading of Information Bank 13, 'Management of Resources'.

When you have done this you are ready to tackle the Ongoing Assignment 3, Task 3.3 'Managing the Resources' and/or the Extended Task below.

Extended task: Staff assessment

Consider a small business where you have recently been a customer which employs staff other than the owner-manager (for example a food or drinks outlet such as a restaurant, wine bar or public house considered in previous extended tasks.)

How would you rate the service provided by the staff, and their general attitude to the customer?

Write a short analysis of the motivation of the staff and the type of management control which you feel this illustrates.

If you were the owner-manager of this business, how could you change staff attitudes and motivation for the benefit of the customer?

Unit 14: Marketing

Marketing has been established as a key ingredient in the strategy of a small business, even if the owner-manager has no great ambitions beyond long term survival. Yet many small business owners would probably say that they do not "do much marketing" or that they "leave that to the larger companies".

Quick answer question: Why limited marketing?

Why do you think that some small firms do not approach marketing very positively, believing that it is more appropriate for large, rather than small firms?

In fact, small firms cannot avoid marketing, even if they would prefer to do so. Customers will receive marketing communications from a small business whether they are intended or not. Patterns emerge from the way a small firm presents and prices its products or services, and how these are sold and delivered to a customer. These patterns amount to the marketing strategy of a small firm, even if it is only in the perception of the customer. The owner-manager who has no time to consider marketing strategy will be adopting one by default.

Why limited marketing?

Managers of small firms may shy away from positive applications of marketing because:

❏ They lack specialised knowledge and skills; often owner-managers are more familiar with the product or technical aspects of their business, and have no training or experience in marketing.

❏ They lack interest because of their personal motivations. Some owner-managers do not want to grow their business. Others find impersonal marketing communication distasteful. Most are so busy with day to day operational problems, they have no time to consider longer term marketing plans.

❏ They believe it to be too expensive. A shortage of funds and high costs in other areas, particularly in the start up phase of a new business, can mean that marketing expenditure is considered as something of a luxury, which only larger companies, achieving economies of scale, can justify.

❏ They believe it to be ineffective. Some small firms are highly specialised, serving very narrow market segments. In these circumstances the appropriate marketing approach may not be obvious and standard promotions may be wasteful and ineffective.

Regardless of the level of marketing effort, a small enterprise will benefit from a marketing plan. Without one they will be leaving their strategy to emerge in ways which may not be advantageous.

Quick answer question: What is in a marketing plan?

Write down what you think should be the main components of a marketing plan?

There is evidence that the marketing style of many small firms is different to larger organisations as marketing is often:

◻ restricted in scope and activity;

◻ simplistic and haphazard;

◻ product and price oriented;

◻ centralised on the experience of the owner-manager.

What is in a marketing plan?

The main components of a marketing plan are:

◻ *The marketing environment:* A background analysis of the strengths and weaknesses of the small firm, in relation to the opportunities and threats in the market place, including competitive and external influences and a definition of the customer and their needs.

◻ *The marketing objective:* A precise summary of the results that a small enterprise expects from its marketing activities – what products or services are to be sold in which markets, in what quantities and when.

◻ *The marketing methods:* A plan of how the elements in the marketing mix are to be used - what product, at which prices, in what place, supported by which promotions.

Scenario 1: Bryony Hannam's marketing plans – product and pricing problems

Bryony Hannam was enjoying her involvement in a picture framing business, Gray's Framing Studios. She found that having a partner, who looked after the production and operations in the workshop, left her free to concentrate on the marketing side of the business. When they had purchased the business, the basic product and services offered were:

1. *A bespoke picture framing service.*

   60% of sales were made by providing a framing service for customers' own images, ranging from photographs to fine art. As all the operations were carried out in their own workshop, this type of business generated a good gross margin of 70%: in other words the variable costs of the mouldings, board, glass and other materials involved in the framing process averaged 30% of the final selling price.

2. *Framed and unframed pictures.*

   As well as the framing service, a range of pictures, including inexpensive prints and posters, limited editions, original water colours and oils, were offered through the three retail shops. Although these were usually sold framed, they could be purchased unframed. The gross margin on a framed picture averaged 50%, as the cost of purchasing the image lowered the profit available on the framing. However, stock costs were not necessarily a problem, as some local artists were happy to leave their work on display on a sale or return basis.

Initially Bryony had thought that the only way to expand the business was to open more shops. Now she had another plan. The customers they attracted at the moment were primarily householders buying pictures for home decorations. They occasionally attracted orders from businesses, however, who wanted a quantity of framing for a variety of applications. Bryony decided to focus her expansion plans on this commercial market. In talking to local businesses, she discovered that some had a need for a high volume of standard framing. A restaurant owner, for example, wanted to hang pictures in the same type of frame all over his interior walls; a local hotel had a continuous demand for framed pictures, and repairs to damaged ones. Potential customers like these seemed to appreciate Bryony's personal approach and service, and she had soon generated a steady stream of orders.

In visiting business premises, she noticed also that many did not have pictures on their walls. Reception areas were left bare and uninviting; offices cried out for the added touch of a well chosen picture. By probing office managers, Bryony found that many were receptive to the idea of improving the environment, but did not have the time or budget (or both) to do anything about it.

Bryony had come up with the idea of a 'hire purchase' scheme. She took all the problems away from the office manager, by advising them on the pictures and frames to select, and allowing them to be purchased over one year by an instalment plan.

This product innovation proved very popular, and their commercial business steadily increased until it became 25% of the total sales of the business. Problems began to emerge however. The partner who ran the workshop, Tony Meeham, asked for an urgent meeting with Bryony to discuss some of them.

"This order for 50 frames from the Crown Hotel can't be done this week, unless we lengthen the turn round time for our regular customers. It's going to block up the entire workshop for a day or two. And are you really sure its worth it?" began Tony.

"How do you mean? I thought you were pleased to have so much business." Bryony looked slightly offended.

"Don't get me wrong. We needed some new business; we were really slack for a while, and your new orders have certainly made a difference. But because they're big one-off orders, they' re really making it difficult to schedule our normal workload. The shops are beginning to get complaints from customers who sometimes have to wait over two weeks for their framing, if we have a big job on. And the prices on those orders are a lot lower – are you sure we're covering our costs?

"It depends which costs you mean," answered Bryony. "I have worked out the cost of materials for commercial orders and we're still making a good margin. Our normal retail price for the frames for the Crown Hotel would be £30 ex VAT. There is plenty of competition for commercial work, so of course I have to give discounts, but we're still selling at £15 per frame. As we make a 70% margin on our retail framing, I feel I can go at least as low as that."

"Yes, we're certainly more than covering our materials costs, but what about the overheads: wages, rent, electricity. When you take all that into account, I don't think we're making much money at that price. How many frames do you think I have to make each day just to pay the overheads?" asked Tony.

"Look," said Bryony feeling a growing sense of irritation that her work was not being appreciated, "when I came here, you yourself said that the workshop could easily cope with more work. I think you even mentioned that you could finish all the production in 4 days a week if you really pushed yourselves. Well the overheads are the same now as then. The only extra costs, are the costs of materials for these frames. Of course we're making money on this order."

"OK I see your point," said Tony sensing the need to tread carefully. "But how far do you think we can go with this commercial business. If it becomes really big, and we lose some of our retail business, then our profitability is bound to suffer isn't it?"

Bryony picked up some papers from the desk. "Have a look at these sales figures I worked out for our last twelve months," she said. "I think you can see we have plenty of room for manoeuvre. I price our commercial work all on the same basis as the Crown job, so I know we make a reasonable margin on it overall. Our overheads are £200,000 including you and I, so I'm sure we are in profit."

Bryony produced the following sales break down:

Sales by type:	£'000s
Retail sales: framing	180
Retail sales: pictures	120
Total retail	300
Commercial	100
Total sales	400

Tony studied the sales figures. "Yes, the sales are certainly looking a lot healthier, with this new commercial business," he commented. "But the retail side is suffering a bit you know. We were forecasting more shop sales than this 12 months ago. The other problem seems to be cash flow. You're not counting interest charges in your overhead figure, and our borrowings are going up. Those commercial customers are not paying in the same way as our cash customers in the shop. Some are taking 90 days to pay. And then of course there are the hire purchase customers where we don't get our money in full for one year. They are getting your normal commercial discounts and free credit."

"Yes but its proving very popular, " replied Bryony. "Business customers expect discounts and credit. We have to price according to the different markets we're in."

Tasks

1. *Bryony has moved into a new market by extending their basic products and services to suit customer needs. What are the core benefits that she is offering these commercial customers? In what ways has Bryony extended the product or service to attract these customers? Can you think of any additional ways?*

See the information bank in *Section III: Unit 14, 4.1, 4.2 and 4.3,* page 347–348.

2. *Bryony has priced their products and services in the commercial market by offering a standard discount. What gross margin are they making on orders such as the one for the Crown Hotel? How else could Bryony go about making pricing decisions? What would you recommend as a pricing strategy for the commercial market?*

See the information bank in *Section III: Unit 14, 5.1, 5.2 and 5.3,* page 350–353.

3. *The company has an issue over the mix of products and customer types, which could considerably affect its profitability. Is Bryony right to say that they are still in profit? Calculate the gross margins that apply to each of the sales figures produced by Bryony, and verify if the total gross margin covers the overheads. Assuming the average sales price per unit is £25, use the average gross margin, and known total overheads, to calculate the number of units required to break even.*

See the information bank in *Section III: Unit 14, 5.4,* page 353–358.

4. *Bryony's marketing decisions are having a negative impact on the cash flow of the business. What can Bryony do to redress the balance?*

See the information bank in *Section III: Unit 14, 5.4,* page 353–358.

Quick answer question: Low risk innovation

How can small firms, with limited resources, research and develop new products?

Small firms are often faced with a dilemma over product development and innovation. Without new products, a small business in a competitive environment cannot hope to survive. Yet the costs and risks involved in researching and developing new products are substantial.

Low risk innovation

☐ A small firm can stick to existing products and services, but innovate in terms of how they are offered to various market segments. The last scenario illustrated how a basic service can be modified into something very different, with very little development costs.

☐ Licensing agreements can give a small firm access to new products, manufacturing processes, or services.

☐ Collaborative ventures are being encouraged between the business and scientific community. A growing number of small firms are gaining access to the innovations of Universities, Polytechnics and research establishments, and providing the commercial expertise to exploit concepts developed elsewhere.

☐ Franchising can provide a small firm with the development resource of the franchisor, with the costs amortised across a large number of franchisees.

Scenario 2: Bryony Hannam's marketing plans – promotional and distribution issues

Bryony was feeling pleased with her day's work. She had just signed up her first distributor, Sherwoods Office Furniture. The commercial side of their business had flourished but Bryony had found that the local area was limited in its potential. There were only a certain number of businesses , and after an initial sales campaign she had found that there were diminishing returns from revisiting the same prospects. Instead she had looked further afield and found easier pickings nearer larger cities. Unfortunately, she had no local knowledge or contacts in these areas, which made consistent sales difficult. However, on one call, she had met Stan Renton, who was also looking for customers for his company Sherwoods Office Furniture. Bryony had quickly recognised the potential synergy between their organisations, which had culminated in the distribution agreement they had just signed. Sherwoods would have the exclusive right in a defined territory to sell pictures and framing which Bryony would supply them. Renton had readily accepted her approaches, as he was visiting commercial companies in the area, and he saw the possibilities of selling some pictures as an add-on to his normal business.

As she drove back, Bryony thought through some of the details of their meeting. "He will be quite demanding," she thought. "Although that's probably a good thing. I don't think Tony will be very pleased that I've given away another 33% of our margin, but that's not much for a distributor. It will mean I can't afford much for promotional materials – the existing retail leaflets will just have to do, despite what Renton thinks. I don't think we can agree with him about changing our name either; that sounds too complicated and expensive, even if he did say it doesn't sound very business like. Maybe he is right about using direct mail, however. I like the way he used it to promote his own business, in conjunction with personal selling. I've never liked it myself, but it's worked very well for him. I wonder how many more distributors I should set up.........."

Tasks

1. *What do you think will be the advantages and disadvantages for Bryony's firm in using a distributors like Sherwoods?*

| HELP **?** | See the information bank in **S***ection III: Unit 14, 7.3 and 7.4,* page 370–371. |

2. *Do you agree with Bryony's caution about new promotional material, and a name change? What promotional activities would you undertake to reach the commercial market, both directly and in support of a distributor?*

| HELP **?** | See the information bank in *Section III: Unit 14, 6.2–6.4,* page 360–367. |

In conclusion

Now complete your reading of the Information Bank, Unit 14 'Marketing'.

When you have done this you are ready to tackle the Ongoing Assignment 3, Task 3.4 'Planning the Marketing' and/or the Extended Task below.

Extended task: A marketing evaluation

Consider two small businesses (preferably involved in the food and drinks industry) with which you are familiar. (See the Extended Task in Unit 1 and subsequently.)

Compare and contrast the marketing strategy of these two businesses. List their activities under the categories of the 4Ps of product, price, promotion and place.

In what ways do you think they are good practitioners of marketing philosophy?

How could you improve upon their marketing strategies, and their implementation of marketing methods?

Unit 15: Money

This Unit considers money in the four aspects of:

1. The financial requirements of a small business.
2. The sources of finance available.
3. The control of financial resources.
4. Financial analysis for a small firm.

Quick answer questions: Financial requirements

What are the different financial needs of a small firm? What does it need money for?

Small firms need money for a large variety of purposes, which will depend not only on the nature of the business, but also the stage that the business has reached in its life cycle. There are also many sources of finance for a small business, and it is important to match the funding of certain needs with an appropriate source of finance.

Financial requirements

A small firm's finance needs can be classified into:

❑ *Permanent capital:* used for start-up expenses, expansion or refinancing after positive or negative developments. This represents the long term capital base of the company and usually comes from equity investment by the owners or external investors.

❑ *Working capital:* required to fund the gap between being paid by debtors, and paying out to suppliers. It may also be needed to cope with seasonal fluctuations in trade, or to pay for short lived assets. It is funded by short term borrowings of up to 3 years.

❑ *Asset finance:* required to buy the tangible assets of the business, such as machinery, equipment, premises and vehicles. It is funded by medium to long term borrowings of 3 years or more.

❑ *International trade:* may need to be specifically financed, to overcome problems of security of payment and currency uncertainties when dealing with overseas customers.

Quick answer questions: Sources of finance

*What are the different sources of finance available to the small firm?
For what purposes are they best suited?*

Finance for small firms has been a live political issue since the UK government began actively promoting small business in the 1980s. Until the 1970s, the sources of finance were limited to personal investment by owners, loans from banks, and hire purchase from finance houses, with alternative sources relatively rare. Although personal investment and bank borrowings are still the most common source, the alternatives have grown considerably in the last decade or so.

Sources of finance

The funding options and their appropriate uses include:

1. *Personal investment by owner-managers:* This still represents the most common source of permanent, equity capital for a small firm.

2. *External private investment:* The government recognised the importance of attracting private investment in small business by introducing incentives such as the Business Expansion Scheme (BES), and support through schemes such as LINC, a service designed to match up investors with potential business partners. The Unlisted Securities Market (USM) was launched in 1980, to provide equity finance for the growing smaller business.

   These routes were all designed primarily to attract longer term equity investment, to assist small firms at start-up or significant development points.

3. *Venture capital:* Organisations such as 3i, Candover Investments, and some Enterprise Boards and Development Agencies offer venture capital, in return mainly for equity in the young and growing business. In 1990 £1.4 billion was invested in start-ups (12% of the money invested), expansion developments (31%), and management buy-outs and buy-ins (52%).

   This type of finance is targeted at longer term financing requirements, although an exit route (a method by which the venture capital organisation can cash in their investment) has to be visible.

4. *Clearing banks:* The major high street banks and other clearing banks, have all developed services aimed at the small firm. Overdrafts are still the most common way of providing working capital. Bank loans are widely used to finance medium to long term requirements.

5. *Public sector sources:* A wide range of financial support is available to the small business from public sector sources, including the Enterprise Allowance Scheme, British Technology Group, Development Boards, Enterprise

Agencies, EC funds, Rural Development Commission, Tourist Boards, the Princes Youth Business Trust and the Enterprise Initiative.

6. *Finance houses and leasing companies:* Leasing and hire purchase of assets, such as equipment and vehicles, is available to small firms from finance houses and leasing companies.

7. *Factoring:* A small firm can generate working capital by handing its debtors over to a factoring company, which quickly pays a percentage of a firm's invoice value, in return for the right to collect the full amount.

8. *Export finance:* The Export Credits Guarantee Department of the DTI arranges insurance in the event of non-payment by an overseas customer, which is an important first step in obtaining finance to support international trade from banks or export houses.

Scenario 1: It all adds up for Susan

Susan Howells had found that mathematics homework in her household was a traumatic experience. It started when her children were asked by their school to do simple sums at home, and then learn their multiplication tables. This proved a stressful time in the Howells' household until Susan invented a series of games which turned a duty into fun. Her children liked her mathematics games so much that they introduced them to their friends. Requests for Susan to produce more copies of the games soon followed.

Over the next few years, Susan developed this experience into a small business. Working from home as a sole trader, she built up a respectable turnover in her childrens' activity games, based on making mathematics more fun. Towards the end of the third year, she decided it was time to set up her business on a more permanent basis in separate premises. Her family certainly agreed; they would be pleased to have their kitchen and living room back for their own use when the piles of Susan's products and literature left.

Susan explained her plans to her accountant. "I want to set up from January 1st next year as a limited company, Kal Kulate Ltd, using my brand name. I have found some new premises for a small workshop and storage facilities, where I can employ the staff I need. But I will have to buy some new equipment. We need to become more organised and efficient in our production, which means buying more benches, tools and the like. I have had a preliminary talk with my bank manager, who was encouraging, but said I had to produce a cash flow forecast in order to apply for a larger overdraft. Unfortunately I've no idea where to start, although he did give me some leaflets, with outline headings for a forecast. Can you help?"

"Yes, of course," replied the accountant, "but you will have to do quite a lot of work to provide the information. A cash flow forecast is quite simple really. It tries to estimate how much cash will be coming into and going out of your business each month. From this we can judge what you can afford to invest in new equipment, and to risk in new overheads such as your premises."

"Well, I've done a rough calculation of my profit for the year, and it looks as though I can more or less break even after paying myself some sort of salary. But that's not the same as a cash flow forecast is it?"

"No, it's different," replied the accountant, "although one can be derived from the other. In fact it's usually easier to do forecasts of profit and cash at the same time. They use a lot of common information. The crucial difference is that a profit forecast looks at the difference between your sales and your costs at the moment those sales are made, or those costs incurred. It calculates a profit, or loss, based on invoices as they are sent, or received, not on when they are paid. The cash flow is only concerned with cash – when sales and purchases are actually paid for."

"Right, I think I see what you're getting at," replied Susan, "but I'm sure it will be even clearer when we have the figures in front of us. Exactly what information do you need?"

"Here is a list of the headings we're looking at. I think you should spend a few days working on this information, and then we can talk about it again."

A week later, Susan returned to see the accountant, and brought the information he had asked for with her. It is summarised below:

Kal Kulate Ltd: Profit & Loss/Cash Flow input information

1. *Sales forecast.* Total net sales for year: £211,500

£'s	Jan	Feb	March	April	May	June
	19000	13000	14000	20500	15500	20000

July	Aug	Sept	Oct	Nov	Dec
15500	17500	17000	18000	21000	20500

2. *Materials used:* Raw materials purchased are estimated to represent 50% of the net sales value sold in the month.

3. *Production wages:* Wages of production operatives will be £3000 per month in total, including employer's NIC.

4. *Overheads:* Overheads are estimated as follows:

    Salaries of directors and administrative staff £2000 per month in total

    Rent £12000 per annum

    Rates and insurances £500 per month

    Publicity £500 per month

    Other costs £1000 per month

5. *Bank interest:* It is assumed there will be an overdraft of £15000 at 15% p.a. interest, plus bank charges of £750 per annum.

6. *Depreciation:* Depreciation will be based on fixed assets of £18000 net costs depreciated over 3 years, or £6000 per annum.

7. *Receipts:* Sales will be invoiced with VAT at 17.5% and paid for in 60 days, or during the second month after invoice date (January invoices paid in March etc).

8. *Payment* of overheads: Purchases will be paid for on the following basis:

   ❏ Materials used, publicity and other costs – 60 days from date of use, or during the 2nd month after receipt of invoice. These costs will all be subject to VAT at 17.5%.

   ❏ Rent will be paid quarterly (March, June, Oct and Dec)

   ❏ Rates and insurances will be paid monthly by standing order.

9. *VAT:* Will also be added to some purchases when they are paid for. This will be at the rate of 17.5% and apply to materials used, publicity and other costs.

10. *VAT due:* Kal Kulate Ltd. will be registered for VAT from January 1st and will need to submit VAT returns for each quarter, and pay any VAT due during the month following the quarter end. (The first quarter will be January to March with payments due in April.)

11. *Capital:* Capital Assets which total £18000 plus £3150 VAT will be paid for in January.

12. *Opening position:* Kal Kulate's opening cash balance will be nil, as it is not intended to bring any cash forward into the new limited company. Shares will be purchased for £5000 in December, which will be used to pay for any initial costs, such as prepayment of rent and legal charges.

   However debtors and creditors will be brought forward as follows:

Debtors:	Nov. sales £20000 + VAT
	Dec. sales £20000 + VAT
Creditors:	Nov. and Dec. purchases at 50% of the above sales + VAT
	Nov. and Dec. publicity and other costs at the monthly rate of £1500 + VAT.
Prepayments:	Rent will be paid for in advance, with the first quarter paid for in December, prior to incorporation.

13. *Stocks* will equate to one month's sales, i.e. the materials needed for one month's sales (50% of the relevant month's sales value).

"This is a very good start," replied the accountant, "we should be able to produce a profit and loss, and cash flow forecast and balance sheet from this information. How are you going to finance your capital purchases of £21,150 by the way?"

"Well if I pay cash there are some real bargains at the moment," replied Susan, "so I thought I would use an overdraft at the bank."

Tasks

1. Can you prepare the profit and loss and cash flow for Kal Kulate Ltd. from this information?

See the information bank in **Section III: Unit 15, 4.2,** pages 390–402.

2. Looking at the profit and loss account, and the cash flow forecast, why is there only a small profit for the year, yet a larger positive cash flow?

See the information bank in **Section III: Unit 15, 4.1,** page 389–390.

3. Using the cash flow forecast, make some recommendations for Susan's borrowing strategy. Is she right to want an overdraft to finance her new equipment?

See the information bank in **Section III: Unit 15, 1.,** page 377–379.

4. Can you produce a projected balance sheet for the end of the first year (December) from this information?

See the information bank in **Section III: Unit 15, 4.2,** pages 390–402.

Control of finance resources

Whilst obtaining sufficient finance is an important first step, the efficient use of funds acquired by a small firm will ultimately determine its success or failure.

Quick answer question: Financial issues

Can you give some examples of financial issues which are common in small firms? At what stage in a small firm's life cycle are they likely to be most common?

Small firms have been criticised for generating little or poor information with which to control and plan their financial resources. Systems rarely keep pace with changes which can take place very rapidly in a small business which is expanding fast.

Financial issues

Some of the issues likely to confront a small firm as it grows include:

☐ *Under capitalisation* – often at start-up or significant growth stages.

☐ *Control of costs* – especially during early development stages.

☐ *Control of debtors* – a common problem in rapid development stages.

☐ *Control of stocks* – often a continuous issue, but particularly during growth.

☐ *Information systems* – an issue from the early days.

☐ *Lack of profits and return on investment* – at the introduction of a new business, and again later on when it matures or declines.

Scenario 2: Susan mis-calculates

It had been a hectic year for Susan Howells. She had completed her first trading year as Kal Kulate Ltd, and felt really proud of her achievements. She had exceeded her sales targets by 30% in the year, and had considerably increased her customer base.

She was therefore very disappointed when her accountant painted a very different picture. He showed her some preliminary accounts showing actual performance against the budget which they had put together at the beginning of the year.

"I can't believe it," said Susan, looking at the figures he showed her.

KAL KULATE LTD.
Profit and Loss Budget Vs Actual.

12 months	Budget	Actual
Sales (net)	211,500	274,950
Materials used	105,750	154,970
Production wages	36,000	44,990
Gross profit	69,750	74,990
Overheads:		
Salaries	24,000	26,100
Rent	12,000	12,000
Rates and insurance	6,000	5,800
Other costs	12,000	12,850
Publicity	6,000	7,770
Total overheads	60,000	64,520
Interest and Bank charges	3,000	3,790
Depreciation	6,000	6,000
Profit before tax	750	680

"I've sold far more than I thought possible but made less money. What's gone wrong?"

"Before I answer that," said the accountant, "perhaps we had better have the rest of the bad news. Your debtors have grown considerably in the last year. This aged analysis gives you the breakdown." The accountant handed Susan the following debtors' report:

KAL KULATE LTD.
Debtors' report – summary (Dec)

	£
Current month	30,110
One month	30,840
Two months	13,219
Three months	4,990
Over three months	1,105
Total	80,264

"I know the problem," sighed Susan, "it's partly the big customers who never seem to pay on time, and partly the smaller ones who never seem to pay at all. Our small customers are a particular problem as some of them are very old debts now, and I'm worried they may even go out of business."

"Yes there is certainly that concern," said the accountant, "and also your cash. You are very near your overdraft limit now. Apart from the interest costs, the bank will be getting nervous unless you can reduce your borrowing."

"I have been trying to collect the money," said Susan, "but some of these debts are such small amounts. I wonder if its worth the cost of writing them letters and telephoning. I know they all add up to a lot of money, but each one individually is quite small."

Tasks

1. *Why is Kal Kulate making less than budgeted profits when its sales are 30% up. How can it improve profitability?*

See the information bank in **Section III: Unit 15, 3.,** pages 384–389.

2. *The debtor issue is a common one for small firms who do not have the resources to pursue a large number of customers for payment. What steps could Susan consider to improve her cash flow?*

See the information bank in **Section III: Unit 15, 3.2,** pages 386–388.

In conclusion

Now complete your reading of the Information Bank, Unit 15 'Money'.

When you have done this you are ready to tackle the Ongoing Assignment 3, Task 3.5 'Forecasting the Money' and/or the Extended Task below.

Extended task: The cost of money

Try to find out the availability of various types of finance and its costs. For example, a local bank can usually provide information on commercial loans, and overdrafts, with rates of interest and any fixed costs charged for the facility.

From the information you have gathered, why is it important to match the type of borrowing to the use of the funds? Can you give specific examples of what you would use the different types of finance for (e.g. loan, overdrafts, lease etc)?

Ongoing assignment 3: The business plan

If you have completed Units 11 to 15 inclusive in Sections I and III and Tasks 3.1 to 3.5 inclusive in Section II, you should now conclude the Ongoing Assignment 3: 'The Business Plan' by completing Task 3.6 'Summary of the Business Plan'.

Extended task: The cost of money

Try to find out the availability of various types of finance and its costs. For example, a local bank can usually provide information on commercial loans, and overdrafts, with rates of interest and any fixed costs charged for the facility.

From the information you have gathered, why is it important to match the type of borrowing to the use of the funds? Compile some specific examples of what you would use the different types of finance for (e.g. loan, overdrafts, lease etc.)?

Ongoing assignment 3: The business plan

If you have completed Units 11 to 15 inclusive in Sections I and III and Tasks 3.1 to 3.5 inclusive in Section II, you should now conclude the Ongoing Assignment 3: The Business Plan, by completing Task 3.6 Summary of the Business Plan.

Section II

ONGOING ASSIGNMENTS

How to use this section

1. This section contains three assignments each sub-divided into a series of tasks. The three assignments concern the selection of a business idea by the reader, and the development of that idea in tasks progressing with the Units of the book.

2. Each task links to a Unit in Section I, Activities and Scenarios and Section III, Information Bank (see layout of the book in the Preface).

3. The assignments, and the tasks should be undertaken in the sequence of the book, and preferably after the reader has studied the appropriate Unit in Section I and III.

4. The 3 assignments are:

    Assignment 1   ***The feasibility study***

    6 tasks linked to units 1– 6 and one summary

    Assignment 2   ***The route to market entry***

    4 tasks linked to units 7–10 and one summary

    Assignment 3   ***The business plan***

    5 tasks linked to Units 11–15 and a summary

5. The three assignments and tasks develop an idea from the category of 'unknown risk' to 'reasonable prospects' in Assignment 1, to the selection of a 'suitable vehicle' in Assignment 2, and to a level of 'acceptable risk' in Assignment 3.

    The plan of assignments and tasks shown overleaf illustrates this progression.

Assignment 1: The feasibility study

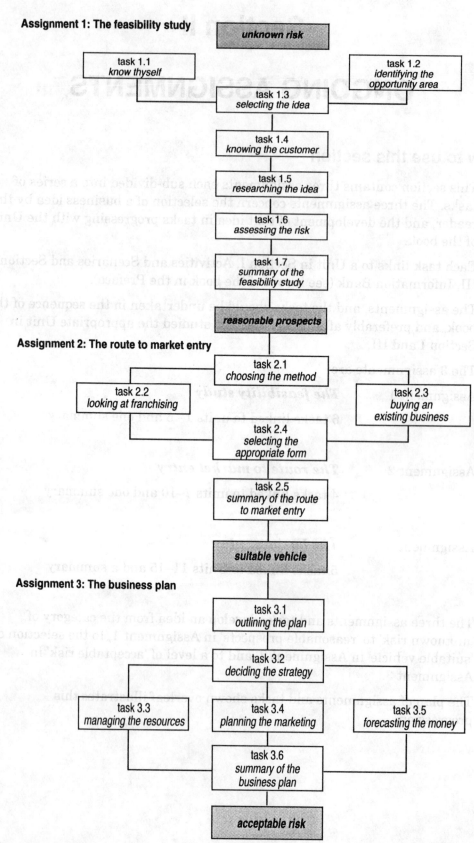

unknown risk

task 1.1
know thyself

task 1.2
identifying the
opportunity area

task 1.3
selecting the idea

task 1.4
knowing the customer

task 1.5
researching the idea

task 1.6
assessing the risk

task 1.7
summary of the
feasibility study

reasonable prospects

Assignment 2: The route to market entry

task 2.1
choosing the method

task 2.2
looking at franchising

task 2.3
buying an
existing business

task 2.4
selecting the
appropriate form

task 2.5
summary of the route
to market entry

suitable vehicle

Assignment 3: The business plan

task 3.1
outlining the plan

task 3.2
deciding the strategy

task 3.3
managing the resources

task 3.4
planning the marketing

task 3.5
forecasting the money

task 3.6
summary of the
business plan

acceptable risk

Ongoing assignments

Assignment 1: The feasibility study

Introduction

The objective of this first assignment is to decide on an idea for a new business venture and to assess the viability of that idea in the market place.

The tasks take you through the process of formulating an idea, which when first identified will be in a position of 'unknown risk'.

Further tasks ask you to assess more closely the feasibility and practicality of the idea. By the end of the assignment, you should be able to judge whether or not the idea has 'reasonable prospects'.

The Assignment is organised into six Tasks and a Summary Task, as shown below.

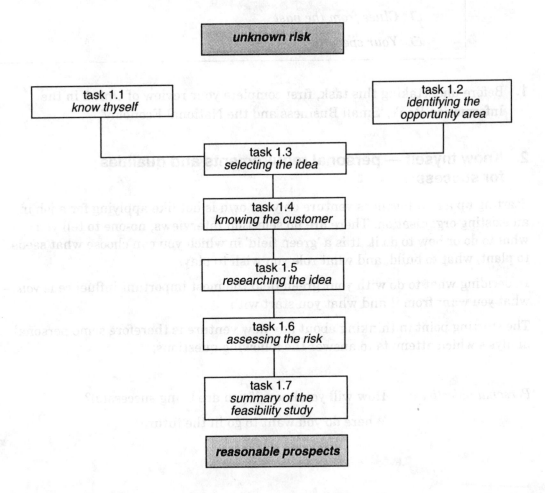

Task 1.1: Know thyself

> ### *Summary of what is required*
>
> 1. *Review Information Bank, Unit 1 'Small Business and the National Economy'.*
>
> 2. *Analyse yourself in terms of:*
>
>   ❑ *Personal objectives*
>
>   ❑ *Personal resources*
>
>   ❑ *Clues from the past*
>
>   ❑ *Your speciality*

1. Before undertaking this task, first complete your review of Unit 1 in the Information Bank, 'Small Business and the National Economy'.

2. Know thyself — personal requirements and qualities for success

Starting up a new business venture on your own is not like applying for a job in an existing organisation. There are no selection interviews, no-one to tell you what to do or how to do it. It is a 'green field' in which you can choose what seeds to plant, what to build, and what role you wish to play.

In deciding what to do with your green field the most important influence is *you*— what you want from it and what you start with.

The starting point in thinking about any new venture is therefore some personal analysis which attempts to answer the following questions:

Personal objectives: How will you know if you are being successful?

Where do you want to go in the future?

Personal resources: Where do you start from? What are your personal strengths, weaknesses and resources within yourself?

Clues from the past: What can you learn from your past? What lessons have you learned that may help take you from where you are now to where you wish to go?

Your speciality: What are your unique qualities that could help you reach your personal objectives? We are all different and therefore unique in some way. How can you use your uniqueness to give you enjoyment and satisfaction? Can you identify special talents you find most satisfying in practice?

Use the following worksheets to help you think about these questions.

It is important to establish these personal parameters for success as criteria against which to judge ideas for any new venture. As you develop ideas you will be asked to evaluate them according to your personal objectives and talents.

The level of commitment needed to make a new enterprise succeed is rooted in its ability to meet your personal requirements and in its potential for personal fulfilment through use of your special qualities. If your personal needs are not met, the motive force to make innovations succeed in practice will be lacking.

☐   **Personal objectives**

Write down what you want in your life in the short, medium, and long term:

	In 1 year	*In 3 years*	*In 10 years*
1. What do I want to be?			
2. What do I want to do?			
3. What do I want to have?			

☐ **Personal resources**

Assess where you are now. Summarise what you have to offer (strengths) and what you need to learn or minimise (weaknesses), in terms of knowledge (general and specific business knowledge), skills (what you can do) and qualities (your personal characteristics).

	Strengths	*Weaknesses*
1. **Knowledge**		
2. **Skills**		
3. **Qualities**		

☐ **Clues from the past**

Review your past life, and write down some specific moments when you felt purposeful, and focused in a way that gave you satisfaction at the time and in retrospect. Also look at times when you felt less directed and adrift.

	Personal qualities used/misused
Satisfying moments:	
Dissatisfying moments:	

What clues do these give about what you want, what you have to offer now and what you wish to avoid?

❏ **Your speciality**

Make an assessment of your knowledge, skills and qualities to try and discover some things in you that are unique and give you enjoyment and satisfaction. Review your personal objectives, personal resources, and clues from the past. Select those qualities and talents that you feel make you stand out from the crowd. These are the talents that give you the greatest sense of enjoyment and satisfaction when you use them well.

My special talents are:
1.
2.
3.
4.
5.
6.

Task 1.2: Identifying the opportunity area

Summary of what is required

1. *Review Information Bank, Unit 2, 'The Entrepreneur and the Owner-Manager'.*

2. ***Define*** *your opportunity area in a short sentence.*

3. *List the* ***sources of opportunity*** *by identifying supporting trends.*

4. *Give some* ***initial ideas*** *with specific examples of possible opportunities.*

1. Before undertaking this task, first complete your review of Unit 2 in the Information Bank, 'The Entrepreneur and the Owner-Manager'.

2. The opportunity area: definition

The second task in our feasibility study is to identify an *opportunity area*. This is a general area of opportunity which not only has the potential to fulfil your personal requirements, and use your personal strengths, but which can also give rise to new solutions to problems in the external environment or novel ways of meeting market needs.

An 'opportunity area' is a focal point for ideas for your new enterprise. It is a single focus which concentrates creative thinking into one opportunity area; it is however general enough to allow for plenty of different specific ideas at this stage.

The key criteria for your opportunity area:

☐ *personal requirements:* Has it potential to meet your personal objectives and aspirations identified in Task 1.1?

☐ *personal qualities:* Will it offer the opportunity to build on your personal strengths and unique qualities and not over expose the weaknesses identified in Task 1.1?

- *innovation:* Can it contain new solutions to specific problems, or fulfil identifiable needs in the external environment in a new way?

- *viable innovation:* Does it represent longer term developments and trends in the social, technological, economic and political environment or could it be a short term fad?

Description

Define your 'opportunity area' in a short sentence which links products, services, technology or resources, to market needs or problem areas.

Examples: Opportunity area definitions

- Healthy foods acceptable to younger people.

- Training programmes to support the public service manager in a changing environment.

- Desk top publishing for fast, creative presentations.

- Personal and accommodation protection for elderly people.

---

3. Sources of opportunity

What are the underlying trends in the environment which give your area potential opportunities? What are the supporting trends in social, technological, economic, political or legal developments? Why may these provide market opportunity? Summarise why your selected area is a good source of potential opportunities.

Example: Sources of opportunity – *'personal and accommodation protection for elderly people'*

- Demographic trends show increasing percentage of the population will be 70 years plus in 1990s onwards.

- Rapidly increasing crime rates against the elderly, seen as 'soft targets'.

- Conventional sheltered accommodation using permanent staff increasingly expensive and difficult to recruit wardens.

- Increasing numbers of elderly who are active and not dependent on others for normal living, but need protection and psychological support.

- Technological developments in building and personal protection devices which are expensive on individual basis.

- Trend to decentralise emergency systems for elderly; public services offering 'hot line' systems for elderly to call for help from their independent living accommodation, rather than live in homes with permanent help available.
- Increasing numbers of retired people as owner occupiers of houses.
- Decreasing percentage of 'young' population and therefore people resources to look after elderly.

4. Initial ideas

Give some first examples and ideas of new product or services which could provide you with an entry point to exploit the opportunities offered by the opportunity area.

---

*Example: Initial **ideas** – 'personal and accommodation protection for elderly people'*

- Personal security warning devices – whistles to electronic alarms.
- Individual housing security devices, 'user friendly' for elderly.
- 'Impersonal' sheltered housing: flats for elderly in electronic surveillance security accommodation.
- 'Help' service for elderly on subscription basis – clearing house for 'approved' services, e.g. plumbers, transport, etc.
- House conversion service – specialist conversions of larger premises owned by elderly, to small accommodation with rental/sale of surplus.

Assignment 1: The feasibility study

Task 1.3: Selecting the idea

Summary of what is required

1. *Review Information Bank, Unit 3, 'Small Business and Innovation'*

2. *Build on ideas by creative thinking within your opportunity area.*

3. *Make a short list from these ideas by elimination and evaluation against key criteria.*

4. *Select a final idea.*

1. Before undertaking this task, first complete your review of Unit 3 in the Information Bank, 'Small Business and Innovation'.

2. Build on ideas

The next step is to select one idea, by first expanding your base of possible opportunities as widely as possible, and then narrowing it down by reference to your own objectives and other criteria.

Expand on your list of initial ideas by creating as many thoughts as possible relating to the opportunity area identified in Task 1.2. The aim is not to come up with "the best" idea.

The objective is to produce a large number of new, imaginative ideas.

These can be later discarded, or built on to produce something creative and practical. (Refer to Unit 3, 3. 'What is Innovation?')

Creative thinking comes from seeing or making new connections. These connections are often between existing ideas or concepts that are too far apart for one person to visualise together.

The basis of 'brain storming' is to use a group of people to build on one another's ideas, so that these improbable connections are made. If you can work with others to develop your list of ideas, then do so. If you cannot, write down as many ideas as you can on your own.

Use the following guidelines if working in a group to brainstorm ideas:

❏ generate as many ideas as possible – the more the better;

❏ improve and build on each other's ideas: as well as suggesting new ideas, try and develop someone else's ideas by proposing improvements or ways of combining ideas;

❏ encourage long shots: crazy-sounding ideas can often spark off original and practical thoughts;

❏ encourage rather than criticise others: praise other group member's ideas to encourage them to come up with more rather than turning off their creative tap by adverse comments;

❏ always record all ideas on a sheet of paper or a flip chart.

3. Make a short list

The large number of ideas which you have generated within your opportunity area now need sorting and shortlisting.

It usually helps to group them into different categories or types. If any are still half-formed, try and build them into something practical or group them with others to see if there are any possible new combinations. From this list, first eliminate any that you consider cannot be translated into productive use (i.e. they are totally impractical).

Next, review each remaining idea against the key criteria established in tasks 1.1 and 1.2.

❏ *Personal requirements:* How well does it fit with your personal objectives and requirements?

❏ *Personal qualities:* Will it offer you the opportunity to maximise your strengths and unique qualities?

❏ *Innovation:* Does it meet identifiable needs in a new way?

❏ *Viability:* Is it supported by longer term trends or could it be short lived?

Decide on a short list of 3 or 4 ideas which you believe will best meet these criteria.

4. Select a final idea

Carefully evaluate each idea once again. It may be useful to give them a ranking (1 to 5) against each criteria.

Before final selection of the one idea you wish to test through the feasibility study, it is sometimes useful to use groups again where possible and invite others to comment on your short listed ideas in relation to the selection criteria.

Make a decision and select one idea to test through a feasibility study.

Task 1.4: Knowing the customer

> **Summary of what is required**
>
> 1. *Review Information Bank, Unit 4, 'The Customer'*
> 2. *Identify the target **customer** for your business idea.*
> 3. *Rate the **benefits** sought by customers, and offered by you.*
> 4. *Identify your **competitive edge.***

1. Before undertaking this task, first complete your review of Unit 4 in the Information Bank, 'The Customer'.

2. Knowing the customer

Now that you have selected your idea to investigate as a small business, the next stage is to identify the target customer group. This has to be done very precisely: 'man in the street' or 'other businesses' will not do!

Use the *Domestic Markets Checklist* to describe your targeted customer if you are selling to domestic or consumer markets. Use the *Industrial Markets Checklist* to describe your customer if you are selling to industrial markets or other businesses. Note it is important to identify the person(s) who makes the purchase decision. Also use these checklists to consider the *benefits* which these customers seek from the type of product or service you are offering. When you have identified the benefits the customer is seeking, consider how well these benefits are met by existing products or services and give them a rating between 0 to 10.

Finally use the *Competitive Edge Checklist* to identify your competitive edge: specify the benefits of your product or service, and how important these are to the customer, compared to competitive offerings.

Identifying your target customer

Decide if you will be selling to largely domestic or industrial markets. Then use the appropriate checklist below to specify your customer target. (They are for guidance only; you may wish to add other parameters or you may feel so[m]e not relevant.)

Checklist: Domestic markets – target customers

Sex	Male	Female
Age group		
Under 15	....	....
15 – 25	....	....
25 – 40	....	....
40 – 65	....	....
Over 65	....	....

Type of employment		
Managerial		.....
Manual		....
Office/Clerical		....
Housewife		....
Self-employed		....
Retired		....
Other (specify)		....

General

Income range	....
Householder or Rented Accommodation	....
Area of residence	....
Personality type	....
Interests and Hobbies	....
Socio-economic grouping	....

Benefits target customer seeks from my product or service:	*Existing product or service provision*:*
1	.....
2	.....
3	.....
4	.....
5	.....

* For each benefit stated, how do you rate existing products or services available to the target customer. Use a scale of 0 to 10 where 0 = benefit not provided and 10 = benefit fully provided.

Checklist: Industrial markets – target customers

Industry type: ....

Legal identity: Limited...   Partnership...   Charity...

Size of organisation: Turnover range...........
                            Number of employees......

Location of companies: Geographic area UK...........
                            Overseas....................

Job title of decision makers(s) for my product or service:..............

Frequency of purchase:...............

Benefits target customer seeks from my product or service:	*Existing product or service provision*:*
1	.....
2	.....
3	.....
4	.....
5	.....

* For each benefit stated, how do you rate existing products or services available to the target customer. Use a scale of 0 to 10 where 0 = benefit not provided and 10 = benefit fully provided.

3. Rate the benefits sought by customers, and offered by you

What are the principle features and benefits of your product or service?

	Feature	Benefit
1.		
2.		
3.		
4.		
5.		

How do your target customers rate these benefits? Indicate for each benefit which you think is the most important in their buying decision, the second most important and so on.

In the *Domestic Markets Checklist* or the *Industrial Markets Checklist* you have also indicated how you rated existing products or services available in terms of benefits sought by the target customer.

Comparing these two ratings of the relative importance of benefits to customers, and your assessment of the competitive delivery of benefits, what will be your competitive edge?

What will you be offering that is better than the competition and valued by your target customer?

4. My competitive edge is:

1.	
2	
3.	

Task 1.5: Researching the idea

Summary of what is required

1. Review Information Bank, Unit 5, 'Market Research'
2. Set research objectives
3. Find out more about the customer
4. Find out more about the competition
5. Find out more about the environment
6. Report back

1. Before undertaking this task, first complete your review of Unit 5 in the Information Bank, 'Market Research'.

In tasks 1.3 and 1.4, you selected an idea and identified the target customer group. The next stage is to refine the idea by finding out more about the target customer segment, the competition you will face, and the characteristics of the environment in which the market operates.

This can only be done by carrying out some preliminary research. Use checklists 1 to 5 to structure the research, carry it out and report back.

Checklist 1: Setting the objectives for research

The overall objective of the research is to provide you with more information to assess the feasibility of your idea as a viable enterprise. It is suggested that this is structured around two specific questions to which you may wish to add more:

1. What opportunities and threats exist in the market place now, and in the future, for my idea?

2. How much will the customer buy from me in my first three years of trading?

These research objectives can be looked at in relation to the customer, the competition and the environment.

Checklist 2: Researching the customer

I **What specific questions do I need to ask about the target customer segment?**

☐ What is the size of the total market?

☐ How many individual customers are there?

☐ Will I be dealing with more than one customer segment?

☐ How often do they buy?

☐ How much do they buy at one time?

☐ Do they buy randomly or at specific times?

☐ Do some customers account for a high percentage of purchases?

☐ If so which ones, and what percentages?

☐ What percentage of the market can I expect in Year 1? Year 2? Year 3?

☐ What are the existing distribution channels and structure of the market?

☐ Other questions?

II **Which research methods can I use to find out some answers?**

Secondary research:

Primary research:

Checklist 3: Researching the competition

I **What specific questions do I need to ask about the competitors in my target market?**

- ☐ Who are the competitors?
- ☐ What percentage of the market do they have?
- ☐ What is their estimated sales turnover?
- ☐ How long have they been in business?
- ☐ Is the market stable or changing, with new competitors entering and/or leaving?
- ☐ What is the competitive edge (or main benefits) of the principle competitors?
- ☐ How profitable and efficient are they?
- ☐ How do customers rate the principle competitors?
- ☐ Are they active in the market place?
- ☐ If yes, in what ways?
- ☐ Other questions

II **Which research methods can I use to find out some answers?**

Secondary research:

Primary research:

Checklist 4: Researching the environment

I **What specific questions do I need to ask about the environment of my target market?**

- ❐ What are the boundaries of my target market?
- ❐ What are the social trends?
- ❐ What are the economic factors?
- ❐ What are the political factors?
- ❐ What are the technological trends?
- ❐ What are the demographics of the market?
- ❐ What will be the key external influences in the market place in the next three years?
- ❐ How will these influences affect the competition?
- ❐ How will these influences affect me?
- ❐ Other questions

II **Which research methods can I use to find out some answers?**

Secondary research:

Primary research:

Checklist 5: Reporting back

Collect together the research you have done, and see how it matches up against your research objectives. In particular, answer the questions below as best you can:

❑   What does my information suggest will be my likely sales turnover?

	Year 1	Year 2	Year 3
Pessimistic			
Optimistic			
Most likely			

❑   What information have I found out about the market that represents opportunities and/or threats?

   ❑   Short term and long term trends representing opportunities and/or threats?

   ❑   Competitive opportunities, and threats?

   ❑   Customer opportunities and threats?

   ❑   Other?

❑   How does my information meet other research objectives that I set myself?

Assignment 1: The feasibility study

Task 1.6: Assessing the risk

Summary of what is required

1. Review Information Bank, Unit 6 'The Small Business Environment'

2. Estimate the fixed costs of operating your enterprise in years 1, 2 and 3.

3. Estimate the variable costs of operating your enterprise in years 1, 2 and 3.

4. Estimate your one-off start-up costs and likely sources of finance.

5. Use your cost estimates to calculate a break even point.

6. Compare your costs to your optimistic, most likely and pessimistic sales forecasts for years 1, 2 and 3, which will give an indication of the probability of success.

7. Evaluate other significant barriers to entry.

1. Before undertaking this task, first complete your review of Unit 6 in the Information Bank, 'The Small Business Environment'.

By the end of this task you should have a clearer idea of the probability of success for your business – an indication of the level of risk you are taking in setting it up, and the barriers you will have to overcome to do so.

One indicator of risk is the break even point of the business – the level of sales required to cover the variable and fixed costs of doing business. If the level of sales needed to cover costs looks high compared with your estimates of market demand, then the risk of failure is obviously high. If, on the other hand, even your pessimistic sales forecast more than covers costs, then the risk looks much smaller.

At this stage, costs and sales can be approximate estimates. More detailed planning comes later, in putting together a full business plan. Here you need a first appraisal of how feasible your new enterprise looks in practice. Is the probability of success high enough to merit taking it to the next stage? Can you overcome the barriers to market entry?

Estimate the start-up, fixed and variable costs of operating the enterprise for years 1, 2 and 3

☐ *Fixed costs* remain almost unchanged whatever you sell. They are fixed in the sense of not being altered by the volume of goods or services you sell.

☐ *Variable costs* varying according to the volume of goods or services you produce. In practice the distinction is not usually clear cut: some items are semi-variable. Often fixed costs are only fixed to a certain level of sales; above that they too increase; for example, more equipment, or staff, would be needed to cope with higher levels of demand.

☐ *Start-up costs:* Estimates need to be made over the first three years of the business in order to establish a pattern of profit or loss. In the first year, particularly, these will be one off costs associated with establishing the business. As such, they need to be identified separately from the ongoing fixed and variable costs of the business.

Inflation over the three years can be dealt with by calculating all figures at 'today's prices', i.e. assume that you will be able to increase your prices in line with the inflation of your costs.

2. Fixed costs and overheads

Fixed costs are usually the overheads of the enterprise. Use the following checklist to estimate your overheads for the first three years. Your list of costs will inevitably be different; this is intended as a prompt so that you don't leave out any important cost areas.

	Year		
	1	2	3
Salaries and wages: include employers 'on-costs' (i.e. any costs of employment in addition to salaries and wages which are paid by the employer, e.g. employer's National Insurance contribution.)			
Rent and rates: include other premises costs e.g. heating, lighting, repairs and maintenance			
Office costs; e.g. telephone, postage, stationery, printing			
Publicity: e.g. advertising, promotions, leaflets, exhibitions			
Legal and professional costs: e.g. bank charges, insurances, legal/accounting charges			
Travel and entertainment: e.g. petrol, car rental			
Financial costs: e.g. interest, depreciation			
Total overheads			

3. Variable costs and gross profit

Net sales value less variable costs is often called *gross profit*. As a percentage of sales this will vary considerably depending on the type of business. A manufacturing company for example might have considerable variable costs in its raw materials and consumables used in production. Some labour costs could also be variable if arranged on a part time basis, which could be varied quickly with the level of demand. The gross profit in such a manufacturing company could be less than 50% of the net sales value.

In a service company, the variable costs will be considerably less. There may even be no really variable costs, only semi-variable or fixed costs, for example in a consultancy firm. In such cases the gross profit as a percentage of sales will be very high.

Usually it is possible to establish a gross profit as a percentage of sales on an ongoing basis. Once sales are estimated for a given period, the gross profit can be calculated.

4. One-off start-up costs

A new enterprise will inevitably require some one-off expenditure which will not be repeated on an annual basis. These may include the legal costs of setting up a company or the acquisition costs of premises, for example.

You need a rough estimate of these at an early stage to:

☐ Determine if it is feasible to raise this money.

☐ Calculate any interest payments to include in your fixed costs.

5. Break even analysis

Once fixed costs and variable costs are known, a level of sales can be calculated to meet these level of costs. For example, if you estimate your fixed costs for the year as £50,000 you will obviously required a gross profit of £50,000 to break even. If you also know that your gross profit is 50% of your net sales, then your break even sales value will be £100,000. What will be the break even point for your business? Review your fixed costs and your gross profit to arrive at an approximate level of sales which represents break even.

6. Sales forecasts

As part of Task 1.4 you were asked to identify your customer and as part of Task 1.5 you were asked to estimate how much that customer was likely to buy from you and why. As a continuation of this exercise estimate your sales for the first three years in the following way:

	Year		
	1	2	3
Optimistic			
Most likely			
Pessimistic			

Compare your sales figures in the above categories, with the break even point for your business. Consider the implications of these calculations on the viability of your enterprise.

7. Barriers to entry

Apart from reaching financial viability, what other barriers to market entry exist for your business? (See Unit 6, 2.1 Barriers to Entry for a list of possible problem areas.) How will you overcome the barriers specific to your industry or market sector. How will these influence your viability?

Task 1.7: Summary of the feasibility study

Summary of what is required

1. *Define the proposed business or enterprise*
2. *Check the 3 Ms of Management, Market and Money for feasibility*
3. *Decide on future research requirements*

The conclusion of your feasibility study should only be undertaken when Tasks 1.1–1.6 are complete, as they form the basis for this final step of the study – reviewing the proposal and checking for feasibility.

1. Define the proposed business or enterprise

You should now be in a position to write down, in simple terms, the nature of your proposed business or enterprise. While this should be a brief statement of one or two sentences, it should be precise and not vague, covering the main features of the business. It should answer such questions as:

❑   What will you sell?

❑   Who will be your customers?

❑   How will you reach the market place (in terms of distribution and communication)?

❑   How will you obtain products, or provide services?

❑   What methods or technologies will be involved?

For example a manufacturer might define their business as:

> "The design and manufacture of printed circuits sold directly to manufacturers of electronic instruments, using CAD and CAM techniques to add value to components purchased from industry suppliers."

A service business might describe themselves thus:

> "The provision of high quality training courses to the small business sector in S.E. England, largely in conjunction with Training and Enterprise Councils conducted from rented premises in the Farnborough area."

The value of this exercise is to look at the scope of your idea again and give it some initial parameters. It should enable you to question the nature of the business, so that you understand more precisely what you are trying to do.

2. Check for feasibility

Successful strategies for small business rely crucially on three factors:

Management   dealing with the influences of the small business environment.

Market   matching customer needs to the strengths of the enterprise.

Money   financial foresight to ensure sufficient ongoing resources.

Before moving to the next stages of selecting the route to market entry and detailed planning of the business, you need to review your strengths and weaknesses in these three crucial areas. Look back at the relevant tasks (1.1–1.6) and summarise your idea in relation to these '3 Ms', using the 'Feasibility Checklist for a successful small enterprise strategy'.

Management: Objectives – Strengths – Weaknesses

☐   What are your personal objectives? What are the objectives of the enterprise?

☐   What are your own, and your team's, strengths in relation to the opportunity you have identified?

☐   Which weaknesses will need to be addressed and when?

☐   How will you deal with the influences of the small enterprise environment?

Market: Opportunities – Threats – Barriers

☐   What are the opportunities and threats posed by your chosen market place?

☐   Who is your intended customer (precisely) and what is your competitive edge?

☐   What are the competitive threats?

☐   What are the barriers to market entry?

Money: Sources – Rewards – Risks

☐ What are the likely financial rewards or benefits of your idea likely to be in the short and medium term?

☐ How quickly will you make a profit?

☐ What are the financial risks?

☐ What is the probability of survival and success?

☐ How much money will you need, and what are the likely sources of finance?

Feasibility checklist for a small business – the '3 Ms'

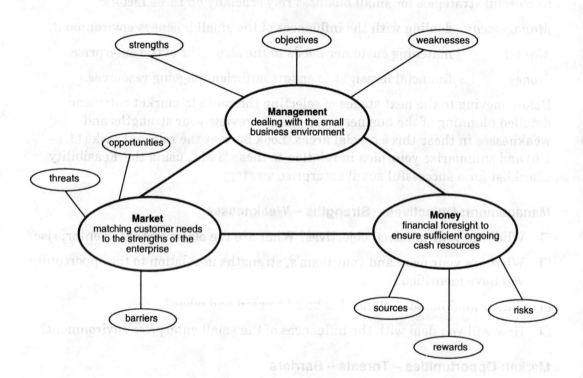

3. Decide on future research

Assuming that you have concluded from your study that your idea is worth pursuing, this is the time to consider future research needs for a more detailed business plan.

In Task 1.5 you began researching your idea to provide basic information to test for viability and progress the concept.

In the next detailed planning stage, what more will you need to know? What research objectives do you have now? What questions will you need answering to develop an in depth plan for your enterprise?

If your conclusions are that the idea is not worth taking further then consider what modifications can be made to make it more feasible. First ideas are often changed, sometimes radically, in the light of further information and analysis.

If you consider that you need to start again because your idea now seems highly unrealistic, even with modification, then this in itself is a valuable learning experience. In order to progress through the next two assignments, without the need to start all over again, consider investigating a franchise, or buying an existing business, rather than going back to the beginning of a brand new venture.

Ongoing assignments

Assignment 2: The route to market entry

Introduction

In Assignment 1, 'The Feasibility Study' you developed a business idea from a situation of unknown risk to a position of reasonable prospects.

In Assignment 2 you further develop the idea by deciding on an appropriate route to market entry. This involves exploring the possibilities of the new venture as a start-up, a franchise, or buying an existing business.

If your feasibility study showed that prospects were not 'reasonable', then you can consider alternative routes using established ideas with proven track records.

You are also required to consider the legal identity of the venture. The Assignment is organised into 4 Tasks, and a Summary Task as shown below.

Assignment 1: The feasibility study

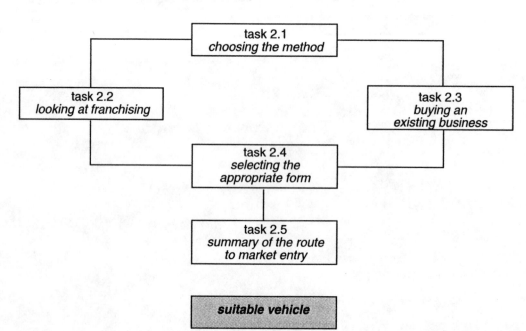

Assignment 2: The route to market entry

Task 2.1: Choosing the method

Summary of what is required

1. *Review Information Bank, Unit 7, 'Routes to Market Entry'*

2. *Consider possible routes to market entry for your business idea*

3. *Investigate the advantages and disadvantages of a new business start-up*

1. Before undertaking this task, first complete your review of Unit 7 in the Information Bank, 'Routes to Market Entry'.

2. List the possible routes to market entry that may be available to you in pursuing your business idea.

3. Consider a new business start-up as an option. Conduct an audit of the advantages and disadvantages of this option for your specific idea, carrying out any necessary research.

4. If your conclusions from Assignment 1 'The Feasibility Study' were that your idea did not represent 'reasonable prospects' then look at alternative routes to market entry. This may involve considering the options discussed more fully in the following units.

Task 2.2: Looking at franchising

Summary of what is required

1. *Review Information Bank, Unit 8, 'Franchising'*

2. *Consider the possibilities of the franchise system – either as franchisor, or franchisee – for your business idea.*

3. *Investigate a franchise in a business area similar to your own.*

1. Before undertaking this task, first complete your review of Unit 8 in the Information Bank on 'Franchising'.

2. Consider the development of your business idea using a franchise network, with you as the franchisor. If this is feasible list the advantages and disadvantages.

3. Consider taking up a franchise as a franchisee as a possible route for developing your idea. Do suitable franchises exist? Obtain details of a franchise in a business area similar to your own and list the advantages and disadvantages of this course of action.

4. If your original idea did not look feasible from your initial analysis, are there more established ideas which you can take up through a franchise? What existing franchises appeal to you as a business concept, and do they represent a better proposition for you to investigate?

Assignment 2: The route to market entry

Task 2.3: Buying an existing business

Summary of what is required

1.   *Review Information Bank Unit 9 "Buying an Existing Business."*

2.   *Consider what type of business you could consider buying (all or part of) that would be consistent with the development of your business idea.*

3.   *Obtain information on suitable businesses for sale.*

4.   *Evaluate the advantages and disadvantages of the specific business(es) offered for sale.*

5.   *Decide if this is the appropriate route of market entry for you and your business idea.*

1. Before undertaking this task, first complete your review of Unit 9 in the Information Bank, 'Buying an Existing Business'.

2. Before committing yourself to a business start-up, it is worth considering buying an existing business. Consider what types of business for sale would help the development of your business idea. This does not necessarily mean that the businesses you think of buying are trading in the market or style you have chosen. For example, if your business idea is a themed cocktail bar and restaurant, it may be beneficial to buy a restaurant with a very different appeal to the one you have considered. The advantages will be that some of the barriers to entry will be more easily overcome (such as licensing permissions), and equipment, for food preparation and storage, could still be appropriate for a different end product. Even if you are considering a totally different business, it is worth looking for some assets that maybe useful. If your business involves retail premises you will certainly need to consider taking over the lease of an existing retail outlet, then changing it over to your use rather than waiting for the right new premises to become available.

You may also wish to consider not just an outright purchase, but buying into an existing business, with or without the participation of the existing management.

If your original idea did not look feasible from your initial analysis, is there an established business which you could consider buying instead? Are there businesses for sale in an area of interest to you?

3. Once you have decided the type of business to look for, obtain information on suitable opportunities. There are a number of sources to consider:

❏ **Business transfer agents.**

There are listings of local and national agents in *Yellow Pages, Business Pages* and *The Thompson Directory*. Business Transfer Agents act rather like estate agents in that a seller will register with them, and provide details of their business for sale; in the event of a sale the seller pays the agent a commission.

Most agents will send particulars of specific businesses for sale on request.

Some specialise in local businesses, others in a particular trade, with confectioners, tobacconists and newsagents (CTNs), and licensed premises firm favourites because these change hands relatively frequently.

Christie & Co (Head office 2 York St, London W1A 1BP, tel. 071-486-4231, fax 071-935-4032) are perhaps the country's leading transfer agents, dealing with the licensed trade (pubs, wine bars, restaurants), CTNs, hotels, residential nursing homes, the retail trade including fast food outlets and other commercial property.

Commercial estate agents also provide details of available commercial property including some which are offered as going concerns.

❏ **Periodicals and newspapers**

National and local press often carry 'business opportunity' sections. These include:

❑ *Financial Times,* (especially 'The Management Page' on Tuesdays)

❑ *Sunday Times* ('Business to Business' in the Business News)

❐ *Organisations*

Accountants, solicitors and government agencies all assist in the transfer of businesses. Some are organised into nationwide services:

❐ *ABN (Accountants Business Network):* Most large accountancy practices participate in this service of linking buyers and sellers from their client network. Contact the local office of Price Waterhouse, Arthur Anderson, Peat Marwick McLintock, and other national accountancy firms.

❐ *The Business Exchange* (21 John Adam Street, London WC2N 6JG Tel. 071-930-8963): A database of businesses for sale fed in by accountants, solicitors and actuaries.

❐ *LINC (Local Investment Networking Company):* Run by 12 Enterprise agencies as a business introduction service. Contact your Local Enterprise Agency.

4. Having obtained what details you can of a business for sale, or an opportunity of investing as a new partner, consider the merits of this as an option for pursuing your business idea. Use the information in the Information Bank, (Unit 9, 'Buying an Existing Business') on general advantages and disadvantages to help you in your evaluation.

5. Decide if you wish to choose this method of market entry for your particular idea, and if you do, how you will investigate it further.

Task 2.4: Selecting the appropriate form

> **Summary of what is required**
>
> 1. Review Information Bank, Unit 10 "Forms of Small Business Organisation"
>
> 2. Review the forms of small business organisation now open to you
>
> 3. Consider the advantages and disadvantages of each option
>
> 4. Decide on the appropriate business form for your organisation

1. Before undertaking this task, first complete your review of Unit 10 in the Information Bank, 'Forms of Small Business Organisation'.

2. The appropriate business form – limited company, sole trader, partnership or co-operative – will be conditioned by the route you have selected. For example, if you have decided to buy an existing business, it may be that you will be acquiring shares in a limited company, which dictates your choice.

A franchisor may also prescribe the legal form you adopt. If the business is to be co-owned, you obviously cannot operate as a sole trader.

The first step is therefore to review the options that are now open to you.

3. Use the 'Checklist for Choosing the Appropriate Form', and further details in the Information Bank, Unit 10 'Forms of Small Business Organisation', to assess the advantages and disadvantages of each form open to you against each of the categories shown. Are there other conditions which are not listed?

4. Decide on the most appropriate form of organisation for your small business, and note your reasons.

Task 2.5: Summary of the route to market entry

Summary of what is required

1. *Review the possible routes to market entry for your business idea. Choose the appropriate route*

2. *Review the possible legal identities which your idea can take. Choose the appropriate legal format for your idea in the chosen route.*

By the end of this task, you should have identified the method you will be using to exploit the opportunity you have identified in terms of:

1. The route to market entry
2. The legal identity.

1. The route to market entry

Now that you have a specific idea to develop as a small enterprise it is important to consider the options you have for entering the market place. Do you have to begin a brand new business? Would it be more appropriate to buy an existing business?

If you are starting a new business, does it have to be a start-up, or are there franchises available?

❐   Review the options outlined in Unit 7, 'Possible Routes to Market Entry' and list those available to you.

❐   Consider the advantages of the options available for your specific idea, which you have outlined in tasks 2.2, 2.3 and 2.4.

❐   Decide on the appropriate route to market entry which you wish to pursue at this stage.

2. The legal identity

The legal identity you wish to adopt – sole trader, partnership, limited company, or co-operative – will be conditioned by the route you have selected. For example if you have decided to buy an existing business, it may be that you will be acquiring a limited company, which effectively limits your choices. A franchise may also prescribe the legal format you adopt.

This stage is therefore to:

☐ Review the legal identity options that are now open to you.

☐ Conduct an audit of the advantages and disadvantages of each of the types available to you.

☐ Decide on your legal identity.

Ongoing assignments

Assignment 3: The business plan

Introduction

Assignment 1, 'The Feasibility Study' developed a business idea from a situation of unknown risk to a position of reasonable prospects.

Assignment 2, 'The Route to Market Entry' identified a suitable vehicle for market entry for the idea.

Assignment 3, 'The Business Plan', takes this idea (with reasonable prospects and an identified route to market entry) to a position of acceptable risk by more detailed planning. This involves researching and writing up a business plan, which uses the information gathered in the first two assignments, but develops it further by looking at the overall strategy as well as management, marketing and money plans.

The Assignment is organised into 5 Tasks, and a Summary Task as shown below.

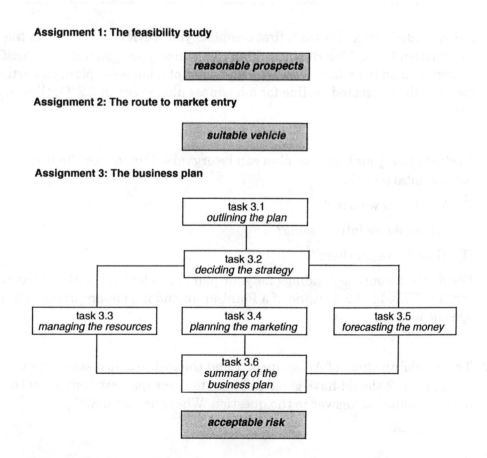

Task 3.1: Outlining the plan

Summary of what is required

1.   Review Information Bank, Unit 11, The Business Plan

2.   Consider the outline of headings which a business plan should cover

3.   Decide the format for your plan

4.   Complete the 'Where are we now?' sections by transferring information from Assignment 1, The Feasibility Study, and Assignment 2, The Route to Market Entry

1.   Before undertaking this task, first complete your review of Unit 11 in the Information Bank, 'The Business Plan'. This unit gives general and specific information on the when, who, why and what of a business plan. In particular consider the suggested outline for a business plan given in 2.2 'Outline of a Plan'.

2.   Evaluate how your business plan can be organised to answer the three fundamental questions:

❑   Where are we now?

❑   Where do we intend going?

❑   How do we get there?

Decide on the outline headings for your plan, i.e. adopt the outline format given in Unit 11, 2.2 'Outline of a Plan', or amend it as appropriate to your specific idea.

3.   The feasibility study of Assignment 1 and the methods investigated in Assignment 2 should have given answers to cover the first sections of the outline format, in answer to the question 'Where are we now?'

Transfer this information into the business plan. This should cover the first three sections in the suggested outline format:

1. The business identity

2. The key people

3. The nature of the business

This information should not be lengthy, but should give a concise summary of what the business idea is, the vehicle intended to take it to the market place, the key people involved in it and the nature of the market place and competition.

Assignment 3: The business plan

Task 3.2: Deciding the strategy

> ### Summary of what is required
>
> 1. Review Information Bank, Unit 12, *Successful and Unsuccessful Small Business Strategies*
> 2. Confirm personal motives for entry into a small enterprise
> 3. Set general objectives
> 4. Set specific objectives
> 5. Define policy
> 6. Draw up a timetable of key activities

1. Before undertaking this task, first complete your review of Unit 12 in the Information Bank, 'Successful and Unsuccessful Small Business Strategies'.

Completion of this task should answer the question, "Where do we want to be in the short and long term?" It is setting out the strategic direction and parameters of the enterprise.

2. Confirm personal motives

The first step is to re-examine personal motives for entry into a small enterprise. You will have distinctive motives and expectations. Now is the time to confirm what these are, as they will be crucial in determining the strategies and objectives of the business. Go back to Tasks 1.1 and 1.2 in Assignment 1 to check your self-analysis, and its fit with the opportunity as you have defined it.

Are these personal motivations still valid?

Are there new, or additional factors which you should now consider before translating these into business objectives?

3. Set general objectives

What are the general objectives of the enterprise? 'General', in this context, means broad in scope and timespan. For example, general objectives could specify overall economic goals (e.g. to achieve sales in excess of £1 million and profits of £100,000), industry goals (to develop a particular process), lifestyle goals (e.g. to provide a satisfying and democratic place of work), environmental goals (e.g. to produce products which are environmentally safe), market goals (to achieve market leadership in a given segment) and so on. (For more examples see Information Bank, Unit 1 'The Objectives of Small Business Owners'.)

Clearly these general objectives of the enterprise will be strongly linked to your personal motives as an individual.

The general objectives are:
1.
2.
3.
4.

4. Set specific objectives

What are the specific objectives of the enterprise? 'Specific' means narrow in
scope and timespan. For example, specific objectives could detail sales and profit
targets for years 1, 2 and 3. They could quantify the number of outlets to be
opened by year, the number of employees or partners by which an enterprise
grows each year, the size of the customer base, the number of new accounts to be
opened in each year, the percentage market share targeted by year, the number of
new products, and other quantifiable goals.

The specific objectives will build into the general objectives set earlier.

Specific objectives are:
1.
2.
3.
4.
5.
6.

5. Define policy

What will be the policies of your enterprise? What general rules, or guidelines will you set for yourself? For example, will you have money policies (e.g. to be risk adverse, to extend no credit, to carry 90 days stock, to borrow only against the assets of the business, to lease equipment rather than purchase it outright)?

Will you have management policies (e.g. to employ only young/experienced/part-time staff, to pay salespeople commission only, to allocate responsibilities between partners in a predetermined way, to operate a shift system, to pay staff bonuses)?

Will you have marketing policies (e.g. not to quote on the basis of price alone, or never be knowingly underbid, to maintain a specific product mix, to spend a fixed percentage of sales revenue on advertising, to use agents on commission, and not employ salespeople, to sell direct to consumers, to distribute via wholesalers)?

Financial policies include:
1.
2.
3.

Management policies include:
1.
2.
3.

Marketing policies include:
1.
2.
3.

5. Draw up a timetable of key activities

The final step in setting the parameters of strategy is to timetable some
activities. What are the key stages that need to be followed in setting up this
enterprise, in what order and by when?

What is the target opening date?

What has to happen before this and when (e.g. negotiation of finance, registration
of company, acquisition of premises/equipment/staff, training of staff)?

What has to happen immediately after this and when (e.g. marketing campaign,
production initiation, further training, targeted first order, delivery and invoice
date)?

Timetable of key activities

Date/Month	Activity

Task 3.3: Managing the resources

> **Summary of what is required**
>
> 1. Review Information Bank, Unit 13, Management of Resources
> 2. Complete the management section of the business plan by:
>   a) planning operations
>   b) formulating a 'people plan'

1. Before undertaking this task, first complete your review of Unit 13 in the Information Bank, 'Management of Resources'.

2. Summarise your operations plan

Outline your plans for premises, materials, equipment, management information systems and other appropriate operating resources.

3. Summarise your 'people plan'

a) Outline how you plan to manage other people within your new venture, at the beginning and as it grows.

b) Consider how you will recruit, retain and motivate staff. How will you ensure a team spirit emerges and endures?

c) What will be your employment practices and how will you operate payroll and personnel systems?

Assignment 3: The business plan

Task 3.4: Planning the marketing

Summary of what is required

1. Review Information Bank, Unit 14, Marketing

Complete the Marketing section of the business plan by

2. Completing your analysis of the marketing environment
3. Setting marketing objectives
4. Outlining marketing methods
5. Producing an example of promotional literature

1. Before undertaking this task, first complete your review of Unit 14 in the Information Bank, 'Marketing'.

This task is to complete the marketing section of the business plan.

2. The marketing environment – your competitive environment

Marketing research should now be completed, so that the marketing environment is now understood. In particular, the *competitive edge* of the business should be confirmed.

Earlier tasks should have done so already, but check that the following questions have now been answered:

a) Who precisely is the customer?

b) What is the market size, and the discernible trends?

c) What is the nature and extent of the competition?

d) What other trends in the technological, economic, and political environment will be important?

e) Why will the customer buy from you? What is your unique selling point?

2. Marketing objectives

What are you aiming to do in marketing terms?

Specify marketing objectives for your enterprise. These should clarify the relationship you wish to achieve between your product or service, and the target market. In other words:

a) They should summarise the product or service offered: for example "office equipment and supplies."

b) They should identify the target market: for example "offices in a 25 mile radius."

c) They should be measurable: for example "gain 10% market share," or "achieve sales of £500,000."

d) They should be time specific: for example "within two years."

3. The marketing methods

Outline the marketing methods you will use to achieve these objectives.

a) Product:
- ❏ What are the core and extended product or services offered?
- ❏ What will be the product mix?
- ❏ How will new products be found?

b) Pricing:
- ❏ What will be the pricing strategy?
- ❏ What will be the basis for pricing decisions?
- ❏ What margins will be achieved?
- ❏ What differential prices will be established?
- ❏ What will be the discount policy?

c) Promotion:
- ❏ What personal and impersonal promotional methods will you use?
- ❏ How will you ensure a consistent message?
- ❏ How will you overcome traditional small business problems in relation to promotional activity?

d) Distribution   ❏ How will you get your product or service in front of the target market?

❏ Will you distribute directly, or through intermediaries?

4. Marketing communications

In order to illustrate the benefits of the product or service on offer, it is most helpful to produce an example of promotional literature, such as a draft leaflet or brochure. This need not be a graphic masterpiece, but should attempt to illustrate how the competitive edge of your business will be put across to the target customer group.

Assignment 3: The business plan

Task 3.5: Forecasting the money

Summary of what is required

1. *Review Information Bank, Unit 15, Money*

Complete the Money section of the business plan by:

2. *Assessing the amount and type of funds required by your business*

3. *Completing profit and loss and cash flow forecasts for the 1st year in detail and the second and third years in at least outline form*

4. *Completing the balance sheet for the first year*

5. *Considering the financial policies and control systems the business will need*

1. Before undertaking this task, first complete your review of Unit 15 in the Information Bank, 'Money'.

This task is to complete the 'Money' section of the business plan.

2. Financial requirements

You should now be in a position to assess the funding requirements of your business idea. In particular, you need to establish how much of the different types of finance you will require, and the likely sources.

❑ How much *permanent capital,* in the form of equity or personal investment, will be available?

❑ How much short term, *working capital* is needed, and where will it come from?

❑ How much finance is required for *assets,* and what are the likely sources?

❑ If you are planning on *international trade,* how will this be financed?

3. Financial forecasts

Financial forecasts need to be undertaken to cover the first three years of the business:

☐ Profit and Loss and Cash Flow forecasts

– for Year 1 by month

– for Year 2 and 3 as a summary for each year as a minimum. It is preferable to complete forecasts for these 2 years by quarters.

☐ Projected Balance Sheet

– an opening and closing balance sheet for Year 1.

– end of year balance sheets for Year 2, and Year 3, are optional, but very informative about the development of the business.

4. Financial policy and control systems

In your financial analyses, you will have made a number of assumptions which will effectively form policies for your business, covering such important areas as:

☐ debtors – what will be your average debtor period?

☐ creditors – how soon will you pay your suppliers?

☐ margins and costs – what relationship will these bear to sales turnover?

☐ stocks and work-in-progress – what levels will these run at in relation to your sales?

It is important to list these assumptions as an appendix to your financial forecasts.

How will you ensure these policies are implemented? Consider what financial control mechanisms and information you will require to ensure you can carry through your assumptions.

Assignment 3: The business plan

Task 3.6: Summary of the business plan

Summary of what is required

1.   *Review Information Bank, Unit 11 to 15*

2.   *Review Assignment 3, Tasks 3.1 to 3.5*

3.   *Write up the Business Plan*

4.   *Write a summary*

You should now be in a position to write up your Business Plan.

Before you do, review Units 11 to 15 in the Information Bank, and Tasks 3.1 to 3.5 of Assignment 3.

Presentation of your final Business Plan should take into account the need for:

❏   *Conciseness:* Make your plan as concise as possible for an external audience such as financiers. Keep the main body of the report for essential information only, using appendices where possible to enlarge on assumptions or research.

❏   *Presentation:* Good presentation is seen as a sign of organised management, a quality you will need as an owner-manager.

❏   *Enthusiasm:* your plan should be interesting to read, as your enthusiasm for the project needs to show through. If you can't be enthusiastic about it, then no-one else will be!

❏   *Realism:* Optimistic plans fool no-one except the writer. Where there are major uncertainties, identify them. Don't try to cover them up as they will look worse if 'discovered' by the reader.

❏   *Illustration:* Where possible show examples by use of sample leaflets, photographs of products, locations etc. Pictures speak a thousand words.

❏   *Summary:* You will need to make a short summary of your plan; this is commonly found at the front of the document.

Section III

INFORMATION BANK

How to use this section

1. This section is divided into 15 Units which link directly with those in Section I, Activities and Scenarios. They are also referenced to specific tasks in Section II, Ongoing Assignments.

2. Each Unit contains information around a major subject area, which can be read in total, or in part as specific help to tasks in Sections I and II.

3. At the beginning of each Unit is a list of contents which summarises the topics covered and the numbering system.

Unit 1: Small business and the national economy

This Unit considers the place of the small business in the national economy. It traces the changing perceptions of small business from the time of the Bolton Report to the rapid revival we are witnessing today. The Unit also considers definitions of a small firm.

Contents

1. Why bother with *small* business?

1.1 Shifting perceptions of small business

Until recently, small business was widely regarded as a rather out of date concept. The development of management theory and studies has been based mainly on the large firm. Social scientists and policy makers devoted their attention to large units of production, which they believed would be the increasingly predominant form of industrial organisation. There was a wide-spread belief that the small firm was rather superfluous to economic growth. Mass production techniques, economies of scale, and global marketing had handed the key to economic prosperity to larger organisations and specifically to the multi-national corporation. Modern technology demanded a concentration of resources, confining small firms to a peripheral role, supporting the dominant position of larger organisations.

Early business education overlooked centuries of history in which the small enterprise had been the basic unit (through agrarian and industrial revolutions) and focused its attention and teaching on the manager working in a large company. The manager of a small firm was seen in a rather inferior light, managing limited resources with backward technologies in an amateur way. The major publications on basic business disciplines such as marketing, finance and strategy were written in the context of large organisations.

Since the 1970s the situation has changed; research into the behaviour of small enterprises has dramatically increased. The literature[1] has boomed, with written material published on virtually every aspect of the small business; there are regular newspaper columns[2] giving advice to small business owners and information on their environment.

Politicians of differing ideologies in many countries have developed a remarkable enthusiasm for the small firm. All three major political parties in the UK support policies promoting small businesses. In the 1980s leaders on both sides of the Atlantic proclaimed the dawn of a new age of enterprise, lead by an army of entrepreneurs in small firms.

By 1985, Peter Drucker[3] (one of the most influential management writers in the pre- and post-war periods, when management was seen only as the concern of big business) was welcoming the shift from a "managerial" to an "entrepreneurial" economy in which growth was being fuelled by small and medium sized enterprises.

1.2 Bolton Report, 1971

In the UK, a watershed in the perceptions of the small firm was the highly influential 'Bolton Report'[4]. This was the outcome of the "Committee of Inquiry on Small Firms", under the chairmanship of J E Bolton, set up in 1969 by the Labour government and reporting to the Conservative government in 1971. During its two years of research, it commissioned many reports which have formed the basis for the large body of work carried out since. It represented the first significant attempt to assess the importance and functions of the small firms sector in the UK.

The report recognised that small enterprises made a special contribution to the health of the economy, identifying eight important roles:

1. a productive outlet for enterprising and independent individuals (some of whom may be frustrated under-achievers in a larger, more controlled environment);

2. the most efficient form of business organisation in some industries or markets where the optimum size of the production unit or sales outlet is small;

3. specialist suppliers, or sub-contractors to larger companies;

4. contributors to the variety of products and services made available to customers in specialised markets, too small for larger companies to consider worthwhile;

5. competition to the monopolistic tendencies of large companies;

6. innovators of new products, services and processes;

7. the breeding ground for new industries; and

8. the seedbed from which tomorrow's larger companies will grow, providing entry points for entrepreneurial talent who will become the industrial captains of the future.

These important roles were underpinned by the conclusion of the Committee that small firms could be extremely efficient, having the advantage of the commitment of their owner-managers, plus the ability in certain circumstances to better exploit business opportunities than their larger brethren.

However, the Committee provided evidence of the decline of the small business sector in the UK economy, concluding that further weakening of small firms was inevitable due to the economies of scale of larger firms. In view of the actual and potential contribution of small firms to the overall health of the economy, the major recommendation of the Report was therefore the creation of a Small Firms Division under a Minister for Small Firms. This was implemented by the establishment of the Small Firms Service within the Department of Industry.

The particular concern of the Report was that government policies should encourage and support the sector, not accelerate its decline through an unfair burden of regulations, paperwork and taxes:

> "We believe that the health of the economy requires the birth of new enterprises in substantial numbers and the growth of some to a position from which they are able to challenge and supplant the existing leaders of industry...This seedbed function, therefore, appears to be a vital contribution of the small firms sector to the long-run health of the economy. We cannot assume that the ordinary working of market forces will necessarily preserve a small firm sector large enough to perform this function in future."

2. The resurgence of small enterprise

In fact, the Bolton report proved unduly pessimistic about the future of small firms. If their survival as an organisational form was the issue in 1971, the concern now is that the expectations are too high. Small firms are currently heralded as leaders in providing employment and growth in a restructuring of advanced economies. In retrospect, we can see that the tide was turning before the Bolton Report.

2.1 The American experience

In the USA, small enterprises began their revival in the 1960s. Since the late 1960s, the creation of new jobs has shifted from the country's largest organisations, to small and medium sized firms, many of them new businesses[3]. The growth in employment in the USA between the mid 60s and mid 80s was phenomenal. The total workforce grew from 71 million in 1965 to 106 million in 1985, an increase of 50%, or 35 million new jobs. Yet at the same time the traditional powerhouses of the American economy, the Fortune 500 representing the very largest businesses, were actually shedding jobs, an estimated loss of 5 million permanent jobs by 1985. In other words, taking into account this loss, 40 million new jobs were created in the two decades to 1985 by small and medium sized businesses. Much of the growth has come from new enterprises, with an estimated 600,000 new businesses being started every year during the boom times of the 1980s.

2.2 The UK statistics

The pick up of small enterprises in the UK may have come later but has been no less impressive. Figure 1.1 illustrates the growth in small firms in the 1980s and the numbers employed in them. Between 1979 and 1986, there was a substantial jump in the total number of firms in the UK from 1.791 million to 2.471 million, an increase of 38%. Virtually all of the increase came from small firms employing under 100 people, which increased in numbers from 1.767 million to 2.445 million, a net growth of 678,000 firms in seven years. Those small firms of under 100 people employed 39% of the workforce in 1979. By 1986 they accounted for 50% of total employment.

Of course, larger companies account for a proportionally higher amount of sales than smaller firms. Although firms employing over 100 people represented only 1% of all firms in 1986, their combined turnovers has been estimated at 54% of total sales[6]. Nevertheless, this implies that smaller firms of under 100 people, not only provide half of the private sector employment, but they account for 46% of aggregate turnover as well.

A sector which had been largely ignored or dismissed as an out of date irrelevance by business and management analysts had grown to represent almost half of total sales, and half of total employment. No wonder there has been a reawakening of interest and a rush of literature!

Figure 1.1: UK firms by size and their employment 1979–1986

Numbers employed in firm	Number of firms 1979	Number of firms 1986	% of total private sector employment 1979	% of total private sector employment 1986
1–2	1,099,132	1,579,389	6.6	9.7
3–5	318,917	472,676	5.9	8.9
6–10	178,628	189,618	6.7	7.3
11–19	108,827	139,824	7.6	10.1
20–49	46,237	44,033	6.9	6.7
50–99	15,585	19,732	5.3	6.9
100–199	14,865	14,066	10.2	9.9
200–499	5,365	7,657	8.1	11.9
500–999	2,169	2,974	7.5	10.5
1000+	<u>1,774</u>	<u>892</u>	<u>35.3</u>	<u>18.2</u>
Total	1,791,499	2,470,861	100.0	100.0

Source: Graham Bannock and Partners Ltd[5]

2.3 Self-employment and small firms

It is noticeable from Figure 1.1 that the largest increase in small firms is in the very smallest category, that is those employing 1 or 2 people, which increased by 44% in the period. It is important to make a distinction between self-employment and the creation of a small business; the former could be just another form of working for larger organisations with no prospects of directly creating employment for others. For example, many professional specialists or skilled workers have taken redundancy to become self-employed as consultants or tradesmen. Often they then work for larger firms on a fee or subcontract basis. This has become a particular feature of recessionary times when employers try to maintain the maximum flexibility over the costs of employment, by using self-employed labour. Some welcome the opportunity for self-employment in this way. Others, it has been suggested up to one-third[7], accept self-employment reluctantly because of redundancy or lack of alternative employment.

The total number of self-employed has risen steeply in the UK in the last decade, from 1.9 million in 1979 to 3.4 million in 1990. However the growth in employment by smaller firms has outstripped this increase in the numbers of self-employed. (Between 1979 and 1986 the growth in the number of self-employed accounted for only 49% of the increase in employment in firms of less than 20 people[5].)

The UK experience has mirrored that of the USA, in that large companies have shed jobs, whilst smaller ones have created them. Total employment in the UK fell by 0.5 million between 1979 and 1986. But large businesses employing 1000 people or more reduced their workforces by 3.5 million, whilst smaller companies of under 1000 people, increased their total employment by 3 million.

2.4   The International scene

The increase in employment in small firms has been a feature of the economies of virtually all developed countries in the 1980s, and 1990s just as most had shown a decline in the sector prior to 1970.

In fact, the Bolton report showed that, although the small business sector was in decline internationally at that time, the concentration of resources in large companies had gone further in the UK than anywhere else. Only the USA had more multinationals in the world's top 500 companies than Britain in the 1960s.

Although the increase in small firms in the UK has subsequently been greater than elsewhere, this is largely because of the rise in self-employment which has not happened on such a scale outside the UK. Thus, the contribution of small firms to both employment and output in the UK still lags well behind that of the USA, Japan and Germany.

3. Interpretations of the small business revival

3.1   Three theories

By the 1980s the small firm found itself at centre stage of a political and economic debate which offered radically different interpretations over its role, and its recent revival. The contenders in this debate have been classified by Goss[8] into three distinct camps.

❑ *Free Market theory*

Right wing governments in the UK and the USA simultaneously seized upon the small firm as a symbol of a new order, the Enterprise Culture, which was ushering out an age of collectivism and government economic intervention. President Reagan hailed the small business as the economic saviour of America, whilst Prime Minister Thatcher pronounced them a barometer of freedom, insisting that "the freer the society, the more small businesses there will be".

The free market economy promoted by the Right relies on the widespread competition provided by new ventures and smaller companies to prevent the monopolistic distortions of large organisations. Entrepreneurial action, stemming from an "on your bike", self sufficient philosophy, is seen as the antidote to the adversity of job loss and regional economic realignment. The virtues of innovation and job creation in small enterprises is contrasted to the lethargy and stagnation of large nationalised industries.

❑ *Marxian analysis*

According to Marxist theory, capitalism degenerates into economies dominated by a small number of monopolistic companies, as society polarises between those that own the large units of production and those that work in them. Far from being inconvenient evidence, the revival of the small firm is explained as part of this inevitable tendency. Small firms represent a subtler form of economic domination by the large firms, and another instrument for the exploitation of labour. Central to this argument is the dependent status of small business on larger organisations which only allow them to thrive when it is more profitable that way.

So, for example, the growth in small firms in the 1980s is seen as part of a strategy by which large firms effectively sub-contract their less profitable activities to smaller firms in difficult times. These can operate on a lower cost base because of their lack of unionisation, and poorer terms and conditions of work. The tendency for small firm formation to increase during recessions illustrates that the core sector of big business is merely using small business as a secondary sector, to cushion itself against market fluctuations. Moreover this secondary sector only survives because it can exploit its unorganised, non-unionised labour with lower pay, poorer working conditions and safety records.

❑ *The Green Movement*

'Mass production', 'bureaucracy', 'centralisation', and 'short term material gain', have all become dirty words, describing a crisis in industrial society which only a return to a more 'natural' order can reverse. This is the thinking behind 'alternative' movements which have also put small business to the forefront of their ideology. The 'small is beautiful' slogan of Fritz Schumacher[9] has been taken up, representing the feeling that the quality of life must come before the materialistic motives of big business. Small enterprises are seen as more democratic and responsive to society than the remote, large organisations following strategies of high growth, which take little account of their effects either on the world environment or local communities.

3.2 Reasons for the small business revival

Factors which have influenced the growth and revival of small business in the UK include:

❑ *Unemployment*

The revival of self-employment and small business ownership in developed countries coincided with a period of recession and high levels of unemployment from the late 1970s, through the early 1980s. There does seem to have been a link between the rate of unemployment and entry into business ownership in the UK. Redundancy, especially with a golden handshake, has pushed many reluctant entrepreneurs into self-employment, and provided the stimulus for others who had already considered starting their own business, but were reluctant to give up the security of their employment.

Whilst this does seem to have been a factor in the early 1980s, unemployment fell sharply in the late 1980s with little slackening in the rate of new business formations[10].

❑ *Growth of the service sector*

The vast majority of all small firms operate in the service and construction sectors of the economy. One estimate is that 90% of firms employing less than 25 people are in services and construction[11].

There has been a strong structural shift in the economy away from manufacturing based industries and towards services; figure 1.2 illustrates the movement between 1969 and 1987 showing that services account for 69% of GDP. Hence small firms are most active in the most dynamic sector of the economy.

Small firms have competitive advantages in many service sectors, which accounts for their strong representation in this area of business. Many services, such as communication and professional advice services (e.g. advertising, accounting, computer services and other consultancies), rely on a personalised, tailor made service very suited to the flexibility and responsiveness of small business.

Other services involve consumption at the point of purchase (restaurants, wine bars, free houses), which favours smaller, localised outlets, requiring individual management.

Figure 1.2: The shift towards services % of GDP by sector

	Manufacturing	Private services & construction	Public services	Total services
1969	33%	45%	12%	57%
1987	23%	54%	15%	69%

Source: Annual Abstracts of Statistics

❐ *Sub-contracting and contraction*

The recession of the early 1980s stimulated some fragmentation of production and services as larger firms reorganised themselves; 'leaner and fitter' became the watchwords as companies adjusted to the new economic realities. In an effort to reduce fixed costs and develop flexibility to cope with fluctuations in demand, some larger organisations have sub-contracted some of their activities to smaller enterprises. In other cases large companies have withdrawn altogether from some activities to concentrate on what they see as their 'core' business, selling off or closing down peripheral businesses. These trends can be interpreted in two fundamentally different ways[12].

i) Large organisations still retain primary control over economic activity but it has served their interests to shift some employment and output to smaller firms. It does not therefore represent a fundamental, long term realignment of forces in favour of smaller business, but a strategy to increase the profitability and flexibility of larger ones (along the lines of Marxian analysis described at 3.1). This "fragmentation model" sees small firms as still very dependent on large firms.

ii) Fundamental changes are happening in the economy, as the mass production methods of large companies become less appropriate to new patterns of demand. Consumers now expect individual preferences to be catered for in detail as business has learned the value of segmenting markets to differentiate their products. A walk down any high street past shops specialising in socks, expensive chocolates, video games and door knobs confirms this point.

At the same time new technology has reduced the fixed costs of some manufacturing processes, so that production can profitably be based in smaller, more flexible units. For example, traditional printing methods involved capital intensive equipment, operated by expensive skilled labour, which became very uneconomic for short run, or one-off jobs. New printing technology, with more flexible presses and computerised text setting, has allowed 'instant printing' to flourish by offering shorter economic print quantities, and faster availability.

This 'flexible specialisation' model of economic development obviously favours small business, which is seen as becoming an increasingly powerful sector, less dependent on big business in the years ahead.

❐ *Public sector reorganisation*

The public sector in the UK has been subject to reorganisations in the 1980s and 1990s which have provided opportunities for small business involvement. A variety of measures has caused public bodies to open up some of the services they purchase to private sector involvement. The creation of 'internal markets', a clearer distinction between departments that purchase services and those that provide them, and compulsive competitive tendering for some functions hitherto provided internally, has meant more sub-contracting possibilities for small firms. For example, grounds maintenance and cleaning and catering services in schools and hospitals are now contracted out to the lowest bidder. Independent architects, solicitors, trainers and consultants have all benefited from additional work from public bodies which have cut back their own internal departments previously providing these professional services.

❐ *The "Enterprise Culture"*

A rare consensus has emerged in British politics, as all three major political parties have proclaimed their support for a healthy small business sector.

In keeping with their market economy ideology, the Conservative administration which came to power in 1979 introduced a series of measures designed to stimulate new businesses. These ranged from investment incentives to information and advice. (See Unit 6, 'The Small Business Environment', 4. 'Government Policy', for a fuller description of government measures.)

As the revival of the small firm was well under way before 1979, this policy served to further stimulate or prolong growth, not initiate it. But the estimated £1 billion spent by the Exchequer between 1980 and 1985, through over 200 policy measures in support of small firms, has clearly had a positive effect on the growth of the sector.

How far the government has succeeded in establishing an 'enterprise culture', which encourages and values entrepreneurial attitudes and self-employment, is more debatable. One survey[13] found that although young people were very aware of entrepreneurial opportunities they were cautious over the risks involved.

❐ *The "New Age"*

The growth in numbers of small firms has coincided with an increased awareness of environmental and lifestyle issues, heralded as a 'New Age' in the values of society. Endorsing the philosophies of the 'Green Movement' people have also sought to further the cause through employment. A whole new variety of self-employment possibilities have been created including:

❐ practitioners of alternative medicine from reflexology to rolfing massage;

❐ health food producers, wholesalers and retailers;

❐ trainers, counsellors, writers, publishers and retailers selling courses, books, magazines, video and audio cassettes on 'New Age' themes; and

❐ producers and retailers of alternative beauty products.

Whilst no statistics are available on the level of self-employment created by the popularity of these activities, their impact has been noticeable in some small business areas; for example, the growth in number of worker co-operatives is partially explained by 'alternative' movements. (See Unit 10 'Forms of Small Business Organisation', 6.1–6.4, 'Co-operatives'.)

4. What is a small firm?

A basic assumption of any study of the small firm sector (and indeed of this book), is that a small business has certain characteristics which distinguish it from a big business. Whilst this is undoubtedly true, it is hard to define these characteristics in practice, and even harder to draw a precise line between small, medium and large firms. The cause of the problem is clear: small firms are a very diverse group of business units. They come in all shapes and sizes from manufacturers to publicans, from professional managers to husband and wife teams, from high growth, high tech start-ups funded by venture capitalists, to tradesmen funding themselves and content just to make a living. It is this diversity which makes generalisations of any kind, including a definition of the sector, extremely difficult, and often unwise.

4.1 Bolton Report definition

The Bolton Committee proposed that a small firm had three essential characteristics:

❐ "A small firm is managed by it owner(s) in a personalised way."

❐ "It has a relatively small share of the market in economic terms."

❐ "It is independent in the sense that it does not form part of a larger enterprise and its ownership is relatively free from outside control in its principal decisions."

As well as these general qualities, small firms were defined by more specific measurements. The diversity of the sector was recognised as definitions depended on the industry type. For example:

Small firm type	Definition used
manufacturing	200 employees or less
construction	25 employees or less
road transport	5 vehicles or less
retailing	£50,000 p.a. turnover or less
miscellaneous services	£50,000 p.a. turnover or less

(Turnover thresholds are subject to inflation since 1971; £50,000 equates to approximately £500,000 today.)

Although these definitions have formed the basis of subsequent research, they are open to several criticisms including:

❐ low market share is not always a characteristic; small firms can operate in highly specialised niches, or limited geographic markets, where they have a relatively high share;

❐ 'independence' is difficult to measure. Bolton's definition excluded franchises for example, which do form part of a larger enterprise, but included sub-contractors very dependent on one customer;

❐ whilst different size measures are very justifiable (200 employees makes a small manufacturer, but a large consultancy or retailer for instance), they have bedevilled statistical comparisons, especially internationally as countries employ different definitions.

4.2 Definition used in this book

Whilst it is important to establish the scope of our subject, this publication is not bound by rigid statistical definitions. Small business management is different in several respects to management in larger organisations, because of different social structures and relationships, and because of the levels of resources available. Whilst these differences may derive from the numbers of employees, and size of turnover, it is the management implications of these differences that will be our primary concern. For example, the owner-manager, who has no specialist department to turn to, takes phone calls from creditors emphasising the shortage of cash resources and has to choose between keeping an appointment with a customer or attending to an important production issue, is faced with a situation typical of small business management, but unlikely to be found in other environments.

In this sense 'small business' management can be extended to 'small enterprise' management; small non-profit making units share certain common problems with small firms. A doctor in a small medical practice, the head teacher of a primary school, or the manager of a small charity may work in a similar management environment, and face similar management decisions as the owner-manager of a small firm. Whilst an organisation may not fit with an accepted definition of a small business, the management environment can still be typical of a small enterprise.

5. A turbulent sector

More recent statistics on the small firms sector of the economy illustrate that although it is maintaining its newly found importance, it is also a sector which has experienced considerable turbulence, which is continuing into the 1990s. Businesses registering or deregistering for VAT are likely to be mainly small firms, and so some idea of the movement in and out of the sector can be seen from the statistics which are shown in figure 1.3.

Figure 1.3: VAT registrations and deregistrations 1980–1990

1980 stock 1,289,000			*1990 stock* 1,709,000
		1980–1990	
	Registrations	*Deregistrations*	*Net change*
	2,147,000	1,727,000	420,000

Source: Employment Gazette, March 1991 [14]

These figures confirm the rapid rise in the total numbers of firms with the net increase of 420,000 in the decade. Whilst this has dropped recently, from its 1989 record level of almost 16,000 registrations a week to about 1,000 a week in 1990, the beginnings of recession in the economy only slackened the rate of new firm formation.

These figures also highlight the turbulence among small firms. There were high levels of deregistrations in the decade as many of those experiencing small business employment or self-employment moved back into employment elsewhere, or unemployment. Deregistrations in 1990 showed a rising trend at 185,000, compared to registrations at 235,000, a net 'gain' of 50,000 registrations in the year, compared to 83,000 in 1989.

Small businesses have provided independence and longer term employment for some, but disillusionment and changing fortunes for others.

6. References and further reading

6.1 References and further information

1. An excellent summary is provided by the *London Business School Small Business Bibliography* published regularly by the London Business School. Testifying to the still increasing literature on the small enterprise, the 1985–86 update contained 1500 new items.

2. For example the Guardian carries a "New Business" section every Monday, edited by Clive Woodcock.

3. Drucker, P, *Innovation and Entrepreneurship,* Heinemann, 1986.

4. Bolton Report, *Committee of Inquiry on Small Firms,* HMSO, Cmnd 4811, London 1971.

5. See Stanworth, J, and Gray, C (eds), *Bolton 20 Years On: the Small Firm in the 1990s,* PCP Ltd, 1991. Chapter 1.

6. Bannock, G, and Daly, M, "Size Distribution of UK firms," in *Employment Gazette,* HMSO, May 1990.

7. Hakim, C, "New recruits to self-employment in the 1980s", in *Employment Gazette,* HMSO, June 1989.

8. Goss, D, *Small Business and Society,* Routledge, 1991. Chapter 1.

9. Schumacher, F, *Small is Beautiful,* Abacus, 1974.

10. See Johnson, S, "Small Firms and the UK. Labour market", in Curran, J and Blackburn, R (eds), *Paths of Enterprise, The Future of Small Business,* Routledge, 1991.

11. Curran, J and Burrows, R, *Enterprise Britain: A National Profile of Small Business Owners and the Self-Employed,* Small Business Research Trust, 1988.

12. For a full summary of the debate see Curran, J and Blackburn, R (eds), *Paths of Enterprise, The Future of Small Business,* Routledge, 1991.

13. Blackburn, R and Curran, J, *The Future of the Small Firm: Attitudes of Young People to Entrepreneurship,* paper to 12th UK Small Firms Policy and Research Conference, 1989.

14. Daly, M, "VAT Registrations and Deregistrations in 1990", *Employment Gazette,* Department of Employment, November 1991.

6.2 Recommended further reading

Stanworth, J and Gray, C (eds), *Bolton 20 Years On: the Small Firm in the 1990s,* PCP 1991. Chapter 1 'An Economic Survey'.

Goss, D, *Small Business and Society,* Routledge, 1991. Chapter 2 'The Empirical Investigation of UK Small Business.'

Unit 2: The entrepreneur and the owner-manager

This Unit looks at the personality and backgrounds of entrepreneurs and owner-managers. After considering the definitions of 'entrepreneur' and 'owner-manager', it then explores their personality traits, motivation and backgrounds, before summarising some of the key influences and characteristics in theory and in practice.

Contents

1. Entrepreneur and owner-manager: is there a difference?

The terms 'entrepreneur' and 'owner-manager' are often used to describe somebody who is engaged in the management of a small business. Strictly these terms have different meanings, yet are often interchanged as though they mean the same thing. Thus, anyone who starts up their own business is labelled as an 'entrepreneur', and 'entrepreneurship' is inextricably linked to small business management.

There is great diversity among those engaged in managing small enterprises and, in order to understand them better, it is necessary to define how we label them more clearly.

1.1 'Entrepreneur': a definition

J B Say[1] apparently coined the term around 1800, as meaning someone who consciously moves economic resources from "an area of lower and into an area of higher productivity and greater yield". In other words, the entrepreneur takes existing resources, such as people, materials, buildings, and money, and redeploys them in such a way as to make them more productive and give them greater value.

This original definition implies changing what already exists; it sees the entrepreneur as an instrument of change, someone who does not seek to perfect, or optimise existing ways of doing things, but searches instead for new methods, and new markets – different ways of doing things. About a hundred years later, Joseph Schumpeter[2] took up this theme of the entrepreneur as a necessary destabilising force. According to Schumpeter, economic equilibrium, which optimises what already exists, does not create 'healthy' economies. A dynamic economy takes as its norm the disequilibrium brought about by the constant change and innovation of entrepreneurship.

In the 1980s Peter Drucker[3] developed these earlier ideas, seeing the emergence of an entrepreneurial economy in the USA as a "most significant and hopeful event". He defined an entrepreneur as someone who "always searches for change, responds to it, and exploits it as an opportunity". He thus made innovation a necessary part of entrepreneurship.

1.2 Entrepreneurs in small – and large – business

The term 'entrepreneur' is commonly linked with small business management. However, these definitions present two problems.

❏ Most small business owners do not innovate or seek out change in a continuous or purposeful way. Some do of course. There are inventive people, labelled "boffin business men" by some researchers[4], who seek to exploit new ideas through commercial activity. But these are the exceptions as most small businesses are founded on existing ideas and practices. The couple that open their own wine bar, the redundant employee who forms a training consultancy or the craftsman who starts up a joinery firm, are all taking risks but only by doing what has been done many times before. They do not necessarily attempt to innovate or seek out change, but base their business on hopes of increased consumption of the same products or services also on offer elsewhere.

Many small firms lack creative spirit. The majority of start-ups are based on established industries. Research into the choice of product for a new business in relation to the owner-manager's previous experience showed that the vast majority stuck to the same industry. Only four percent had innovated a new product or technique in one survey[5]. There seems to be a natural tendency to play safe, staying with known business areas, when considering a new business.

Once established, small firms can also lack innovative entrepreneurship. Owner-managers are invariably close to the day to day problems of their business as it grows – often too close to see opportunities or the need for change. Small business management can easily become a reactive process in which new ideas are pushed out by the need to cope with more pressing realities. In these circumstances, the entrepreneur has to adapt and react, rather than direct and create. From its innovative origins, entrepreneurship has been watered down to imply adaptability and constant manoeuvring to fit the circumstances of the day. Entrepreneurs have taken on a 'wheeler-dealer' image in which creativity is used only for survival rather than progress.

❏ Entrepreneurs can exist in large as well as small economic units. Small business does not have a monopoly of entrepreneurial talent. There is a perception, to some extent confirmed by research, that small business is more innovative, and therefore more entrepreneurial, than larger organisations. (The role of innovation in small business is more fully discussed in Unit 3 'Innovation'.) The lack of policy and rules in a small, informal structure can provide a more creative environment than a large, hierarchical organisation. Many large organisations, however, exhibit more sustained entrepreneurial tendencies than small business. Some have deliberately tried to remain entrepreneurial by encouraging managers to innovate rather than administer. Companies such as DEC and 3M have a track record of innovative entrepreneurship which is hard to match in any business sector. Because the word 'entrepreneur' has been so linked to small business a new word was coined, 'intrapreneur', to describe someone who behaves in an entrepreneurial fashion in a larger organisation.

Entrepreneurial activity is not confined to the small business sector, nor is it always found in small firms.

1.3 The "heroic" entrepreneur

Entrepreneurs are frequently presented as heroic individuals. Picture an entrepreneur: we tend to think of an individual who masters the odds stacked against them, single-handedly overcoming traditional barriers until, by sheer force of personality, they manage to change what exists and offer the customer the something different that they really wanted all along. The 'enterprise culture' promoted by the Thatcherite government in the UK certainly encouraged this portrayal. Economic policy was developed on the premise that individuals needed only the right environment to become entrepreneurs, and that the economy could be led by 'heroic individuals' whose entrepreneurial talent would lead the way to a new era of growth in British industry. The likes of Richard Branson and Lord Hanson were seen as examples for small business managers to emulate.

The reality is that whilst large numbers of new small businesses have been started, only a tiny minority will grow into substantial enterprises. Many will cease after only a few years trading, as the heroic vision fades. The substantial growth in numbers of small businesses has masked an even greater amount of activity in and out of the sector. The growth in overall numbers has only been achieved through a high level of new entrants to small business who quickly returned to other types of employment, or sadly unemployment.

1.4 The owner-manager

The term "owner-manager" is also commonly used to describe those involved in running a small business. It encapsulates a condition which is typical of many small firms – the predominant role of the owner as manager. The majority of small business are *very* small; of the approximate 2.5 million firms in the UK in 1986, over 2 million (83%) of them, employed only 5 people or less (see Unit 1, 'Small Business and the National Economy', Figure 1.1: UK firms by size and their employment 1979–86). The owners of these firms are predominantly the managers as well, and likely to be the only manager. The 'owner-manager' describes the reality for a large number of small firms which are totally reliant on, and dominated by, the owner.

Although less confusing than 'entrepreneur' to describe small business managers, 'owner-manager' is also a limiting term which implies a uniformity of management which does not exist in practice. 'Owner-managers' are not an homogeneous group which can be easily classified, or expected to behave in certain ways.

2. Types of owner-managers and entrepreneurs

The diversity of types of owner-managers and entrepreneurs has led to several attempts to classify them. An early effort[6] simply split them into 'craftsmen' and 'opportunists', to reflect the different backgrounds and aspirations of these types. This basic classification has been extended by later commentators to lengths which indicate the great diversity of small business managers. Figure 2.1 below illustrates a list of entrepreneurial 'types', adapted from Douglas Gray, whose book[7] offers self assessment profiles to judge the readers 'suitability' to entrepreneurial activity.

Figure 2.1: Entrepreneurial types

1. *Soloist*	A self employed person operating alone, for example in a specific trade or profession.
2. *Key partner*	One stage on from the soloist, as an autonomous individual, but with a partner in the background, sometimes as a financial backer only.
3. *Grouper*	Those who prefer working in small groups with other partners who share the decision making; for example craftsmen working in their own firm as equals.
4. *Professional*	Self employed experts; e.g., traditional professionals (accountants, solicitors, doctors, architects etc). Whilst not traditionally considered to be 'entrepreneurs' they do tend to work in small firms.

5. **Inventor-researcher**	Creative inventors, who may, or may not, have the practical skills to turn creativity into innovation.
6. **High-tech**	New technological developments have created opportunities for those with the technical expertise, e.g. in electronics or computers.
7. **Work force builder**	The delegator who manages the labour and expertise of others in an effective way; e.g. in the building trade.
8. **Inveterate initiator**	The start-up expert who only really enjoys the challenge of initiating new enterprises, then loses interest, often selling the business in order to start another.
9. **Concept multiplier**	Someone who identifies a successful concept that can be duplicated by others, for example through franchising, or licensing arrangements.
10. **Acquirer**	Those that prefer to take over a business that already exists, rather than start from scratch.
11. **Speculator**	There are many property based opportunities to buy and sell at a profit, as well as 'collectables' such as art, stamps and antique furniture which have spawned many dealers as owner-managers of small firms.
12. **Turn-about artist**	An acquirer who buys small businesses with problems, but potential for profit.
13. **Value manipulator**	An entrepreneur who acquires assets at a low price and who then, through manipulation of the financial structure, is able to sell at a higher price.
14. **Lifestyle entrepreneur**	Small business is a means to the end of making possible the 'good-life' however this is defined. Consistent cash flow is the primary business requirement rather than high growth which might involve too much time commitment.
15. **Committed manager**	The small business is regarded as a lifetime's work, something to be built up carefully. Personal satisfaction comes from the process of nurturing the fledgling firm through all its various stages of growth.
16. **Conglomerator**	An entrepreneur who builds up a portfolio of ownership in small businesses, sometimes using shares or assets of one company to provide the financial base to acquire another.
17. **Capital aggregator**	A business owner with the necessary financial leverage to acquire other substantial attractive businesses.
18. **Matriarch or patriarch**	The head of a family owned business, which often employs several members of the family.
19. **Going public**	Entrepreneurs who start-up in business with the clear aim of achieving a quotation on the stock exchange, usually via the Unlisted Securities Market (see Unit 15, 2.5 'Public Equity – the USM').
20. **The alternative entrepreneur**	Alternative 'new age' belief in a return to simpler, more environmentally sound lifestyles have been expressed in a wish to avoid conventional employment. Commercial activities have developed in areas such as health foods, alternative healing and medicines, alternative beauty products, and 'new age' publications and audio tapes.

Adapted from *The Entrepreneur's Complete Self-Assessment Guide,* by Douglas Gray[7].

3. The search for entrepreneurial traits

Is it possible to predict someone's aptitude to entrepreneurship? Can anyone become a small business manager, or does it require a certain type of person to make it really work? If it does require certain attributes, are they innate or can we acquire them? In other words are successful entrepreneurs and owner-managers born or made?

The influence of the owner-manager on a small business is crucial. Particularly in the early days enterprises are inseparable from their owner-managers; they are conceived by them, born of their labours, and survive because of their dedication. In later stages of growth, a management team may emerge which make the enterprise more autonomous, capable of continuity without the originating force.

But it is the owner-manager who has to grow the enterprise to the stage where it has the critical mass to survive as an entity in its own right. As this impact is so vital, it would be very helpful to identify personality types who are more likely to succeed, in order to encourage those who were the right 'fit' and discourage others who did not have the necessary characteristics.

A number of 'traits' or personality characteristics have been put forward as important influences in successful entrepreneurship.

3.1 Need for achievement

A well known investigation into the entrepreneurial personality by McClelland[8] concluded that the driving force is 'need for achievement'. Parental influences are significant in the development of this 'need achievement' personality. According to this study, entrepreneurs are likely to have parents who expected them to be self-reliant at an early age, whilst remaining supportive and not rejecting of their offspring. An entrepreneur's need for achievement manifests itself in a number of ways:

❑ risk taking

❑ confidence of success

❑ desire for independence

❑ energy in pursuing goals

❑ measurement of success by wealth

3.2 "The dark side" of entrepreneurship

Kets de Vries[9] also concluded that family background and experiences were significant in forming an entrepreneurial personality, but from a very different perspective. He paints a picture of hardships endured in childhood which leave an adult troubled by images of the past, leading to low self-esteem, insecurity and lack of confidence. Driving ambition and hyperactivity emerge as compensating characteristics, but in a non-conformist, rebellious person who is thus driven to self-employment through lack of acceptance in conventional employment. The entrepreneur who emerges from such a background is therefore driven by a need to escape from their roots, but their aggressive, impulsive behaviour, which does not accept the authority of others, means they have to create their own organisation to succeed. Whilst an inner compulsion may lead to some business success, longer term problems are likely to emerge as a result of these deviant personality traits.

3.3   Self-determination

Successful entrepreneurs are convinced that they can control their own destinies according to some research studies[10]. Behavioural scientists describe those who believe they have the ability to control their environment as having an 'internal locus of control', compared to others with an 'external locus of control' who believe that their lives are dominated by chance and fate. Some studies[10] concluded that small business survival and success is linked to the internal locus of control beliefs of the owner-managers. The stronger commitment to self determination has enabled some owner-managers to overcome difficulties which defeated others.

3.4   Risk taking

Without a significant level of belief in themselves, owner-managers are unlikely to have taken the initial risk of starting their own business. Entrepreneurs are often characterised as risk-takers who instinctively know that gains do not accrue to those who always play safety first.

However, there is debate over the levels of risk taken, which highlights a distinction between the entrepreneur and the owner-manager. At one extreme there is the 'opportunist entrepreneur' who relentlessly pursues every possibility with little regard to the resources available to them at the time. According to the Kets de Vries version of their personality[9], this compulsive competitiveness stems from their deep insecurity which drives them to prove themselves time and time again by taking risks. Others might argue that their internal locus of control gives them the self confidence to take on any challenge.

At the other end of the spectrum is the 'conservative owner-manager', who took some risk to establish their business, but whose only aim now is to preserve what they have achieved. Risks are to be avoided for this type of small business manager, whose traits match those of an administrator more than an entrepreneur.

In between there are many shades of risk taking, from the reckless to the calculated, which depend on the context as well as an individual's character. A young, unemployed person with no family would be seen as taking less risk in starting a new venture than an older person in a secure job with a family.

3.5   Desire for independence

A trait which is commonly recognised as prevalent among entrepreneurs and owner-managers alike is their strong desire for independence, the freedom to create their own futures. This can be linked to their internal locus of control: belief in their ability to control their own destiny can lead to a desire for the necessary independence to make it happen 'their way'.

3.6   Innovation

Definitions developed earlier (1.1 'Entrepreneur: a definition) singled out innovative activity as a hallmark of entrepreneurship, but not necessarily of the owner-manager. Innovative behaviour is key to the entrepreneurial personality according to many commentators. Can this be learned or are we born with, or without, an ability to innovate? Drucker[3] insists that we can develop our innovation skills.

He regards entrepreneurship and innovation as tasks that can be – and should be – organised in a purposeful, systematic way. In other words, they are part of any manager's job, whether he or she works in a small, or a large, enterprise. The entrepreneurial manager is constantly looking for innovations, not by waiting for a flash of inspiration, but through an organised and continuous search for new ideas. Drucker presents entrepreneurs, not as people who are born with certain character traits, but as managers who know where to look for innovation, and how to develop it into useful products or markets once they have found it.

Drucker's entrepreneurship is not so much an art that you either have, or you don't, but rather a practice which you constantly follow or you choose to ignore. It can thus be developed, and learned; its core activity is innovation and a continuous, purposeful search for new ideas, and their practical applications.

3.7 Limitations of the trait approach

The attempt to find single personality traits which characterise either entrepreneurs or owner-managers has not succeeded. The ideas discussed above are useful in describing certain types of entrepreneurs or owner-managers, but none can claim general application.

The diversity of types of entrepreneurs (who, as we have seen, are not limited to small businesses) and owner-managers means that there can be no rules without significant exceptions.

4. Motivations for starting a business

Some of the reasons for the difficulties in classifying those involved in small business management is the wide variety of motives for their involvement in small firms. The reasons for small firm formation can be divided between 'pull' and 'push' influences.

4.1 'Pull' influences

Some individuals are attracted towards small business ownership by positive motives such as a specific idea which they are convinced will work. 'Pull' motives include:

❑ *Desire for independence:* This features prominently in several research studies[11] as the key motivator. The Bolton Report singled out the need to gain and keep independence as a distinguishing feature of small business owner-managers. A study of female entrepreneurs in Britain found that women were motivated particularly by the need for autonomy, which had been frustrated by the individuals prior training and background[12].

❑ *Desire to exploit an opportunity:* The identification of a perceived gap in the market place through personal observation or experience is also a common reason for starting a business. For example, a study of new manufacturing firms in South Hampshire[11] reported that 60% of founders quoted their desire to exploit a perceived market. Whilst other studies have shown lower percentages, the wish to satisfy a perceived market gap remains a powerful motive. Entrepreneurs may seek to exploit this opportunity through specialist knowledge, product development or they may hire the appropriate technology and skills.

❑ *Turning a hobby or previous work experience into a business:* Many new entrepreneurs seek fulfilment by spending more time involved in a cherished hobby, or part of their work that they particularly enjoy. Although research confirms that founders tend to establish businesses in activities of which they have direct prior experience, this is often precipitated by a 'push' motive, such as redundancy (see 4.2 below), rather than part of a considered decision process.

☐ *Financial incentive:* The rewards of starting a business can be high, and are well publicised by those selling 'how to' information to would-be entrepreneurs. The promise of long term financial independence can clearly be a motive in starting a new firm, although it is usually not quoted as frequently as other factors.

4.2 'Push' influences

Many people are pushed into founding a new enterprise by a variety of factors including:

☐ *Redundancy:* This has proved a considerable push into entrepreneurship particularly when accompanied by a generous hand shake in a locality where other employment possibilities are low.

☐ *Unemployment (or threat of):* Job insecurity and unemployment varies in significance by region, and by prevailing economic climate. A study reported that 25% of business founders in the late 1970s were pushed in this way, whilst later research showed a figure of 50% when unemployment nationally was much higher[13].

☐ *Disagreement with previous employer:* Uncomfortable relations at work has also pushed new entrants into small business.

The dividing line between those 'pulled' and those 'pushed' is often blurred. Many people considering an opportunity or having a desire for independence still need some form of push to help them make their decision.

What is clear is that the diversity of motivations for starting a business will influence the owner-manager once they have set up. For example, the desire for independence may inhibit growth, as this can be seen as a threat to autonomy; once a firm becomes less than small it might take on some of the characteristics of larger organisations from which the owner-manager is trying to escape. Entrepreneurial tendencies to develop the business through new opportunities may therefore conflict with an owner-manager motivation to retain control by remaining small.

5. Owner-manager backgrounds

There has been considerable research interest recently into the backgrounds of owner-managers. Whilst the results reveal some interesting overall trends, there are significant differences common to owner-managers in different industry sectors.

5.1 Age

There seems to be two 'age-windows' for self-employment and owner-management. The first is in the 30 to 45 age group and the second after normal retirement at 65[14]. It seems that owner-managers need the experience, stable background and capital assets (especially home ownership) that is more likely to come with middle-age.

The post retirement peak is caused by twin influences: the self-employed needing to work on past retirement because of pension insufficiencies; and the employed who wish to work but who are compulsorily retired from their jobs.

Types of enterprise will influence age ranges however. Recent research into the profiles of small enterprises in different service sectors found that 'younger' sectors such as computer services and video hire attracted relatively younger owner-managers, whereas established business types such as plant and equipment hire, free houses, wine bars and restaurants were owned by relatively older managers[15].

5.2 Gender

Women are under-represented in small business ownership. Although they represent over 40% of the employed workforce, they account for only one-third of the self-employed, and under 25% of small business owners who employ others[14]. Recently women have been entering self-employment at about twice the rate of men, but mostly without employees so the ratio of male to female owner-managers who employ others has not changed significantly. Women are much more likely to go into service sector enterprises than manufacturing being strongly represented in such businesses as employment, secretarial and training agencies.

5.3 Marital status

Marriage, it would seem, is good for small business ownership as single people are less likely to be owner-managers or self-employed than those who are married. This reflects not only the more mature age range of small business owners, but also the possibilities of either husband-wife teams in business partnership, or one supporting the other whilst a new venture is formed.

5.4 Social and class backgrounds

The lower-middle-classes provide more small business owners than other social backgrounds. This is partly explained by attempts at upward mobility by manual and routine white collar employees, who may see self-employment as the means for advancement in society, especially if they lack formal educational qualifications.

It is also influenced by the fact that those born into families of small business owners tend to follow in their parents footsteps. This overall trend is however subject to considerable variation by types of business; longer established forms of small enterprise such as free houses, wine bars and restaurants are much more likely to be owned by the children of self-employed parents, than more recent types of small business such as advertising and computer services[15].

5.5 Education

There is a traditional view that small business management requires an aptitude for practical activities in which formal educational qualifications are less relevant. In this sense owner-management was seen as an alternative route for advancement for those who had more practical and less academic skills. The Bolton Report[16] quoted data which supported this view by suggesting that small business owner-managers were less well educated than the average in the population. Recent research has painted a much more complicated picture, as this 'qualification gap' seems to have significantly narrowed, with changing attitudes towards small business and the growth of knowledge-based small enterprises in the service sectors. Owner-managers involved in high-tech industries such as computer-services, or those in marketing and design sectors, are likely to be well qualified with 'A' level or equivalent qualifications, or degrees[15].

5.6 Ethnicity

There is a traditional view that some ethnic minorities turn to self-employment and entrepreneurial activities because of inequality of opportunity in the jobs market. Recent research [14] has generally confirmed this trend, but there are significant variations among non-white groups, with those originating from the Mediterranean or Indian sub-continent more likely to be in self-employment than those of Afro-Caribbean backgrounds.

6. Entrepreneurial influences

Investigations into the types, characteristics and backgrounds of entrepreneurs and owner-managers reveals a very mixed picture, dependent not only on the motives of the people involved but also the type of enterprise undertaken. Clearly, there is no simple or direct answer to the question: "What makes the difference between really successful entrepreneurs and 'run of the mill' owner-managers?"

6.1 The successful entrepreneur

Whilst no clear 'identikit' of a successful entrepreneur emerges, a list of characteristics which seem common to success can be attempted. Success seems to follow individuals who are motivated, prepared to take risks, creative, hard-working, adaptable, financially shrewd, enthusiastic, resourceful, organised, get on well with people.... the list can go on, and will be strongly influenced by personal objectives for the business. Assuming that there is a motive for continuous growth which eventually will take the enterprise out of the 'small' category, an entrepreneur would be most helped by these important characteristics:

❐ *Innovative:* Innovation is needed if a business is to develop that is different from the competition, and continues to seek advantages over other firms. This requires a constant search for tangible benefits for the customer, not just in terms of new products or services, but more efficient and effective ways of making them available in the market place.

Characteristics which help innovation include the creativity to spot new ideas, allied to a practical and adaptable mind which can convert them to productive use.

As new ideas are unlikely to be immediately successful, the entrepreneur needs the conviction to cope with failure, and the shrewdness to minimise its impact on the survival chances of the enterprises.

❐ *Commitment:* A common motive which pulls entrepreneurs into a small business is a desire for independence and control over their own destinies. To succeed this needs translating into a commitment to ride the inevitable ups and downs which this freedom brings. Such commitment brings the necessary motivation to cope with the inevitable risks and hard work that follows. It demonstrates itself in an enthusiasm to make the enterprise succeed, and a determination to organise the resources necessary for success. Innovation, the first of the key entrepreneurial influences, has been typified as "an unreasonable conviction based on inadequate evidence." This flavour of risk-taking determination flows from a whole-hearted commitment to an enterprise.

❏ *Team leadership:* Whilst some owner-managers seem lonely figures relying only on their own abilities, successful entrepreneurs know that long term growth relies on leading a team of people who influence the enterprise.

The lone owner-manager is unable to develop a business beyond a certain size, if it is reliant totally on his or her efforts. Effective delegation, and training of others are important prerequisites for sustained growth. The team does not stop at the internal members of an enterprise; other 'stakeholders' in the business, such as financial backers, banks, suppliers, key customers, the immediate family of both entrepreneur and employees all exert an influence which have to be managed and encouraged in positive directions. The entrepreneur requires leadership qualities to maintain this team, supporting the individuals within it, to ensure successful outcomes for the tasks in hand.

6.2 The realities of owner-management

In practice owner-managers are highly unlikely to exhibit all of these characteristics. Most do not constantly seek new opportunities through innovation. Their commitment is variable, as the large scale movement in and out of the small business and self-employment sectors show. Autocratic styles rather than team leadership are more common, with most small firms remaining very small (with under 5 employees). The 'heroic', high growth entrepreneur is a rare species, indicating that most owner-managers need help and support in order to survive.

The idea of 'networking', in which owner-managers give each other mutual support and gain further assistance from local institutions such as Chambers of Commerce and Training and Enterprise Councils, has recently been put forward as a way of dealing with these deficiencies. Whilst the number of support bodies available to owner-managers has increased substantially in recent years, the advantages of these networks have been minimised by another characteristic of small business owners – they are not joiners, preferring to keep themselves and their business problems to themselves.

7. References and further reading

7.1 References and further information

1. Say, J B, a French economist writing at the beginning of the nineteenth century.

2. Schumpeter, J *The Theory of Economic Development,* Harvard University Press, 1934.

3. Drucker, P, *Innovation and Entrepreneurship,* Heinemann, 1986.

4. See Storey, D, *Entrepreneurship and the New Firm,* Croom Helm, 1982.

5. Binks, M and Jennings, A, "New Firms as a Source of Industrial Regeneration", in Scott, M et al (eds), *Small Firms Growth and Development,* Gower 1986.

6. Smith, N, *The Entrepreneur and His Firm: The Relationship between Type of Man and Type of Company,* Michigan State University Press, 1967.

7. Gray, D, *The Entrepreneur's Complete Self-Assessment Guide,* Kogan Page, 1987.

8. McClelland, D, *The Achieving Society,* Van Nostrand, 1961.

9. Kets de Vries, M, *The Dark Side of Entrepreneurship,* Harvard Business Review, Nov–Dec 1985.

10. Brockhaus, R and Horwitz P, "The Psychology of the Entrepreneur", in Sexton, D and Smilor, R (eds), *The Art and Science of Entrepreneurship,* Ballinger, 1986.

11. See Mason, C and Lloyd, P, "New Manufacturing Firms in a prosperous UK sub-region: The case of South Hampshire", and Binks, M and Jennings, A, "New Firms as a Source of Industrial Regeneration", both in Scott, M et al (eds), *Small Firms Growth and Development,* Gower, 1986.

12. Watkins, D and Watkins, J "The Female Entrepreneur in Britain", in Scott, M et al (eds), *Small Firms Growth and Development,* Gower, 1986.

13. Storey, D, *Entrepreneurship and the New Firm,* Croom Helm, 1982.

14. Curran, J, and Burrows, R, *Enterprise in Britain: A National Profile of Small Business-Owners and the Self-Employed,* Small Business Research Trust, 1988.

15. Curran, J, Blackburn, R and Woods, A, *Profiles of the Small Enterprise in the Service Sector,* ESRC Centre for Research on Small Service Sector Enterprises, Kingston Business School, 1991.

16. Bolton Report, *Committee of Inquiry on Small Firms,* HMSO, Cmnd 4811, 1971.

7.2   Recommended further reading

Goss, D, *Small Business and Society,* Routledge 1991. Chapter 3, "Small Business and the Entrepreneur".

Stanworth, J and Gray, C, *Bolton 20 Years On: the Small Firm in the 1990s,* PCP, 1991. Chapter 7, "The Small Business Owner-Manager".

Gray, D, *The Entrepreneur's Complete Self-Assessment Guide,* Kogan Page, 1987. Part 1: "So You Want to Be an Entrepreneur".

Chell, E, "The Entrepreneurial Personality: A Review and Some Theoretical Developments", in Curran, J et al (eds), *The Survival of The Small Firm,* Vol. 1, Gower, 1986.

Unit 3: Small business and innovation

This Unit considers innovation in the small business context. It looks at the advantages and disadvantages of small and large firms in innovation, and gives two case studies of innovative entrepreneurs. The Unit goes on to examine some misinterpretations about innovation, and how innovative opportunities can be purposefully pursued.

1. Small firms as innovators

1.1 'Small is innovative'?

The small firm today is seen as playing an important role in industrial innovation and technological change. Small and medium sized companies are often regarded as being more innovative than large ones because of their flexibility and willingness to try new approaches[1].

The point is reinforced by well-publicised success stories of innovative entrepreneurs who were forced to start their own new business because their ideas were rejected by large established companies. Hewlett Packard turned down Steve Wozniak's invention of a small portable computer, so he took the idea to his friend Steven Jobs and together they began making Apple Computers in a garage.

This notion that small firms contribute relatively more to innovation than larger ones was not always in vogue. In the 1960s, the UK and other European governments encouraged larger companies to form, through merger and acquisition, in order to promote the research and development of new products and technologies. It was thought that only large industrial units could afford the high fixed cost of investment in research and development. The monopoly power and economies of scale of large organisations were thought to be necessary to provide the resources needed for the high costs of new technology.

In practice, there are advantages and disadvantages for the small and large business involved in innovative activity. Figure 3.1 summarises some of these, from the research of Rothwell[2] into the role of small firms in innovation. In summary small firms have advantages in management, internal communications and marketing, stemming from their flexible and opportunist behavioural patterns, especially influenced by entrepreneurial owner-managers. They have the disadvantages of lack of in-depth resources of qualified people and finance. Larger firms have greater material resources which gives them advantages in attracting the necessary staff and funding the growth and other activities to which successful innovation can lead.

Figure 3.1: Small vs large firms in innovation – advantages and disadvantages

FUNCTION	SMALL FIRMS		LARGE FIRMS	
	Advantage	*Disadvantage*	*Advantage*	*Disadvantage*
Management	Entrepreneurial managers seeking new opportunities and taking risks	Unable to cope with high growth and adapt to increased complexity	Professional managers controlling complex organisations	Managers become 'administrators' controlled by risk-averse accountants
Personnel		Lack of technical specialists which limits scale of R&D effort	Attract highly skilled specialists. Can support large R&D facility	
Finance		Difficulties in raising risk capital and inability to spread risk over portfolio of projects	Able to raise venture capital, spread risk and fund any resulting diversification	
Communications	Internal communication fast and efficient, able to adapt to solve problems	Difficult to link with outside sources of expertise	Able to plug into external sources of expertise, and can buy crucial technical information and services	Internal communications bureaucratic and slow to react
Marketing	Fast reaction time to changing market requirements	Lack resources to set up expensive distribution systems	Marketing of existing products with comprehensive distribution and servicing networks	Management remote from market place
Patents and legal requirements		Difficult to cope with patents and subsequent litigation. High unit cost of meeting complex regulations in some industries	Able to employ patent and legal specialists. Able to defend patents and spread costs of compliance with complex regulations	

Adapted from R Rothwell, *The Role of Small Firms in Technological Innovation*[2].

1.2   Industrial life cycles

In several respects, comparisons between large and small firms ignore the realities of specific industries and market sectors. In the early stages of an industry's life cycle, firms tend to be small and innovative. The technology of an emergent industry is often new and therefore requires participating companies to be innovative. New industries also tend to be fragmented as competitors, including new small businesses, jostle for position.

As industries mature, the companies involved tend to become bigger through organic growth as well as consolidation amongst competitors. Innovation in established industries usually requires higher costs in development and marketing, thus favouring larger companies.

The micro-electronics and computer industry has epitomised this process in the post war years, moving through several phases of growth and maturity which have alternatively favoured small and large firms. In the 1950s and 60s the industry was dominated by a few large main frame computer manufacturers, such as IBM, who had the resources to invest in research and development. Entrepreneurs, such as those at Apple played significant roles in establishing new branches of the industry in the 1970s and 1980s. Today the shake out in the personal computer market has swung the balance back to larger firms who are making the innovative running.

1.3 Innovation records

A record of innovations introduced by British companies, giving details of the size of firms involved[3], produced the results shown below in figure 3.2.

Figure 3.2: Innovation share (%) by size of firm in the UK

	No. of employees in firm				
PERIOD	1–199	200–499	500–999	1000–9999	10000+
1965–69	15.4	8.2	8.5	24.2	43.7
1970–74	17.5	9.0	6.3	20.7	46.5
1975–79	19.6	9.6	7.5	16.2	47.2
1980–83	26.8	12.1	4.3	14.9	41.9

Source: Science Policy Research Unit[3]

This shows that small firms with under 200 employees, and those with under 500 employees have significantly increased their share of innovations since 1975, at the expense of firms above 500 employees and particularly those with over 10000 employees. This implies that small firms have become relatively more efficient at innovating than their larger counterparts.

1.4 Small business units

Figure 3.3 shows the share of innovations by size of unit, i.e. subsidiary, division or business unit.

Figure 3.3: Innovation share (%) by size of unit in the UK

	No. of employees in firm				
PERIOD	1–199	200–499	500–999	1000–9999	10000+
1965–69	21.4	14.2	11.4	37.9	15.1
1970–74	24.5	14.0	12.2	34.0	15.3
1975–79	31.3	13.6	13.0	29.8	12.3
1980–83	32.1	17.7	10.1	29.3	10.9

Source: Science Policy Research Unit[3]

This shows an even more marked shift of share of innovations towards small and medium sized units, with units employing under 500 people accounting for almost half (49.8%) of innovations in the period 1980–83. This perhaps reflects the attempts by larger companies to benefit from the advantages of both large and small firms shown in figure 3.1: to keep the large firm benefits deriving from their resources, whilst gaining the benefits of flexibility and adaptability by organising their activities into smaller units.

2. Entrepreneurs as innovators

2.1 The creative hero

The entrepreneur has tended to take on an heroic mantle in our pursuit of economic prosperity (see Unit 2, 1.3 'The Heroic Entrepreneur'). This has been particularly emphasised in the role of the entrepreneur as innovator. The idea that small firms are hot beds of creativity compared to large firms which specialise in efficiency and policy but not innovation, has reinforced the myth of the entrepreneurial innovator versus the industrial drone[4].

The myth portrays the entrepreneur as the personification of creativity, coming up with significant new ideas that solve old problems. These entrepreneurial innovators are non-conformists who do not fit into conventional educational patterns or industrial organisations. Large companies constrain their creative talents, which need the freedom of the small firm to fully develop.

Two such innovators have captured the imagination of the British public in recent years.

2.2 Clive Sinclair

Clive Sinclair's career to date fits well into the archetype of misfit entrepreneurial innovator. He left school at seventeen, with only modest qualifications, starting work as a technical journalist writing handbooks for the electronics hobbyist.

In 1962 he started a company, Sinclair Radionics, which began in business by selling amplifier kits by mail order. It was Sinclair's innovation of cheap pocket calculators that first brought him industrial fame as his company became the UK market leader.

Diversifying quickly into digital watches, pocket televisions sets and digital metering equipment, Sinclair Radionics ran into financial difficulties and in 1979 Sinclair left.

His innovative genius soon found another outlet when in 1980 his new company, Sinclair Research, launched the ZX81, the inexpensive home computer that temporarily gave the UK world wide leadership in this market by selling over 1 million units in the first 18 months. Sinclair soon added the equally successful Spectrum and the more sophisticated QL to the range. Then the business suffered from a period of bad publicity over delivery delays, followed by a down turn in the home computer market in 1985. Sinclair's reaction was typical – another innovation, the C5 electric car. The marketing philosophy of the C5 was based on the same principles as his earlier innovations of turning technologically advanced but expensive products into something which could be afforded by mass markets. This time he misjudged the market and the C5 was a financial disaster, forcing Sinclair to sell off his computer assets to Amstrad.

His innovations have not stopped there. In 1987 his new business Cambridge Computer Company launched an early portable computer, the Z88. He is now in the process of launching a motorised bicycle, again priced to attract mass markets.

2.3   Anita Roddick

Anita Roddick's innovations have been in areas far removed from the high technology of electronics and computers. Indeed her basic concept is not to be 'original' at all.

The daughter of Italian immigrants living in coastal Sussex, Anita Roddick had a mixed career before the Body Shop, varying between teacher, traveller and restaurateur. When her husband went off on a long trip to South America, she decided she needed 'just a little shop' to provide her with a living in his absence.

She had long been irritated by the marketing of cosmetics which were sold on a message of hope in expensive packaging.

"One of the great challenges for entrepreneurs is to identify a simple need. People tend not to trust their gut instincts enough, especially about those things that irritate them", says Roddick in her autobiography[5]. The 'simple need' that she identified had two main aspects. Firstly she saw the need for cosmetics in cheap containers of different sizes with simple labels, which took away the hyped images of fantasy and expectation that characterised conventional perfumery and toiletries. Secondly she believed in products made from natural ingredients, rather than chemically produced cosmetics which often relied on animal testing. In this sense she was a forerunner of the green movement, sharing the perceived need of a growing percentage of the population for environmentally-sound, 'return-to-nature' style products. She called her shop 'The Body Shop' to reflect this simpler, honest approach to body care, even though it was named after panel-beating garages she had seen on her travels in the USA! The first shop opened in Brighton in 1976 and the second in Chichester six months later.

But fast growth came through use of another innovation, franchising. By using the commitment and cash of franchisees, the franchisor is able to devote their resources to expand the coverage of a business concept much faster than by internal organic growth. In 1984 the Body Shop was floated on the Unlisted Securities Market; in 1988 there were more than 200 stores in 33 countries, and franchises were opened in the USA. By 1991 The Body Shop had grown from one shop to more than six hundred outlets trading in 38 countries in less than 15 years.

2.4   Collective creativity

For every Sinclair and Roddick, there are thousands of unheralded owner-managers who have innovated in a small way in creating their small enterprise. Their innovation may have been to only adapt existing ideas and practices to a local market; their appetite and talent for innovation may have stopped with their original idea. These are much more common experiences than the individual success story. Whilst the histories of entrepreneurial innovators like Sinclair and Roddick may inspire others to follow in their creative footsteps, it is a myth to suppose that their example can become the rule rather than the exception. Many may try, very few will succeed, and most will remain as small businesses.

To help those that remain small and yet wish to innovate, it has been suggested that co-operation and collaboration among smaller enterprises can help overcome some of their resource disadvantages. The idea of 'networked' innovation has become increasingly popular, at least in concept. At the initiative of the European Commission, 'Business and Innovation Centres' have been set up to promote regional development. Targeted on innovative industrial activities, the aim is to promote individual projects by pooling ideas, technology and commercial experiences[6]. The Department of Trade and Industry in the UK. also encourage collaborative innovation through the Enterprise Initiative which has set up Regional Technology Centres to help firms find out about, and benefit from new technology and processes[7].

Whilst new innovative heroes will undoubtedly emerge, the way forward for the majority of small businesses who wish to innovate may lie in collective creativity rather than reliance on one individual talent.

3. What is "innovation"?

Innovation is widely recognised as a crucial factor in successful small business management and a key entrepreneurial activity. But innovation has been misinterpreted.

3.1   Misinterpretation 1: innovation = invention

Innovation is strongly linked to invention but, although they overlap, they are not the same. An invention is essentially a creative idea. Innovation takes that idea, and puts it to work. Innovative activity encourages the development of new ideas, but it also turns them into useful products or services[8].

The British have been prolific inventors, but often failed to take their new ideas successfully to the market place. Joseph Swan in England developed a light bulb at the same time as Edison in the USA. Edison thought through the system required to generate and distribute power to customers for the light bulb, and developed an industry. Swan produced a superior light bulb (Edison recognised this by buying up his patents), for which others developed a market.

The career of Clive Sinclair has highlighted the distinction between invention and innovation. His pocket calculators, digital watches and home computers were highly successful innovations. So far his electric car remains an invention still in search of practical application.

3.2   Misinterpretation 2: innovation = new products or services only

Innovation may result in new products or services, but it is not confined solely to their development. Certainly the most publicised innovations are often related to new product developments. Small companies have become international giants through successful product innovation. For example 3 M's 'Scotch Tape', Xerox's plain paper copiers and Letraset's rub down transfers turned fledgling companies into international corporations.

Innovation does not stop at products. It embraces new developments in other fields including:

❐ *New markets:* It is innovative to take existing products or services and sell them into new markets. These new markets may be differentiated by types of end user; for example 3M first launched 'Scotch Tape' in 1930 into the industrial packaging market. Their second and, in terms of company sales, more important innovation come later when cellotape was launched into the office and domestic markets — essentially the same product but complete with dispenser.

A new market may be differentiated only by geography. Small business often innovates in this way, spotting a geographic market overlooked by larger companies, or using an idea from another town or country before it is widely introduced. Instant print shops which expanded very quickly in the USA in the 1970s are an example of this. The success was spotted by several UK entrepreneurs who suitably modified the idea to local conditions, and established a strong market position which the belated launch of the American originators failed to dent.

☐ *New marketing methods:* The product or service can remain the same and the market does not change; the key innovation can come from the marketing of the product to the customer.

Like 3M's 'Scotch Tape', Xerox copiers required two innovations to become successful. When the first plain paper copier was patented, many companies turned down the opportunity to market it. The first machines were expensive – the equivalent of about £40,000 today – and conventional wisdom said that no-one would pay that kind of money for a gadget to help the office secretary when carbon paper cost practically nothing.

Xerox – then an obscure New York company called Halloid – thought differently. Although they helped develop the machine, their real innovation was in pricing. They sold not the machine, but what it produced, copies. Providing copiers on a rental basis for a few pennies per copy, made plain paper copying widely available at a price which looked like petty cash, not a major capital investment.

Distribution, another key marketing activity, has been fertile ground for innovative change for small businesses, as they have developed more convenient ways of making goods and services available to the customer. Successful innovations in this category include the home delivery of products from pizzas to flowers, or the lunch time sandwich van visiting business parks.

☐ *New methods of operating:* An enterprise can innovate in how it operates internally. It can change its systems or its way of doing business. Although these changes may be internal, their influence can be felt externally in the market place.

For example, technology is transforming how we pay for goods or services. Automated till facilities can not only directly debit a purchaser's bank account, but also provide the supplier with very detailed sales records and stock analyses. These innovations can give a business a distinct competitive edge through increased efficiency or customer knowledge.

The small business world has been increasingly affected by another operational innovation – franchising. A wide range of business concepts, from fast food restaurants to energy conservation systems, have been made available in a short time to a very wide audience through the franchising concept.

3.3 Misinterpretation 3: innovation = original

Innovation does not take place in a vacuum. New ideas always have roots in the old; they start with what already exists, and become 'original' from the unique way in which they combine or connect these existing ideas and knowledge.

The most prolific innovator of all, Nature, creates and recreates using different combinations of a very small number of elements; we have so far only discovered just over 90 separate elements in the Universe, and living matter (which includes us) is made from only 16 of them! Although we are all 'unique', we are made from different arrangements of these small numbers of elements.

Creative thinking, starts by trying to make connections between concepts that already exist, but that are too far apart for others to see. It has been said that the secret of entrepreneurial success is to use OPB (Other People's Brains). This is not to encourage imitation which does not create anything new. It is accepting that innovators pick up other people's ideas, whether old or new, and piece them together to form a unique pattern, which is only 'original' in that no-one else has put them to use in this way before.

Dai Davies, the creator of Letraset, saw the need for faster lettering for graphic artists in order to save them time in creating advertising captions and headlines. He took an existing idea, water-based transfers which had previously been used for children's products, and adapted them for use by the professional graphic artist. Anita Roddick, on her travels, watched the women in Tahiti rub their bodies with cocoa butter, and wash their hair in mud in Morocco. These, and other natural treatments were to form the basis of the product range of the Body Shop.

3.4 Misinterpretation 4: innovation = one-off inspiration

Innovation does not rely on one sudden flash of inspiration to give the blueprint for a new development. Innovation is a gradual process which builds into something new and worthwhile over a period of time, through a variety of stages. We have already mentioned 3M's 'Scotch Tape', and Xerox's plain paper copiers, which became world wide products, not through one innovation, but several. Similarly, Letraset's development was a process, not one immediate success. The initial water transfers were messy and time consuming to use. The company did not see real success until a 'second' product had emerged – a dry transfer lettering system which could be easily and speedily rubbed down onto the page.

Unfortunately many small enterprises stop at the first innovation. A good marketable idea leads to a new business start up, which meets with early success. The founding entrepreneur can perhaps be forgiven for believing that the initial innovation was all that was required. Besides, the 'innovator' has now become a 'manager'; having conceived the original idea, the founder now has a business to manage. Management likes order, not chaos, certainties rather than novelties. Unfortunately creativity thrives on disorder, which throws up more chances for novel combinations between hitherto unconnected parts. The danger for the small business is that the opportunity for continuous innovation becomes stifled by organised management. Policies and rules are drawn up to help keep the business on the rails in the early days but which restrict the creative thinking necessary to feed the innovative growth of the future.

4. The seven sources for innovative opportunity

How can the owner-manager ensure a continuous, systematic search for innovation? The would-be innovator can look at changes in what already exists to give clues to what opportunities may exist in future.

Innovation uses and builds on changes that are already taking place. The Wright Brother's aeroplane exploited the earlier invention of the internal combustion engine by linking it to advances in the understanding of aerodynamics. The development of out-of-town superstores capitalised on changes caused by the widespread ownership of the motor car: the advantage of increased personal mobility, linked to the disadvantage of congestion in town centres.

The successful entrepreneur investigates and analyses change in order to find opportunities for innovation. Drucker[9] has identified seven sources for innovative opportunity.

Drucker's seven sources: 1. The unexpected

2. The incongruous

3. Process need

4. Industry and market structures

5. Demographics

6. Changes in perception

7. New knowledge

4.1   The unexpected

A very common indicator of underlying change is the unexpected result – either success or failure. Unexpected success, or failure, often gives clues to underlying trends which can lead to innovation.

❑ *Unexpected success*

Early computers were designed exclusively for scientific purposes. IBM demonstrated one of the first machines, which it also targeted at the scientific market. To their surprise, their established business customers showed keen interest in using this highly complex equipment for very ordinary tasks such as bookkeeping and payroll. Whilst other computer manufacturers regarded this mundane application with some disdain, IBM took this unexpected success very seriously. They developed equipment and software specifically for business customers, who in the end proved to be the most significant market for computers. By innovating in response to this unexpected interest, IBM were able to establish themselves as market leaders, a position they retain to this day.

❑ *Unexpected failure*

A restauranteur was initially irritated when increasing numbers of customers ordered only a jacket potato, a side dish with no main course, from his extensive menu. On investigation he found however that the unexpected demand for jacket potatoes could be turned to his advantage by innovating a whole range of toppings to make it a profitable, stand alone meal which became a significant part of his lunch time menu.

A local school was unexpectedly suffering from a decline in pupil numbers, despite its convenient location in a well populated, affluent neighbourhood, and its excellent academic record. The new head teacher investigated this unforeseen failure by talking to local parents. She found that they preferred other schools, often in the private sector, whose academic standing was no better, but which offered many more after-school activities and interests. By creating new, stimulating school clubs and societies, some even run by parents, the headteacher was soon able to report a waiting list for entry to her school.

Both the restauranteur and the headteacher based their innovations on changes to their market place, which were already under-way. The move towards a simple, healthier, meat-free diet, expressed itself in unusual selections from the restaurant's menu. The demand for all round social and physical development from a child's education, not just academic results, unexpectedly affected pupil enrolments. In both cases the entrepreneur used the discovery of change through the unexpected as an opportunity for innovation.

4.2   The incongruous

An incongruous event or result is a discrepancy between what is and what everyone expects; it occurs when there is a difference between reality, and everyone's assumption about that reality. It is also an important source of innovation because incongruity is a further sign that changes are taking place. Unlike the unexpected it is, however, more difficult to quantify; it is not likely to show up in a report of sales figures. Rather, it represents shifts in perception or attitudes.

Often the incongruity exists in the perception of customer values and requirements.

❑   A self-employed investment consultant used an incongruous response from the small business sector to uncover a misunderstanding in his perception of customer needs. He decided to concentrate his efforts on selling investment packages to the small businessman – the successful entrepreneur who had generated some surplus cash from their labours, and needed an investment home for it. He expected these entrepreneurs, who had already taken considerable risks to earn money from their own business, to be prepared to take further risks to increase their surplus cash still further – only this time without all the effort of running their own business. Their response in no way matched his expectations; the risk takers did not buy his investment packages, which they viewed as too risky! This incongruous reaction gave the consultant an opportunity to innovate. By talking to these self-made entrepreneurs, he found that most of them had set up on their own, not just to make money, but more importantly to achieve independence. Once they had taken the risk to achieve that independence, they were not prepared to take a further risk, through investments, which might jeopardise it. They became, in fact, extremely cautious and conservative demanding security for their money above all else. The investment consultant 'innovated' by offering them a risk-free package with moderate returns, which they found much more acceptable. Thus he created an opportunity from the incongruity of entrepreneurial risk takers who turned down higher risk investments.

4.3   Process need

The importance of need as a source of innovation is captured in the proverb: 'Necessity is the mother of invention'.

Drucker highlights one particular need, the 'process need', as a major area of opportunity, because it is a very specific and easily identified need. Innovation from 'process need' improves an existing process which is recognised as having significant limitations; it takes new, often unrelated, developments to revolutionise an existing process or way of doing something.

❑   For years, there were two basic types of glass; sheet glass which was cheap but optically imperfect, and plate glass which was ground and hand polished to optical perfection and therefore expensive. There was a recognised need for cheaper, high quality distortion free glass. But it was not until Alastair Pilkington developed 'float glass', allegedly inspired by a floating plate in his washing up bowl, that the process need was met. Molten glass is floated on a bath of molten tin which keeps it flat and regular as it cools, eliminating the need for later labour-intensive polishing.

☐ Dai Davies's invention, Letraset, likewise recognised a process need. Davies was a graphic artist, used to working to tight deadlines designing high quality presentations and artwork, usually for the advertising industry. He recognised that the process of carefully hand lettering each presentation or headline was time consuming and repetitive. So he used developments in transfer technology to transform the design process by making available easily applied lettering in a wide variety of typefaces and sizes.

In each case, it was the understanding of the need to improve a process which lead to the innovation. The new knowledge required to develop the process was obviously important, but the first, crucial step was the recognition of the need in the first place. Once the 'need' is felt, a programme of focused research can be instigated to develop the required innovation. Provided that the technology is available and the objective clearly defined and specified, such research can usually find the answer.

4.4 Industry and market structures

Whole industry and market structures can change rapidly, sometimes after a long period of stability. Such changes offer exceptional opportunities to innovators, and considerable threat to those who incorrectly read the changes.

☐ The structure of the printing industry has been through such a change. After a long period of stability, the basic technologies of printing changed. The pre-print activities of producing artwork and printing plates, which until the 1970s relied on photo-mechanical methods, were increasingly replaced by computer-aided technology. At the same time traditional printing methods using 'hot-metal' and letterpress have been updated by more flexible offset lithography. Long training in the mysteries of the printer's art are no longer necessary. One effect in the market place has been the emergence of 'instant-print' shops. The lower set-up costs and skills needed to start a printing business using the new technologies allowed a new type of printer to emerge. Instant print shops were an innovation in that they were located nearer the customer and offered more flexible, faster response times.

Changing industry and market structures often give the small business entrepreneur opportunities to benefit from the sluggishness of larger, existing suppliers who often view structural change as threats to be resisted, rather than a chance to innovate.

4.5 Demographics

Changes to the environment of an enterprise inevitably contain many possibilities for innovation, but are often hard to see, or understand, until they are past and the opportunity missed. Demographic changes, however, are clear and unambiguous, and signalled well in advance. Demography is the study of statistics of the population – births, deaths, diseases, employment, education, income – and the trends which these figures show. These statistic are universally accepted as key indicators of demand changes within society which are often highly predictable. A high birth rate in one year will inevitably mean an increased need for First School places four to five years later. Lower death rates, and longer life expectancy will be sure to create more demand for retirement homes and old age care facilities. These new requirements create many opportunities for innovation which can be seen well in advance; yet often these key numbers are overlooked in the search for entrepreneurial ideas.

❏ The 'swinging 60s' gave rise to a host of innovations, many in the fashion, leisure and entertainments industry. Whilst this may have seemed like a sudden revolution in attitudes and patterns of demand it should have come as no real surprise to the student of demographics, who could have pointed to the post war baby boom, which in turn meant a dramatically increased percentage of teenagers in the population by the 1960s. Their pre-dominance in that decade ensured that activities would reflect youthful values and demands. Similarly in the 1990s, we know that the age profile of the population will become older, with an increase in the percentage of people 70 years old and over, and a decrease in number of young people. The alert innovator will be developing enterprises with these trends firmly in mind.

4.6   Changes in perception

Some changes are not really changes at all. The facts do not change, but people's perception of the facts change, which has an equally powerful effect.

The fashion industry relies heavily on changes in perception. Clothes from an earlier generation do not change, but our perceptions of them does. We regard the trendy garments of yesterday as comically out of date today.

Changes in perception give the entrepreneur many new openings.

❏ Ten years ago, vegetarian restaurants and health food shops were viewed as strictly for a minority fringe element of the population. The food has not changed dramatically, but now every restaurant has to have at least one vegetarian dish, as our perception of what we ought to eat has shifted.

❏ Today we perceive an urgent need to protect our environment, a notion that had little following a decade or so ago. Anita Roddick sensed this shift in values well before it became common policy to have green products, in creating the Body Shop.

The skilful innovator will be careful to differentiate between temporary changes in perception, or 'fads', and longer lasting developments. The entertainments industry, for example, throws up a continuous stream of new 'heroes', from masked cowboys to mutant turtles. Focusing an enterprise entirely on any one of these novelties would be a very short term strategy, as young peoples' fidelity to any one heroic concept is extremely fickle. However there is a well established long term need for 'heroes' on which the innovators in Hollywood have built up a world wide industry.

4.7   New knowledge

The most famous innovations are often based on new knowledge, or 'inventions'. The first telephone made by Alexander Graham Bell, the light bulb demonstrated by Thomas Edison, the radio messages of Guglielmo Marconi and the early television transmissions of John Logie Baird are all well known.

But despite the publicity, knowledge based innovations are the most problematic and, in many respects, the least attractive to entrepreneurs.

The time between new knowledge being available, and its successful development into marketable products is long. The idea of using radio waves to transmit visual information was around in the early days of radio in the 1890s, but only became practical as the first television transmission in 1926.

197

Innovations based on new knowledge also require not just one independent discovery, but the bringing together of several developments. Baird's first television, itself based on earlier research on radio waves, scanned an image into lines of dots of light by a mechanical method. More sophisticated, electronic systems were required before television could become an acceptable product, a decade or so after the first transmission.

5. References and further reading

5.1. References and further information

1. See for example, Davis, W, "The Innovators" in Henry, J and Walker, D (eds), *Managing Innovation,* Sage Publications, 1991.

2. Rothwell, R, "The Role of Small Firms in Technological Innovation" in Curran, J et al (eds), *The Survival of the Small Firm,* Vol. 2., Gower, 1986.

3. Robson, M and Townsend, J, *Trends and Characteristics of Significant Innovations and their Innovators in the UK. since 1945,* Science Policy Research Unit, 1984. The data reproduced here is taken from a summary produced in reference 2 above.

4. See Reich, R, *Entrepreneurship Reconsidered: The Team as Hero,* Harvard Business Review (May–June), 1987.

5. Roddick, A, *Body and Soul,* Ebury Press, 1991.

6. The first Business and Innovation Centres were set up in 1985. They publish a newsletter, *Network,* obtainable from 'European Business and Innovation Centres Network' (EBN), Avenue de Tervueren 188A, B-1150 Brussels, Belgium.

7. See *Introducing the Enterprise Initiative,* DTI, 1991 – an introductory brochure to all the Enterprise Initiative services.

8. See Adair, J, *The Challenge of Innovation,* Talbot Adair Press, 1990.

9. Drucker, P, *Innovation and Entrepreneurship,* Heinemann, 1986.

5.2 Recommended further reading

Henry, J and Walker, D (eds), *Managing Innovation,* Sage Publications, 1991, Chapter 6, "Entrepreneurship Reconsidered: The Team As Hero" (Reich, R), and Chapter 14 "The Innovators" (Davis, W).

Drucker, P, *Innovation and Entrepreneurship,* Heinemann, 1986, Section 1 "The Practice of Innovation".

Goss, D, *Small Business and Society,* Routledge, 1991, Chapter 6, "Small Business, New Technology and Innovation".

Adair, J, *The Challenge of Innovation,* Talbot Adair Press, 1990, Chapter 8 "Team Creativity".

Roddick, A, *Body and Soul,* Ebury Press 1991.

Unit 4: The customer

This Unit looks at the small business from the perspective of that all important – yet often elusive entity – the customer. It examines different approaches to the market place by small firms, emphasising the need for careful identification of customer groups, and the benefits they seek from a small enterprise.

1. Focus on the market

1.1 Missing the market

One of the most common reasons given for the failure of a small enterprise is that it did not identify its market or, more particularly, its customers. At first this may seem a strange failing. After all it is only common sense to realise that a business, even a non-profit making one, cannot survive for very long without customers in the market place.

Entrepreneurs originated because of the need to shift resources from where they were under-used, or surplus, to areas where there was demand because of relative shortages. This was done through the 'market place', where those with a surplus – something to sell – could meet with those who had a shortage – a need to buy.

Business and commerce has its roots in this concept of the market place.

The ancient bazaars of the Middle East, the medieval merchants of the Mediterranean and the shopkeepers of Victorian England, all based their trade on understanding what customers in the market place wanted, finding it for them, and making it available in an acceptable way at the right price. They were small businesses by today's standards, whose size made regular contact with customers inevitable, helping them identify with the markets they served.

If the natural instinct of the small business owner and the traditions of commerce over the centuries are based on the market place, and the needs of customers within it, why did modern business 'unlearn' this fundamental lesson and need retraining in 'customer-orientation'? Some of the reasons are:

❏ Business has got bigger. As an enterprise grows it needs more levels of management. This tends to make key decision makers, even in relatively small companies, more remote from the market place and the customer.

❏ Modern business has become a very complicated mixture of forces and influences. A small business manager has to consider not just the demands of customers but the requirements of many other forces, including the government, employees, suppliers, banks, other financial partners, existing competitors, and potentially new competition. The owner-manager doesn't have time to fully consider all these influences, and sometimes it is the customer who is forgotten.

❏ The complex nature of modern business requires systems and policies to help manage and control the confusion. Order reduces the chaos of conflicting demands and makes the accomplishment of necessary tasks more likely. Unfortunately order tends to create inflexibility; 'ways of doing things,' once established, are difficult to change. The market place however is constantly changing: customer's preferences change; competitive products and services come and go; technology creates new opportunities; the law imposes new constraints. The small enterprise with limited resources can be tempted to over-organise its activities so that it fails to understand and respond to these changes.

❏ Technology and other advances in human knowledge and skills have made many more new products or services possible. It is increasingly tempting to launch a new business based on an idea just because it becomes possible, rather than because there is an identifiable, sustained demand from the market place. Even larger organisations can fall into this trap; the development of Concorde may have been a great technological advance, but it has been a very limited business success.

1.2 Approaches to the market

There are two extremes in how enterprises approach the market place – the product based approach or the market based approach. Figure 4.1 illustrates these two approaches. The product based approach implies that the enterprise is more concerned with the basic product, or the internal demands of production, than with the needs of the customer. It can lead to inflexible, even arrogant attitudes towards the ultimate buyer of the product or service ("I wish all the people who want to shop at lunch time, would realise we have to eat as well," a store manager).

The market based approach on the other hand seeks to find out what the customer wants and is willing to pay for. It implies that the enterprise is focused around the needs of the customer, rather than its own internal requirements[1].

Figure 4.1: Product-based and market-based approaches to the market

PRODUCT-BASED		*Approaches to the market*	MARKET-BASED	
Stage 1	Product *idea* by firm or individual		**Stage 1**	Market *analysis* by firm or individual
Stage 2	Product *developed*		**Stage 2**	Market *identified* and needs estimated
Stage 3	Product *sold*		**Stage 3**	Product *criteria* established
Stage 4	Product *adapted* according to sales levels		**Stage 4**	Product *developed* and tested with target market
			Stage 5	Product *marketed* to customer

In practice, a small business is unlikely to start from the extreme market-based approach, however desirable that may be, for a variety of reasons, including:

1. Owner-managers starting a business usually have a specific skill or knowledge which they wish to exploit.

2. The business is already established and wishes to add to its existing product range without diversification.

3. The business has established products which it wishes to sell to new customers.

A successful approach to the market is a combination of understanding the resources available and matching them to an idea for a new product or service, which fills a gap in the market place. This is illustrated in figure 4.2.

Figure 4.2: Market focus in practice

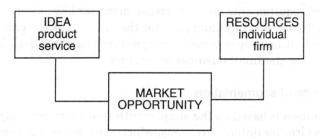

This summaries the matching process that takes place when an idea, based on customer demand or needs, is linked to the existing or future resources of an enterprise. This acknowledges not just the importance of the customer, but also the enterprise's strengths and weaknesses in relation to the market opportunity.

2. Who is the customer?

2.1 Market segments and niches

It is possible for a small business to regard customers as the focal point of its strategies and activities yet still fail.

Failure can come from an inability to define precisely who is the target customer. It is always tempting to believe that products or services can have a universal appeal, or that it is safer to offer them to as wide a market as possible.

However, there is overwhelming evidence that successful companies, large as well as small, carefully target markets. These companies will identify sub divisions of markets – referred to as 'segments' – and specialised subdivisions of segments – referred to as 'niches'.

Data on hundreds of companies world wide has been analysed for many years by the Strategic Planning Institute of Cambridge, Massachusetts, USA, in a project called PIMS (Profit Impact of Market Strategy). This study shows that firms achieve long term profitability by selling high value-added products or services to viable market niches, and establishing a leadership position within them. In other words, it is better to have a high share of a relatively small market than a small share of a relatively large market. This is particularly valid for small enterprises whose limited resources make the precisely targeted approach to the customer even more preferable.

2.2 Customer or consumer?

Finding out in precise terms exactly who a small business's customers are, or could be, may not be straightforward.

There is often a distinction between customer and consumer or end-user. A small business may be serving the final user of a product or service directly; for example, the customer of a book shop will often be the reader of the book they purchase – the consumer. In some cases however, the customer will purchase a book for someone else – as a present or for their children perhaps. The small business could be a publisher of books whose customers are book wholesalers and large retail chains, thus removing them still further from the ultimate consumer.

Whose needs and requirements does the owner-manager have to understand and seek to fulfil – the customer who buys and pays for the product, or the consumer or end-user whose opinion will ultimately determine the product's success? Both influences are clearly important for the small business to consider.

2.3 The purpose of segmentation

Market segmentation is based on the simple truth that customers buy similar types of products and services for different reasons, which give rise to different expectations of what they are buying. People buy books, for example, for many reasons: for pleasure, for study, for reference, for presents, even for show. Each end use will require differing qualities and specifications from the books purchased, not just in the content of the book, but also its size, appearance, durability, price and so on.

The principle of segmentation categorises customers and consumers into groups with similar needs and expectations from their purchases. The more precise the definition of the customer group, the more precise can be the definition of their needs and requirements.

The whole purpose of market segmentation is to allow a small business to use its resources where they count most. Segmentation allows the small enterprise to look for the most promising openings for its special talents and advantages, a niche where its strengths will be of most value and its weaknesses of little account.

The process is to discover natural groupings amongst both customers and consumers, which match the special abilities of a small firm.

2.4   The segmentation process for a small firm

Definition of the target segments for a small business can be achieved in stages as illustrated in figure 4.3.

Figure 4.3: Segmentation process for a small business

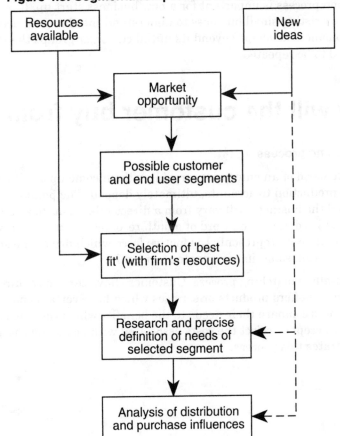

A balancing of the resources available to a small enterprise with new ideas for possible innovations establishes a general definition of a 'market opportunity'. This is refined into possible customer and consumer segments. A selection is then made of the segment which best fits with the resources available to the firm[2].

For example a small business, having focused on the market opportunity of publishing books covering business subjects, decides to further specialise in students in higher and further education as the most promising way of using its special talents and strengths.

This is one of the most crucial decisions that a small business makes, influencing how it operates and where and what it sells.

Further research into the selected segment makes possible a more precise definition of the purchasing habits and requirements of the target market. This research includes considering the distribution chain and analysing other possible major influences on the purchase decision. At these stages new ideas may again be considered. The choice of the student segment by our publishing business actually determines who will be the customer, as the firm will need to sell through the established distribution channels of wholesalers and retailers specialising in student sales. Setting up a new access system to the target market would be a much harder route. The decision also reveals other influences in the purchase decision which will need careful consideration; in this case, lecturers of business studies play an important role in determining student purchases through recommended reading lists.

The segmentation process is important for a new business start up. It is equally important for an existing small business to understand the changing needs of its target market. If the business develops beyond its initial customer groups the segmentation process will need to be repeated.

3. Why will the customer buy from me?

3.1 The matching process

Sales are the life blood of an enterprise, providing the income upon which all other functions, from production to accounts, ultimately depend. The point of contact between the customer and the business will vary from a direct sales visit, to a retail shop in the high street, to mail order, or even word of mouth recommendations. But whatever form it takes, the sales activity represents the motive force which drives the small business on, or causes it to stall, sometimes never to start again.

Selling is essentially a matching process. Customers have certain requirements or needs. An enterprise offers products or services which have certain characteristics or features. Customers compare their needs to the benefits which these features offer them, and either accept or reject the costs associated with acquiring those benefits. Figure 4.4 illustrates this process.

Figure 4.4: The sales process in a small business

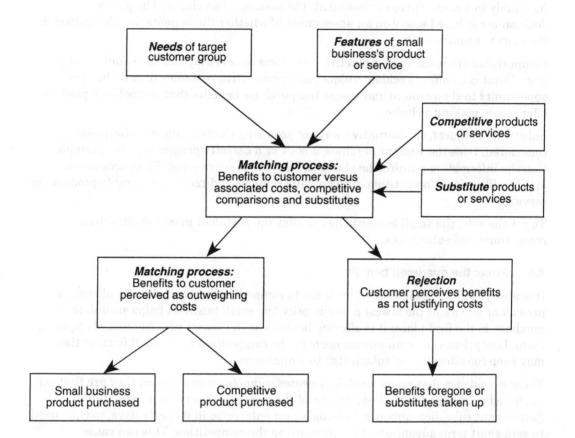

3.2 Features and benefits

In the matching process, the customers' decision hinges on the *benefits* offered by a product or service, not its *features*.

A *feature* is a characteristic of a product or service. For example, a student's text book has a soft, laminated cover; this is a feature of the product.

A *benefit* is the *value* of a product feature to a customer. For example, the benefits of a soft laminated cover are that it is hard wearing, and therefore lasts well, whilst being light and easy to carry.

These are benefits which are relevant to students; they might be inappropriate to other customer groups, and therefore not really benefits. For example a book that was targeted at the 'coffee table' market, for display purposes, would probably require benefits of high quality finish and attractiveness rather than lightness and durability.

A successful small business meets the needs of the targeted customer group by ensuring the features of its products or services translate into benefits appropriate to the customer.

3.3   Competition and substitutes

Inevitably in a competitive environment, the customer has choice. The purchase decision is not based solely on an assessment of whether the benefits on offer outweigh the costs to acquire them.

Comparisons are made with competitive products or services, and the benefits they offer. What is on offer is seldom unique, so a prospective customer usually has the opportunity to shop around and assess the purchase benefits that competitive products offer before making a choice.

Substitute products, or alternative ways of acquiring the benefits, are often also considered. Does the student purchase a book or a cassette programme, for example? Can the information required be obtained from other sources e.g. TV programmes, articles, libraries? Competition does not only come from directly comparable products or services.

To get the sale, the small business has to offer the customer more benefits than competitors and substitutes.

3.4   Price: the overused benefit

It is always tempting for a small business to compete mainly on price. By offering a product or service at the lowest possible price the small business helps stimulate a purchase in the first place; it is offering benefits at the lowest possible cost of acquiring them. Low prices can be an advantage over the competition for a small firm, or they may keep consideration of substitutes to a minimum.

There is evidence that many small businesses compete on price when they are first set up, based primarily on the cheap labour of the owner. There is even concern that government subsidies, aimed at helping a new enterprise in its early days, may be used to gain short term advantages by undercutting the competition. This can cause problems, sometimes terminal ones, for established businesses and the new business cannot sustain its price advantage once the subsidies are removed[3].

Unless a business has established economies of scale not available to its competitors it is unlikely to gain long term competitive advantage through pricing policies alone. As economies of scale are not usually available to a small business (because of their size) low prices are most likely to come from short term cost savings: for example the owner does not expect a market wage, particularly in the start-up phase of the business, or little investment is made in product development or marketing. As other businesses are likely to react by lowering their prices, the small firm may find that the only result of price competition is to reduce the profitability of the total business segment. Under-pricing has certainly been a major factor in small business failures.

The 'cost' to a customer does not only consist of the price paid for a product or service. Other, more hidden, cost factors such as time, convenience or reliability, may be more important to the buyer.

3.5   The competitive edge

If a small firm is unlikely to gain long term advantages over the competition through low prices, it still has to find a competitive edge if it is to survive and grow.

A competitive edge is the means by which the small firm differentiates itself from the competition. It comes ultimately from the careful selection of a target market in which the small enterprise can offer something better than anyone else. It answers the question: *'Why will this particular group of customers buy from me rather than anyone else?'*.

The competitive edge of a small firm can be described in terms of benefits, with two main characteristics:

i)   they are benefits significant to the target market segment;

ii) in total, they amount to a greater package of benefits than those offered by competitors.

To return to our example of the book publisher, this firm considered the needs of its target customers – students of business studies in higher and further education – and produced the following list of desirable benefits for books offered:

- easy to understand, readable contents;
- easy to follow (and memorise) layout;
- affordable prices;
- light and hard wearing;
- available when required;
- up to date information;
- texts aligned to courses taught.

When investigating how well existing suppliers met these needs, the small firm discovered two problem areas: many books covered broad subject areas, not necessarily in line with the content of specific courses; students complained that recommended texts were frequently out of stock at the beginning of term.

From this the small firm developed its competitive edge. By working closely with lecturing staff it developed texts which followed courses of study, not just subject areas. By specialising in business studies it was able to concentrate on specific outlets and, by giving them a fast delivery service, to ensure adequate stocks of recommended texts at the beginning of courses.

The firm's books became the market leaders as text books in the limited areas covered. They gained a large share of a small market by understanding the target market better than any of their competitors, and offering products and services that were different in ways that were of significant benefit to the customer.

4. References and further reading

4.1 References and further information

1. For a full discussion of these concepts, see one of the many texts on marketing. Good introductory books include:

   Morden, A, *Elements of Marketing,* DPP, 1991; and

   Kotler, P and Armstrong, G, *Marketing, an Introduction,* Prentice Hall, 1990.

2. For a more detailed description of segmentation see Waterworth, D, *Marketing for the Small Business,* MacMillan, 1987, especially Chapter 4 "Selection of a Customer Mix".

3. These arguments are pursued in Unit 6, The Small Business Environment and Unit 14, 'Marketing', 5.1 'Pricing–the Weak Link?'.

4.2 Recommended further reading

Barrow, C and Barrow, P, *The Business Plan Workbook,* Kogan Page, 1990. Pages 61–83 'Customers' and 'Competition'

Unit 5: Market research

This Unit considers what information owner-managers need about their market place. The methods of research appropriate to small business resources are examined.

Contents

1. The role of market research

There are two key factors in the survival and success of a small firm which relate to research into the market place:

❏ Is there sufficient demand for the products or services of a new enterprise so that it can establish itself as a viable business? Before start-up, the prospective owner-manager can attempt to reduce the unknown risk of a new venture to the level of acceptable risk by researching the market place. During business planning, such research should establish the prospects of the perceived opportunity in practice.

❏ Can an established small business adapt to the ever-changing environment to take advantage of any opportunities that may arise and withstand any threats to its existence?

Successful owner-managers have a good understanding of the environment in which their enterprise operates. They know their customers well; they keep an eye on competitive activity; they are aware of underlying trends which may effect their business. Researchers have suggested that the key factor in business survival is how quickly new owner-managers can understand their environment, and then learn from their experience of dealing with it[1]. Such research has also shown that future growth is critically affected by how well the owner-manager stays in touch with external influences; successful development begins with an awareness of the total situation surrounding an enterprise, and the modification of initial objectives to suit this ever changing environment.

There are many problems with this need for an understanding of the environment, including:

❏ owner-managers tend to concentrate on immediate day to day problems, overlooking the wider, often long term issues.

❏ small firms often operate with a relatively small customer base. Information can be over-dependent on feedback from a small number of customers, leading to a blindness about the real environment.

❏ owner-managers seem suspicious of formalised market research. Accessible market information is not necessarily relevant to the position of a small firm. There is a reluctance to commission more relevant research because of its costs. Owner-managers tend to rely on informal information gathering methods of highly variable reliability. Even successful entrepreneurs use informal networks to keep up to date, using extensive contacts to develop a rich 'mental map' of their environment[2].

2. Information requirements

Even an informal information gathering process has to start by asking the right questions. So what does a small enterprise need to know about its market place?

2.1   Market information

Market information is essentially about existing customers and competitors. It seeks to give a small business answers to questions including the following:

1. What are the *characteristics* of existing customers and potential new customers?

    a) *Who* makes the buying decision?

    b) *What* are the differences between customer groups? e.g. between those who buy a lot and those who buy a little.

    c) *When* are purchases made? e.g. on a regular or cyclical basis.

2. What is the *size* of the target market?

    a) the number of customers?

    b) volume of purchases?

    c) value of purchases?

    d) what are estimates for the above in one years time, and subsequently?

3. Who is the direct *competition?*

    a) how many competitors?

    b) how big?

    c) how successful?

4. What are the *substitutes* for the product or service? What choices does the buyer have to in terms of:

    a) indirect alternatives?

    b) substitutes for discretionary expenditure?

2.2   Marketing information

Marketing information is about those factors which can change the existing position of customers and competitors. It seeks to find out what will influence customers in their decision making through such questions as:

1. What benefits is the customer seeking to acquire from the product or service offered?

2. How will the buying decision be made? (Who will have an influence on the decision and how will this be exerted?)

3. Where does the customer buy existing products or services? What distribution channels are used?

4. What price parameters are there?

5. How does the customer find out about the product or service?

    a) word of mouth?

    b) advertising and other promotional activities?

6. How well do competitors meet the requirements of the target customers group? What are their strengths and weaknesses in relation to customer preferences?

7. How do competitors use marketing activities in relation to the target market?

    a) what is their pricing policy?

    b) how do they promote?

    c) how do they distribute?

    d) what is their product strategy?

Such information is just as important to the developing enterprise as it is to the new business start up. Time and cost factors will restrict the volume and accuracy of answers available to these questions, but the successful owner-manager will continually be looking for answers through formal and informal methods.

3. The research process

Entrepreneurs tend to regard market and marketing research as long winded and expensive, but there are many inexpensive, and uncomplicated ways a small business can research the market place.

An example of a research process which can be undertaken by a small firm is shown in figure 5.1. The stages of this process are:

1. Describe the target customer segment (see Unit 4, 2 'Who is the Customer?'). Any description of the customer group under investigation needs to be as precise as possible, to avoid wasting resources in gathering unnecessary data.

2. Define research objectives: what will the information be used for once it has been obtained? What questions, if answered, will meet the aims of the research?

3. Check existing knowledge and data: there is always a wealth of existing data available especially in an ongoing business. Some of this may not always be obvious even to the owner-manager. Customer records, sales people, sales assistants, invoice records, sales ledgers, financial statistics – these are all very important potential sources of information about the market place.

4. Define new information required. What new information will be required if the questions arising from the research objectives are to be answered?

5. Decide methods to be used to gather data. The following sections of this Unit discuss what methods are available.

6. Collect data   }   New and existing data is usually raw information
                        }   which needs collating and turning into intelligent

7. Analyse existing   }   information, i.e. data which has been interpreted
    and new data   }   and summarised.

8. Evaluate and review strategy in the light of information gained through research: this is the stage at which decisions relating to the objectives of the research can be made. It may involve a rethink about the customer segment under investigation. Does the information support the targeting of the selected segment and, if so, how can this be best pursued? Should the firm's resources be concentrated on a different segment, in which case which one, and what research now needs to undertaken?

Figure 5.1: A market research process for a small enterprise

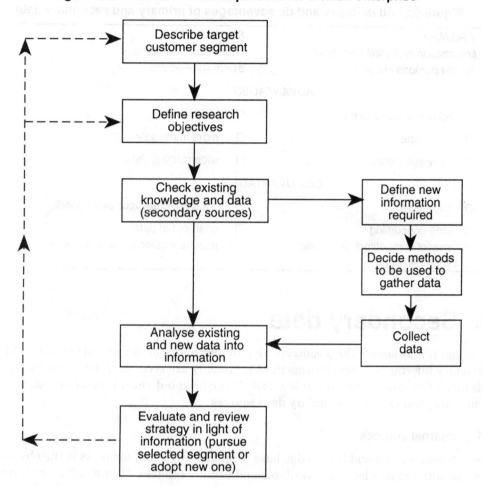

4. Research methods

The questions which are posed by the research objectives will determine which methods can be used for collecting the data. Data is divided into two basic categories:

❏ *Primary:* new data specifically collected for the project, usually through field research;

❏ *Secondary:* data that already exists which can be collected by desk research.

The comparative advantages and disadvantages of each type are summarised in figure 5.2 below:

Figure 5.2: Advantages and disadvantages of primary and secondary data

PRIMARY Information collected specifically for the purpose in hand	SECONDARY Information that already exists somewhere
ADVANTAGES	
❏ reflects specific need	❏ lower cost
❏ up to date	❏ more immediate
❏ individual control	❏ wide ranging data
DISADVANTAGES	
❏ expensive	❏ does not meet your exact needs
❏ time-consuming	❏ often out of date
❏ risk of competitors finding out your intentions	❏ may be incomplete or inaccurate

5. Secondary data

Although it may sound like a contradiction in terms, research invariably starts with secondary information. Small firms most commonly use secondary data sources because it is immediate and either free or low cost. It can be sub-divided further into internal, competitor, and external secondary data sources.

5.1   Internal sources

The internal records and knowledge base of an existing small business is the obvious place to start, as it is low cost, available and usually reliable. Most small firms have at least basic records of customers, sales and costs; they may also keep records of prospective customers e.g. from sales visit reports. Non-written information may also exist, for example from the knowledge of staff who deal with customers.

5.2   Competitor sources

Most businesses publish information about themselves, usually intended for customers, but also obtainable by other small firms. Accessible published information includes product information leaflets, reports and accounts. Trade shows and exhibitions can be good sources of competitive information; the catalogue will provide a good summary of the existing companies in the field and literature can be collected easily from one place.

5.3   External secondary sources

Government statistics and those published by other official bodies can have the disadvantage of being out of date, and not in line with exact needs. There are some general guides to information available (see listing in sub-section 7. 'External Secondary Data Sources for Small Business Research' at the end of this Unit); these are a good place to start for anyone unfamiliar with the range of data available.

There are many other sources of data available, some free of charge in a library. Where information has to be purchased it is still relatively low cost as the data collection is amortised over many subscribers. Trade associations, banks, universities, polytechnics, colleges of further and higher education and research institutions are good sources of information for specific fields. Newspapers and periodicals tend to provide more general data but can be useful for background information. (For some general sources of secondary data, see sub-section 7. 'External Secondary Data Sources for Small Business Research', later in this Unit.)

6. Primary data

Most small firms shy away from collecting primary research data, but although it is invariably time consuming to collect and collate it need not be expensive; in some instances it can cost nothing except time. Primary research approaches are described below.

6.1   Observation

Some opportunities lend themselves to research by observing what is happening in the market place. For example, a small business owner could observe the quantity and type of shoppers using locations at which he or she was interested in opening a retail unit. Competitive information can be gained from observation; the size, staffing and activity levels of stands at exhibitions and trade shows are useful indicators of competitive strengths and weaknesses. Other tactics are less open–such as following around a competitor's delivery van to find out where their customers are!

Where possible, observations should be quantified to ensure objectivity and comparability. For example, pedestrians can be counted at different times, in different locations, to build up a comparative audit of shopping traffic, which could give vital clues to potential demand in given areas.

6.2   Surveys and questionnaires

Common impressions of market research involve answering a questionnaire posed by someone with a clipboard carrying out a survey. Surveys are indeed a common form of research, but they can take many forms.

A market survey asks questions of a number of respondents selected to correspond to the target market under investigation. Its main instrument is the questionnaire, which is probably the most widely known and used market research tool.

Questionnaires can be used to measure:

❑ Buying patterns and trends (Have you purchased XYZ in last 12 months/ 6 months/ 1 month?);

❑ Attitudes to products and services (How would you rate the performance of XYZ on a scale of 1 to 5?);

❑ Expectations related to products and services (When you purchase XYZ, which of the following benefits is most/least important?);

❑ Competitor's activities (which of the following products have you purchased in last 12 months?)

❑ Media exposure and influence (which of the following journals do you read regularly?)

Small firms have tended to overlook many of the opportunities of gathering information by surveys; they have been regarded as the province of bigger companies with more resources to collect large statistically valid samples. There are three principle contact methods for surveys using questionnaires, which are listed below with examples of how they can be used inexpensively by small businesses:

❑ *Personal*

The best form of research is often on existing customers or visitors to business premises. For example finding out about customer dissatisfaction is a major problem for restaurant owners; most unhappy customers say nothing at the time – they just don't come back and complain to their friends, thereby amplifying the damage without giving the restaurant owner an opportunity to put the damage right. A simple questionnaire, allowing customers to remain 'incognito' can help overcome the problem. Surveys of existing customer perceptions of a small firm can be particularly revealing and inexpensive if conducted at the point of sale.

❑ *Telephone*

Surveys by telephone can be quick and usually give high response rates. Small firms can survey their competitor's prices by phoning round for quotes on a standard item or piece of work for example.

❑ *Mail*

Questionnaires by post can be useful to reach a wider audience and remove many problems of bias through the interviewer. A small inducement may be necessary to provoke the quantity of response desired. However surveys by mail should not be confused with any form of selling, which, although tempting to mitigate the costs, will inevitably bias the results. For example, a training consultant mailed a brief questionnaire to companies in his area to find out more about their perceived training needs and intentions. Although he offered a discount voucher for forthcoming workshops as an incentive to respond to the questionnaire, he resisted the temptation to confuse his research objectives with a specific sales message about his training programmes.

Which method to choose?

These three contact methods have advantages and disadvantages, summarised in figure 5.3, which will determine which application they are best suited to. For example, if a speedy response with tight control of who is surveyed is a priority, then telephone is probably the best method. A small firm might use this route, for instance, to find out more about competitive activity to which an immediate reaction is necessary (for example, price cutting). If the need for confidentiality and impartiality is paramount, then a mail survey is usually the preferred route. This is likely to be the case when personal details, of health or income for example, are required; this might therefore be the preferred method for surveys by small firms offering financial services, or computer dating.

If the survey requires a flexible approach, allowing respondents the opportunity to comment in a qualitative, open-ended manner, then the personal interview will be necessary. This could be the case, for example, where a small publishing company wished to test various concepts for educational books by interviewing lecturers and teachers of the subjects concerned.

**Figure 5.3: Primary research by questionnaire –
Summary of the comparative advantages of three methods**

Criterion	Contact Methods		
	Mail	Telephone	Personal
Quantity of data	Poor	Good	Excellent
Interviewer effect†	Good	Fair	Excellent
Control of sample	Excellent	Fair	Poor
Speed	Poor	Excellent	Good
Response Rate	Poor	Good	Good
Costs	Fair	Fair	Poor

† This refers to the possibility of interviewers biasing results because of their pre-conceived ideas.

6.3 The structure of a questionnaire

The construction of the questionnaire in terms of wording and layout will largely determine how useful it is as a guide for decision making. Although a trained researcher should be used where possible, there is nothing to stop the small business manager drafting a valid questionnaire without expert help, provided it is kept simple and basic rules are observed.

The most common approach to an overall structure is through 'funnelling'. This involves asking the most general questions first and then gradually restricting the focus through more specific questions, leaving the most direct questions until last. This 'funnel technique' is used to reduce elements of bias which could come from asking specific questions up front.

The first consideration in designing a questionnaire is to define what information is required. The questions asked will flow from this and will be of two basic types:

❐ *Closed questions* are those which can attract only a limited response such as Yes/No or a rating on a scale (Do you own your own house? or, How do you rate our service – excellent, good fair, below average or poor?) Closed questions can be used when quantitative analysis is required from the surveys and result in a very structured approach.

❐ *Open questions* are those which invite a freer response, such as an opinion or individual information (What do you think of......? Which sports do you play?) They are particularly useful in researching attitudes and buying motivations.

Questionnaires often use a mix of these styles of questions. A typical questionnaire might start with structured questions to qualify the respondent (e.g. Do you live within five miles of this town, 5 to 10 miles, more than 10 miles?) and finish with unstructured questions inviting comments on a key aspect of the research objectives (Why do you shop in this area?).

Bias in questions

The wording of a questionnaire needs careful examination to avoid biasing the response. This can result, for example, from social pressure on respondents to answer in a certain way because of implied expectations. The question, "Do you dislike smoke from other people's tables when you are eating?", encourages a positive response, which may over-emphasise genuine objections to other people smoking in a restaurant, for example. One word can radically change the impact of a question. Consider the following two questions for inclusion in a survey of the parents of a first school:

a) "Do you think all after school activities should be free of charge?"

b) "Do you think all after school activities could be free of charge?"

The change of the word 'should' for 'could' switches the whole emphasis of the question: 'should be free of charge' will prompt the answer 'yes'; 'could be free of charge' may lead to more realistic replies.

6.4 Omnibus surveys

If the market to be researched is large, or there is a need for continuous information, a small enterprise can consider omnibus research. This is a service offered by research agencies who regularly conduct surveys in a specific industry or market sector. The results are then sold to subscribing companies, which spreads the costs of the research over a wider client base. Subscribers can also add their own specific requirements to the survey, which is a good way of obtaining cost effective data providing the information needed is straightforward and can be obtained from a small number of questions.

Omnibus surveys are either based on national samples of adult purchasers, or specialist populations, for example regional markets or house owners. They are particularly useful if continuous research is needed. If regular feedback from a large customer base is important, this can be obtained from surveys which are regularly repeated.

6.5 Group discussions

Group discussions are a good example of qualitative research available to the small business. A group of people, conforming to the parameters of the target market, are invited to an informal discussion, led by a facilitator to guide the conversation around desired topics. The session is normally taped, and may also be observed. The aim is to give insights into perception and motivation of potential customer groups. One of the prime uses, for example, is in testing concepts for new products or services. The results are not statistical, but more unstructured and subtle, probing for reactions to various propositions. A small business can consider using them as they are not prohibitively expensive, the principle costs being that of the facilitator, an interpretative report on proceedings if required, and the recruitment of the group (they are normally not paid, but offered suitable refreshments). A useful insight into customer perceptions can usually be gained from each group, at a cost in hundreds, rather than thousands of pounds. For example, a small firm specialising in marketing free publications to doctors financed by pharmaceutical advertising, conducted discussion groups of general practitioners to test the concept of a new magazine. They obtained useful feed back not only on the acceptability of the idea, but its proposed content, layout, design and name as well.

6.6 Experimentation

Experiments, or tests, are sometimes conducted in the small business field to obtain 'live' feedback from the market place. A small retail chain of two or three shops might vary their marketing activities in one outlet; for instance, prices may be changed in one shop only and sales patterns compared to the other shops in an effort to gauge the effectiveness of the price change.

7. External secondary data sources for small business research

Secondary sources of information used will very much depend on the types of information required. However, some useful places to start are listed below. The general guides can be used to find out what data exists. *The New Small Business Guide* is a particularly good starting point for sources of information.

Most of the sources listed below are available from specialist libraries if your local library is unable to help. A list of specialist business libraries (there are over 300) is published in the ASLIB Economic and Business Information Group Membership Directory. This is available from one of the most comprehensive business libraries, the London Business School Library, Sussex Place, Regents Park, London NW1 4SA, Tel 071 262 5050.

7.1 General guides

Information

The New Small Business Guide: Sources of Information for New and Small Businesses, by Colin Barrow (BBC Publications 1989, 3rd Edition) is an invaluable reference book. Section 5 "Finding out about your Market", lists the principle sources of information available and where to find them.

Organisations

Central Statistical Office (CSO), Great George Street. London SW1

The Business Statistics Office (BSO), Cardiff Road, Newport, Gwent.

Government publications

Guide to Official Statistics (HMSO)

Regional Statistics (HMSO)

Government Statistics: A Brief Guide to Sources (CSO)

7.2 Sources of official information

Monthly Digest of Statistics – monthly information on population, housing, manufacturing etc.

Annual Abstract of Statistics – as above but annual summary

Abstract of Regional Statistics – economic and social statistics for UK regions

Economic Trends – monthly economic review

Social Trends – annual key social statistics

National Income and Expenditure Blue Book (yearly)

Census of Distribution – information on retail sector

Business Monitors – government business statistics collected from over 20,000 UK firms.

British Business – published weekly by the DTI with statistics on UK markets, commercial and industrial trends, and other business information

7.3 Non-official sources

Mintel Market Intelligence reports – monthly information mainly on consumer markets

Retail Intelligence – specific studies of market sectors published by Mintel

The Economist Intelligence Unit – part of The Economist Group, which publishes regular reports on specific industrial sectors

Financial Business Information Service – detailed information on many business sectors. Provider of electronic information via PRESTEL the Post Office viewdata system

Jordans Industrial and Financial Surveys – comparative performance indicators in market sectors.

7.4 Year books and directories

Kelly's Business Directory (Kelly's Directories) – listing of all manufacturers and distributors, by trade classification.

Dun and Bradstreet's directories e.g. *Key British Enterprises, Who owns Whom*

The Retail Directory (Newman) – lists stores and other distributive outlets

Kompass, (in association with CBI) – information on products and services, plus companies (with financial data)

7.5 On-line services

Pergamon Infoline – databases including sales prospecting

Kompass On-line – company name, address, telephone number, description of business, number of employees, and named executives

7.6 Professional institutions

British Institute of Management (BIM),
Africa House, 64–78 Kingsway, London WC2B 6BL

Confederation of British Industry (CBI)
21 Tothill Street, London SW1

Association for Information Management (ASLIB)
26–27 Boswell Street, London WC1N 3JZ

8. References and further reading

8.1 References and further information

1. See for example Watkins, D, "Management Development and the Owner-Manager", in Webb et al (eds.), *Small Business Research: The Development of Entrepreneurs,* Gower, 1982. This follows the line of earlier research in identifying adaptability of the business to the changing requirements of the economy as important, whilst noting a general lack of outward-looking information gathering by owner-managers, who tended to be inward looking and focused on day to day problems.

2. See Milne, T and Thompson, M "The Infant Business Development Process", in Scott et al (eds.), *Small Firms Growth and Development,* Gower, 1986. Their research concluded that owner-managers are "impatient with formality including formal market research. But the successful ones are doing the research in an extremely powerful and efficient personal contact manner".

8.2 Recommended further reading

Barrow, C, *The New Small Business Guide,* BBC Books, 1989, especially Section 5, 'Finding Out About Your Market'.

Barrow, C and Barrow, P, *The Business Plan Workbook,* Kogan Page, 1988, especially pages 83–109, "A Plan for Market Research".

Chisnall, P, *The Essence of Marketing Research,* Prentice Hall, 1991. (A good general introduction to research including some examples of questionnaires and case histories.)

Unit 6: The small business environment

This Unit considers the peculiarities of the small business environment, and concludes that differences in sector are as important as size influences. The role of government policy since Bolton is analysed and assessed.

Contents

1. The hostile environment

1.1   Victims of circumstances?

Small business owners are often described as being at the mercy of a hostile environment which threatens them from many directions. 'Unfair' competition from larger firms, the burden of government regulations, penal bank charges, high interest

222

rates and the recession all contribute to make life in the small business a constant struggle. Is this really so? Does smallness, and therefore lack of resources, mean that small firms will always be the most vulnerable members of the business community. Certainly the declining numbers of small firms up to the 1970s was attributed to external influences, just as their revival has been put down to changes in the social, economic and political environment. A major concern of the Bolton Committee was to protect the small business sector, which it saw as unable to fully sustain itself without government help.

But small firms are not always victims of circumstances beyond their control. Even in recessionary times there are some small businesses doing better than others.

1.2   Market sector conditions

Although general external influences in society and the economy are important, it is the specific market conditions faced by a small firm that determine basic healthiness.

Small enterprises operate in virtually every market or industry, so they face a wide variety of environments, some more favourable to the small business form than others.

In some industry sectors small firms are more commonplace than others. This is not by chance. Smallness is the most appropriate size of trading unit in certain markets, where the environment, far from being hostile, favours small firms. In others areas larger firms have distinct advantages and the small business has to find a niche in order to survive.

Sectors in which small firms are numerous include:

❑ Construction

❑ Retail distribution

❑ Hotels and catering

❑ Transport and communications

❑ Finance and insurance

❑ Business services

❑ Other services

As we have already noted, 90% of small firms operate in the services sector, where the environment seems generally more favourable.

These sectorial differences in the small business environment confirm the problems in over-generalised notions of small enterprises. Even within the services sector some environments are friendlier than others. 28% of total retail businesses are single outlets, i.e. small firms. But single outlet retailers account for 62% of newspapers and periodicals sold, indicating perhaps that the unsociable hours involved in this type of business do not suit the larger multiples.

The key aspect of a small firms environment, then, is the industry, or market, in which it operates. Forces outside of the specific industry, such as government policy, and general economic conditions are of course important, but only in a relative sense. As outside forces usually affect all firms within an industry, the issue becomes their differing abilities to deal with them.

2. Structural analysis

The underlying economic structure of an industry or market place determines how favourably it is disposed towards large, medium or small-sized units.

Porter's well-known model[1] of the forces which drive industry competition can be used to assess the structural features which influence an industry's suitability to the small business form.

Figure 6.1: The five forces model of industry competition

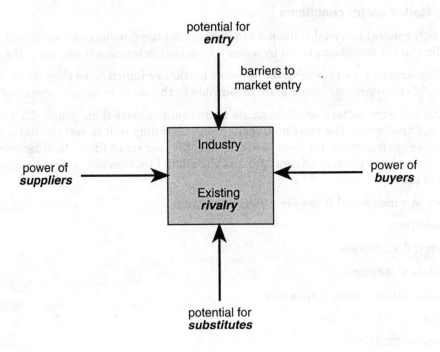

These five forces of Entry, Rivalry, Substitutes, Buyers and Suppliers jointly govern the intensity of competition, and profit potential for a small and large firm in a given industry or market sector.

2.1 Barriers to entry

The initial attractiveness of a specific market to a small business will be determined by the barriers to entry. These represent a variety of issues encountered by anyone wishing to start business in a given market place. As illustrated in figure 6.2, these include:

Figure 6.2: Barriers to market entry for a small firm

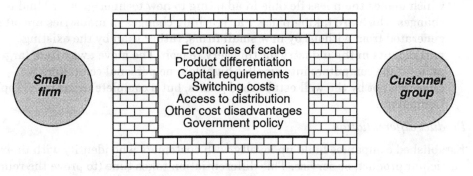

☐ *Economies of scale*

Where significant cost reductions result from high levels of output in an industry, then small firms find it difficult to compete. It was believed that the increasing existence of such economies in mass markets would lead to the inevitable decline of smaller firms. Certainly a large firm enjoying economies of scale can use this cost advantage in a number of ways. By establishing low market prices, large companies can force competitors to operate on low margins which make it an unattractive market to new entrants. If prices are kept up, then the additional profits enjoyed by the large supplier can be reinvested in marketing, or research and development of new products, again reducing the competitiveness of small firms. It is for such reasons that the economies of scale created by automation in car manufacturing have effectively blocked entry to smaller companies.

However, although an industry may be subject to economies of scale, particular operations or processes within it may not. Many small firms exist as suppliers to car manufacturers who find it more efficient to subcontract some specialised areas, such as design and development. For example, a small firm recently won an award for its innovative design of a supercharger, licensed to the large car manufacturers[2a].

In relying on economies of scale, the larger company can have problems which can be successfully exploited by the smaller firm:

☐ To achieve scale economies, the larger firm may have to sacrifice differentiation of products or services. It may not go as far as Henry Ford's famous restriction on the colour range of the Model T, but it may encourage a standardisation of products or services leaving niche markets open to less uniform treatment.

For example, the cosmetic and toiletries industry is dominated by some very large organisations, such as Unilever, Proctor and Gamble, Avon and Revlon, who achieve significant economies in production, distribution and marketing.

A small firm[2b] has successfully entered this market by offering soaps shaped and decorated in the image of favourite children's characters (such as Minnie Mouse and Winnie the Pooh). Such specialised products do not easily lend themselves to large scale production, partly because of their individual shapes and colours, but also because of their life span. The average life of these character-based concepts is short, so the need for a constant flow of new up-to-date designs is more important than the efficiency of production in this particular market segment.

❑ Scale economies may be achieved by a larger firm using an existing technology, which makes them less flexible in adapting to new technologies, or blind to the changes which are taking place. Far reaching changes in industries are often generated from without by new small firms, rather than by the existing participants in the industry for this very reason. The move away from large, main frame computers into smaller high volume personal computers was triggered not by the well established giants, but a complete newcomer, Apple Computers.

❑ *Product differentiation*

Established companies build up loyalty with customers who identify with their particular product, or service. This differentiation takes time (to prove the reliability of a product or service) and money (for advertising, packaging, signage, branding), and therefore represents a significant barrier for any new entrant to overcome.

Direct competition with nationally branded products, supported by the resources of large companies, is not feasible for smaller firms. Nevertheless there are always segments less affected by large scale loyalty, as we have already seen in the example of the small toiletries firm. The Body Shop successfully overcame the brand loyalty of the cosmetic giants by rejecting the basic ideas of "beauty products" on which that loyalty was based. Their cheap plastic containers and simple descriptions appealed by their contrast to the lifestyle image approach of established brands, and provided the perfect market entry for a small firm with no resources to compete head on.

Small firms also build up their own loyalties which differentiate them sufficiently to deter new competitors. Allegiances to an existing small business are sometimes sufficiently great, and the local market sufficiently small, to make market entry impossible except by purchasing the business. Well liked publicans in small communities effectively differentiate their public houses by their own character, thereby blocking new entrants through personal loyalties.

In fact the brewing industry is a good example of large, and small scale product differentiation. At a national and regional level the large brewers have created differentiated, branded products which, coupled with economies of scale in production and distribution, have established high barriers. At the local level public houses and other outlets are differentiated by location, management and environment, which often works to the benefit of an owner-manager.

❑ *Capital requirements*

A very tangible barrier into some markets is the large set-up cost involved. Industry classifications with a low representation of small firms are usually those requiring substantial start-up investment, often those involved in production and manufacturing. This barrier can be reduced by the availability of second-hand plant and equipment. Bankruptcy and trading difficulties increase the availability of second-hand machinery, often sold cheaply through auction, which is a further factor in the higher level of small business starts during times of recession[3].

❑ *Switching costs*

When buyers switch from one company's product to another, they may incur one-off switching costs. These may be in the retraining of staff; for example the most significant costs in changing computer software may be in the retraining needed for the users. Other switching costs could be incurred by a manufacturer changing supplier of raw materials which involves product redesign, or increased stock obsolescence. Where significant costs exist, the potential new supplier has to offer more than just marginal benefits to persuade a buyer to change.

Some firms deliberately exploit switching costs as a marketing ploy to attract and retain existing customers. Suppliers of coffee offer commercial customers the free loan of coffee making equipment, for example, immediately establishing a barrier to any competitors.

For small firms, switching costs often represent a real, but hidden, barrier. A concept which has been researched only hypothetically may not pass the ultimate test of being purchased in place of a competitive product, because of the emotional switching costs of severing a relationship with an existing supplier. Sales training emphasises the need to build strong personal relationships with existing customers so these emotional switching costs will be increased, and the temptation to buy elsewhere decreased.

❏ *Access to distribution channels*

Another market barrier, sometimes overlooked in the concept stage of a small business, is the need to have access to established channels of distribution. For example anyone wishing to publish a consumer magazine will have to persuade retailers to give their new publication shelf space – not an easy task as space is limited and fiercely fought over by many publications.

A small business marketing a new food product will similarly face an uphill struggle to win space on the shelves of the major retailers.

❏ *Other cost disadvantages*

Some cost advantages enjoyed by established companies are independent of scale. Perhaps the two most significant of these for smaller firms are:

  ❏ *'Learning curve'.* Improvements come with experience, and this can be translated into cost economies. Manufacturers will often benefit from higher machine productivity for example, as they gain production experience. A restaurant owner will learn how to reduce the food waste in serving a particular menu only with time and practice. The new business can expect higher unit costs in its early days than its more established competitors.

  ❏ *Location.* In many markets, location of premises is a crucial marketing factor. Existing firms often have good locations which will be expensive for the new entrant to equal. For example leasehold retail premises in good locations can command a 'premium' when they change hands; that is the incoming tenant pays the outgoing one for the privilege of taking over the lease. Established companies may have paid no such premium because they were an original tenant, or the location had not been popular when they moved in.

❏ *Government policy*

Certain industries are controlled by national or local government regulations, which create total or partial barriers to entry. Some postal delivery services have only recently been opened up to new business entrants, whilst other areas still remain prohibited. The licensing laws present barriers to entrants who wish to open a restaurant, run a public house, or operate an off-licence.

227

Other regulations increase the capital costs of market entry. Conforming to Health and Safety regulations often requires expenditure in adapting premises; for example, in the provision of toilets and fire escapes. Hygiene regulations lay down strict requirements on the preparation of food for public consumption, which increases the start-up and ongoing costs for several types of small business, from exclusive restaurants to sandwich bars.

Owners of small businesses often complain that conforming to government regulations gives larger firms an unfair economy of scale; the costs of conforming to the paperwork of tax returns, for example, is a relatively fixed cost, which the larger firm can amortise over higher sales turnover than the small firm. Since the Bolton Report, the UK government has become increasingly aware of these problems, and a number of measures have been taken to try and level the 'playing field' (see sub-section 6 'Government Policy', later in this Unit).

2.2   Power of buyers

Buyers, or customers, 'compete' with a small firm by trying to get the best possible deal for themselves; they will try to negotiate discounts, additional services, higher quality, more after sales support and other benefits which are added costs for the supplier.

Buyers differ in the power they can bring to bear on a small firm, which will in turn condition the attractiveness of doing business with the buyer group of a particular industry.

❑   Some buyers have little choice. The costs of switching to another supplier are too great; for example, the existing supplier has locked them in by providing 'free on loan' equipment to use their product; or the supplier is the only stockist in town, and it is not convenient to travel elsewhere.

❑   Other buyers are not inclined to negotiate. The purchase is of such little significance in their cost structure that they are not sensitive to price. Graphic Art suppliers, for example, are able to charge high prices because the materials they sell to a designer represents a small fraction of the price charged to the client by the designer.

❑   Some buyers are all powerful. They can effectively dictate terms to a small firm which becomes dependent on them. This happens when buying is concentrated in the hands of a small number of large customers, who purchase high volumes from a large number of small suppliers. Superstore retailers have achieved this position. A small firm wishing to supply Sainsburys or Tesco will have little choice over most marketing variables, such as product quality, packaging, delivery times and methods, and even prices.

The buyer groups, or potential customers, to which a small firm can sell, do not usually exercise equal power. Choice of buyer groups is therefore a key decision, which will influence the business environment of the firm. For instance, a garment manufacturer may have a choice of selling large quantities with little marketing control to multiples such as Marks and Spencer, or lower volumes but setting their own strategies through a variety of smaller fragmented outlets.

2.3   Power of suppliers

Suppliers to a small firm also influence its environment in their pricing and other marketing policies. As the small firm is now in the position of buyer, its powers in relation to the supplier will be influenced by the factors considered already. Small firms tend to buy in a fragmented way so their power relative to large suppliers tends to be low. Franchising has attempted to overcome this by grouping a large number of outlets into one buying source. A franchisee can therefore expect higher discounts than an independent outlet of similar size.

Other small firms attempt to enhance their power over suppliers by coming together as formal or informal groups. For example, an office equipment company which distributed its products through a series of owner-managed agents throughout the country was able to dictate its own terms when the network was first set up. When the agents had successfully developed their territories they used their improved negotiating position to jointly strike a better deal with the supplier.

2.4 Rivalry

Rivalry between established firms is evidenced by traditional forms of competition: selling and promotional campaigns, discount offers, new product launches, extending distribution channels and so on. Small firms may do this in spirits of rivalry which range from the very friendly to the fiercely competitive.

The intensity of rivalry is affected by the *exit barriers* in the industry. These are the factors that keep a firm from quitting altogether, even though returns are inadequate or negative. Exit barriers for small firms can be economic – the costs of liquidation or sale and loss of income – or psychological – attachment to the enterprise, loyalty to employees and pride that comes from ownership. Where these barriers are high, then a firm will continue for as long as possible before exiting, thus increasing the intensity of rivalry in the market place.

2.5 Threat of substitute products or services

Substitution of a firm's products or services can come in two ways:

❑ a substitute which performs the same function, but in a different way. A taxi service is competing not only with other taxi firms, but also bus companies, for instance;

❑ a substitute way of spending money.

The competition for disposable income comes from widely differing products and services. For example, a restaurant is competing not only with other restaurants and take-aways, but a whole range of other leisure opportunities from the theatre to the pub.

Industries where there are fewer real substitutes tend to be more stable than those that can be easily substituted by other products or services, or those that rely on disposable income. In recessionary times, for example, taxis in areas where cheaper public transport is readily available will be affected more quickly than those that serve a more captive market such as tourists.

3. Large versus small

3.1 Dependent or independent small firms?

There has been considerable debate over the viability of the small business sector in relation to large companies. Opinions have polarised between those believing that small firms represent a dependent secondary sector, always subject to the greater power of the core sector of big business, and those seeing the emergence of a healthy independent small firms sector as a symbol of a new culture of enterprise. (See Unit 1, 'Small Business and the National Economy', 3.1 'Three Theories', for a fuller exposition of these views.)

In fact the viability of small firms will depend largely on the structural factors we have examined using Porter's model. In some industries, large firms will have advantages as buyers, suppliers, or rivals to small firms. In other sectors, however, larger organisations will have little natural advantage, and the common form of business unit will be small.

3.2   Fragmented industries

Industries are fragmented into a large number of smaller firms for a variety of reasons:

☐ *Low entry barriers:* Most industries with a large population of small firms have low entry barriers. These include many of the service sectors where small enterprises predominate, such as training, recruitment and secretarial agencies, household services, and the construction industry. Low barriers on their own do not always create fragmentation however, as there are usually other forces in favour of the small firm.

☐ *Diseconomies of scale:* Where customer preferences necessitate constantly changing products and styles, smaller, more flexible firms can be more efficient than larger, bureaucratic companies. Women's clothes, and other industries where fashion is a major ingredient, would be typical here.

☐ *High creative content:* Architects, interior design firms, and specialist product development companies tend to be small as it is often more difficult to produce conditions of high creativity in large organisations.

☐ *Personal service:* Where an individualised, personal service is required, for example in consultancy, or picture framing, then small operations tend to be able to offer more responsive, tailor-made services than large firms.

☐ *Close local control:* Restaurants, wine bars and night clubs are good examples where the close local supervision of an owner-manager often works better than the absentee management of a large company.

☐ *Newness:* A new or emerging industry can be fragmented because no companies have been able to take a significant market share. Technological innovations, or shifting consumer needs which create these newly formed industries are sometimes exploited first by newly formed small businesses. There are currently many small businesses operating in 'environmental' markets such as solar heating and water filtering.

3.3   Franchising and fragmentation

In some markets, franchising is being used to overcome some of the forces towards fragmentation. For example, where economies of scale potentially exist in production or purchasing, an industry may still remain fragmented because the market place demands personal service or local sources of supply. The brewing industry overcame this problem with an early form of franchising, retaining centralised production but using tenants with some autonomy to manage the local outlet.

'Format franchising' has enabled parts of the retail industry to centralise production or buying, whilst retaining the benefits of local service and location. Fast food chains such as McDonalds and Kentucky Fried Chicken are able to market themselves as providing a convenient, neighbourly service whilst offering the low prices and uniform standards of a larger organisation.

4. Government policy

Central and local government exert a general influence on the environment of small enterprises. Since the Bolton Report, both Labour and Conservative governments have followed policies aimed at supporting the small business sector.

4.1 The need for support

The rationale for actively discriminating in favour of the small firm stems from a number of beliefs about the role of the small firm:

❑ *Creation of jobs:* most European countries encourage small firms, and particularly new firms, as a way of reducing unemployment.

❑ *Source of innovation:* although small firms have proved to be an abundant source of inventive ideas, they can lack the resources to put them into practise without external assistance.

❑ *Competition to larger firms:* as part of an anti-monopoly policy, small firms are needed to compete with larger companies by providing alternative sources of supply.

❑ A *"level playing field":* Some legislation is aimed at removing the unfair advantages that large firms might enjoy over small. These include the fixed cost of implementing government regulations in taxation, health and safety and employing additional personnel, which are a relatively higher burden for the small firm to carry. Small firms' access to external finance is also seen as more restricted as financiers prefer lending to larger companies, where the risk is less and the returns greater, (costs of setting up loans are similar for greater or smaller amounts).

The Conservative government in power from 1979 is particularly active in promoting small firms. Measures have been introduced in three main areas of financial assistance, lightening the tax and administration load, and information and advice.

4.2 Financial assistance

Three major schemes and other smaller schemes have been introduced:

❑ *The Enterprise Allowance Scheme (EAS)*

This encourages unemployed people to start their own business, by paying them £40 a week for a year to offset the loss of unemployment benefit once they are in business. To qualify, you need:

✓ to have at least £1000 to invest in the business;

✓ to have been unemployed, and drawing benefits, for at least 13 weeks;

✓ to be able to work full time (at least 36 hours per week) in the new business;

✓ to be over 18 and under retirement age; and

✓ to have a plan for a new business which will be independent, small and 'suitable' for public funding (that is, not involving such activities as politics, gambling, sex or religion).

This scheme seems to have encouraged more self-employment than small business development in that for every participant in the scheme only one third of a full time job has been created for others.

❏ *Loan Guarantee Scheme (LGS)*

In certain circumstances the government will agree to guarantee 80% of a bank loan. Loans can be up to £100,000 repayable over 2 to 7 years; there is a premium of 2.5% payable by the borrower in addition to normal bank interest rates.

The Loan Guarantee Scheme is intended for those not able to arrange loans under normal banking policies. A measure of its popularity is indicated by the fact that over £700 million of loans, to more than 21,000 small firms, have been guaranteed by the scheme since its introduction in 1981.

❏ *The Business Expansion Scheme (BES)*

This was designed to attract outside investment in small businesses by UK tax payers, who can deduct up to £40,000 in any one year from their tax liability to match the size of their investment.

To qualify, investors must:

✓ *not* be paid directors or employees of the business;

✓ *not* own more than 30% of its equity;

✓ invest a minimum of £500 and a maximum of £50,000 for at least five years.

The effect of the scheme was that a £40,000 investment made by a top-rate (40%) taxpayer can cost only £24,000 to the investor, the balance effectively coming from the Inland Revenue.

The scheme has attracted not only direct investment by individuals but also BES portfolios, offered by some financial institutions who select a range of businesses for investment, thereby spreading the risk of the investment and putting it under professional management. The 1992 Budget announced the end of the scheme in 1993 (see also Unit 15, 'Money' 2.2 'The Business Expansion Scheme').

4.3 Lightening the tax and administration load

Government policy has been to remove as much of the burden of taxation and the bureaucratic regulation of business activities as possible, claiming in the 1985 White Paper, "Lifting the Burdens", that this was necessary to encourage economic development and growth.

Small business has been singled out for special treatment in several areas:

❏ *Taxation*

The Bolton committee were particularly concerned that taxation policy reflected the need to encourage entrepreneurial activity and improve the liquidity position of small businesses. These concerns have been taken up in a number of ways:

A special rate of corporation tax for small companies with profits less than £250,000 has been progressively lightened to the level of 25% (1992/3).

Personal income tax reductions have directly affected small businesses which are sole traders and partnerships, as any surpluses are liable to income tax whether drawn from the business or not.

Inflation accounting, rather that historic cost accounting can now be used in assessing tax liability, with a resulting benefit for most profitable small firms.

❐ *Retirement*

Measures have also improved the arrangements possible for the retirement of a small business owner:

Pensions: Although still not equal to the tax-free provisions available to employees, the self-employed can now obtain tax relief on up to 17.5% of earned income (or progressively higher levels up to 40%, depending on age over 35 years).

Capital Gains Tax: Relief on capital gains of up to £150,000 is now available to owners disposing of their business on retirement.

❐ *Tax collection*

Businesses are major collectors of Pay-As-You-Earn Income Tax (PAYE), National Insurance Contributions (NIC), and Value Added Tax (VAT). By requiring even very small businesses to act as unpaid tax collectors, the government places a very high burden on them, which for the very smallest has been calculated to cost as much as one third of the value of the tax collected[4].

Although still a major burden there has been some mitigation:

VAT: In the 1991 Budget, the threshold for registration for VAT was lifted to £35,000 from £25,400 in 1990, thereby substantially raising the annual turnover level which small firms have to achieve before they are compelled to register for, and thereby collect and account for, VAT. For 1992/3, the minimum level is £36,600.

VAT is normally accounted for quarterly, against invoiced sales and purchases. The Cash Accounting Scheme, which permits firms to only pay VAT on those transactions which have been paid for, and not just invoiced, and the Annual Accounting Scheme, which allows for one return only for the year with estimated monthly payments, have helped to reduce the financial and administrative costs of these procedures for very small firms.

PAYE: Small employers with monthly PAYE deductions of less than £400 can now account for this tax on a quarterly return not the monthly basis which is normally required.

❐ *Health and safety at work*

Like all businesses, small firms are responsible for working conditions on all their premises for employees and visitors alike. The Safety at Work Act (1974), the Offices, Shops and Railway Premises Act (1963), and the Factories Act (1961) give employers extensive responsibilities, covering such areas as fire precautions, means of escape, hygiene, temperature, toilet and washing facilities, workspace and machinery safety. The government recognised the difficulties for small firms of applying these regulations in detail, by removing the requirement to prepare a written safety policy from small firms with less than 25 employees. Health and

Safety Inspectors have also been encouraged "to increase their awareness of smaller firm's interests".

☐ *Employment protection*

On the assumption that small firms were being discouraged from taking on more employees because of their inability to dismiss unsatisfactory ones, the government removed the right to complain of unfair dismissal from people in firms with less than 20 staff.

4.4   Information and advice

The third major area in which the government has sought to help small firms is in the provision of information and advice.

☐ *The Small Firms Service*

On the recommendation of the Bolton Committee, the Small Firms Service (SFS) was set up in 1972 within the Department of Trade and Industry, to provide information through a network of 13 Small Firms Centres (SFCs). This was developed in 1978, by the addition of a counselling service through over 100 Area Counselling Offices.

Although originally conceived as a means of encouraging efficiency and profitability, the key role of the sector in creating new jobs was recognised in 1987 when the government transferred the SFS to the Department of Employment, under a Minister of State for Employment with special responsibility for small firms. In 1989/90, the SFS handled over 317,000 inquiries on "anything and everything to do with business", and provided over 50,000 counselling sessions[5]. This was the last full year of the SFS, as responsibility for this service is now being transferred to the Training and Enterprise Councils.

☐ *Training and Enterprise Councils*

The Training and Enterprise Councils (TECS) were set up with the aim of improving efficiency in delivering training and other government initiatives, directed at regenerating local economies. TECS are partnerships between the government, which provides funds via the Training Agency (formerly the Manpower Services Commission), employer-led organisations and private business, charged with the responsibility to co-ordinate training needs, and to help new and expanding businesses in their area. The 82 TECS, each with an average of a £20 million contract with central government and 50 staff, have taken over responsibility for the work of the SFS, although the majority of their resources will be devoted to various training initiatives. For example, AZTEC became the first operational London TEC in January 1991 covering the area of Kingston, Merton and Wandsworth with the strategic aim to "promote business growth, improve skill levels and develop individuals to reach their full potential"[6].

☐ *Local Enterprise Agencies*

Local Enterprise Agencies (LEAs) are small, local advisory organisations, funded from private and public sources. A network of about 350 has emerged in the last decade or so, sponsored by local government, chambers of commerce, universities and colleges, and a mixture of private companies including banks and building societies. The primary objective is to provide help and advice to local business communities. The work of each LEA varies considerably from the provision of small premises to training courses and advice clinics[7].

❏ *The Enterprise Initiative*

The Enterprise Initiative is a package of "advice, guidance and practical help for British Business"[8], launched by the Department of Trade and Industry in 1988. It is based around a number of consultancy services in marketing, manufacturing, design, finance, quality, collaborative research and exporting, delivered by specialist organisations such as 3i Enterprise Support Ltd., the Chartered Institute of Marketing, the Design Council and PERA, (the Production Engineering Research Association). A small or medium-sized firm employing less than 500 people can receive from 5 to 15 days of consultancy with half the costs paid for by the DTI (two thirds in Assisted and Urban Programme Areas).

❏ *Business Growth Training*

Business Growth Training (BGT) consolidated a number of existing and new training programmes under one roof. BGT has five training options to suit differing circumstances, industries and sizes of business, from basic business planning kits, through business skills training for owner-managers, to the development of in-house training programmes for medium sized companies.

❏ *Other assistance*

The government's emphasis on small firms has been echoed by other institutions in the public and private sectors.

Banks have set up their own small business advisory units, led by National Westminster Bank which now claims to have a small business advisor in each of its 3000 UK branches. Lloyds, Midland and Barclays offer similar services.

Local Government offer various kinds of assistance to small firms. This can be through their Economic Development Units (EDUs) which offer cheap premises and relaxed planning controls. Some offer financial assistance in loans or grants to certain kinds of business, such as co-operatives. About two-thirds of all local authorities offer some type of advisory or information service.

The *Rural Development Commission (RDC)* formed in 1988 to advise government on rural issues, have a Business Service based at over 31 offices offering a wide range of advice, and sometimes finance, to small businesses in rural areas[7].

British Steel Industry and *British Coal Enterprise* were both set up by their respective parent bodies to encourage job regeneration and enterprise in areas where they are reducing their activities. They offer advice, finance and premises to suitable projects.

4.5 The effects of government policy

During the 1980s there has been substantial growth in the types of assistance offered to small firms in these three major areas of financial assistance, lightening the tax and administrative load, and information and advice.

There is considerable debate over the impact and effectiveness of all this activity. In particular there is no really conclusive evidence that these measures have induced growth in the small business sector which would not have happened anyway. Measurement of the success of policies has been largely by reference to the numbers of small firms using a particular service – the number of loans guaranteed by the LGS, or the number of inquiries to the SFS for example – without research into whether those small firms would have existed, or survived, without such assistance.

There can be little doubt that a general environment has been developed which does encourage, rather than dampen, enthusiasm for starting and growing a small business. However, a number of important criticisms have been made of the effectiveness of government policy:

❏ *Regional bias*

Most of the schemes described are nationally available. Although some special assistance does exist for regions which have high rates of unemployment or require additional development assistance for historic reasons (e.g. inner cities, docklands, mining or steel areas), the major government initiatives have an equal availability in all areas. Storey[9] in particular has criticised this policy on the basis that it is regionally divisive, because it favours areas that are already better off. New firm formation rates do vary by region. For example, in 1980–81 they were highest in the South West and South East, areas of comparatively low unemployment, and lowest in the North and Scotland, which are areas with traditionally high levels of unemployment[10]. This produces unequal benefits from such schemes as the Loan Guarantee Scheme, which has a much higher take up rate in the South East than in Scotland for example.

Recent training and consultancy initiatives, such as the Enterprise Initiative, have proved more popular in the North than the South which has thrown some doubt on the extent of regional bias. However, overall the more wealthy Southern areas have benefited more from financial assistance than poorer Northern ones.

❏ *Backing winners or losers?*

Assistance to small firms is also widely spread amongst all varieties of business and industries. There is some evidence that this merely encourages the unemployed to set up in competition with existing businesses, which they reduce to marginal levels of profitability or failure. They can do this because they devote their own labour to the enterprise at below market rates and initially they are subsidised by government sponsored schemes, such as the Enterprise Allowance Scheme[11].

Some commentators have suggested that policy should be more selective in assisting 'winners', that is small firms with a proven record of growth and the potential to create new jobs.

More recent government initiatives have moved in this direction by offering training, consultancy and advice to established businesses, rather than financial incentives for new ventures.

❏ *Confusion and overlap*

A further area for concern is the sheer number of services now available to the small business owner-manager, which can result in confusion and inefficiency. The integration of the SFS into TECs has tended to add to the confused atmosphere. Whilst there is evidence of co-operation between LEAs and TECs the possibilities for overlap are numerous.

5. The owner-manager perspective

5.1 The influence of smallness

How do small business owner-managers regard their environment? We have already observed that the environment of small firms will first and foremost be conditioned by the market place or industry within which they operate. But the small scale of a business does bring some common problems and influences. The key influences are listed in figure 6.3 below.

Figure 6.3: Influences of small size on management

❏ Small management team
❏ "Total" management with multi-functional roles for managers
❏ No specialist personnel or support functions
❏ Scope for autocratic leadership style by owner-manager
❏ Informal control systems
❏ Closeness of working group
❏ Limited control of environment
❏ Limited resources to research environment
❏ Limited market and usually small market share
❏ Limited product range, although flexibility within it
❏ Technology limited in terms of scale
❏ Limited leverage in obtaining financial resources

Adapted from "The Small Business Challenge to Management Education"[12]

(These major implications of smallness are developed further in Units 13, "Management of Resources", Unit 14, "Marketing" and Unit 15 "Money".)

Some of these influences relate to the lack of specialist management in the firm; 'total' management of an autocratic style, using informal control systems arises from the very real pressure of time in a small business environment. Other influences reflect a sense of helplessness in the face of external forces, with no real resources to research the environment, let alone control it. All the influences imply limited resources in terms of money, marketing and management.

5.2 The small business research trust survey

These influences are reflected in the problems and issues that owner-managers perceive as important. A *Quarterly Survey of Small Firms in Britain* has been carried out by the Small Business Research Trust, which asks owner-managers about the important problems facing their business. The results of one such survey are shown in figure 6.4 below.

Figure 6.4: Problems of the small business

Problem	% of replies
Interest rates	29%
Cash flow & payments	16%
Low turnover	15%
Lack of skilled employees	6%
Total tax burden	5%
Premises, rent & rates	5%
Inflation	4%
Govt. regulations & paperwork	3%
Access to finance	3%
Competition from big business	3%
High rates of pay	2%
Other	5%
No response	2%
	100%

From the *Quarterly Survey of Small Firms,* SBRT Survey Third quarter 1990, (1027 replies)

The risks faced by small enterprises are summed up by their financial concerns, at a time when interest rates were at a very high level. Their individual weakness against economic trends and competition from larger companies is witness to their lack of resources. The pressure on the time of the owner-manager leads to a general intolerance of what are regarded as "unnecessary" activities such as paperwork and conformity to government regulations.

How do small businesses overcome these problems? Small firms do have considerable strengths which derive from the central influence of the owner-manager, seeking to gain and retain a measure of independence which they perceive as unavailable in larger organisations. For most of them this overrides the inherent problems of smallness and the particular difficulties of their market.

6. References and further reading

6.1 References and further information

1. Porter, M, *Competitive Strategy. Techniques for Analysing Industries and Competitors,* The Free Press, 1980.

2. As reported in, *Ten Case Studies of Owner-Managed Businesses,* Department of Employment, 1990.

    a) Fleming Thermodynamics Ltd– an engineering design and development company founded in 1983 with a turnover of £500,000 and 17 employees in

1989. Although the company was originally engaged in manufacture, it withdrew to concentrate on design and development work.

b) Prelude Concepts and Designs Ltd, designs, markets and manufacturers toiletries and textiles, with a turnover of £1.8 million and 40 employees in 1990. The two founders concentrate on new product development, which they consider to be the key to their business, leaving a management team to look after the operational side.

3. See Binks, M and Jennings, A, "New Firms as a Source of Industrial Regeneration", in Scott, M et al (eds), *Small Firms Growth and Development,* Gower, 1986.

4. Sandford, C, Godwin, M and Hardwick P, *Administrative and Compliance Costs of Taxation,* Fiscal Publications 1989. This study calculated that firms collecting less than £1000 PAYE and NIC in one year incurred costs equivalent to one third of the tax collected. This fell to less than 1% where the annual collection was more than £280,000.

5. According to the SFS *Annual Report 1989/90,* Department of Employment, 1990.

6. Taken from their newsletter the *Aztec Messenger.* To contact your local TEC see the phone book. There is also a full listing in *Employment Gazette,* November 1991, HMSO, "The TEC Network".

7. There is a useful list of sources of direct help and advice in Barrow, C, *The New Small Business Guide,* BBC Books, 1989, Chapter 2, including a full listing of LEA's, and RDC offices.

8. *Introducing the Enterprise Initiative,* Department of Trade and Industry, 1989. This booklet summarises each of the different 'Consultancy Initiatives' and support services, with contact addresses.

9. Storey, D, *Entrepreneurship and the New firm,* London 1982.

10. Whittinton R, "Regional Bias in New Firm Formation", in Scott M et al (eds) *Small Firms Growth and Development,* Gower, 1986.

11. Binks M, and Jennings A, "Small Firms as a Source of Economic Rejuvenation", in Curran J. et al (eds), *The Survival of the Small Firm,* Vol. 1, Gower, 1986.

12. Gibb A, "The Small Business Challenge to Management Education" in *Journal of European Industrial Training,* Vol 7, No. 5, 1983.

6.2   Recommended further reading

Stanworth, J and Coray, C (eds), *Bolton 20 Years On: the Small Firm in the 1990s,* PCP, 1991. Chapter 2 "Change and Continuity in Small Firm Policy since Bolton" and Chapter 3 "Problems and Preoccupations".

Porter, M, *Competitive Strategy. Techniques for Analysing Industries and Competitors,* The Free Press, 1980. Chapter 9 "Competitive Strategy in Fragmented Industry".

Unit 7: Routes to market entry

This Unit identifies the alternative routes of developing an opportunity from concept into business reality. It also considers the specific advantages and disadvantages of the business start-up compared to other possible routes.

Contents

1. The alternative routes to market entry
1.1 Start-ups
1.2 Franchise
1.3 Outright purchase
1.4 'Buy-out'
1.5 'Buy-in'

2. The start-up
2.1 The wide scope of start-up
2.2 The advantages and disadvantages of start-up

3. References and further reading
3.1 References and further information
3.2 Recommended further reading

1. The alternative routes to market entry

Would-be owner-managers can choose between several different methods, or several different routes to market entry as a small enterprise.

The fundamental choice will be between starting a new business, or buying an existing one. Both possibilities then lead to further alternatives. Figure 7.1 illustrates the main choices open to the new entrant.

Figure 7.1: Possible routes to market entry for the small firm

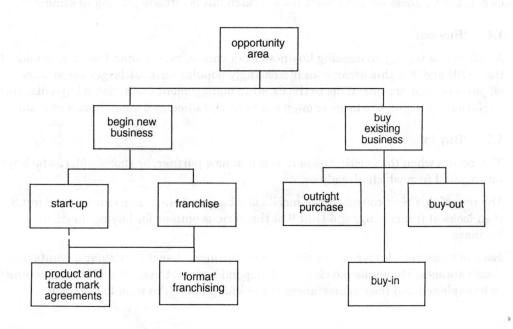

Inevitably there are overlaps and areas of greyness between these various forms.

1.1 Start-up

A business start-up means creating a new business, which stands alone, and is not tied to other organisations, except in the normal course of trading. It does not mean that the idea is necessarily new, only the vehicle which is set up to exploit it.

1.2 Franchise

A franchise is a method for starting a new business within the framework of an existing, larger business entity. It is a legally separate enterprise operating in some way under the umbrella of another organisation.

❏ *'Product and trademark' agreements*

A franchise can mean an agency to sell another company's products in a certain way, or within a certain territory. This may involve use of a registered trademark. It may involve distribution only (e.g. of cars), or it could include production under a licensed process. It includes straightforward agencies and more elaborate systems such as multi-level marketing. Some franchise agreements do not preclude other activities, and may thus form part of a business start-up's portfolio of products or services.

❏ *Format franchising*

Franchising has come to commonly mean a system for a business to set up using a complete format developed by another company, including trading name, standardised business presentation, products or services and operating systems. Some franchises have become household names, such as McDonalds, the Body Shop and DynoRod, but outlets are operated as separate legal entities by their owners.

1.3 Out-right purchase

This involves buying an existing business from somebody else; although there is a new owner, the business does not start from scratch but is already trading in some way.

1.4 'Buy-out'

A 'buy-out' is buying an existing business from within, rather than from the outside. In the 1970s and '80s this became an increasingly popular form, as larger corporations sold off parts of their organisations to the existing management team. Some buy-outs, such as National Freight, are large enough not to be classified as a small business at all.

1.5 'Buy-in'

This occurs when the existing owners accept a new partner, or shareholder, who buys into a small firm which already exists.

The rest of this Unit considers the merits of a business start-up as an option. Unit 8 then looks at franchising, and Unit 9 at the various options for buying an existing business.

Each of these vehicles for establishing a new business, has it particular advantages and disadvantages. The preferred choice will depend both on the nature of the opportunity to be exploited and the circumstances of the individuals who wish to pursue it.

2. The start-up

2.1 The wide scope of start-up

The business start-up means exactly what it says; it is a new enterprise, starting up and trading in its chosen field – a "green field" in which the seeds of ideas have a chance to grow and develop. For many new ideas there is no other option; existing businesses have not developed the idea that a would-be entrant wishes to exploit. Alternatively the new entrant may try to minimise risk in starting something new by only incurring significant liabilities after the idea has been tested in the market place.

In fact the scope of new businesses varies significantly, in line with the objectives of the founder, linked to their willingness and ability to invest in the enterprise. The level of risk taken in a start-up ranges from virtually nothing to highly significant personal financial and time investment. This investment can be made by an individual on their own, as the sole owner of the business, or it can be shared with others, who are either directly involved as equal partners, or less committed but still investing money, or time, in starting the business. This can be seen as a spectrum, as in Figure 7.2.

Figure 7.2: Illustration of the business start-up spectrum

Investment/risk	Scope of start-up	Examples
SOLE RISK		
Minimal personal risk with low initial investment	Part-time business activity	Hobby or skill used to generate additional income or to test idea
Increased initial investment required	Self-employment in existing trade or profession	Consultant or plumber using home as office
High individual risk	Sole trader creating new business entity	Retail outlet, restaurant, small manufacturer
SHARED RISK		
Initial investment minimised	Partnership of self-employed	Accounting or other professional practice, craft partnership
Increased initial investment from partners	New business organisation owned by two or more	Manufacturer, small hotel
High level of shared risk with significant up front investment	'Consortium' start-up	High-tech company with technical, management and financial partners

One end is typified by someone who begins in business on a part-time basis. The risk, whilst all their own, is minimal as income is generated elsewhere and investment requirements are small. The motivation may be to turn an existing hobby or skill into financial gain, or to put a toe in the water, before making the jump to full-time employment in the business.

At a higher level of risk on the spectrum is the tradesman, or professional, who decides to become self-employed, whilst keeping their liabilities low by minimal investment in equipment or overheads other than their own personal drawings and expenses.

A start-up, such as a new shop or manufacturing company, may require greater investment in capital equipment, premises, office equipment, staff in addition to the owner and other overheads. If this investment is made by a sole trader it can represent a very high level of individual risk.

Such investment can be shared, again at different levels, depending on the scope of the start-up. Some new enterprises require such significant initial investment that a consortium of partners come together to share the risk. For example, a new business wishing to exploit a technologically advanced process is formed as a partnership between the full time founders of the enterprise, a venture capital company who contribute long term finance and non-executive management, and a bank who provide an overdraft as working capital[1].

The scope of the start-up will be determined by the nature of the business, and the objectives of the owners. Businesses vary considerably in their investment requirements, from the self employed plumber who has to buy some basic tools and an answer machine, to a capital intensive manufacturer, needing hundreds of thousands of pounds to get off the ground. The objectives of the founders in relation to the speed of anticipated growth, will also influence the investment requirements. Perhaps the objectives extend only to personal self-employment with no other staff or overheads; or maybe the scope is more ambitious, foreseeing the need to develop a team of people to cope with the business activity[2].

2.2   The advantages and disadvantages of start-up

Some of the advantages and disadvantages of the business start-up, compared to other methods of becoming a small business owner (such as buying an existing business), are summarised in figure 7.3. Notice that, as is common with this kind of 'balance sheet' analysis, advantages have corresponding disadvantages. So, for example, the advantage that a start-up is the creation of the owners, which gives them freedom of choice, has the corresponding disadvantage that it is unproven by anyone else.

The advantage of control over decision-making becomes the disadvantage that these decisions could be misplaced, as the high failure rate suggests. Starting with a clean sheet has the downside of no market share or goodwill at the out-set.

Figure 7.3: The advantages and disadvantages of the start-up as a small business entrant

Advantages	Disadvantages
Creation of the owners: freedom of choice over what the business does, how it operates, and what its values are.	*Unproven idea:* the idea may be creative, but will it work? Even after the most thorough research, a new business can only prove itself in practice.
Control of the owners: personal decisions count, external influences can be minimised.	*High failure rate:* the failure rate of start ups is high; less than 50% survive the first 5 years. Other methods, e.g. franchising, have better track records.
Satisfaction of the owners: success due to the skill and efforts of owners, which gives them heightened sense of satisfaction when (if) success comes.	*Hard, lonely work:* unsociable working hours are often linked to feelings of being alone as, even in a partnership, there are no support departments and services in the firm. Entrepreneurs do it themselves.
Clean sheet: the business starts with no backlog of problems; it will create plenty, but at least they will be new ones and not inherited from the past.	*No market share or goodwill:* compared to buying an existing business or franchising, the start-up has the problem of establishing its name from scratch – the goodwill in an established company name or loyalty of existing customers takes some time to build up.

Advantages	Disadvantages
Help from various agencies: Government assistance and help from other agencies is available to encourage new business start-ups.	*Barriers to entry:* there are many barriers to market entry. One-off start up costs can be significant. Legislation has to be considered, premises found, accounts with suppliers opened, credit worthiness proved—these, and many other obstacles have to be overcome before trading begins[3].
Match between founder and enterprise: the founders of new enterprises can ensure that their individual strengths are well used, and their weaknesses minimised, by choosing a business well matched to their own qualities and experiences.	*Difficult to forecast:* with no track record, a start-up is very hard to predict for financial and other outcomes.
Less funds required: a start-up that works costs less than buying a similar franchise or existing business.	*Difficult to finance:* banks and other lenders are always keener to give money to proven concepts than to new ideas.

3. References and further reading

3.1 References and further information

1. A special category of small firm – the new technology based firm (NTBF) – has been identified by researchers looking at businesses that start up in newly emerging, and fast moving areas of technology. The role of these NTBFs is discussed for example in: Rothwell, R, "The Role of Small Firms in Technological Innovation," in Curran, J et al (eds), *The Survival of the Small Firm,* Vol 2, Gower 1986.

2. This theme of diversity in types of owner-managers of small business is explored in more depth in Unit 2, 2. 'Types of Owner-Managers and Entrepreneurs'.

   The different types of motivation for business ownership are discussed in Unit 12, 1.3 'The Objectives of Small Business Owner-Managers'.

3. Barriers to market entry are also considered in Unit 6, 2.1 'Barriers to Entry'.

3.2 Recommended further reading

Rosthorn, J et al, *The Small Business Action Kit,* Kogan Page, 1991. Chapter 2, 'What are the Options?' This book has a series of work sheets to guide the new start-up along its chosen course. (It is therefore a very practical book, well suited to prospective owner-managers and their advisors, and less appropriate for a student interested in a more theoretical approach.)

Williams, S, *Lloyds Bank Small Business Guide,* Penguin, 1991. Section II 'Getting A Head Start'. This is one of the best of the bank-sponsored publications on how to set up and run a small business.

Unit 8: Franchising

This Unit looks at Franchising – its definition, background, development, financial implications and place among the categories of small business types. The advantages and disadvantages are considered compared to other small business forms.

Contents

1. **What is franchising?**

2. **Product and trademark agreements**

3. **Business format franchising**

4. **The franchising market**

5. **How much does it cost?**
   5.1 Start-up costs
   5.2 Annual charges

6. **Advantages and disadvantages**
   6.1 Advantages for franchisees
   6.2 Disadvantages for franchisees
   6.3 Advantages for franchisors
   6.4 Disadvantages for franchisors

7. **But is it a small business?**

8. **References and further reading**
   8.1 References and further information
   8.2 Recommended further reading

1. What is franchising?

Franchising is a business arrangement in which one party (the franchisor) allows others (the franchisees) to use a business name, or sell products, in such a way that the franchisees can operate their own legally separate business.

It can mean as little as a simple agreement to sell a company's products in a specified area. However it is now more commonly used to describe business format franchising in which the franchisor offers a complete business package[1].

2. Product and trademark agreements

The early forms of franchising were agreements in which manufacturers distributed their products through licensed dealers.

In the early days of the Singer Sewing Machine Company, for example, distribution was carried out in this way. Breweries, oil companies and car manufacturers all developed the distribution of their products through different forms of licensing arrangements. Under such arrangements local tenants or dealers took responsibility for sales in a given territory in return for some element of the local profit. The producers developed their products and the goodwill associated with their trademarks; the local distributor contributed local knowledge, contacts, and effort. Such distribution arrangements are still common, particularly for the marketing of drinks (soft and alcoholic), petrol and cars.

Certain manufacturing processes, particularly where a patent exists, are also licensed. The patent holder may wish to exploit their innovation on a wider basis than their own resources allow. They therefore permit other manufacturers to use the process under licence in return for a royalty. This is particularly common in international markets where local laws prohibit foreign ownership of production, or where local conditions make it impractical.

Some small businesses specialise as import agencies, often negotiating a number of agreements to import foreign goods, and act as the national, or regional distributor.

If these goods are branded, the producer will usually attempt to protect their trademark by an agreement which not only outlines the terms and conditions of trade, but also sets minimum standards covering sales and after-sales aspects.

Other forms of agreement cover the use of registered trademarks or celebrity names. The right to use well-known names – fictional or real – can be purchased under a licensing agreement which specifies how the name is to be used, and what royalties will be paid for the privilege. Many children's products, for example, are sold in the image of the latest popular hero, manufactured and distributed under a licensing arrangement with the creator. Real live celebrities may also allow their name to be associated with a product or service under an endorsement agreement.

Although up front payments and on-going royalties can be onerous, the small business, with no established identity of its own, can often benefit from a relevant association with an established, known name. For example, a small manufacturer of leisure clothes and equipment may seek endorsement of their products by a local sports personality, to add stature and gain new outlets.

For some small businesses, product and trademark arrangements are essential. Many public houses are 'tied' to a major brewery, even though the business is sometimes owned by the tenant; the publicans benefit from the national marketing by the brewery, but there are restrictions on what else they can sell. A small manufacturer of toys and games will inevitably seek licensing arrangements so that their products can be merchandised using the latest cartoon characters; sales can be dramatically influenced by the well-timed launch of a product endorsed by the latest heroes.

3. Business format franchising

Today the word franchising is more commonly used to describe business format franchising. This is a more in-depth relationship between franchisor and franchisee than a simple product or trademark licensing arrangement.

The International Franchise Association[2] describes this type of franchise as:

> "A continuing relationship in which the franchisor provides a licensed privilege to do business plus assistance in organising training, merchandising and management in return for a consideration from the franchisee."

In other words, this type of franchise goes beyond the supply of products and trade names, and covers many other aspects of how the business is run. The business format offered by the franchisor can cover such aspect as:

- ❑ trade name, business style, logo, house colours;

- ❑ detailed product or service specification;

- ❑ analysis of location, and lease negotiations;

- ❑ design of premises, and purchase of equipment;

- ❑ financial advice to establish the business;

- ❑ operating systems and manuals;

- ❑ management control systems;

- ❑ training and help to set up;

- ❑ continuing assistance including research and development and management counselling;

- ❑ national and local marketing;

- ❑ centralised purchasing;

- ❑ current market research results.

This represents a complete package which allows the franchisee to use a format proven by the franchisor, whilst retaining independence as a business. There is an agreement between the two parties which sets out how the business will be run, and the obligations of both parties.

The major banks also offer specific advice and information on franchising; for certain proven franchises they will be able to offer loans more easily than for other types of new business with no track record.

4. The franchising market

Business format franchising has grown most dramatically in the USA. Originating in the 1950s, it now accounts for around one third of all retail sales, with a turnover of $750 billion, according to the United States Department of Commerce[3].

Kentucky Fried Chicken became one of the pioneers when Colonel Sanders travelled around America teaching people how to cook chicken his way. Today, Pepsi-Cola own the Kentucky Fried Chicken chain of over 7,000 franchised outlets around the world.

Another fast food chain was started in the 1950s by Ray Kroc based on the standardised hamburger production techniques developed by the McDonald brothers. McDonalds now represent the largest group of retail outlets in the world with over 12,000 franchises. Wimpy was the first major franchise in the UK, developed by J Lyons and Company from 1956.

Franchising is still expanding rapidly in the UK, by the late 1980s franchising had become the fastest growing sector among retail and service outlets, accounting for almost 4% of total retail sales.

A survey jointly commissioned by the British Franchise Association[4] and National Westminster Bank reported retail sales of £3.8 billion in 1988 (up 33% on 1987), with 16,000 franchised businesses, employing 181,500 people, with average sales of £269,000 per unit. The authors of the survey projected turnover to reach £20 billion by the year 2000. In 1991 there were an estimated 18,000 outlets, operated by over 400 franchisors, with total retail sales in excess of £5 billion (these statistics relate to format franchising only).

In Europe there were a reported 92,000 franchised outlets in 1987 with sales of £20 billion. In some countries such as France, Holland and Belgium, penetration of franchising seems more advanced than the UK.

Three major markets account for a little over two-thirds of today's franchises in the UK:

❏ Food and drink – 30%

❏ Business services – 20%

❏ Home improvements – 10%

It is still a relatively young industry: three-quarters of the franchises on offer in 1985 were less than three years old.

Older franchises include: Wimpy, Servicemaster, Apollo Window Blinds, Dyno-Rod and Prontaprint.

Recent, successful franchises include: The Body Shop, Pancake Place, Tie Rack, Beneton and Fast Frame.

Despite the concentration in the retail and service sectors, the range of franchised businesses is extremely wide. Some of the more unusual franchises offered in the UK include[5]:

❏ Brenderup Ltd – marketing a range of domestic and industrial trailers.

❏ Country Cousins & Emergency Mothers – a residential care service.

❏ Create-a-Book – personalised children's books.

❏ Fatty Arbuckles – themed American restaurants serving very generous portions of food.

❏ Giltsharp Technology – a high-tech scissor sharpening service.

❏ Just Wills – home-visit will writing service.

❏ Nationwide Investigations Group – private detective agencies.

❏ Somerford Claims Association – settling loss of earnings claims through insurance companies for the taxi industry.

5. How much does it cost?

In addition to the usual overhead costs of running a business, the franchisee will have to find some additional funds.

5.1 Start-up costs

These include an initial franchise fee as a one-off payment to the franchisor for the privilege of becoming a franchisee. In addition, other start-up investment is required to cover the costs of buying equipment, fitting out premises, trade signs, initial stocks of materials, stationery, promotional literature, and all the other items which the franchisor deems necessary to run the business. There may be some element of profit to the franchisor in providing the new franchisee with these.

The advertised finance required for some well known, and not so well known, franchises in 1991 was as follows[5]:

Franchise	Minimum Start-up Investment	Initial Franchise Fee
Budget Rent-a-Car	£75,000	£25,000
Burger King	£700,000	£25,000
Climat de France (2 star hotel chain)	£400,00	£5,500 (+ £400 per bedroom)
Fast Frame	£16,000	£10,000
Brenderup	£7,000	–
Country Cousins & Emergency Mothers	£29,000	£7,500
Create-a-Book	£2,000	£2,000
Fatty Arbuckles	£100,000	£10,000
Gilt Sharp Technology	£11,950	£4,000
Home-Tune	£16,000	£8,250
Just Wills Ltd	£5,000	£15,000
Kalamazoo	£30,000	£15,000
Nationwide Investigations	£12,000	£7,500
PDC International (instant print shops)	£31,000	£5,000
Pizza Express	£250,000	£17,500
Somerford Claims Association	£3,000	£7,500
Unigate Dairies (milk round)	£4,500	£1,000

5.2 Annual charges

Franchisors will also levy a service fee, and possibly other charges on an ongoing basis. The service charge is normally calculated as a percentage of net invoiced sales, varying from 5% to 15% plus, and averaging in the 10 to 12% range. Where the supply of goods on a continuous basis is part of the franchise arrangement (e.g. Body shop and McDonalds) then the franchisor will have some level of profit in the transfer price of these goods.

Fixed charges representing a contribution to national advertising and 'management' are also common.

6. Advantages and disadvantages

6.1 Advantages for franchisees

☐ The business concept is proven, or should be. The British Franchise Association have laid down guidelines as to what constitutes 'proven', which includes more than just one business outlet for a short period.

☐ The way to operate the business has already been worked out and tested. Starting up should be easier and faster.

☐ Training and support is given including technical training, business training, site selection and choice of suppliers.

☐ Statistically less franchises fail than other business start-ups; therefore it can be easier to obtain finance for the franchise. Annual failure rates are estimated to be between 5 to 7 per cent, much lower than for small firms generally[6].

☐ National branding will often have been established.

☐ Research and development, and competitive analysis will usually be undertaken by the franchisor to keep abreast of environmental changes.

☐ Economies of scale may apply, for example in nationally agreed terms with suppliers which take account of the total franchised business.

☐ Economies of experience should apply, for example in knowing the marketing techniques that have worked best for other franchisees.

6.2 Disadvantages to franchisees

☐ Not your own creation. This is someone else's idea; the franchisee is implementing not creating.

☐ Lack of independence. The franchisor makes the rules which the franchisee has to follow.

☐ The financial costs can be considerable with large up front fees and high royalties. Set up costs can also be higher as they have to follow a prescribed formula.

☐ The franchise may not be suited to your area.

☐ The goodwill your business builds up is never all yours, as it is dependent on a continuing franchise agreement. This could cause problems when you decide to sell the business.

☐ The franchisor needs to ensure regular disclosure of information by the franchisee to protect their royalties and the franchise agreement. This can become intrusive into the financial affairs of the franchisee.

☐ The brand image of the franchisor can become a distinct liability if things go wrong. The franchisee is dependent on the stability of the franchisor; a national problem with the franchise can dramatically affect the franchisee who has no control over events.

Franchises vary greatly in quality, from the well-established proven formulae of household names, to new creations which have yet to establish their viability. In the USA franchising is regulated by legislation, which ensures that franchisors have to register with the authorities, filing a 'franchise offering circular'. This is similar to a share prospectus, and contains information essential for the prospective franchisee, such as details of the history and officers of the franchisor company. In the UK such disclosure is voluntary, as is the regulation of the industry. Most established franchisors are members of the British Franchise Association, which has a code of conduct and accreditation rules, based on codes developed by the European Franchise Federation. One of the key guiding principles is that the franchisor "shall have operated a business concept with success for a reasonable time, and in at least one pilot unit before starting its franchise network"[7].

A prospective franchisee will clearly want to know more about these aspects to protect themselves from the possibility of taking on many of the disadvantages of franchising without the compensating advantages.

6.3   Advantages for franchisors

❏   Franchising is a way of expanding a small business into a big business in a relatively short time. The burden of raising capital to develop a business concept is shared with franchisees and fast expansion becomes easier to fund.

❏   Another common barrier to expansion, the recruitment, motivation and reward of key staff, is also eased; a proven opportunity usually has a queue of potential franchisees waiting to start. Franchisees tend to be motivated individuals prepared to accept rewards in line with the results of their business.

6.4   Disadvantages for franchisors

❏   Franchising inevitably means loss of control compared to a conventional branch outlet. Franchisees are more independent than a branch manager.

❏   If the franchisor offers a franchise based on the recommended practices of the BFA, then it will take time, effort and resources to operate the concept as a pilot franchise unit.

❏   The franchisor may take on many obligations in the franchise agreement, such as continuing commercial and technical assistance during the life time of the agreement, which will necessitate developing central support resources.

❏   Franchisees are becoming more organised as groups in their dealings with franchisors. Their ability to exert pressure on franchisors will probably increase as the industry matures.

❏   Failure of a single franchisee, through no fault of the franchisor, can do considerable damage to the reputation of the franchisor.

Ultimately the franchisor has a powerful vested interest to ensure the survival and success of its franchised outlets; without them the franchise will fail.

The self-interest of the franchisor will be best served by meeting in full its obligations to prove the idea it wishes to network, and provide the required support to ensure the prosperity of the franchisees.

7. But is it a small business?

Is a franchised outlet a small business? Or should it be classified as a f
branch of a larger organisation?

The Bolton Committee excluded franchises from its review of the UK
sector. One of its key criteria in defining a small business was independence from otner
organisations. As a franchise is not independent from the franchisor, the total
franchised network could be considered as one business, rather than a collection of
separate, small firms (franchisees) and one larger business (the franchisor).

In practice, all small firms exhibit differing degrees of independence. None are truly
autonomous, as all will depend to some extent on forces outside their full control.

Customers can be a powerful controlling factor, particularly if a small business is
reliant on a few of them. A small producer supplying a large supermarket chain, for
example, may not have full control over many important operations of its business
including quality control, delivery schedule and pricing policies. Financial backers of an
enterprise may also exert considerable influence on the management of a small
business, particularly one that is in difficulties.

In reality the independence of small firms is not a fixed factor, but rather a point on a
continuum. A firm's position on the continuum depends on a number of factors,
including the level of competitive activity in its chosen market, the power of its buyers
and suppliers, and its relative financial success or failure[8].

Franchisees occupy a place on this continuum, but not necessarily at the end of minimal
control. Nor will all franchisees be at the same point; some will be more controlled by
their franchisors than others. Indeed the perceptions of the franchisor and its
franchisees over who controls what have been shown to significantly differ. A survey of
three franchise networks[9] indicated that, whilst franchisors felt that their franchise
contracts were strictly enforced, franchisees believed that contractual obligations were
not rigorously applied. They did agree however that franchisees had the principle
responsibility for hours of opening, employment of personnel, bookkeeping and quality
standards, which represent a significant part of the operational running of the business.

A critical ingredient in the make-up of the relationships in a franchised network is that
the franchisee operates a legally separate business. This business may be constrained
by the terms of the franchise contract, but in the eyes of the law it is a separate entity.
The experience of franchisors is that they need to manage their franchisees by
persuasion not mandate, as the desire for independence is strong among franchisees.
The degree of independence exercised by the owner of a successful franchised outlet is
not so significantly different from a more conventional small business that it can be
considered a totally different business type.

Many of the principles for the successful management of small businesses hold true for
franchised outlets. The performance of individual outlets operating the same franchise
varies more significantly than can be explained by location factors alone. Some
franchisees always struggle. Others become successful owner-managers, with a chain of
franchised outlets.

8. References and further reading

8.1 References and further information

1. This is the definition used by the Small Firms Service in their booklet *Franchising*, Small Firms Service, Department of Employment. This is a useful introductory leaflet, outlining the key aspects of Format Franchising.

2. The International Franchise Association, based in Washington DC, USA, was founded in 1960 as a non-profit making body and it now represents over 400 franchisors in the USA and worldwide.

3. For a short history of franchising, and some information on its place in the economy see Acheson, D, "What is Franchising?" in the *Franchise Handbook 1992*, CGB Publishing, 1992.

4. The British Franchise Association, (BFA), Thames View, Newtown Road, Henley on Thames, Oxon, RG9 1HG (Tel. 0491 578049)

   The BFA was formed in 1977 by several leading franchisors in the UK, with the aim of "establishing a clear definition of ethical franchising standards to help members of the public, press, potential investors, and government bodies to identify sound business opportunities". (From a BFA leaflet, *Your First Steps in Franchising*.)

5. Details of these, and other franchise opportunities are to be found in the *Franchise Handbook 1992*, CGB Publishing, 1992.

6. Stanworth, J and Curran, J, "Franchising", in Woodcock, C (ed.) *The Guardian Guide to Running a Small Business*, Kogan Page, 1990. For a discussion on franchise survival rates see section 7.5 "Franchising for the Future".

7. The European Code of Ethics for Franchising has been adapted by an agreed 'Extension and Interpretation' to form the "Code of Ethical Conduct" of the British Franchise Association. For further details see the *Franchise Handbook 1992*. CGB Publishing, 1992, Pages 27–34.

8. The relative independence of small business types is further discussed in Information Bank, Unit 6, 3.1 Dependent or Independent Small Firms?

9. Stanworth, J, Curran, J and Hough, J, "The Franchised Small Enterprise: Formal and Operational Dimensions of Independence", in Curran, J et al (eds), *The Survival of The Small Firm*, Gower, 1986.

8.2 Recommended further reading

Franchise Handbook 1992, CGB Publishing, 1992.

Barrow, C, *The New Small Business Guide,* BBC Books, 1989. Pages 105–126 contain useful addresses of franchise associations and publications, as well as a directory of franchise opportunities.

Stanworth, J, Curran, J and Hough, J, "The Franchised Small Enterprise: Formal and Operational Dimensions of Independence" (see reference 9 above). This paper discusses the issue of whether the franchised small business is genuinely independent.

There are also some magazines sold at newsagents such as WH Smith which specialise in franchising and are worth looking through to understand the scope of the system. For example, *Business Franchise Magazine,* CGB Publishing and *The Franchise Magazine,* Franchise Development Services Ltd.

Unit 9: Buying an existing business

This Unit is concerned with the possibility of buying an existing business, as opposed to starting up from scratch. The opportunities for purchasing (and selling) businesses are explored, along with the main problem areas to look out for.

Contents

1. The scope for buying existing businesses

The would-be owner-manager does not necessarily have to start a brand new business. There are various opportunities to become part of an existing business. A buyer may choose to purchase an existing firm outright, or they may opt to become involved in it in some way as a partner. The sellers of existing small businesses vary from small to large enterprises, conventional to franchised businesses and from the successful to the failed.

The different possibilities arising from the intentions of a buyer, and the status of a seller, create many permutations of ways of buying an existing business, or part of it. This is illustrated in Figure 9.1 as a "Matrix of Possibilities for Entry into an Existing Small Business."

Figure 9.1: Matrix of possibilities for entry into an existing small business

	Seller			
	Small firm	Larger firm	Franchise	Forced sale
Buyer				
Outright purchase	✔	✔	✔	✔
Buy-in	✔	?	✔	✔
Buy-out	✔	✔	✔	✔

2. The seller

2.1 Small firm

The seller may be a small business person who, for one reason or another, wishes to dispose of the enterprise, or their share in it.

The reasons for the sale may include:

❑ recognition of lack of success, and low probability of it in the future;

❑ problems, not related to the business, which force its sale, including health problems, marital break-up or other personal issues;

❑ other business activities which make a sale desirable; for example the need to raise money for another failing/succeeding enterprise, or the desire to free-up time for other business involvements;

❑ desire for a career change out of small business;

❑ retirement of an owner, with no family succession plans;

❑ desire to cash-in on the success of a business;

❑ a dispute which has lead to the breakdown of a business partnership where one side cannot, or does not wish to, buy out the other.

The seller may own all of the business or only a part.

2.2   Larger firm

Larger companies sometimes dispose of a part of their business which by itself constitutes a small firm. Again their motives will be varied, including:

☐ financial targets set by the parent company are consistently not met by the small business unit. The return on the investment is considered inadequate, and there is a desire to re-invest the capital and management time elsewhere;

☐ the parent company adopts a new strategy, which means that the small business unit no longer contributes to meeting group objectives. Particularly in times of recession, larger companies which have diversified into new areas of higher risk, may seek to return to what they consider to be their 'core business'. This has motivated the scaling down of some companies, and the break-up of some conglomerates into parts which can be classified once again as a small business;

☐ the parent company needs to raise money for other activities, because of financial difficulties, or for other reasons;

☐ the parent company is itself taken over, and the new owners do not see the small business unit as contributing to their overall strategy, or they may wish to sell parts of the acquisition to help fund the purchase;

☐ legislation may force a large company to sell some parts of its business.

2.3   Franchise

As well as starting a new outlet in a franchise network, it is also possible to buy either the business of an existing franchisee, or a branch outlet from a franchisor. Existing franchisees may wish to sell their business for any of the reasons given for small firms above. In addition, they may simply be disillusioned with the franchise system, because it does not provide sufficient independence to the franchisee, for instance. The franchisor will have to agree to such a sale, as the franchise agreement will need to be assigned to a new owner. However, it is usually in their interests to facilitate the change of ownership for two main reasons:

☐ the franchisee wishing to sell will hardly be motivated to properly manage the franchise having failed to secure a buyer because of the intransigence of the franchisor;

☐ it is motivational for other franchisees to see the exit possibilities from their business; they will like to feel they are building up a capital gain, as well as ongoing income from their business. Franchisors are therefore usually keen to build up a second market for the sale of franchised outlets, providing they can approve the quality of the incoming franchisee.

Franchisors may also wish to sell off an outlet which they themselves own, and manage. This may have been an original pilot operation to prove the franchise concept. Or the franchisor may have developed as a series of owned outlets before moving into franchising, the success of which then triggers a sale of the managed outlets to franchisees.

2.4   Forced sales

The high failure rate of small businesses unfortunately gives rise to many opportunities to purchase the assets of a failed enterprise from a liquidator, receiver, or

administrator. The forced sale of a business and its assets takes different forms
dependent on the legal status of the failed company[1].

❏ *Liquidation* describes the legal process of closing down a bankrupt company, and the
   sale of its assets to pay off as many debts as possible. The owner no longer controls
   the business; a liquidator is appointed who will sell off the assets of the business for
   the highest possible price. Insolvency has usually gone too far at this stage for there
   to be much interest in the on-going trading of the business. The liquidator simply
   disposes of the individual assets as quickly and economically as possible.
   Liquidation is not so much a possibility to buy a business as an opportunity to buy
   some assets, such as equipment, or office furniture, at low prices.

❏ *Receivership* allows more possibilities to acquire the on-going business of a company
   in trouble. A receiver is normally appointed by a lender, such as a bank, who has
   secured their loan by a charge against certain of the company's assets, often the
   debtors. The receiver comes in to realise the assets in order to repay as much as
   possible of the debt.

   Unlike a liquidator, a receiver can keep a business trading if it is considered in the
   best interest of the creditors.

❏ *Administration*. The Insolvency Act of 1986 introduced a further possibility for
   creditors, who might otherwise have had to force a company into liquidation.

   Before the 1986 Act, the only way of dealing with company failure where there were
   no specific charges on company assets, was through liquidation; potentially viable
   businesses were accordingly forced into liquidation because the creditors had no
   other process available to them for the efficient recovery of their money. The 1986
   Act introduced 'Administration Orders', which are court orders appointing an
   administrator empowered to salvage as much of the company as possible, or to sell
   its assets on a more profitable basis than under the circumstances of a liquidation.

   Whilst it would be unwise in most circumstances to buy the shares of a company in
   receivership or under administration, it is possible to acquire those assets of the
   business which enable it to continue trading, thereby in effect buying the business.

3. The buyer

The intentions of the buyer add further to the scope of entry permutations into an
existing business.

3.1 Outright purchase

A would-be entrepreneur may choose to buy an on-going business in its entirety, as a
means of market entry.

An existing small business owner can also decide to expand by purchasing another
small enterprise.

In some trades, the barriers to entry for a new start-up are sufficiently high to make the
purchase of existing businesses the most common route.

The case of the licensed trade

This has been the case for example in the licensed trades, particularly public houses. It is very difficult to obtain the necessary permission to sell alcoholic drinks from premises which do not have an existing licence, especially where this is not tied to the consumption of food, as in a pub, or wine bar. However there is a well established market in the buying and selling of existing licensed premises. Specialist licensed property estate agents, or 'transfer agents', act on behalf of owners wishing to sell the freehold or leasehold of their premises.

A buyer can find vendors in any of the seller categories listed in the 'Matrix of possibilities for entry into small businesses' (figure 9.1):

❑ *Small firm:* Some pubs are 'free houses', owned outright by the publican, and not tied by contract to any one brewer. These are bought and sold much like other small firms, often with the added attraction of having a freehold property as an asset.

❑ *Larger firms:* Larger firms have also recently been forced to sell some public houses which they own. A Monopolies and Mergers Commission report into the supply of beer found that large brewers controlled too many of the outlets for their products. Their recommendations have forced brewers to sell off hundreds of licensed outlets.

❑ *Franchise:* Some pubs are sold effectively as a franchise because the publican trades from licensed premises which are 'tied' by a lease to one particular brewery.

❑ *Forced Sales:* Recently, forced sales of public houses have become more commonplace. Free house prices have been doubly hit by the general depression in the property market and the increase in premises for sale forced on the brewers.

Owners who bought when prices were much higher have been affected by high interest rates, and the decline in the value of their property asset, usually the main collateral for loans to buy the business. This has also coincided with a downturn in demand for pubs' services. Increased competition from other leisure service providers, and stricter enforcement of drink drive legislation, has lead to a general decline in sales. These factors have combined to cause a rise in the number of forced sales. A survey by the Business Sales Group, specialist licensed transfer agents, in 1991 suggested that one third of free house pub sales were forced on the owners.[2]

3.2 Buy-in

Buyers may not wish to purchase an existing business in its entirety. They may instead 'buy into' an existing business, and become a new partner, or shareholder, with those that already exist.

Again this is more commonplace in some types of small business than others. It often happens, for example, in professional practices such as accountants, solicitors, doctors and other medical practitioners such as physiotherapists. These are often large partnerships, where it is normal to have a turnover of partners who leave, or retire. In such circumstances, it is not necessary to dissolve the partnership, because the partnership agreement allows for the recruitment of another partner into the practice.

Other types of small firms, including franchises, may also wish to allow in a new partner or shareholder. For example an expanding firm out-grows the resources of the founding entrepreneur(s) who sees the need to build a team to manage the business; in order that the new team members may share the founders' objectives and commitment, they are invited to purchase into the equity of the business. A similar scenario might also arise if a small firm found itself in difficulties; the addition of different skills and capital from a new partner or shareholder represents a possible recovery strategy of the 'forced sale' kind. A strategy which falls between these two extremes was adopted by Anita Roddick in the early days of the Body Shop. The success of her first shop in Brighton encouraged her to open a second. She was unable to raise the necessary capital, and so instead found a new partner who put up the necessary £4,000 in return for 50% of the equity of the business. It proved a very sound investment.

Buying into a business being sold off by a larger firm is also possible. This is becoming more common, especially in conjunction with buy-outs by the management (see below).

3.3   Buy-out

'Buy-outs' commonly refer to the purchase of a business, or a significant part of it, by its existing management. Relatively rare in the 1970s, management buy-outs became increasingly common in the 1980s. Although buy-outs can occur from small firms and franchises and have also happened as a result of a forced sale by the parent company, larger firms are usually the sellers. Indeed many buy-outs are larger firms buying themselves out of even bigger companies. For example, MFI was bought out of Asda for £718 million, the most expensive deal of its kind in the UK.

Management buy-outs became very fashionable in the 1980s. Made possible by readily available finance from venture capital funds, buy-outs were further fuelled by some well publicised success stories, such as the buy-out of Premier Brands for £97 million from Cadbury Schweppes, in which 4500 of the 5000 employees bought shares at 1p each. When the company was sold in 1989, these shares were worth £5 each, turning a factory workers stake of £10 into £5000, and giving the managing director a reported profit of £45 million. Such large scale buy-outs encouraged many more smaller ones.

More recently, changes in local government legislation, introducing more competition in the provision of services, has stimulated some buy-outs in the public sector as well. For example a local council, the City and District of St. Albans recently sub-contracted the management of its leisure facilities to St. Albans Leisure Ltd, a company formed by the management, who had previously been employed by the council to run those same facilities. The council benefit from a fixed cost base for the provision of leisure services, rather than unpredictable losses which they had experienced hitherto. The management team are able to market the facilities more aggressively, and believe they are financially more efficient now that they are out of local authority control[3].

But not all buy-outs are success stories. There have been many casualties. High interest rates, and falling demand in recessionary times, work against buy-outs particularly, where high levels of borrowing, and expectations of rapid growth are typical. In 1991, the Management Buy-Out Research Unit at Nottingham University reported record levels of buy-outs in receivership.

3.4   Buy-in Management Buy-Out' ('BIMBO')

A variation on the Management Buy-Out theme is the 'Buy-In Management Buy-Out' (or 'BIMBO' as it is sometimes called), which combines outside and inside management in the purchase of a company. The risk of buying into a company from the outside can be reduced if the existing management of the company are also involved. In theory at least, it is possible to have the benefit of a fresh approach and wider experiences from the buying-in manager(s), linked to the in-depth knowledge of the company and its markets provided by the buy-out manager(s).

The motives of the vendor follow the general lines of the larger firm as seller outlined above. Disposals often follow strategy changes brought on by financial problems or changes of ownership.

For example, Letraset grew from a small firm in the 1960s to a quoted international company in the 1970s, and then found it difficult to sustain growth in its core graphic art business. By the early 1980s it had diversified into toys, leisure and collectables, and quickly hit problems in these new businesses.

A recovery strategy involved selling three companies in the toy and leisure field to their existing management as buy-outs. But it was too late. Letraset was acquired by Esselte, the Swedish office products group. Wanting only the core graphic arts activities, Esselte promptly put up for sale the remaining unrelated business, Stanley Gibbons, the stamp dealing and philatelic publishing group. Stanley Gibbons was eventually bought by a consortium of its own internal management plus some external stamp trade specialists – an early BIMBO.

4. Assets for sale

In buying an existing business, whoever the seller or buyer, it is important to recognise what exactly is for sale. This will depend not only on the wishes of the parties to the negotiation, but also on the legal status of the business. Sole traders and partnerships have no legal existence separate from their owners; therefore only the assets of such businesses can be sold. Limited companies, on the other hand, are separate legal bodies; they have an existence distinct from their owners. Once a limited company has been given birth it can change parents; shares can be bought and sold. However, in order to avoid inheriting unwanted or unknown liabilities it is also common for only the assets of limited companies to be acquired.

The assets of a business for sale, whether it is a sole trader, partnership or limited company, will be the focus of attention of any prospective buyer. These assets can be reviewed under several headings not all of which will appear in the balance sheet.

4.1 Freehold property

The business may own the freehold of the property from which it trades. This is often the case where the position of the property is a key factor in its success in the market place. Hotels, restaurants, public houses, wine bars, squash clubs and other leisure facilities will all depend on their geographic location to attract customers. If location is such an important element in the marketing strategy of a small enterprise, then it is sensible to gain security of tenure over the property by buying the freehold, or at least securing a long lease, with first option to renew. Other business, less dependent on location, also purchase freehold property as a long term investment, preferring to have a mortgage on an appreciating asset rather than pay rent. Property owned by a small firm improves the look of its balance sheet, and may make it easier to raise finance at a later date.

When such a business changes hands, the property is sometimes the most valuable asset. The bricks and mortar and land of a small hotel, for example, will almost certainly be of more value than the beds, furniture, kitchen equipment and other fixtures which make it possible to trade as a hotel.

Purchasing a freehold property as part of buying a business requires all the care and caution of buying any other property. In addition to the usual checks on ownership, planning permissions, restrictive covenants, mortgages and other charges, any prospective purchaser will particularly want to assure themselves of the suitability of the premises to the business. Moving from owned premises can be a longwinded affair taking months, or even years in a slow property market.

4.2   Leasehold property

Property rented under a leasehold agreement can also be a valuable asset to a business. Most independent retailers, for instance, operate from leasehold premises. The situation of those premises sometimes commands a 'premium' when the business or even just the premises, change hands. Commercial estate agents, dealing in the transfer of such properties will quote a price for 'the benefit of the leasehold interest', which in times of a strong market can be tens of thousands of pounds even for a small property with a relatively short lease if it is well situated. Any purchaser looking at the history of the leasehold property market, will understand that it is, however, more volatile than the freehold market. High premiums paid for premises can disappear to nothing in times of recession, when even 'reverse premiums' become possible. In 1990/91 the slowness of trading in high streets caused increased closures of retail firms, such that existing tenants became prepared to pay prospective owners to take the liability of their lease from them. The owners of properties proving difficult to rent, may offer rent-free periods to new tenants as an inducement to take on a new lease.

By its very nature a lease is a declining asset, compared to a freehold which will probably be an increasing one over the long term. Its value as an asset in the purchase of an existing business will therefore depend on the desirability of the premises, and the state of the property market at the time of purchase. Thereafter the value is likely to fluctuate. Other factors which will influence the value of a lease include:

❐ *Transferability.* Most leases are not automatically transferable. Landlords will want to control the suitability of any incoming tenants. Although most leases state that permission for transfer should not be 'unreasonably withheld', restrictions on transferability will devalue a lease.

❐ *Term of the lease.* Most commercial properties are held on shorter terms than residential properties. Twenty-one year leases are quite common, so that a business changing hands within the term of a lease will sometimes have only a few years left to run on the lease. However, a landlord will find it quite difficult to eject a sitting tenant, and many leases provide for the existing tenant to have first refusal on a new lease. These rights can be overridden however, for example by a landlord wishing to redevelop, or use the property for their personal use.

❐ *Repairs and dilapidations.* Most commercial leases are on a 'full repairing' basis; that is the tenant is responsible to pay for the upkeep not only of the interior, but also the exterior of the buildings and any surrounding land. A 'dilapidations' clause in the lease will also usually make the tenant responsible for returning the premises to the landlord in a specified condition at the end of a lease. The cost of these ongoing, and end of lease, repairs and refurbishments can constitute a considerable burden on the tenant, especially if the premises are old, and near the end of the lease. Such factors will again influence the value of a lease. In some instances (for example where a high level of dilapidations are expected soon) the lease can have a negative value as its liabilities outweigh its usefulness.

❏ *Rent and provision for reviews:* Where the rent due on a property is considered to be below market levels, then this will add to the value of a lease. Most leases provide for rent reviews on a three or five year basis. The date of the next review, and provisions in the lease on how it is to be carried out, are also important. Many leases provide for 'upward only' reviews, with prescribed arbitration procedures in the event of a failure to agree on a new rent. Such clauses will limit the benefit of any sub-market rent situations.

4.3 Furniture, fixtures and fittings

Buying an existing business implies that any premises from which it operates will be fitted out and furnished. A freehold or leasehold property, when taken on from new, is usually a bare shell, adaptable to the use of the incoming tenant. The cost of these fittings, whether it be shopfittings in the case of retail premises, or partitioning and modifications for manufacturing or office premises, is usually considerable. When a business is to be sold these fixtures and fittings are an asset whose value depends on their extent, condition and appropriateness.

The type of the business will determine the nature of the furniture, as well as fixture and fittings. It is likely that those small enterprises where the customer receives a service on the premises will have a relatively high level of value in this kind of asset. For example, a restaurant will require tables, chairs, and other furnishings and decor appropriate to its target market, which can be expensive to purchase. The value of these to a prospective purchaser will depend on whether they wish to focus the business in the same way (on the same group of customers) or switch to a new theme and style which might involve a complete refit of the premises.

Those service industries where customers are not usually dealt with on the premises, and which require only a small area of office space, are likely to have a lower value in these assets. Manufacturing companies will vary, and sometimes will have spent the minimum possible on furnishings and fixtures. Higher technology firms often however need to invest in sophisticated fittings, for example to create a dust free 'clean room' for certain processes.

4.4 Machinery, equipment and vehicles

The machinery and equipment necessary to perform the functions of a business will invariably be acquired with it. The type and extent will obviously depend on the business and could include:

❏ *manufacturing plant* (e.g. printing presses, automated packaging machinery), workshop machinery and tools (e.g. lathes, compressors, saws and other small tools);

❏ *commercial equipment* (e.g. kitchen equipment, freezers, desk top publishing equipment);

❏ *office equipment* (e.g. computers, copiers, telephones and exchange);

❏ *vehicles* (e.g. delivery vans, fork lift trucks, company cars).

The alternatives for evaluating these types of assets all have flaws:

❏ *the written down book value* will tend to be somewhat arbitrary depending on the depreciation policies of the business which may have been optimistic or cautious;

❏ *the market value* could be a pessimistic figure as these assets tend to be worthless when sold off individually and not as part of an ongoing business;

- *the replacement value* is a useful measure to appreciate what it might cost to start up an equivalent new business, but it will not take account of the age and useful life of the equipment.

- *the original cost of the equipment* is again a useful measure to have in valuing these fixed assets but will not take account of inflation in new prices, nor devaluation of an asset through age.

Ownership is an important consideration in the acquisition of any assets under this heading. Frequently hire purchase, leasing or rental agreements cover such equipment, which determine who owns it and how much there is to be paid for the continued use of the equipment on an ongoing basis.

4.5   Stock and work in progress

The vendor of a small firm will usually wish to sell the stocks of the business to the new owner. This stock can be classified into three main types:

- *Raw materials stock* –the materials a business buys in from suppliers which it then uses or converts into something else. (For example, a picture framing business will have a stock of glass, mountboard, and uncut lengths of wood and metal mouldings for frames.)

- *Work in progress* –on the day of handover from one owner to the next, some jobs will be partly finished, representing work still in progress. (For example, the picture framer may have frames which are not fully finished sitting on the workbench.)

- *Finished stock* –there will be a stock of product which is ready for sale to the customer, but which remains unsold or unshipped and not invoiced on the day of transfer. (For example, the picture framer will have finished pictures awaiting collection by customers. There may also be unsold framed pictures displayed in a shop area, along with unsold ready-made frames and unframed prints.)

The valuation of such stock is often more straightforward than other assets with fewer negotiating points.

The basis of valuation for raw materials stock is normally the original cost paid for the stock. If there have been price rises subsequent to the purchase of the stock the seller may wish to negotiate a higher price based on its replacement value. The buyer, on the other hand, may wish to ask for a reduced price if they consider some materials damaged, obsolete or overstocked and perishable. Work in progress is more complicated to value, but is normally done on a similar basis to raw materials stock, with an additional amount to represent the value already added to the product.

Finished goods stock is normally valued at its selling price at the time, taking account of any overstocked positions which may decrease the value of some lines.

Stocks are normally valued on the day of transfer of the business, so that it does not represent a fixed sum of money during the negotiations. Stocks are taken over 'at valuation', and it is the basis only that is negotiated prior to handover.

Some types of business may need an independent valuer, either because of the complexity or time consuming nature of the valuation of stock. The 'stock' of a farm to be taken over will include crops already planted, requiring an expert to assess their value. A busy catering business, such as a restaurant or hotel, may have a large number of different items, some partly consumed, which require outside assistance to quantify on the day of the sale of the business.

4.6 Debtors

Those people or companies who still owe money to a business for sale, on account of goods received or services rendered, represent a real asset in the books of any business which extends credit to its customers. The problem is not so much negotiating a value for debtors; their worth is clearly the amount of money which they eventually pay. The issue is whether or not they will pay, and how long they will take. This uncertainty over the validity of debtors is often overcome by the vendor of the business either retaining ownership of the debtors, and collecting the money themselves after the sale of the business, or guaranteeing the amount that is collected from debtors by the new owner.

As with stocks, debtors will be valued on the date of transfer of the business to represent an up-to-date figure.

4.7 Intangible assets and goodwill

A distinction is drawn between the tangible and intangible assets of a business for sale. The assets discussed so far are tangible in that they can be physically identified and quantified. The intangible assets of a successful business will often be more important for they relate to why these physical assets have any meaning in the marketplace. The intangible assets are the sum of what makes a collection of property, fixtures fittings, plant equipment and stocks work together to add value to products and services, in a way that is meaningful to customers, and profitable to the business. Figure 9.2 summarises the principle tangible and intangible assets of a business. In practice the distinction is not clear-cut; there are many areas of overlap between the types of assets, some of which have been shown.

Figure 9.2: The tangible and intangible assets of a business for sale

Tangible assets	Examples of areas of overlap	Intangible assets
Property (Freehold/leasehold)	Location of premises	Goodwill
Furniture, fixtures and fittings	Signage and logo	Image and reputation
Plant, equipment and vehicles	Systems and training	Employees
Stock and work-in-progress	Research and development	Intellectual property
Debtors	Mailing list	Customers

Intangible assets, only have real value whilst a business continues to trade. Once it has ceased trading, they loose most of their meaning and their worth. An unsuccessful business will tend to have fewer intangible assets as these represent the necessary conditions for success. But even a 'failed' business will not have failed in every respect and can have some valuable intangibles, such as a skilled and loyal workforce. Even these assets soon evaporate once business has ceased, which is why the 1986 Insolvency

Act introduced the concept of 'administration' to allow struggling enterprises the opportunity to re-organise or be sold whilst trading continued.

The intangible assets of a business include:

❏ *Goodwill*

In many respects this is a summary of the value of the intangible assets of a business. It is an accountancy term which can find its way into the balance sheets of a business, but its accuracy will be determined by circumstance and not necessarily reality. If a business has recently been acquired, then the tangible assets, such as property, stocks and debtors, will have an identified value which will probably not equate to the purchase price of the business and therefore the total use of funds in buying it. In these circumstances, 'goodwill' is a balancing figure representing the difference between the book value of specific assets, less any liabilities, and the amount actually paid to acquire them. Immediately after the purchase of a business, the amount of goodwill in the balance sheet will therefore reflect the negotiated value placed on it. But any small business which has not been recently bought or sold will not have had its goodwill valued in this way, and so it will not necessarily be reflected in the accounts.

Goodwill also occurs as a balance sheet item in relation to property. For example an existing retail business moves premises, and pays a premium over and above the value of any fixtures and fittings, to acquire a good commercial site. This premium will be reflected in the balance sheet as 'goodwill' or 'intangible fixed assets'. This is a first area of overlap in distinguishing between tangible and intangible assets. The value of freehold or leasehold property is not just a function of its physical attributes and associated costs, but also its geographic location in relation to the market place. For some small firms this will be the key factor in determining its value. A hotel near an airport or busy seaside town will be worth far more than an identical building in an area that few people visit; if external factors cause a decrease or increase in the number of visitors, then the property value will be affected accordingly. In other circumstances, the value of a property for a small firm is less significant; a manufacturing company with a geographically spread customer base may be successfully located anywhere where there is available labour.

Goodwill is a general term which attempts to value the likelihood of success and therefore the future profitability of an enterprise. When a business is advertised for sale, 'goodwill' is often the word used to describe the vendor's valuation of this future profitability, which is added to any market value of the tangible assets.

❏ *Image and reputation*

The image and reputation developed by a small firm amongst its existing and potential customers will have a profound affect on its probability of success. An enterprise's image can be symbolised more tangibly in its logo style, the permanent signs used to advertise its presence and other fixtures and fittings which give the customer an impression of what the business is like.

For this reason a franchise network will emphasise the need to portray a consistent look in the premises of franchisees by using standard image and furnishings. But for all that, reputation is a fragile asset; the work of years to build an image of quality and reliability can be destroyed in minutes through shoddy or variable products or services.

The new owner of a small firm can become a negative influence on a well established reputation, or provide a well needed change to a more tarnished image.

❏ *Employees*

As well as the owner, the employees of a small business can be a crucial element in its success. Their skills, experience, and way of doing business will directly or indirectly impact on the satisfaction of customers. In part this will be truly intangible, relying on individual expertise and motivation. A more tangible aspect of this asset will be the systems which have been established to guide employees in the various operations of the business, in the use of plant and equipment and the training offered to them to improve the quality of their work, for example.

The seller of a small business has often acted as its manager, and in this sense, may have been the key employee. Their contribution to the business, and the impact of their removal from it, will be an issue that is particularly important in the sale of a small, owner-managed enterprise.

❏ *Intellectual property*

Innovation is a key ingredient in the success of a small enterprise. The results of innovation can become an important part of the intangible assets of a small business, classified as 'intellectual property'. Laws protect these innovations under a number of categories[4]:

Patents afford temporary protection to technological inventions.

Copyright covers literary, artistic and musical creations in the longer term.

Trademarks or brand names used in trading can be registered to protect them from infringement or passing off by other companies.

'Design right' extends protection to registered designs of products which have original features in their shape or configuration.

A small business may have created an asset from such properties in two distinct ways:

1. As the owner of a protected intellectual property.

   For example a small publisher usually copyrights any material which it publishes, and although this does not appear in the balance sheet, it has considerable value if the material can be reused.

2. As the contracted user of intellectual property.

   For example the same small publisher also has contracted rights to publish books by certain authors who themselves own the copyright to the work.

Contracts covering licensing arrangements for products or processes protected by patents, trademarks, or design rights can form an integral part of a small enterprises' activities. A new owner will therefore wish to ensure any necessary assignment of such contracts.

Past investment in research and development is a more tangible demonstration of the worth of a small firm's intellectual property, which otherwise might only be visible in its stocks of finished product, some of which may carry a brand name or be protected by patent.

❐ *Customers*

Customers are perhaps the most tangible of the intangible assets of a small firm; they can be observed and are often organised into a mailing list or appear in a schedule of debtors.

What is intangible is their loyalty and commitment to the business, especially if it changes ownership. The extent and longevity of the customer base will be important aspects in its valuation. A business which relies heavily on a small number of recently acquired customers has a very different asset to one with a large number of well established clients.

5. Liabilities to be avoided

Whilst wanting to retain and build on the existing assets of a small business, a prospective purchaser will wish to avoid any liabilities arising from the past activities of the firm.

The liabilities of a small business might include:

❐ trade creditors;

❐ bank and other borrowings;

❐ tax, VAT, PAYE and National Insurance contributions;

❐ lease and hire purchase agreements;

❐ guarantees or mortgages on assets.

If the business being sold is a sole trader or a partnership, then only the assets can be sold. The previous owner(s) will be left to pay off trade creditors, repay the bank or other borrowings and settle outstanding tax, VAT, PAYE and National Insurance liabilities.

If the shares of a limited company are being purchased, these liabilities belong to the company and will be transferred with it. The unknown quantity of some of these liabilities, especially those involving taxation where uncertainties can exist for several years after purchase, can be dealt with by:

❐ arranging for the vendor to give personal guarantees and warranties on the amount of future liabilities; or

❐ purchasing only the assets of a limited company in the same way as if it were a sole trader or partnership. These assets can be purchased by a shell company with no previous liabilities.

There are some liabilities which cannot be avoided, even when purchasing only the assets of a business, as some of these assets will be inseparable from certain liabilities. These include:

❐ *Obligations to employees.* When a business is sold as a going concern, even if only assets are transferred to a new owner, employment law regards terms of employment and the period of service of an employee as continuous. Employees' contracts specifying their terms and conditions of service, including any notice period required for termination of employment, remain valid.

An employee's period of service with the former owner, is added to that with the new owner, to form one continuous period of employment. This can increase the new owner's obligations for such benefits as redundancy payments and statutory maternity pay which require two years continuous service.

Where a business has contracted out of the state pension scheme and set up its own private pension fund, there is a continuous obligation on the employer to ensure that the fund can meet the minimum benefits of the state scheme.

❑ *Liabilities attached to specific assets:* An acquired asset may not be totally free of liabilities. Equipment can be subject to lease or hire purchase agreements; property or debtors may be part of a guarantee on loans. Such liabilities can be terminated by the seller before passing title to a new owner, or the buyer may agree to take on the liability with the asset.

6. Basis of valuation of an existing business

6.1 Assets or profits

There are two basic ways of valuing an existing business, which follow the nature of the assets to be valued:

1. *Market or other valuation of the assets to be acquired.* Tangible assets, tend to be valued this way. Property, fixtures and fittings, equipment, stocks and debtors, can all be physically, and separately, identified and valued.

2. *Multiple of annual profits.* Rather than evaluating individual assets, a buyer can consider the earning power of the business now and in the future. This is the usual way of assessing the value of intangible assets. If intangibles cannot be physically measured or counted, their effectiveness in the market place can and the usual yardstick for this is profit.

The basis chosen for valuation will depend on the mix of assets of the business, as shown in figure 9.3.

Figure 9.3: The basis of valuation for a small business

Asset mix	Tangible assets only	Mix of tangible and intangible assets	Intangible assets only
Valuation basis	Market value of assets	Assets at valuation plus goodwill valued as multiple of profits	Multiple of profits
Examples	Agricultural smallholding	Small manufacturing firm	Training consultancy
	Freehold retail premises	Leasehold restaurant	Estate agency

Some small businesses are 'asset-rich', and profitability becomes of secondary importance in a valuation. For example, an agricultural business – a small farm or small holding – is valued primarily on the going rate of an acre of land in the neighbourhood. Two farms of the same size would be of similar value, despite the fact that one may be farmed more efficiently, and therefore making more profits (or less losses), than the other. In the same way, freehold retail shops are priced according to the market value of other similar properties in the area. If the business trading from the shop is not profitable, this has little impact on the price, which will be determined more by the potential trade of the locality for any kind of retail operation.

At the other end of the spectrum are businesses with no real tangible assets at all. A consultancy operating from home can only be measured by its profitability, as its assets will be overwhelmingly intangible. Other small firms valued on this basis include many operating in service industries where they act as intermediaries between buyers and sellers, for example estate agents, import agencies and insurance brokers.

In practice, the majority of businesses for sale are valued on the basis of a mix of tangible and intangible assets. Even service industries accumulate fixed assets if they survive in business for long enough – fixtures, fittings and equipment for the office and cars for sales people, for example. Many businesses depend on tangible assets for their processes, and build intangible assets through the goodwill of a customer base. Most small manufacturing firms would come into this category. Other service-oriented enterprises also have valuable fixed assets in equipment and fittings, as well as intangible goodwill. For example, a restaurant will need considerable investment in its kitchen and decor, whilst its profitability will determine its full value as an ongoing business.

6.2   Multiple of profits

If intangible assets are to be judged by profitability, how much profit should be taken into account? This is normally expressed as a multiple of annual profits; for example a business making £30,000 per annum might be judged to have goodwill valued at £90,000 or three times annual profits. The size of the multiplier is a key negotiating point, which will consider the following factors:

☐ *'Quality of earnings'*. Where a small firm has a history of several profitable years in business (usually a minimum of three years) and can demonstrate clearly that it has a sound, continuing level of profitability through a well spread customer base, then it can be said to have good "quality earnings". It will be worth a higher multiple of profits than, say, a business which has just made an annual profit of a similar amount, but for the first time and dependent on one large order. This is really a measure of risk in the likelihood of profits continuing at the current level in the future. When the risk that profits will fall is low , a potential buyer will be more easily persuaded to pay for more years of those profits.

☐ *Interest rates*. Bank interest rates will indicate the maximum multiplier that can be paid for a business, and still be worthwhile. For example, if interest rates are 10% and a small firm is for sale at £100,000 ,representing a multiple of 10 on annual profits of £10,000 then interest payable on a loan to buy the business will cancel out the annual profits. Even a cash buyer who has no need to borrow to make the purchase will do as well with less risk by putting their money on deposit at a bank.

If a limited company uses its own shares to buy another business (i.e. the vendor receives shares in the purchasing company rather than cash), then higher multiples are possible because money interest rates are less relevant.

But with interest rates in the 12.5% range, multiples of between 2.5 to 5 times profits are common in small firm transactions.

❏ *Rate of inflation.* Higher rates of inflation can operate in the same way as higher interest rates; the return or profits from an investment have to keep pace with inflation just to maintain its value. If £100,000 is paid for a business in times when inflation is running very high, at say 20%, then profits will have to be £20,000 p.a. just to maintain the value of the original investment. This fixes a maximum profits multiplier of 5 times earnings if the money invested is not to lose its value.

6.3   Gearing

A buyer of a small business commonly uses a mix of borrowed and personal funds. The relationship between the buyers own money and borrowed funds, or gearing, is an important influence on the risks and rewards of a purchase and therefore the price worth paying.

Higher gearing enables a buyer to purchase more for each pound of his own money invested. If the business is successful, this increases the reward. But it also increases the risk; if the profits of the business fall, the effect on the buyer's personal stake is magnified.

For example, figure 9.4 outlines two possible scenarios for a buyer with £50,000 of his own money to invest.

In Purchase A, the buyer raises a further £50,000 to buy a business for £100,000 representing 4 x profits. After interest, the buyer is left with profits of £19,000, a rate of return on his own money invested of 38%.

In Purchase B, the buyer invests the same £50,000 from personal funds, but this time becomes more highly geared by raising a further £150,000 to buy a business for £200,000, again at a multiple of 4 times annual profits of £50,000. This time the buyer is left with £32,000 profit after interest, a rate of return of 64% on the same personal investment of £50,000.

If business goes well, then the deal gets even better under Purchase B. The first scenario of profits rising by 25% increases the return on investment, and the £50,000 invested is now worth £98,000, compared to £74,000 under Purchase A (assuming the business is still valued at 4 x profits).

If business goes badly, the deal is worse under Purchase B, and can become disastrous sooner than under Purchase A. A profit fall of 25% will still give Purchase B higher profits at £20,000 compared to £13,000 under Purchase A, but a valuation of the business on the same basis of 4 x profits shows that the original investment of £50,000 has virtually all been lost under Purchase B, and only half lost under Purchase A.

Under Purchase B a profit fall of 50% will not only lose the buyer his original stake, but also put him into debt by £50,000 if the business was sold. Under Purchase A, the buyer loses his personal investment but no more.

Although higher gearing improves the rewards of success, it also increases the risks in failure. A cautious buyer will want to be very convinced about the quality of earnings before accepting a high gearing in order to make a purchase.

Figure 9.4: The effects of gearing on a small business purchase

	Purchase A	Purchase B
Purchase price (4 x profits)	100	200
Profit (before interest, depreciation and tax)	25	50
Personal capital	50	50
Borrowings	50	150
Interest @ 12%	6	18
Profit after interest	19	32
1st Scenario: Profits rise by 25%		
Profits	31	62
Profits after interest	25	44
Value of business (4 x profits)	124	248
Personal equity after borrowings repaid	74	98
2nd Scenario: Profits fall by 25%		
Profits	19	38
Profits after interest	13	20
Value of business (4 x profits)	76	152
Personal equity after borrowings repaid	26	2
3rd Scenario: Profits fall by 50%		
Profits	13	25
Profits after interest	7	7
Value of business (4 x profits)	52	100
Personal equity after borrowings	2	(50)

In the mid to late 1980s, the easier availability of loans to buy businesses helped increase the risks involved, not only by tempting purchasers to accept higher gearing, but also by increasing the price of buying a business at a time of relatively low interest rates and a booming economy.

Management buy-outs were particularly affected. By the late 1980s, the success of earlier buyouts made the route more popular and more expensive for buyers. Higher prices meant higher gearing; according to Peat Marwick, McLintock, gearing for large MBOs went from 1:2 (borrowings to equity) in 1981 to 5:1 by 1989.

The recession in the early 1990s has particularly hit those small businesses which were purchased with high gearing, through high interest rates and lower profits. Failures have made banks more cautious and gearing ratios are back to levels more common in the early 1980s.

7. Taxation aspects of a small business purchase

Taxation aspects are important in buying an existing business, not only in the immediate impact they may have on the total costs of purchase, but also the ongoing level of profitability thereafter.

Once a purchase price has been agreed, the next negotiating point is often the allocation of the price to the individual assets purchased. The interests of a buyer and a seller in terms of tax minimisation may not coincide.

7.1 The buyer

When assets are purchased, they qualify for a first year and annual writing down allowance which are deducted from the owner's tax bill. The amount of these allowances varies according to the asset purchased:

❑ *Property:* The cost of acquiring a freehold or leasehold property can be written off over the remaining life of the building, or term of the lease.

❑ *Machinery and equipment:* There is an annual writing down allowance of 4% on both new and second hand equipment. In an Enterprise Zone, an initial 100% allowance may be claimable.

❑ *Stock:* Stock used in the course of trading represents a cost against sales, but it is possible to make a paper profit on the value of stocks held through inflation or because of a low valuation of stocks purchased with the business. Ongoing tax relief may be obtainable on part of this profit.

❑ *Debtors:* If debtors are acquired in a purchase which subsequently are not paid through liquidation, then these bad debts can be written off against profits, and any VAT paid can be reclaimed.

❑ *Goodwill:* From 1st April 1986, new provisions were introduced in the UK to allow payments for goodwill, know-how or patent rights to be written down at 25% per annum on the reducing balance over 6 years.

These allowances apply for sole traders, partnerships and limited companies. Therefore, careful consideration is required in allocating a purchase price to the various assets acquired as future tax liabilities will be affected. A prudent buyer will seek the advice of an accountant in this complicated area.

7.2 The seller

The seller will also wish to carefully consider the taxation implications of a sale. Capital gains tax may be a major concern. Capital gains for both individuals and companies are now taxed as income in the year in which they are made. There is an individual exemption of £5800 (1992/3) in any one tax year, and gains are reduced to reflect changes in the retail price index.

'Roll-over' relief can also apply. If one business is sold, and another purchased within three years, payment of tax is deferred until the new business is finally sold.

If a business is sold because of retirement, then relief may be particularly beneficial. If the seller is 55 years old or over, and has owned the business for more than 10 years, relief of £150,000 plus 50% of the balance up to £600,000 may be claimed (1992/3).

7.3 Tax losses

If a limited company has made trading losses, which have not all been cancelled out by subsequent profits, then those losses remain with the company, and are available for use by a new owner of the shares. Tax losses can thus represent an asset which make it more advantageous to purchase the shares of a limited company rather than just its assets. However if the nature of the trade carried on by the company is significantly altered, the relief against future tax given by past losses may be denied. It is not possible to purchase a company solely for its tax loses, and carry on business in a totally new direction.

8. The advantages and disadvantages of buying an existing business

How does buying an existing business, or part of it, either as an outsider, or an existing manager, compare to other routes to market entry as a small enterprise? See figure 9.5 for a summary.

Figure 9.5: a summary of the possible advantages and disadvantages of buying an existing business

Possible advantages	Potential disadvantages
❑ overcomes barriers to market entry	❑ possibility of liabilities as well as assets
❑ buying immediate turnover and income	❑ uncertainty over records
❑ existing assets of property, equipment and staff in place	❑ risk in intangible assets
❑ goodwill with existing customers already built up	❑ historical problems in the business
❑ existing track record	❑ not "all my own work"
❑ 'insider' knowledge (especially in MBOs)	

8.1 Possible advantages

❑ *Overcomes barriers to market entry.* Where there are significant barriers to market entry for a small business entrant, buying an existing enterprise may be the most realistic alternative. For example, the planning permission, and other legal permits required for restaurants, hotels, nightclubs, wine bars and public houses make market entry through acquisition the most common route.

❑ *Buying immediate turnover and income.* This could be important, especially when the buyer has no other sources of income.

❑ *Buying market share.* One of the key ingredients for a successful small business is to build a high share of a specific market. If existing businesses control a significant percentage of the desired market then it may be advantageous to buy into them, rather than compete.

❏ *Existing assets of property, equipment and staff.* The costs and time required to put these into place as a start-up can be considerable, and it may be more appropriate to focus resources and energy on the market place through an existing operation.

❏ *Goodwill with existing customers.* An existing customer base is evidence of the viability of a business concept, and therefore takes some of the risk out of small business ownership. It can also provide a good platform for future growth.

❏ *Existing track record.* The ability to look over the past performance of a company not only provides comfort to a potential buyer, but also to financial supporters such as banks. A business showing evidence of a good track record over a number of years is easier to fund than one with no history at all.

❏ *'Insider' knowledge.* This advantage only usually applies to situations where the existing management is involved in the purchase. But it may also be in the best interest of existing management to be as open as possible with prospective new owners, rather than suffer the consequences of concealment at a later date.

8.2 Possible disadvantages

❏ *Buying possible liabilities with assets.* Even if only assets are purchased, liabilities can still be attached to them, for example employee liabilities. If shares in a company are bought, then liabilities will certainly exist. Liabilities can form part of an acceptable risk when they are known; the greatest problem is the possibility of liabilities, unrecognised at the time of purchase, emerging at a later date.

❏ *Uncertainty over records.* A business for sale will obviously be presented in the best possible light. Sole traders, and partnerships are not required to have their accounts audited, so some information may be withheld. The onus is on the buyer to ask the right questions, not on the seller to provide all the information.

❏ *Risk in intangible assets.* The goodwill inherent in an existing business can disappear very rapidly if a new owner makes inappropriate changes. A previous owner-manager may represent a substantial part of the goodwill, which goes with them when they leave.

❏ *Historical problems in the business.* An existing business may have some 'negative goodwill' which is not immediately apparent. There may be a history of poor relationships with suppliers or staff, for example, which outlives the departure of the owner.

❏ *Not "all my own work".* Some of the satisfaction an entrepreneur gains from a new business start up derives from taking a business idea from conception to successful implementation. Buying an existing business can diminish the sense of achievement, and therefore the motivation to make it succeed.

8.3 Motives for sale

The key question to ask in buying an existing business is 'why is it for sale?' A buyer needs to establish acceptable reasons why a business should be sold. If they can not, there may be hidden negative factors which may apply equally negatively to the buyer.

9. References and further reading

9.1 References and further information

1. For a more detailed account of bankruptcy and liquidation see Clayton, P, *Law for the Small Business,* Kogan Page, 1991, Chapter 14.

2. As reported in *The Daily Telegraph,* 14 September 1991, page 24. The article "Private woes in the public house" summarised the business difficulties of those involved in running their own pub.

3. These, and other interesting cases, are reported in 'The Management Buy-Out Report' in *Management Week,* Management Week Publishing Ltd., 30th October 1991.

4. A useful review of patent and trade mark law is in Williams, S, *Small Business Guide,* Penguin, 1991 Chapter 12 'Beating the Pirates'.

9.2 Recommended further reading

Farrell, P, *How to Buy a Business,* Kogan Page, 1986.

Clayton, P, *Law for the Small Business,* Kogan Page, 1991. Chapter 5 'Premises', Chapter 11, 'Intellectual Property: Patents, Copyrights and Trademarks', Chapter 14 'Bankruptcy and Liquidation'.

The New Small Business Guide, BBC Books, 1989, Section 3, 'New Products or Businesses', and Section 7, 'Protecting Your Ideas'.

Williams, S, *Small Business Guide,* Penguin, 1991 Chapter 9, 'Off the Peg'.

Unit 10: Forms of small business organisation

This unit contains information about the basic legal forms a small business can take: limited company; sole trader; partnership; and co-operative. The advantages and disadvantages of each format are identified.

Contents

1. Choice of business organisation

A small business can take on four basic legal forms. The choice depends on the circumstances and objectives of the small enterprise. The first choice is between 'going it alone' or working in co-ownership with others. Figure 10.1 summarises the basic alternatives. A limited company can be owned by one or several persons. If this is not the desired form, then single ownership has to be achieved as a sole trader and multiple ownership as a partnership or co-operative.

Figure 10.1 Forms of small business according to ownership

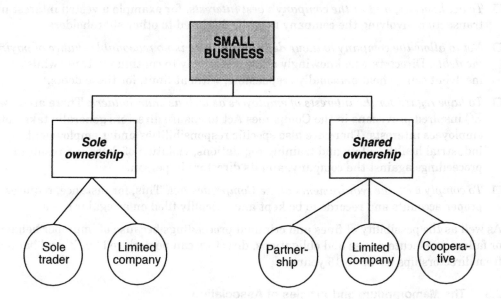

2. Limited company

A limited company, incorporated under the Companies Act, is a legal body, which has a separate identity to that of its owners. It can be bought and sold as a whole, or in part, go bankrupt without its owners suffering the same fate, have legal documents signed on its behalf by a director, and employ staff. Putting business activities into a company literally gives them life as a separate legal entity. This is a key difference to a sole trader or partnership, where the owner(s) are inextricably linked to the business and not separable from it.

A company needs shareholders (the owners) and directors (those empowered to act on the company's behalf by the shareholders). In small companies, shareholders and directors are usually the same people, but not necessarily so. Some investors in a business do not become directors; indeed investments made under the Business Expansion Scheme specifically prohibited management involvement in the enterprise (see Information Bank, Unit 6, 4.2 'UK Government Policy', for more details of the BES).

2.1   Shareholders' responsibilities

The shareholders' responsibility for the company's debt is limited to the paid-up value of their shares. Once they are paid for, the company cannot call on shareholders for more funds (unless by way of a voluntary subscription for more shares), even if it is insolvent.

2.2   Directors' responsibilities

The responsibilities of a director extend beyond that of a shareholder. Although directors can separate their own personal assets from those of the business, this is dependent on responsible business behaviour. Where directors have been deemed to have behaved irresponsibly, they can be held personally responsible for the company's debts. In other words, there are limits to limited liability of directors.

Directors duties and responsibilities include:

☐ *To act honestly, and in the company's best interests:* for example a vested interest in a transaction involving the company must be disclosed to other shareholders.

☐ *Not to allow the company to incur debts when there is no reasonable chance of paying the debts.* Directors who knowingly allow a company to continue to trade whilst insolvent can be held personally responsible, without limit, for those debts.

☐ *To have regard for the interests of employees as well as shareholders.* There are new EC inspired provisions in the Companies Act to ensure directors generally take note of employees interests. There are also specific responsibilities under employment, industrial health, safety and training regulations; violation of these can result in proceedings against the company, and its directors in person.

☐ *To comply with the requirements of the Companies Act.* This, for instance, requires proper accounts and records to be kept and officially filed on a regular basis.

As well as the possibility of fines and criminal proceedings because of improper behaviour or failure to execute duties and obligations, directors can be declared 'unfit' and banned from directorships for up to 15 years.

2.3   The Memorandum and Articles of Association

Although commonly referred to as one, these are in fact two key legal documents, which set out the constitution and management arrangements of the company.

Memorandum Of Association

This is the company's charter which includes:

☐ *The name of the company:* The name of a limited company has to be approved by the Registrar of Companies. It cannot be 'offensive', nor likely to be confused with an existing company. To limit its liabilities, 'limited' must be the last word of the name of a company trading for profit.

☐ *Location of the registered office:* The location of the registered office effectively establishes under which laws a company trades, and where it pays its taxes. It is the address to which official and legal notices will be sent. It need not be the company's principle place of business and for small firms it is frequently the address of the company's solicitors or accountants.

☐ *The objects of the company:* The objectives for which a company has been formed, its powers and area of business, are defined in the objects clause of the Memorandum.

These are normally kept very general (as in "general commercial activities") to avoid activities and transactions being declared 'ultra vires' (outside of the powers of the company), which may then make them the personal liability of the directors or management. Recent legislation has abolished the 'ultra vires' rules for external transactions, so that third parties can now insist a company meet the obligations to which a director or senior manager have committed the company, even if they fall strictly outside of the company's objects. 'Ultra-vires' still holds for internal transactions, however – between directors and shareholders, for example.

❏ *The limited liability of the shareholders:* This clause in the Memorandum limits the liability of shareholders to the value of their shares.

❏ *The share capital and structure:* The amount of authorised capital, and how it is divided into shares, is specified. Shares are normally made up of relatively small denominations, e.g. £1, to retain flexibility in transfer and issuing of new shares.

The amount of capital subscribed for by shareholders, that is shares issued and paid for, is the issued share capital of a company.

Sometimes not all the authorised capital is subscribed for, some shares being authorised but not issued. Shareholders are still however liable for this amount but no more, in the event of liquidation.

❏ *The names of signatories:* At incorporation, there must be two signatories who agree to take out at least one share each. When formed, a company has to have two shareholders, at least one of whom is a director; a company secretary (who may or may not be a shareholder) is also appointed. Share holdings can later change so that one person can own all the shares.

Articles of association

The Articles contain detailed information about the internal management of the company. They deal with the appointment of directors, their powers and fees, and procedures for meetings. They deal with the relationships between the company and shareholders and between individual shareholders. For example, the Articles usually provide for the issue of new shares to be offered first to existing shareholders, in proportion to their existing holding, so that they can protect their percentage stake in the company.

Likewise it is common in small companies for shareholders to give first refusal rights to the other shareholders should they wish to sell any equity.

2.4   Formation of a limited company

Forming a new limited company can take some time. Suitable Memorandum and Articles of Association and other documents must be lodged with the Registrar of Companies, and a Certificate of Incorporation obtained.

It is possible to buy a ready-made company 'off-the-shelf'. This is usually a shell company which has not traded, but is incorporated and, with a suitable name change, can be used by a new small firm.

2.5 Tax, National Insurance and pensions

As a company is a separate legal body, owner-directors are employed by it, and are therefore employees for tax, national insurance and pension purposes. As a corporate body, the company is the employer and taxable on its profits.

This means that:

❑ *PAYE* is operated even for owner-director salaries. As tax is deducted at source, this has cash flow disadvantages over the self-employed status of a sole trader or partner who pay tax annually on a retrospective basis. Income Tax is paid at normal rates.

❑ *National insurance contributions* are paid by directors as employees, and by the company as the employer, which makes them more expensive than for self-employed owners, but entitles the director-employee to the full range of benefits.

❑ *Corporation tax* is paid by the company on profits it makes, after deducting all expenses including directors salaries. For small businesses this will usually be at the lower rate (25% on profits up to £250,000 in 1992/93) which can be an advantage over self-employed owners making good profits, which will be taxed as income at the higher rates.

   Losses can be carried forward in a company to be offset against future profits or capital gains. This can represent an asset if the company is sold.

❑ *Pensions* can be contributed to by both employee-directors and the company. There is no limit to the contributions which a company can make free of tax to a pension scheme on behalf of employees. Director-employees can also contribute up to 15% of their salary to a pension fund, with relief at their highest rate of income tax. Self-employed sole traders and partners will be more restricted, as they have no company to make contributions on their behalf.

❑ *Capital gains* made by a company form part of its profits, and are therefore liable to corporation tax with no relief, unlike a self-employed owner who can use personal relief to offset the tax due.

The principle advantages and disadvantages for a small business to trade as a limited company are shown in figure 10.2.

Figure 10.2: Limited company – summary of advantages and disadvantages

A limited company has an existence separate from its owners. As a corporate body, it has independent legal and tax status.

Advantages

☐ Limited liability for shareholders.

☐ Some formalised structures (e.g. director's meetings) make management clearer.

☐ Income tax paid only on salaries drawn; higher rates of personal tax can be avoided when profits are retained.

☐ No limit to contributions made to a pension scheme with tax relief.

☐ Finance easier to raise externally – especially from equity.

☐ Easier to widen ownership base.

☐ Existence not threatened by death or personal bankruptcy of one of owners.

☐ Possibly higher perceived status.

Disadvantages

☐ More time consuming and expensive to set up.

☐ Complicated and time consuming to conform to requirements of Companies Act.

☐ Loss of confidentiality as some records are publicly filed.

☐ Audit and accounting costs higher.

☐ "Double" tax when company pays corporation tax on profits and capital gains, and shareholders are personally taxed on dividends.

☐ Higher national insurance contributions.

☐ As employees, directors have worse cash flow of taxes under PAYE than self-employed.

☐ Limited liability reduced in early days as creditors seek personal guarantees from directors.

☐ Directors can be held personally liable if company trades while insolvent.

3. Sole trader

A sole trader is unlike a limited company in that the owner is the business; there is no legal separation between the assets and liabilities of the business and the assets and liabilities of the individual who owns it.

This makes for simpler and more informal arrangements for operating a business. It can also increase the risk for an owner, whose total possessions are now on the line with his or her business at all times.

The sole trader can simply choose a business name, and start trading. If they use a name different from their own, they will have to put their own name on their headed paper however.

3.1 Investment

A sole trader can invest in or draw funds from the business as they think fit. However additional resources can only be raised by loans; it is not possible to invite outside equity participation.

3.2 Tax, national insurance and pensions:

As the business will not have any separate status from the owner, the sole trader will be self-employed, and not an employee. This has implications for tax and pension provisions.

Tax is payable on any profits of the business, which are treated as if it were the income of the owner, whether they receive it or not. A sole trader cannot choose to reinvest profits for income tax purposes. If profits are made, the sole trader is taxed as if they were taken as income, whether they were drawn or not.

As profits increase so tax can be payable at higher rates (40% for 1992/3). Being self-employed the sole trader will not pay tax as income is earned, but on a retrospective basis. On the normal preceding year basis tax can be payable up to 20 months after profits are made.

Losses can be offset against not only future profits of the same business, but also against other income of the owner, as they are inseparable from the business. If the owner previously paid taxes under PAYE, then trading losses in the early years can be used to claw back some of these taxes paid before self employment.

National Insurance contributions for self employed are payable as

1. a weekly flat rate of £5.35 for 1992/93 (Class II contributions); and

2. a percentage of profits (Class IV contributions: 6.3% of net profits in 1992/3). Although this usually amounts to less than the total amount payable by company director-employees the benefits are also less: there is no unemployment benefit, widow's benefit, invalidity pension, or the earnings-related portion of the retirement pension.

Pension payments are also more restricted as a self-employed person. Tax relief for pension payments is allowable on 17.5% of 'net relevant earnings' (which for most purposes equates to taxable profits), or higher levels for those over 35 years old rising to 40% for those over 61. This compares to the unlimited, tax deductible payments which a company can make on behalf of its directors.

Capital gains can however be more favourably treated, as the sole trader's personal allowance for tax free capital gains (£5,800 in 1992/93) is available in the event that the business makes a capital profit. A company does not have such allowances.

3.3 Records

The Inland Revenue and Customs and Excise authorities require certain financial records to be kept for taxation purposes. Apart from that, the accounting requirements of the business can be determined by internal management needs. An independent audit is not a legal requirement. Records are private, and need not be revealed to anyone other than the Inland Revenue.

3.4 Setting up as a sole trader

This is very straightforward, requiring only notifications to the local tax and DHSS office of self-employment status. VAT registration is a further possible step, either on a voluntary basis, or because the business trades at above the minimum registration level (£36,600 from March 1992.)

The principle advantages and disadvantages for a small business to operate as a sole trader are set out in figure 10.3.

Figure 10.3: Sole trader – Summary of advantages and disadvantages

The individual and the business are the same. There are no legal or tax distinctions.

Advantages

❏ Straightforward and easy to set up – minimal legal requirements and costs.

❏ Make all the decisions and keep all the profits.

❏ No audit of accounts required legally.

❏ No public disclosures of records (unless registered for VAT).

❏ Business losses can be offset against other income, including clawback of past PAYE.

❏ Self-employment defers income tax, and reduces national insurance contributions.

Disadvantages

❏ Unlimited liability, including personal assets outside of the business.

❏ No additional funds possible from equity investment by others.

❏ Transfer of ownership less flexible – can only sell the assets of the business.

❏ Possible status problems perceived by third parties.

❏ All profits taxed as personal income whether retained in business or taken out.

❏ Self-employed national insurance entitlements have less benefits.

❏ Tax relief on pension contributions restricted.

4. Partnership

Where two or more people set up in business intending to share the profits, then the law deems they are in partnership.

Regulations under the Partnership Act of 1890 provide a framework which applies unless partners specifically agree to the contrary. Some of these provisions assume that:

❏ all partners have an equal vote in how the business should be run;

❏ all partners have invested equally in the business;

❏ all partners have an equal share of profits and losses;

❏ partners will not receive a salary;

❏ partners will not receive interest on their capital invested.

Clearly these assumptions will not be the intentions of every partnership. But unless there is an agreement by the partners to the contrary, the law will assume this to be the case in the event of a dispute.

Partnerships are restricted to 20 partners, except in certain professions, such as law and accountancy.

A partnership is like a sole trader in that it is not a legal entity. It therefore carries unlimited liability. Unlike the sole trader, partners do however have to look beyond just their own liabilities. Each partner is "jointly and severally" responsible with other partners for all the obligations and debts of the partnership – even where they exist directly as a result of another partner's actions. If one partner fails to meet their share of the liabilities, creditors can look to the rest of the partnership to make good the deficit.

The formalities to establish a partnership follow those of the sole trader; they are simple and legally only require the names of partners on any letterhead.

If one partner dies, retires, or becomes bankrupt, the partnership is automatically dissolved, whether or not this is in the best interests of the other partners, unless a separate written agreement is made to the contrary.

4.1 The Partnership Agreement

To regulate matters between the partners (and prevent dissolution as described above), a Partnership Agreement is strongly advised. This is not a legal requirement however; partnerships are legally, and in practice, a matter of trust between the partners. A Partnership Agreement can define some broad areas of responsibility and authority such as:

❏ details of the partners, and the name and nature of the business they carry on;

❏ duration of the partnership – date of commencement and any anticipated termination date;

❏ capital contributed by the partners, and any agreement on interest payable to partners for money introduced;

❏ calculation and division of profits: this needs to be specified particularly where partners contribute unequally, as the 1890 Act assumes they have equal rights to profits;

❏ management and control of the business: this is most needed where partners put in unequal amounts of time in the partnership. Where there is a sleeping partner, management partners may need to guard against future interference, and provide for their own salaries before profits are divided;

❏ dissolution: what happens on retirement, death or withdrawal of a partner has to be spelt out to prevent automatic dissolution of the partnership.

4.2 Partners' responsibilities

A partner in a business is expected by law to behave fairly and in good faith. In practice, partners will control each other to a greater or lesser extent. As all partners act for the partnership, and therefore incur liabilities on behalf of other partners, the choice of partner is an extremely important decision. It can be a decision which has effects even beyond the life of a partner, as their estate can still be responsible for partnership liabilities, unless the partner has taken public leave of the partnership by notifying their retirement to business contacts and advertising it in the 'Business Gazette'.

4.3   Tax, National Insurance and pension

As there is no corporate body to employ them, partners are self-employed. This confers the same advantages and disadvantages as to the sole trader of delayed income tax payments, reduced national insurance contribution (but with the penalty of reduced entitlements from NIC) and smaller tax-free pension contribution possibilities. Losses in the partnership can also be used to offset taxes due on other, non-partnership income.

The principle advantages and disadvantages of operating as a partnership are shown in Figure 10.4.

Figure 10.4: Partnerships – Summary of advantages and disadvantages

Two or more persons undertaking a business activity together are in partnership. There is no separate legal entity, and partners are personally responsible for all liabilities of the partnership.

Advantages

- ❏ Easy to set up.
- ❏ Access to the experience of other partners.
- ❏ No audit of accounts legally required.
- ❏ Confidentiality is maintained, as no public access to accounts.
- ❏ Losses from the business can be offset against other income.
- ❏ Can be relatively easily transferred to a limited company at a later stage.
- ❏ Benefits of self-employment for income tax and National Insurance purposes.

Disadvantages

- ❏ Partners are liable for debts, "jointly and severally".
- ❏ Partners estate can still be liable for their debts after death.
- ❏ Death, bankruptcy or retirement dissolves partnership, unless specific continuation provisions in agreement.
- ❏ Less flexibility in transferring ownership than limited company.
- ❏ High degree of mutual trust required.
- ❏ Profits taxed as income, whether drawn or not.
- ❏ Self-employed national insurance entitlements have less benefits.
- ❏ Tax relief on pension contributions restricted.

5. Choosing the appropriate business form: Sole trader vs. Partnership vs. Limited company

The choice of business identity is usually between these three forms, as co-operatives and other forms are much less common. Their appropriateness depends on the circumstances of the business and the objectives of its owners.

These can be evaluated on a number of categories which are shown in figure 10.5.

Figure 10.5: Checklist for choosing the appropriate form

Categories	Company	Sole trader	Partnership
Liabilities	Liability limited, but personal guarantees and directors' obligations can reduce limitations.	All assets liable including those not involved in the business.	Liability extends to business debts of other partners.
Records & accounts	Legal accounting and audit requirements. Accounts filed open to inspection.	No strict accounting or audit requirements. Records not available for public inspection.	
Setting up	Formalities of registration, although can buy 'off-the-peg'.	No formalities except registering as self-employed.	As for sole trader, except partnership agreement strongly advised to prevent problems, especially of dissolution.
Raising money	Wide choice, including further equity investments.	Options limited to overdraft or loan.	Overdraft, loans or new partners with money.
Selling up	Flexible, as can sell part or all of shares.	Can only sell assets – difficult if only selling part of the business.	
Status	Possibly higher perceived status.	Possibly lower perceived status.	
Tax, National Insurance & pensions	Employee status – PAYE, high National Insurance, but full benefits. Unlimited company contributions to pension. Corporation tax on company profits. Losses retained in company.	Self-employed status: all profits , drawn or not are taxable as income, possibly at higher rates. National Insurance cheaper but less benefits. Tax deductible pension contributions restricted. Losses can be offset against tax on other income.	

The decision of business form may be dictated by one category only. If the nature of the business is such that uninsurable liabilities are possible on a large scale, then a limited company is the only choice. For this reason, many small firms manufacturing components for other companies wish to maintain limited liability. Law suits instigated by end-users over a product deficiency could involve a sub-contractor not involved in the final sale. When products are exported, especially to the USA, this can increase the possibility of legal problems, not within the control of the subcontractor.

At the other extreme, where a small business is offering an individual service which carries no real liabilities, or is covered by full indemnity insurance, then the advantages of the lack of formality in sole trader status will probably be the obvious route. Most tradesmen operate as self-employed sole traders or partners for this reason.

The developing business may wish to change status because of an altered environment. Growth can make it desirable to introduce the more formal structures and money raising possibilities of a limited company.

6. Co-operatives

A co-operative is an enterprise owned and controlled by all the people working for it. It is an alternative form of business structure, where the emphasis is on the work environment and not the accumulation of individual wealth. Established in the eighteenth century, they were almost extinct until a revival began in the 1970s that has continued ever since.

6.1 Legal form

Co-operatives are usually limited companies, co-operative societies or, more rarely, partnerships. Governed by the Industrial and Provident Societies Acts 1965–75, registration as a co-operative requires the following principles to be adopted:

❏ The objectives, management and use of assets are controlled by the members.

❏ Membership is not restricted; it must be open to anyone who fulfils the qualifications laid down.

❏ Each member of the co-operative has an equal vote in how it is to be run.

❏ Surpluses, or profits, are shared between the members, pro-rata to their participation.

❏ Share capital remains at its original value. Members benefit from their participation, not as investors; co-operatives are not about making capital gains.

❏ Interest on loans, or share capital, is limited, even if profits permit higher payments.

A registered co-operative is a separate legal body, with limited liability for its members, and annual accounts must be filed. A minimum of seven members are required to register, but they don't all need to work full time. Registration is not mandatory however, and where co-operatives do not register, they are regarded in law as partnerships with unlimited liability.

6.2 Background

In the 18th and 19th centuries working people formed many self-help groups to cope with poverty and hardship. Co-operatives were part of this movement, and were established either from above, by those seeking to spread a philosophy of co-operation, or at the grass roots by working people themselves in an effort to improve their conditions.

Today the best known co-operative is the supermarket chain. But there is another variety – the worker co-operative. The number of these peaked at around 1000 in the early 1900s and then declined to a very small number by the 1960s. They have since enjoyed a revival, promoted by the Co-operative Development Agency set up by the government in 1978 to give advice to anyone wishing to form a co-operative. Estimates suggest there were over 1500 by the late 1980s, with some 300 or so being established annually. The reasons for the growth lies in the motives for establishing the various types of co-operative.

6.3   Types of co-operative

Like other small businesses, co-operatives do not constitute a uniform group. Research into the characteristics and objectives of co-operatives suggests that there are four main types[1]:

1. *'Endowed' co-operatives:* Some owners transfer their business to their employees, either as a philanthropic gesture or an attempt to keep the firm going, for example, if the owner has no heir. Shares are usually held in trust by the employees.

   This is a relatively uncommon form, the best known example of which is the chemical manufacturer, Scott-Bader Commonwealth.

2. *'Defensive' co-operatives:* If an enterprise is threatened with closure, employees have formed co-operatives in a desperate attempt to keep their company alive and their jobs with it.

   Co-operatives of this type have been small in number, but have often commanded considerable publicity.

   As Industry Minister in the 1970s, Tony Benn encouraged some of the better known examples, such as Triumph Meridien and the Scottish Daily News.

3. *'Job-creation' co-operatives:* In times of high unemployment, increasing numbers of co-operatives have been set up to create new jobs. Encouragement and help from local Co-operative Development Agencies, with financial support from government sponsored job schemes, have stimulated this form in recent years.

4. *'Alternative' co-operatives:* This is the most common form of modern co-operative, arising from various alternative movements, emphasising social and environmental needs rather than profit. Members of these co-operatives are often from the well-educated, middle-classes, looking for a lifestyle that is different to what they perceive as the conventional 'rat-race'. Businesses are often in craft-related industries, health products, such as wholefood distribution, or publishing and printing.

6.4   Advantages and disadvantages

The recent renaissance of co-operatives has stimulated evaluation of their success or failure[2].

Advantages

There are some obvious advantages in the high level of commitment a member of a co-operative is likely to feel towards their work.

Increased motivation comes from putting an ideology into practice, and from sharing equally in the control and rewards of an enterprise. Those working in co-operatives report a higher than average sense of purpose and satisfaction from their work.

Disadvantages

Co-operatives face the same problems as many other small businesses including the lack of management experience and other appropriate skills, insufficient finance, and difficulties in gaining access to the market place. But they also face additional problems:

☐ Many start in difficult economic conditions. Defensive co-operatives emerge from firms already in serious trouble. Job creation co-operatives are stimulated by recession and high unemployment. Many alternative co-operatives operate in markets which are inherently difficult, for example small health food shops. Only endowed co-operatives have the benefit of a successful background as they are usually formed from a well-established business; it is not surprising therefore that their success rate is highest among co-operative types.

☐ Work place democracy requires innovative organisational structures which sometimes work, but often don't. Decision making can become confused. Lengthy debates over the running of the co-operative, can be an unproductive use of time. Finding people to join a co-operative and keeping the ones that have, is more difficult than conventional recruitment and retention practices, and can put an effective brake on growth.

The emphasis on social and environmental factors, particularly in alternative co-operatives, often leads to inefficient, labour intensive work practices.

Despite these difficulties, the new breed of co-operative does not seem to have a survival rate dramatically worse than small business generally. It is not necessarily a criticism that their financial performance tends to be poorer, but rather a reflection of the lower status accorded to making profits in many co-operatives.

7. References and further reading

7.1 References and further information

1. For a summary of this work see Goss, D, *Small Business and Society,* Routledge 1991, Chapter 5, "Alternative Forms of Small Business".

2. For a review of the background, classifications, and success or failure influences see Cornforth, C, "Worker Co-operatives: Factors Affecting their Success and Failure", in Curran, J. et al (eds.), *The Survival of the Small Firm,* Gower 1986.

7.2 Recommended further reading

Williams, S, *Lloyds Bank Small Business Guide,* Penguin, 1991, Chapter 4 'Your Business Identity".

Clayton, P, *Law for the Small Business,* Kogan Page 1991. Chapters 1, 2, 3, 4 and 6.

Barrows, C, *The New Small Business Guide,* BBC Books 1989 Section 3, 'Co-operatives', and Section 7 'Choosing the Form of the Business.

Cornforth, C, *Worker Co-operatives: Factors Affecting their Success and Failure.* (see reference 2 above).

Unit 11: The business plan

This unit looks at the when, who, why and what of business plans for the small enterprise:

- ❑ *when* they are produced or can be used;
- ❑ *who* writes them, and for whom;
- ❑ *why* they are produced, and the benefits that can follow;
- ❑ *what* they look like, the topics covered and a format that can be used.

Contents

1. The purpose of a business plan

Many managers already involved in small business, or those considering it as a possibility, perceive the business plan, first and foremost, as a document that is produced for the bank manager, investor, or venture capital company, in order to raise money.

For this reason, small businesses that do not have an external funding requirement tend not to write formal business plans.

The reasons for this include:

- ❑ a lack of understanding of the process or benefits of business planning;
- ❑ pressure on 'doing', rather than 'thinking' or gathering information, in the small business environment;
- ❑ the belief that strategic planning is for larger organisations and big business resources, and not necessary for smaller firms who can plan effectively 'on the back of an envelope'.

The Keynesian concept of central control and planning of the economy at the macro-level has been rejected by the post 1979 Conservative government. In part this has been reflected at the micro level, by the feeling that entrepreneurial management, of the "seat-of-the-pants", unstructured variety, should be encouraged rather than criticised. This apparent victory for the entrepreneur over the planner, has helped devalue the planning process, except as the means to the end of raising finances.

However a business plan can be used at different times, with benefits for several audiences. This is shown in figure 11.1 which illustrates when a business plan can be used, by and for whom, and why.

Figure 11.1: Purpose of a business plan – the when, who and why

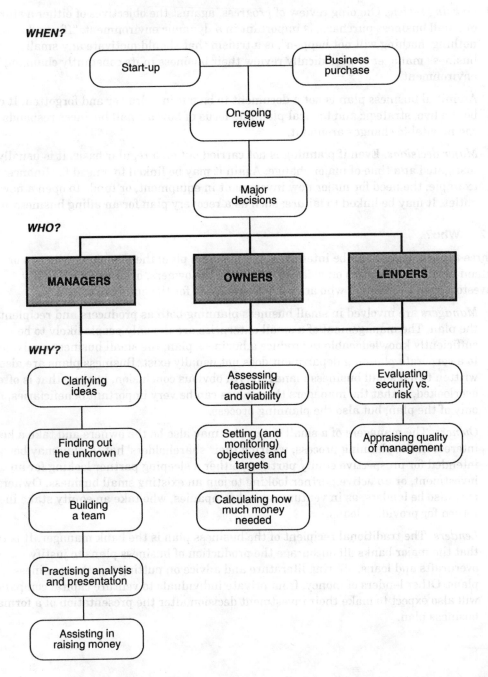

1.1   When?

❏ *Start-up.* After the concept stage of initial idea and feasibility study a new business start up may go through a more detailed planning stage of which the main output is the business plan.

❏ *Business purchase.* Buying an existing business does not negate the need for an initial business plan. A detailed plan, which tests the sensitivity of changes to key business variables (e.g. what if sales drop by 25% ...what if overheads increase by 25% ...etc), greatly increases the prospective purchasers understanding of the level of risk they will be accepting, and the likelihood of rewards being available.

❏ *Ongoing review.* Ongoing review of progress, against the objectives of either a start-up or small business purchase, is important in a dynamic environment. "If you do nothing, nothing will not happen", is a truism that should motivate any small business manager to periodically review their business in its constantly changing environment.

An initial business plan is not a document to be put in a drawer and forgotten. It can be the live, strategic and tactical planning focus of how a small business responds to the inevitable changes around it.

❏ *Major decisions.* Even if planning is not carried out on a regular basis, it is usually instigated at a time of major change. Again it may be linked to a need for finance: for example, the need for major new investment in equipment, or funds to open a new outlet. It may be linked to failure; such as a recovery plan for an ailing business.

1.2   Who?

Three types of people will be interested in a business plan: the managers who run or intend to run the business on a day to day basis; the owners, or prospective equity investors; and the lenders who are considering loans for the enterprise.

❏ *Managers* are involved in small business planning both as producers and recipients of the plan. The management of a small enterprise are the only people likely to be sufficiently knowledgeable to produce a business plan; the small business equivalent to a corporate planning department does not usually exist. Business plans are also written to aid small business managers. An obvious conclusion, but one that is often overlooked, is that the managers themselves can be very important beneficiaries, not only of the plan, but also the planning process.

❏ *Owners.* The managers of a small enterprise may also be the owners and take a keen interest in the planning process, wearing their shareholders' hat. A plan may be intended for prospective equity partners, either a sleeping partner looking for an investment, or an active partner looking to join an existing small business. Owners may also be lenders, as in venture capital companies, who take an equity stake in return for providing loans.

❏ *Lenders.* The traditional recipient of the business plan is the bank manager. It is true that the major banks all encourage the production of business plans to justify overdrafts and loans, offering literature and advice on putting together business plans. Other lenders of money, from private individuals to venture capital companies, will also expect to make their investment decision after the presentation of a formal business plan.

1.3   Why?

These three groups will have some shared, and some more separate, motives for using a business plan. *Managers, owners* and *lenders* will all be seeking to investigate the following issues:

☐ *Assessing the feasibility and viability of the business or project.* Will it work and become commercially and financially viable? It is in everyone's interests to make mistakes on paper, hypothetically testing for feasibility, before trying the real thing.

☐ *Setting objectives and budgets.* What is the overall direction and financial target set by the plan? Having a clear financial vision with believable budgets is a basic requirement of everyone involved in a plan.

☐ *Calculating how much money is needed.* What level and type of finance is required to make the plan work? A detailed cash flow with assumptions is a vital ingredient to precisely quantify earlier guestimates of the likely funds required.

Managers involved in producing the plan can, in addition, gain from the process itself in the following ways:

☐ *Clarifying ideas:* Putting together a business plan often acts as a powerful focus bringing together generalised and random thoughts into a clearer understanding of the concept, and how it can be made to work.

☐ *Finding out the unknown:* The information gathering process of a plan can uncover many interesting and relevant facts. The day to day pressure may obscure much in the business environment – a new competitor about to open; opportunities for cheaper premises or suppliers; new equipment available; successful marketing methods used by others; or useful ideas of other staff.

☐ *Building a team:* Developing a plan can be a catalyst to promote a feeling of participation among all those involved in a small business. Contrary to popular belief, small enterprises do not necessarily benefit from their shorter communication lines by encouraging participation in decision making processes. Some owner-managers are deliberately secretive about their plans; others leave insufficient time to effectively communicate with their staff. Even before a business has been launched, future partners may develop ideas themselves which remain unexpressed to each other.

The business plan provides a useful forum for all people involved in a small enterprise to express their ideas and feelings, in a way which develops a spirit of teamwork among them. The separate parts can find some unity not only in the plan, but also in the process of putting it together.

☐ *Practice in using analysis and presentation:* A plan can be an aid to training and management development. The research and analysis involved in a business plan, with quantification into forecast profit and loss and cash flows, is a widely used learning tool at centres of business education and also in practice elsewhere. For some would-be and practising small business managers the planning process is their first experience of market research and detailed budgeting. The presentation of a business plan to raise funds from banks or investors is good experience in selling a concept of any kind.

☐ *To assist in raising money:* A well presented business plan is no guarantee of raising money, but it helps. Research into why banks decline finance for small business cites "inadequate information" as a common reason[1]. Banks and venture capital companies receive many requests for finance. A professional-looking business plan will at least help overcome the first hurdle of gaining a hearing[2].

Lenders of finance will look to a business plan to provide them with additional information, particularly:

❏ *To evaluate the security offered for funds versus the risks involved.* Any source of funds for a small business will seek the security of tangible assets for their loans, and the comfort of a very high probability of receiving their money back. The assets of a business, such as its debtors and fixed assets, are likely to be investigated for their underlying quality and not just balance sheet value.

Although personal guarantees are frequently needed from owners, these are not necessarily a passport to successful loan negotiation. Financiers will not lend money for ideas they do not believe viable, even when fully backed by security. The higher the assessment of the risk, the greater the security needed to obtain finance.

❏ *To appraise the quality of management.* A lender of loan capital will be aware that in a small business the intangible asset of the quality of its management is more important than tangible assets in guaranteeing the security of a loan. The best opportunity they may have to assess the quality of that management may be in observing the production and presentation of the business plan. It is not just what the plan says but how it is put together, and communicated, that will count for or against a lending decision.

2. The format of a business plan

2.1 The three key questions

What should a business plan look like, and what should be included or excluded? Many outline business plans look formidable documents, running to numerous pages filled with very detailed questions. In fact to do its job a business plan needs to answer three straightforward questions:

❏ *Where are we now?*

❏ *Where do we intend going?*

❏ *How do we get there?*

❏ ***Where are we now?***

An analysis of the current situation of the marketplace, the competition, the business concept and the people involved is a necessary first step. It will include any historical background relevant to the position to date.

❏ ***Where do we intend going?***

The direction that is intended for the business needs to be clear and precise, if others are to share its vision for the future. As well as qualitative expression of the objectives, quantifiable targets will clarify and measure progress towards the intended goals. Identification of likely changes to the business environment will build on the opportunities outlined, and assess possible threats.

❏ *How do we get there?*

Implementation of accepted aims is what all the parties to a plan are interested in as a final result. Plans for marketing and managing the business, with detailed financial analysis, are the advisable preliminaries before putting it all into practice.

2.2   Outline of a business plan

The precise format of a business plan depends on the particular business and the intended audience of the plan. It is not possible to suggest subject headings for a plan which would have universal application. However figure 11b suggests an outline which follows standard practise in answering the three key questions above.

Suggested topics for each section are developed as a more complete outline below.

Figure 11.2: The format of a business plan

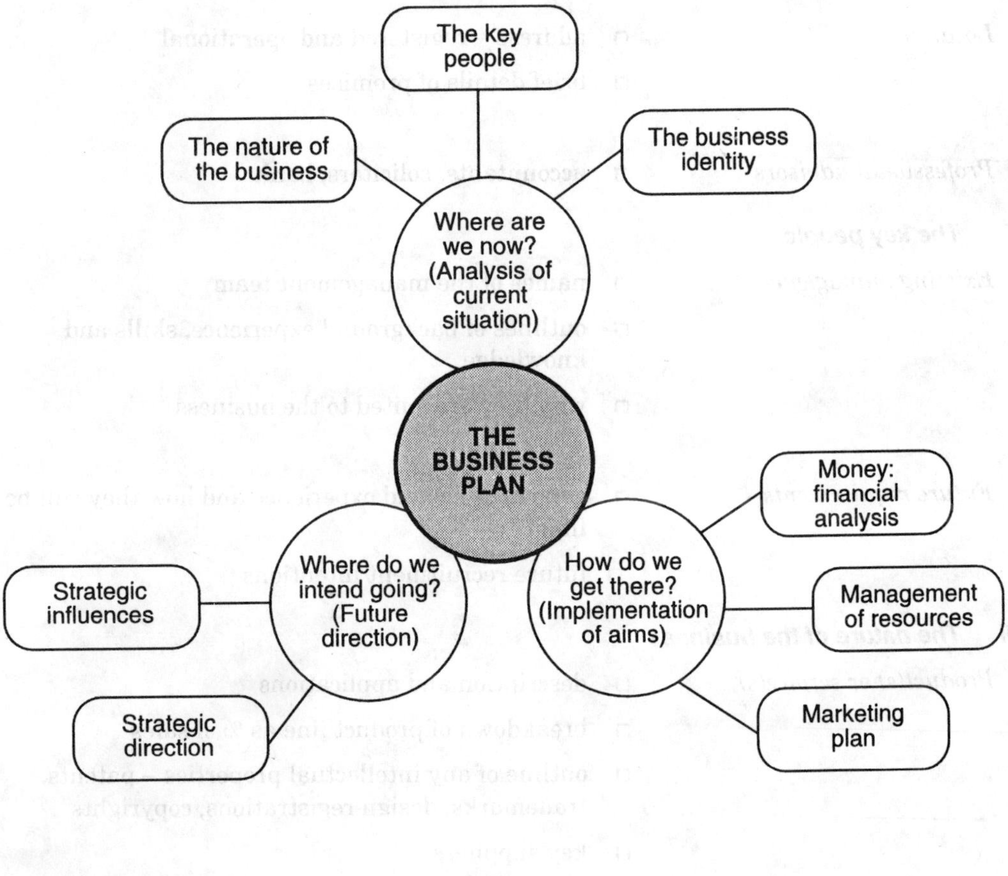

I Analysis of current situation (Where are we now?)

I.i Identity of the business:

☐ *Introduction*
- ☐ relevant history and background
- ☐ date or proposed date for commencement of trading/beginning of a plan

☐ *Names*
- ☐ name of business and trading names
- ☐ names of managers/owners

☐ *Legal identity*
- ☐ company/sole trader/partnership/co-operative
- ☐ details of share or capital structure

☐ *Location*
- ☐ address – registered and operational
- ☐ brief details of premises

☐ *Professional advisors*
- ☐ accountants, solicitors, bank

I.ii The key people

☐ *Existing management*
- ☐ names of the management team
- ☐ outlines of background experience, skills and knowledge
- ☐ why they are suited to the business

☐ *Future requirements*
- ☐ gaps in skills and experience and how they will be filled
- ☐ future recruitment intentions

I.iii The nature of the business

☐ *Product(s) or service(s)*
- ☐ description and applications
- ☐ breakdown of product line as % of sales
- ☐ outline of any intellectual properties – patents, trademarks, design registrations, copyrights
- ☐ key suppliers
- ☐ after sales service, or guarantees and warranties offered
- ☐ planned developments of product or service

☐ *Market and customers* ☐ definition of target market

☐ trends in market place

☐ classification of customers

☐ needs of customers and influences in their buying decisions

☐ benefits offered by business to target customers

☐ *Competition* ☐ description of competitors

☐ strengths and weakness of the major competitors

☐ competitive edge; the uniqueness of your business compared to the competition

II   Future direction (Where do we intend going?)

II.i   Strategic influences

☐ *Opportunities and threats in the business environment* ☐ socio-economic trends

☐ technological trends

☐ legislation and politics

☐ competition

☐ *Strengths and weaknesses of the business* ☐ in its industry

☐ in the general environment

II.ii   Strategic direction

☐ *Objectives* ☐ general

☐ specific

☐ *Policies* ☐ guidelines and rules

☐ *Activities* ☐ action plan

☐ timetable of key activities

III Implementation of aims (How do we get there?)

III.i Management of resources

☐ *Operations*
- ☐ premises
- ☐ materials
- ☐ equipment
- ☐ insurances
- ☐ management information systems

☐ *People*
- ☐ employment practices
- ☐ recruitment
- ☐ retention and motivation
- ☐ payroll and personnel system
- ☐ team management

III.ii Marketing plan

☐ *Competitive edge*
- ☐ unique selling point of business

☐ *Marketing objectives*
- ☐ specific aims for product or service in the market place

☐ *Marketing methods*
- ☐ product   - core and extended
  - product mix
  - product development
- ☐ pricing   - basis
  - margins
  - discount policy
- ☐ promotion - methods to be used
  - consistency of image
- ☐ distribution - channels used
  - direct or intermediaries

☐ *Research*
- ☐ confirmation of demand
- ☐ future research planned

III.iii Money: financial analysis

□ *Funding requirements*	□ start-up capital
	□ working capital
	□ asset capital
	□ timing of funds required
	□ security offered
□ *Profit and loss*	□ 3 year forecast
	□ sales
	□ variable costs
	□ gross profit
	□ overheads
	□ net profit
□ *Cash flow*	□ 3 year forecast
	□ receipts
	□ payments
	□ monthly and cumulative cash flow
□ *Balance sheet*	□ Use of funds
	□ Source of funds
□ *Sensitivity analysis*	□ Break-even point
	□ "What-ifs"
□ *Summary*	□ main assumptions
	□ performance ratios

Note on presentation: although business plans can be long, they should not be an unmanageable length for an external audience. A summary, and perhaps a timetable of activities is advisable. Where detailed information is necessary it should be given in appendices so that the main body of the report can be kept as concise and clear as possible.

3. References and further reading

3.1 References and further information

1. Robbie, M, "Small Business Requests for Bank Finance: Reasons for Decline" in Scott, M et al (eds.), *Small Firms Growth and Development,* Gower, 1986.

2. The major banks provide outline plans for finance applicants. The British Venture Capital Association suggest a "Short Form Business Profile", to obtain an initial expression of interest – see the BVCA Directory (1992) available from BVCA, 3 Catherine Place, London SW1E 6DX Tel. 071-233-5212.

3.2 Recommended further reading

Barrow, C and Barrow P, *The Business Plan Workbook,* Kogan Page, 1988.

Johnson, R, *The 24 hour Business Plan,* Hutchinson Business Books, 1990.

Unit 12: Successful and unsuccessful small business strategies

This unit describes some of the main considerations in formulating small business strategies, in answer to the question, "what internal factors determine a small firm's success or failure?"

Contents

1. **What is successful?**
   1.1 Success equals growth?
   1.2 Models of growth stages
   1.3 The objectives of small business owner-managers

2. **Unsuccessful strategies**
   2.1 Frequency of small business failure
   2.2 Internal reasons for small business failure

3. **Small business strategy**
   3.1 Some definitions
   3.2 Survival strategy
   3.3 Strategies beyond survival
   3.4 Strategies for growth
   3.5 Intended and emergent strategies

4. **References and further reading**
   4.1 References and further information
   4.2 Recommended further reading

1. What is successful?

1.1 "Success equals growth"

It is often assumed that to be truly successful a small firm must manage the transition into a larger company. Small business is, after all, the seed corn for tomorrow's larger enterprises; many of our industrial giants will disappear to be replaced by today's fast growing small firms. Success is inextricably linked to growth. The small business owner who achieves rapid growth to enter the large business category is seen in an heroic light. Examples of successful entrepreneurs are drawn from the likes of Alan Sugar, Richard Branson and Anita Roddick, who had humble origins in small business, but have now moved on to bigger things.

...alysis of successful small business strategies often starts with a large company ...s founders, then works backwards to see how they got there. Little attention is given to the owner-manager who has survived in business, yet remained small.

The size distribution of firms in the economy

Unfortunately this narrow view of success consigns most small businesses into the category of 'unsuccessful'. The vast majority of businesses do not grow beyond their classification as a 'small firm'. Only a few grow to become medium-sized, and even less grow into the new, large companies of the future. Large firms in our economy account for no more than 6% of the total number of enterprises; over 95% of manufacturing firms have less than 200 employees, with the average employment at 30 people[1]. If the size distribution of firms is visualised as a pyramid, the base is extremely broad and the apex very narrow. If success means climbing from the bottom to the top, then it is rare indeed.

1.2   Models of growth stages

This view of small business success or failure has been refined into various models of the growth stages of a small business. The number of stages varies, but a composite model is illustrated in figure 12.1.

Figure 12.1: A model of the growth or decline of a small business

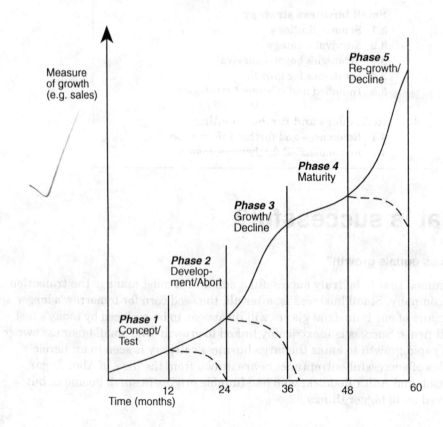

❏ *Phase 1. Concept / Test stage*

The new business idea is conceived, and planned. Full scale operations may (or may not) be preceded by detailed planning and testing in the market place. In some cases the business is run as a part time operation, before the owner places complete dependence on it.

❏ *Phase 2. Development / Abort stage*

The small business begins operation and is developed to viability, or it is aborted at an early stage. This stage is typified as the individual owner-manager launching a new enterprise largely through his own efforts.

Some analyses indicate crucial periods when a small business will survive or fail. One such period is illustrated as the first 18–24 months, when a new enterprise will pass through the critical phase of start-up, and grow to a viable size, or it will not develop satisfactorily and suffer an early death. VAT statistics confirm this high level of early failures with only 74% of registrations surviving the first 2 years.

❏ *Phase 3. Growth / Decline stage*

The second crucial phase is sometimes shown as occurring between the second and third years of operation. The growth that can occur at this time places organisational strains on the enterprise. The one-person entrepreneurial management style is seen as inadequate to fully sustain growth. A division of managerial tasks, the recruitment of non-owner-managers and the development of a functionally organised team are seen as the prerequisites to take the business through this phase, without which it will struggle and often fail.

❏ *Phase 4. Maturity*

A further stage looks at the business maturing, and going through a period of stability, when growth flattens. The small firm loses its simple structure of centralised decision making, and becomes more sophisticated in its control systems and more bureaucratic in its procedures. In other words it takes on some of the characteristics of a larger organisation.

❏ *Phase 5. Re-growth / Decline*

The identification of a further phase, sometimes referred to as the 's-curve hypothesis', suggests that once a small business has established itself in the market place, with a demonstrable competitive advantage, profits or external investment will follow to further exploit this early success. This will trigger a second period of high growth. Without this second surge of growth, the lack of impetus in the maturity phase can turn into stagnation and decline, as competition intensifies.

Whilst these models of the various growth stages of 'successful' small enterprises contain aspects which are indeed descriptive of how businesses develop, they overlook the statistical evidence, that most small businesses do not develop into larger organisations in this way. It is true that many do fail; but many more simply establish themselves and survive as small businesses, without becoming larger companies in either size or organisational structure.

VAT registrations show that 50% of all registrations are still registered after 5 year and 31% after 10 years[2]. Other estimates show that 90% of VAT registered companies are small firms, indicating that survivors are more likely to be small than any other form.

1.3   The objectives of small business owner-managers

The general purpose of the management of any enterprise has been defined as the achievement of the organisation's objectives and a continuous improvement in its performance[3]. Successful management is thus directly linked to the objectives of the organisation. If the objectives of a business include high rates of growth, then this is clearly a yardstick against which success of the management can be judged. If however continuous strong growth is not necessarily one of the aims of an enterprise, then success has to be measured in other ways.

As many small businesses are the psychological extension of the owner-manager, their personal motives and objectives will be crucial in assessing success or failure. Research has cast considerable doubt on whether growth is the common goal driving the small business owner forward. A survey of owner-managed businesses concluded that "for owner-managers growth is only one of a number of desirable objectives and is less important than survival and staying independent"[4]. Another study reported that more than 30% of owners wanted their small firms to stay at their present size[5]. This echoes earlier work done at the time of the Bolton report (1971) which suggested that many owners paid lip service to the ideal of growth, being primarily motivated by the need to preserve independence, which too much growth might threaten[6].

Clearly the motives of owner-managers for entering into the world of small business will vary, giving rise to different objectives for their business. Attempts have been made to classify entrepreneurs in terms of their personal values, in order to distinguish between some of the more obvious types, and their possible objectives (see also Unit 2, 'The Entrepreneur and the Owner-Manager'). Figure 12.2 illustrates some of these[7], in relation to their desire for growth.

Figure 12.2: Examples of personal identities and values which condition the growth objectives of the owner-managed business

Growth objectives	Identity	Personal values
LOW GROWTH Passive owner- managers	1. 'The Isolationist'	❑ escapism from market economy ❑ maintenance of acceptable lifestyle ❑ business seen as 'means to an end'
▲	2. 'The Artisan'	❑ personal autonomy ❑ work satisfaction from quality of product and personal service ❑ ability to choose workmates
▲	3. 'The Manager'	❑ seeking recognition by others of own managerial excellence ❑ security and long term planning
▼	4. 'The Technocentric'	❑ attachment to a given industrial process and its potential for development; managerial orientation
▼	5. 'The Marketeer'	❑ business goals ends in themselves ❑ less importance on nature of business, more on customer satisfaction
▼		
HIGH GROWTH opportunistic owner- managers	6. 'The Classical Entrepreneur'	❑ great importance on profits and earnings ❑ satisfaction from success of risk taking

Identities taken from Stanworth and Curran, *Growth and the Small Firm* and Goss, *Small Business and Society*.[7]

This so-called 'social action' view sees the small firm as a social grouping in which the attitude to growth is determined by the participants' social background, identity and desires. Passive owner-managers, who look upon growth as a necessary evil to ensure survival, will not primarily be motivated by the prospect of high profits. They will be more concerned with the intrinsic satisfaction of the job itself (the 'artisan'), or by the business's ability to deliver an acceptable life style, without having to compete in the 'rat-race' of employment in larger organisations ('the isolationist'). At the other end of the spectrum are those who conform to the capitalist model of a profit seeking opportunist ('classical entrepreneur'), which may involve attachment to the market place ('marketeer'), or a specific product or process ('technocentric'). Others may place more emphasis on recognition by others, with security for themselves and their heirs ('manager'), which makes them less likely to take the risks of high growth, whilst being dissatisfied with minimal growth.

ommon motive that can be attributed to owner-managers with such differing
's and desires is the survival of the business itself, for a sufficiently long
..eliver the objectives sought.

2. Unsuccessful strategies

The management of a small firm which goes out of business after a relatively short time
can usually be described as 'unsuccessful' because survival of the firm is necessary to
deliver the objectives, whatever they are.

In order to understand more about successful strategies, it is necessary to look at the
frequency and causes of unsuccessful small business strategy. In this sense, 'success'
can only be described by looking at its opposite, failure.

2.1 Frequency of small business failure

The real levels of small business failure in the UK have been the subject of much
current debate. Recent statistics have cautioned against the euphoria of the 'enterprise
culture' of the 1980s, which encouraged a new wave of small business start-ups as the
beginning of a new economic dawn. Whilst the 1980s was a decade of rapid rise in self-
employment (see Unit 1), the recession of the early 1990s has witnessed record failure
rates, with 21,827 reported company insolvencies in 1991, the majority of them small
firms, and 25, 640 individual bankruptcies, many the result of small business activity[8].

This has served to increase pessimism over the probability of success for small
businesses in terms of survival.

The problem is that there is no hard data on the failure rates of small business. VAT
registrations and deregistrations provide the broadest statistical data. Some
information has already been quoted and a fuller picture of the longevity of VAT
registered businesses is shown in figure 12.3.

Figure 12.3: Longevity of VAT-registered businesses

Still registered after:	Percentage of all registration
6 months	95%
I year	88%
2 years	74%
3 years	64%
5 years	50%
7 years	41%
9 years	33%
10 years	31%

Source DoE, British Business, 1987

There are however problems in relying on VAT data:

☐ The data excludes many enterprises, including those whose taxable turnover is below the VAT threshold, and some exempt activities such as opticians and undertakers.

☐ The data includes larger enterprises. Whilst new registrations for VAT may be largely small businesses, deregistrations can include many larger firms.

A specific study[9] to confront some of these issues reported more optimistic survival rates with only 16% of the survey sample failing to survive the first 5 years. Although the data was taken from a limited survey in the 1970s, and would probably be less favourable if applied to the new wave of 1980s entrepreneurs, it does point out discrepancies which could lead to misplaced pessimism.

2.2 Internal reasons for small business failure

There is more concensus over the internal reasons for small business failure. For example, a study[10] in Britain and Europe asked financial institutions lending to small manufacturing industries to rank their perceptions of the major threats to the survival of small firms. Their reasons were:

United Kingdom	1.	Availability of finance
	2.	Management capability of owner
	3.	Marketing problems
West Germany	1.	Availability of finance
	2.	Management capability of owner
	3.	Marketing problems
France	1.	Management capability of owner
	2.	Availability of finance
	3.	Difficulty in complying with new laws and regulations

There seems broad agreement that if factors outside of their control are excluded, small businesses fail primarily because of problems under the three headings of Management, Marketing and Money.

☐ *Management*

The competence of the owner-manager is the ultimate determinant of survival or failure. In the early days, the founder's personal competence in selecting the right business and running it will be crucial, as the firm is likely to be indistinguishable from the owner. As the business develops, growth can be prematurely curtailed by an unwillingness or inability to draw others in to help with the management of the enterprise.

☐ *Marketing*

To have a good chance of survival, a small firm needs to answer the basic strategic question: "what markets are we targeting, with what products?" A common weakness in owner-managers lies in their failure to understand key marketing issues. Product and service concepts and standards often reflect only the perceptions of the owner, which may not be mirrored in the market place. Minor fluctuations in markets can topple a newly established small firm, particularly where it is reliant on a small number of customers.

❐ *Money*

Financial difficulties of small firms arise, either because of an inability to raise sufficient funds to properly capitalise the business, or a mismanagement of the funds that do exist (or a combination of both). Access to external funds may be difficult to achieve for the new, or young, small business with no track record, especially for owners without personal assets to offer as security. Venture capital may be inappropriate for very small enterprises. Many new owner-managers, having received funds, misuse them; small businesses are notorious for their lack of proper financial controls and information.

3. Small business strategy

With a low probability of sustained growth, and a high risk of failure, can a small business adopt strategies to improve its chances of success?

Much advice is published on "how to succeed" as a small business owner. There is obviously much to be gained from listening to the practical advice of those who have experience of small enterprises. But can this be formulated into a prescriptive strategy to guide the small business owner?

3.1 Some definitions

First let us be clear what we mean by strategy in this context.

A **strategy** is a *plan* or *pattern* that brings together an enterprise's major *objectives*, *policies* and *activities* into a cohesive whole[11]. It provides the direction necessary to allocate the resources of the enterprise in a unique and viable way, which takes account of internal strengths and weaknesses, and external opportunities and threats.

❐ *Objectives* represent what is to be achieved (but not how). Objectives can be a broad and permanent assessment of the values to which an enterprise and its chief participants aspire (e.g." to remain independent of others"; "to satisfy customers whilst doing what we are best at and enjoy"; "to make a large capital gain"; "to promote the protection of the environment"; "to work in a truly democratic and fair organisation"). Alternatively objectives can be more narrow and less permanent, defining specific targets (e.g. "to reach a turnover of £1 million"; "to open three outlets"; "to pay off the overdaft"; "to take on an extra partner").

❐ *Policies* are rules or guidelines which define the limits within which activities should occur. Again they can be broad ("borrowings should be kept to a minimum, so that our house is not at risk), or more specific ("we will not trade on a Sunday").

❐ *Activities* are the detailed actions necessary to achieve the objectives, within the policy constraints. They can be formalised in *action plans,* which specify the step by step sequence of how objectives will be achieved.

Earlier discussion in this unit around the objectives of a small firm concluded that:

❏ the personal motives of the small business owner will largely determine the objectives of the enterprise;

❏ these motives vary from the craftsman seeking an alternative lifestyle to the opportunistic entrepreneur driven by materialistic gain; and

❏ the objectives of small enterprises will also vary therefore. High or continuous growth cannot be *assumed* as an objective. The only objective common to the whole small business sector seems to be that of survival, as the risk of failure is high.

These conclusions, taken with our definition of strategy, mean that there can be no prescriptive "successful small business strategy", only descriptive guidelines on key strategy influences.

It is possible however to identify the basic influences on a small business strategy in relation to the common objective of survival. We have established that the key determinants of survival, within the controllable environment of a small firm, are management, marketing and money.

These are illustrated in figure 12.4 as the '3 Ms'.

Figure 12.4: Key influences in small firm strategies for survival – 'the 3 Ms'

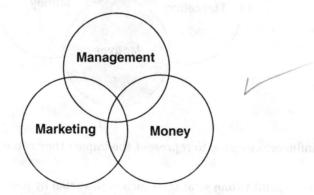

These influences are shown as overlapping, as clearly they do not work in isolation.

❏ *Management* is concerned with the efficient and effective use of resources by the enterprise, in order that it can meet its objectives. Money is one of the resources for management to use, or misuse. Marketing decisions are a crucial aspect of management.

❏ *Marketing* represents the relationship of the enterprise with those customers it seeks to serve. It will determine how much money flows into an enterprise via sales to customers. It will also dictate the kinds and quantities of resources that management will need to satisfy the demand it has stimulated.

❏ *Money* enables the whole system to work. It enables management to purchase the resources it requires; it enables marketing activities to take place.

3.3 Strategies beyond survival

Beyond survival, strategies will depend on the objectives of the enterprise. However, the quality of management and marketing and the quantity of money remain as key influences on the ability of the small firm to meet its objectives, whatever these happen to be. New strategies will need to build on, rather than detract from, these primary influences. The motives of the owner-manager(s) are therefore a fourth influence to be added to the existing three.

Unlike large companies where objectives arise from the influences of a variety of 'stakeholders', small enterprise strategy is driven by a more easily identifiable source, often one person. This additional force in any development of strategy beyond survival is shown in figure 12.5 – 'the 4Ms'.

Figure 12.5: Key influences in small firm strategies beyond survival – 'the 4 Ms'

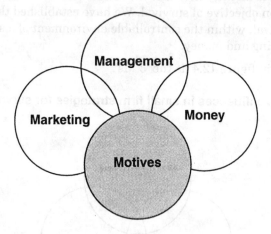

Again the influences overlap to represent the impact they can have on each other. For example:

❏ Motives can point to one strategy which is thwarted by money or marketing considerations. An owner may be motivated to run a business which is completely 'environmentally friendly', only to find that money does not permit this policy to be fully implemented. A restaurant owner may have personal motives to provide only vegetarian food, but finds that the market place does not support this strategy.

❏ Management considerations may indicate a strategy which is thwarted by the motives of the owner. An appropriate management structure for a growing business may never be implemented by an owner motivated by a strong desire for personal control.

❏ Marketing strategies may run counter to motives. An owner's desire to run what they perceive as a completely ethical business may prohibit certain sales approaches. Despite evidence of strong local demand, and competitive advantage, a trader may refuse to open on Sunday for personal reasons.

❏ Money influences may be diminished by personal motives. A desire to retain certain friendships may prevent rigorous pursuit of debtors. An owner with motives to promote their standing in the community may turn down the cheapest deal in favour of the local supplier.

3.4   Strategies for growth

As we have already seen, some commentators assume that continuous growth is an objective of every new business, and evaluate strategy requirements on this basis. As this assumption is not always made explicit, it has to be kept in mind when considering their suggested strategies.

For example, Drucker[12] puts forward four requirements for the successful development of a new venture:

1. Focus on the market.
2. Financial foresight, especially planning cash needs in advance of growth.
3. Building a top management team before it is required.
4. Careful definition of the founders role in the enterprise.

His analysis assumes that growth is the motive force, and illustrates how the significance of marketing, money and management shifts according to the stages of growth of an enterprise.

❐ *Marketing:* the need for a market orientation is paramount whilst a new firm is establishing itself. Lack of market focus is a problem typical of the very young business; failure comes quickly if there is insufficient demand, or inadequate stimulation of it.

❐ *Money:* inappropriate financial policies are the greatest threat to a new enterprise in the next phase of its growth. Here the focus has to be particularly on cash, not profits, as the growing firm outstrips its capital base.

   The business will need to change its financial structure, and improve mechanisms for controlling money if it is to move smoothly into the next phase of its development.

❐ *Management:* once it is established in the market place, and has developed the necessary financial structure and controls, the young enterprise faces a further barrier before it can progress into 'adulthood'. By this stage the business is too big to be managed by its founder(s) alone. It needs a management team. But a team does not form overnight; it has to be built in advance to fully function when it is needed – a brave move for a growing business with limited resources.

A corollary of the emergence of a management team is that the founder(s) then has to redefine their own role in the light of the changed circumstances. It may be that their style is not flexible enough to fit in with a broader spread of control. The only remedy may be their departure from a top executive position to an advisory role. These strategies for the high growth new venture are illustrated in figure 12.6.

Figure 12.6: Phased influences in growth strategies

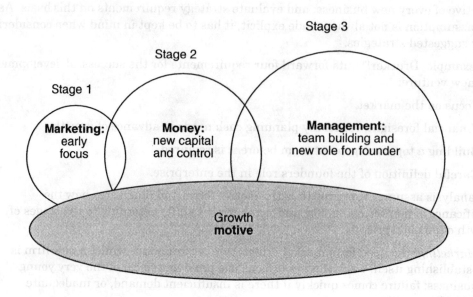

Stage 1

Stage 2

Stage 3

Marketing:
early
focus

Money:
new capital
and control

Management:
team building and
new role for founder

Growth
motive

3.5 Intended and emergent strategies

Strategies can be deliberate, consciously intended courses of action; they can also emerge as a pattern with no advance deliberation. Realised small business strategies are invariably a mixture of both.

❏ *Intended strategy*

Strategy may be formulated as a deliberate plan of stated, or unstated, intentions. Many small businesses produce a business plan (see Unit 11) before start-up, which sets out their intended course of action. Others do not formally document a plan, but intentions are thought through in advance in a deliberate and purposeful way.

❏ *Emergent strategy*

Some strategies are not conceived in advance but emerge as a consistent pattern during the course of events. A small retailer's strategy of having a mid-summer sale each year may have emerged as a pattern over the years, following the success of the early sales. A manufacturer's strategy of using a new technology may have arisen gradually, as a result of an increasing volume of sub-contract orders specifying the technology.

Patterns that emerge from a small firm's activities become strategies, even though they are not formally designed that way.

❏ *Realised strategy*

In practise even the most carefully planned strategy is not fully implemented; there will be an emergent aspect to it. Emergent strategies, once spotted for what they are, often become subject to some form of planning. Strategies which are implemented, or realised, are therefore usually a mixture of intended and emergent strategies. A small business will exist somewhere on the continuum between very planned, deliberate strategies to frequently unplanned, unstructured approaches.

Where exactly they fit will depend on the personality of the owner-manager(s) and the nature of the objectives of the business. An ambitious entrepreneur, who believes in the detailed planning of every move, might operate at the intended end of the spectrum. At the other, emergent extreme, might be a craftsman living day to day, content to keep their business as it is.

'Strategy' may seem a word more applicable to larger organisations than small. However, small businesses are similarly influenced by their strategic choices. The common perception might be that the typical small business is more often than not at the emergent end of the spectrum, whilst larger organisations are more deliberate in their strategic processes. There is little hard evidence to support this view. Some commentators view 'entrepreneurial strategy' as more toward the intended than the emergent end of the spectrum[13]. The focused control of small enterprise certainly makes the process of formulating strategy easier than in larger organisations. The sheer size and complexity of some enterprises means that changing existing patterns to a deliberate new strategy is a difficult task. In a small business, the owner-manager can embark on a new strategy with minimal consultation and communication.

4. References and further reading

4.1 References and further information

1. Curran, J, "The small firm – a neglected area of management" in Cowling A, et al, *Behavioural Sciences for Managers,* Arnold, 1988.

2. See *British Business,* Department of Employment, 1987.

3. According to the *Management Charter Initiative (MCI),* the key purpose of management is: "to achieve the organisations' objectives and continuously monitor its objectives". *Occupational Standards,* MCI, The National Forum for Management Education and Development, 1991.

4. *A Survey of Owner-Managed Businesses,* Department of Employment, September 1990.

5. *The Quarterly Survey of Small Business in Britain,* Small Business Research Trust, Open University (2nd Q. 1991.)

6. See especially Golby, CW and Johns G, *Attitudes and Motivation,* Committee of Inquiry on Small firms, Research Report No.7. HMSO, 1971.

7. Identities of 'artisan', 'classical entrepreneur' and 'manager' are from Stanworth, J and Curran J, 'Growth and the Small Firm' in Curran et al (eds.), *The Survival of the Small Firm,* Volume 2, Gower, 1986.

   Identities of 'technocentric', 'marketeer', and 'isolationist', are from Goss D, *Small Business and Society,* Routledge, 1991.

8. DTI statistics, as reported in The Daily Telegraph Business News, 8 February 1992. Company insolvencies were up 45% and individual bankruptcies up 83%, over 1990. The number of company failures reached a peak of 6072 in the last 3 months of 1992. The 1991 total represented 2.3% of active business on the Companies House Register.

9.   Scott, M, 'Mythology and misplaced pessimism. The real failure record of new small businesses' in Watkins, Stanworth and Westrip (eds), 'Stimulating Small Firms', Gower, 1982.

10. Watkins, D and Morton, T, "Small firms in Britain and Europe: the perceived environment" in Watkins, Stanworth and Westrip (eds), *Stimulating Small Firms*, Gower 1982.

11. See Quinn, J, *Strategies for Change*, Irwin, 1980.

12. Drucker, P, *Innovation and Entrepreneurship*, Heinemann, 1985.

13. See Mintzberg H, "Opening up the definition of Strategy" in Quinn, Mintzberg, James (eds), *The Strategy Process*, Prentice-Hall, 1988. In this Mintzberg describes entrepreneurial strategy as relatively deliberate because it is the personal unarticulated vision of a single leader.

4.2   Recommended further reading

Quinn, J, Mintzberg, H and James R (eds), *The Strategy Process*, Prentice-Hall, 1988. Chapter 1 ' The Strategy Concept'.

Curran et al (eds), *The Survival of the Small Firm*, Gower 1986. Volume 2, Chapter 5 'Growth and the Small Firm'.

Drucker, P, *Innovation and Entrepreneurship*, Heinemann, 1985. Chapter 15 'The New Venture'.

Unit 13: Management of resources

This Unit considers the first of the 3Ms: Management. It looks at how resources –
impersonal and people – are managed in the context of a small firm.

Contents

1. **Small vs large business management – there is a difference**

2. **Use of resources**

3. **Operating resources**
   3.1 Premises
   3.2 Materials
   3.3 Equipment
   3.4 Finance
   3.5 Insurance
   3.6 Management information systems

4. **People**
   4.1 Employment law
   4.2 Harmony versus conflict
   4.3 Types of management control
   4.4 Personnel practices
   4.5 The non-owner-manager

5. **References and further reading**
   5.1 References and further information
   5.2 Recommended further reading

1. Small vs large business management – there is a difference

How does managing a small firm differ from that of a larger organisation? We have
already seen that the small business environment exerts some pressures, which can be
different to the influences on larger organisations. Problems of the availability or cost of
finance, the burden of government regulations and paperwork, and shortages of
suitable premises, are examples of the preoccupations that might concern the manager
of a small enterprise (see Unit 6, 'The Small Business Environment')

However, differences in the environment are probably as great between sectors defined
by products or markets, as they are between those delineated by size of company. For
example, the external influences on a large engineering company manufacturing capital

equipment for industrial customers, will be very different to those on a building society offering financial services to domestic markets. Such environment differences can be just as significant as those between a large and a small company.

It is not then the external environment which sets small business management apart. What makes the difference is the enormity of the range of issues confronting owner-managers, which they have to deal with personally. The internal structure of a small business creates the need for a different management approach. In a larger company, the chief executive is head of a team of specialists in production, finance, marketing, personnel and other functions. There will be a clear distinction between those planning the future of the business in the longer term, and those implementing the strategy on a day to day basis. The small business owner-manager has to do it all. They are generalists who will have to turn their hand to all functions from sales to production. They are the planners and the implementors, responsible for deciding strategy *and* making it happen – and also filling out the VAT form while they're about it.

This scale and diversity of issues to be dealt with is a unique feature of small business management. Of course no manager can hope to be expert in all fields, and advice or training is often needed. However, the required skill is not always the trouble for an owner-manager faced with a multitude of problems, demanding attention simultaneously. Having the experience and understanding necessary to know how to choose which problem to deal with first is often the difficulty.

It is tempting to always tackle the most immediate first; for a small business this may mean overlooking a less obvious, but more significant problem which has a critical impact.

The analogy has been drawn between the owner-manager and the entertainer spinning dozens of plates on poles, all of which need attention to keep them going[1]. One false move, one touch out of sequence, and they all crash down.

By contrast, the chief executive of a larger company is likened to a conductor of an orchestra; their leadership can profoundly influence the result, but their attention can wander without stopping the orchestra from playing.

2. Use of resources

Management is about using resources efficiently in order to meet the objectives of the enterprise.

In the start-up, and early years of a small firm, the owner-manager(s) will be responsible for all significant decisions regarding:

❏ what resources are needed;

❏ where they will come from;

❏ how they will be used;

❏ how their use will be controlled and monitored.

This adds up to an almost endless combination of different responsibilities and activities. Some examples of these is shown in figure 13.1 'Management of Resources in a small firm'[2] which breaks the issues down into the four main areas of operations, people, marketing, and finance.

Figure 13.1: Management of resources in a small firm – some issues to be resol

OPERATIONS

MANUFACTURING PROCESSES
❏ equipment required
❏ costs and methods of finance
❏ operating systems and controls
❏ safety regulations
❏ quality control
❏ operator training
❏ maintenance

MATERIALS
❏ products and services to be bought in
❏ suppliers
❏ costs and credit terms
❏ purchase order systems
❏ storage systems
❏ goods inward

PREMISES
❏ location
❏ space requirements
❏ leasehold vs freehold
❏ rent and rates and insurance
❏ maintenance and cleaning
❏ environmental controls
❏ enterprise zones/assisted areas
❏ security

OFFICE EQUIPMENT
❏ telephone systems
❏ office furniture
❏ computer equipment
❏ wp software
❏ database software
❏ stationery items
❏ photocopier

MANAGEMENT SYSTEMS
❏ accounting systems
❏ financial management information
❏ stock control
❏ debtor and creditor control
❏ cost controls
❏ order book
❏ mail in and out
❏ filing

LEGAL AND INSURANCE
❏ employers liability insurance
❏ fire and theft insurance
❏ loss of profits insurance
❏ public liability
❏ professional indemnity
❏ key man insurance
❏ engineering break down insurance
❏ employment law regulations
 (toilets; first aid; washing water; drinking water; notice board)
❏ certificate display (fire and insurance)
❏ company law requirements

Figure 13.1: Management of resources in a small firm – some issues to be resolved

PEOPLE

RECRUITMENT AND DISMISSAL
- ❏ job titles
- ❏ job definition
- ❏ person specification
- ❏ advertising/agencies
- ❏ interviewing
- ❏ offers/rejections
- ❏ anti-discrimination (race/sex/unions)
- ❏ written statements
- ❏ redundancy
- ❏ notice periods

POLICIES
- ❏ rates of pay
- ❏ full time/part time
- ❏ commission/bonus
- ❏ fringe benefits
- ❏ wage/salary review
- ❏ overtime
- ❏ training
- ❏ pension schemes
- ❏ safe working environment

RECORDS AND SYSTEMS
- ❏ contracts
- ❏ personnel records
- ❏ payroll/PAYE and NIC
- ❏ lateness/sickness
- ❏ holidays
- ❏ grievance procedures
- ❏ sick pay
- ❏ maternity pay

Figure 13.1: Management of resources in a small firm – some issues to be resolved

MARKETING

MARKET RESEARCH
- [ ] evaluation of competitors
- [ ] evaluation of customers
- [ ] evaluation of market needs
- [ ] primary market research
- [ ] secondary market research
- [ ] sales prospects lists
- [ ] enquiries logging
- [ ] customer sales records
- [ ] customer visit records
- [ ] database/mailing list
- [ ] order conversion rates

PRODUCT
- [ ] main benefits
- [ ] key features
- [ ] 'extended' product opportunities
  (after sales service; guarantees/warranties)
- [ ] product development
- [ ] R and D
- [ ] licensing opportunities
- [ ] collaborative ventures

PRICING
- [ ] price lists
- [ ] market/competitor pricing
- [ ] variable costs
- [ ] fixed costs per unit
- [ ] gross margins/mark-ups
- [ ] discounts
- [ ] contract pricing
- [ ] price increases

PROMOTION
- [ ] direct selling
- [ ] use of agents
- [ ] advertising
- [ ] listings in directories
- [ ] direct mail
- [ ] press releases
- [ ] logo
- [ ] house style
- [ ] signage
- [ ] shop layout
- [ ] window display
- [ ] merchandisers
- [ ] selling aids
- [ ] leaflets and brochures

DISTRIBUTION
- [ ] use of intermediaries (wholesale;
  retail; mail order)
- [ ] export agents
- [ ] physical distribution and transport
- [ ] goods out system
- [ ] inspection
- [ ] packaging

SALES ADMINISTRATION
- [ ] order book valuation
- [ ] order acknowledgements
- [ ] quotations/estimates
- [ ] delivery
- [ ] payment terms and conditions
- [ ] invoice/credit note queries
- [ ] customer queries
- [ ] sales leads follow-up
- [ ] export documentation
- [ ] complaints and response

Figure 13.1: Management of resources in a small firm – some issues to be resolved

FINANCE

SALES
- ❑ invoicing
- ❑ sales ledger
- ❑ payments procedures
- ❑ banking (cash; cheques)
- ❑ credit notes
- ❑ sales of assets
- ❑ bad cheques

DEBTORS
- ❑ statements
- ❑ chasing letters
- ❑ telephone follow-up
- ❑ stop supply date
- ❑ legal action date
- ❑ write off date
- ❑ debtor information (aged analysis; by customer; by product)

BANKING
- ❑ current account
- ❑ deposit account
- ❑ cheque book(s)
- ❑ signatories
- ❑ statements
- ❑ reconciliation to cash book
- ❑ bank manager relationships
- ❑ interest
- ❑ bank charges
- ❑ credit cards

TAX
- ❑ VAT
- ❑ PAYE
- ❑ NIC
- ❑ P 11 D
- ❑ Corporation Tax
- ❑ Personal Tax
- ❑ Capital gains
- ❑ Stamp duty

PURCHASES
- ❑ purchase orders
- ❑ authorisation of orders
- ❑ cost control systems
- ❑ expense accounts
- ❑ chasing of suppliers
- ❑ goods-in system

CREDITORS
- ❑ credit terms and references
- ❑ authorisation of invoices
- ❑ payments system
- ❑ creditor information (aged analysis; by supplier; by product)

MANAGEMENT ACCOUNTS
- ❑ ledgers (purchase; sales; nominal)
- ❑ cash book
- ❑ petty cash
- ❑ cash forecast
- ❑ management accounts (P & L; balance sheet)
- ❑ audit arrangements
- ❑ filing of accounts

SOURCES OF FINANCE
- ❑ overdraft facility
- ❑ bank loan
- ❑ shareholders investment
- ❑ director's loans
- ❑ outside investors
- ❑ venture capital
- ❑ government assistance

3. Operating resources

A key management area for the small business owner is the selection, acquisition, use and control of operating resources. Under this heading we include many of the *impersonal* resources that a manager controls, such as premises, materials, machinery, equipment and systems.

3.1 Premises

In a start up situation, the location and type of premises is often a first consideration (even though location of potential customers may be a more advisable start!). Key questions for an owner-manager will be:

❐ *Where is the business to be located?*

Kitchen tables (and even a telephone kiosk in the case of Richard Branson) have provided many new ventures with a first, low-cost working facility. Once independent premises become necessary there are many considerations to be taken into account, such as:

❐ ease of communication (road, rail etc);

❐ availability of labour, especially for any process requiring specific skills;

❐ proximity to centres of population: this is a key factor for retail, catering and hotel businesses;

❐ costs of rent and rates; these still vary considerably even within relatively short distances;

❐ government and local authority assistance: there are a variety of ways in which specific geographic regions try to stimulate the growth of small business. Enterprise Zones[3], for example, offer a variety of benefits including no rates, 100% capital allowances for the first year, and simplified and faster planning applications.

❐ proximity to the home of the founder of the small business. Research[4] has indicated that, in practice, this the most important consideration in deciding the location of a small firm. Very few founders move their homes in order to set up a new business.

❐ *What type of premises are needed?*

The nature of the business will largely dictate the type of premises required. Considerations will include the facilities, the appearance, the size and layout, and the physical environment of the premises.

❐ *What are the legal and financial implications?*

Taking on a lease can be a major commitment for a small business, especially for an owner-manager who may have to give personal guarantees. As well as the obligation to pay rent and rates, the tenant will normally be obliged to pay for the insurance, maintenance and repair of leasehold property (for fuller details of the implications of acquiring freehold and leasehold premises, see Unit 9 'Buying an Existing Business')

❐ *Are the right premises available?*

Finding suitable premises has been a major problem for many small firms. In the 1970s and early 1980s, several surveys showed that difficulties over premises, particularly in inner city areas, were a constraint on the development of small businesses[5]. Armed with a study carried out by Coopers and Lybrand in 1980 which concluded that "there is clear evidence that the shortage of premises has constrained the establishment and development of small firms"[6], central government became increasingly critical of local government planning policies. As a result public authorities and developers have now provided many more units suitable for small businesses. It has also been shown that small firms tend to relocate quite frequently as they grow[4]; requirements can change quite rapidly from small space in a fully serviced, shared unit to larger, more independent premises. Flexibility of tenure is therefore needed, in addition to the right size of premises in a good location, with appropriate facilities. These needs have been increasingly met by local councils, Enterprise Agencies, British Coal and British Steel Enterprises (formed to promote new business activity in areas of high job losses), business centres, business parks and science parks.

3.2 Materials

Purchasing of goods or materials is a key management activity in many small firms, especially manufacturers and retailers. Materials purchased fall into two basic types:

❐ *Goods to be sold, either modified or unchanged.* This includes the stocks of raw materials for a manufacturer, retail stocks in a shop, food ingredients in a restaurant, and building materials in the construction industry.

❐ *Consumable items, indirectly supporting the business.* This includes stationery, publicity material, reference catalogues (and lots of tea and coffee!).

Larger manufacturing companies and retailers will normally employ specialist buyers; the owner-manager usually fulfils this role in the formative years, perhaps handing over routine ordering to an office manager or assistant as the business develops. Good management of this function can assist the small firm in a number of ways:

❐ ensuring that the right material for the job is always purchased;

❐ reduction in costs: time spent on researching and negotiating with suppliers can result in lower buying prices;

❐ availability of stock: poor purchasing systems can easily lose sales because a manufacturer cannot produce on time, a retailer runs out of a popular line, or a construction company develops a reputation for delays

❐ reduction in stock: 'just-in-time' purchasing policies ensure adequate availability, whilst minimising stock levels to keep down the working capital requirements of the small firm.

Despite these benefits, many owner-managers neglect the purchasing function, and fail to build good relationships with suppliers. The demands of other activities which may have more immediate effect, often take precedence; for example, the visiting representative from a supplier is put off or not seen at all, as the owner-manager struggles to keep up with other demands on their time. Alternative supply sources are often not followed up because it is easier not to change from the existing supplier.

3.3　Equipment

The infrastructure of a small firm is made up principally of various categories of equipment, representing a key resource to be managed. These categories include:

❑ *Production machinery and equipment:* this is obviously specific to the type of manufacturing process.

❑ *Communication equipment:* telephone, fax and word processing systems are becoming increasingly sophisticated at the level a small business can afford.

❑ *Office or retail furniture:* image as well as functionality will influence the selection of furniture for public areas of a small firm.

❑ *Systems equipment:* this category represents an area of increasing expenditure for small businesses, as it includes computer hardware and software for a variety of applications, including word processing accounts, databases and stock control. Cash registers and tills for retail outlets are also often part of a wider computerised system, capable of generating accounting, sales and stock control information as well as performing the basic function of monitoring cash intake.

❑ *Personal equipment:* Cars, mobile telephones and portable computers are the main items of equipment that a small business manager may consider, especially if their work involves travelling to visit customers or suppliers.

3.4　Finance

Owner-managers often buy equipment on lease or lease purchase at real rates of interest above those applying to normal bank borrowing. Commentators have therefore been critical of small firm management for its use of financial resources to acquire equipment. Whilst there are, no doubt, cases where small firms do pay more in finance costs than they need, there are often valid objections to looking beyond lease or lease purchase. It is often easier and less time consuming to arrange leasing, and owner-managers may wish to keep their bank borrowing potential available for other purposes, such as the funding of expansion – or losses, for which there are less alternatives.

3.5　Insurance

The purpose of insurance is to minimise risks. As small firms are particularly vulnerable to one-off disasters, an important management issue will be the choice of appropriate insurance policies to mitigate the effect of misfortune.

❑ **Obligatory insurance**

In some areas there is no choice. Insurance is obligatory for:

❑ *Employers' liability:* insurance against claims by employees who suffer injury or illness as a result of their employment is required by law.

❑ *Third party vehicle insurance:* company vehicles are subject to the same legal requirement as private vehicles, and need at least third party insurance.

❑ *Specified insurances:* some contracts will stipulate a requirement for insurance. Leases for premises normally require the tenant to take out property insurance. Lease or lease purchase agreements for equipment usually insist on a specified insurance cover.

❏ *Discretionary insurance*

Other insurances are less obligatory, but more or less desirable according to the circumstances of the business and the owner-managers. They include:

❏ *Fire and theft:* covering premises and their contents.

❏ *Engineering breakdown:* equipment can be insured for the costs of repair in the case of break down or damage.

❏ *Loss of profits:* in the event of fire, theft, breakdown and other misfortunes, a small firm can suffer not just the costs of replacement or repair, but the loss of profits whilst it is out of action. Insurance can cover these other costs of disruptions.

❏ *Public and product liability:* in the event of injury to members of the public or damage to their property. Because of the size and frequency of claims in the USA, this insurance is particularly advisable for companies exporting to North America.

❏ *Professional indemnity:* against claims of misconduct or negligence in performing a professional service.

❏ *Legal costs insurance:* provides cover in the event of a legal dispute with customers, suppliers or employees.

❏ *Key man insurance:* a small firm is usually heavily dependent on one person, or a small number of people, whose death would jeopardise the future of the enterprise. Key man insurance helps by paying a large sum so that at the very least a business can cover its debts if a key person dies.

❏ *Personal insurance:* owner-managers are usually advised to take out life, permanent health and pension policies to protect their family and themselves.

3.6 Management information systems

To help the small business manager in their seemingly impossible task of juggling with all the important variables that could effect their business, management information systems are becoming increasingly available and affordable. Whilst manual systems are still common, and advisable in some situations, computerised systems are helping the small firm more and more to develop not only adequate records, but controls as well.

The economies of scale, available to larger firms in computerisation of important information areas, have been gradually eroded by the availability of hardware and software which has reduced in price, whilst it has increased in scope, power, flexibility and user friendliness. Quite sophisticated systems are now available to a small business to cover all major management functions.

Figure 13.2: Management information systems for the small firm – areas where records are necessary or desirable

SALES

- potential customers
- sources of enquiries
- follow up statistics
- conversion rates
- time management of sales people
- volume and value of sales
  (by customer; by product; by time period)
- order book value and changes
- product margins
- price movements and elasticity of demand
- effectiveness of promotions
- direct mail response/order rates
- sales by distribution agent/retail outlet

FINANCE

- cash book
- petty cash book
- sales ledger
- purchase ledger
- nominal ledger
- banking records and reconciliations
- VAT/PAYE/NIC
- budgets
- cash flow
- management accounts
- debtor analysis
- creditor analysis
- costs analysis
- sales and gross margins
- fixed asset register
- annual accounts

PRODUCTION

- productivity measures
  (by operators; by machine; by time period)
- wastage
- rejects
- breakdowns
- critical path for orders
- quality control
- work in progress
- goods-out

PURCHASING

- stock turn
- stock valuation
- purchase specifications
- supplier quotations
- orders and acknowledgements
- invoice approval
- goods-in
- direct material costs

PERSONNEL

- employee records
- PAYE/NIC references
- wages payments
- time sheets
- overtime
- absenteeism
- holidays booked and taken
- statutory sick pay
- statutory maternity pay
- pension contributions

Many owner-managers, however, have learned the lesson that it is more important to keep basic records in a methodical way right from the start of a new business, than to spend time installing sophisticated systems whilst overlooking more fundamental paperwork flows, and information requirements.

Another common error is to assume that record keeping and systems are primarily financial in function. Whilst accounting records are at the heart of any small firm's systems, every other management function benefits from an information system. Figure 13.2 is a summary of areas where records are necessary, or may be desirable, for a small firm. Whilst not all these categories are applicable to every small firm, the list does appear formidable. Paperwork, especially that generated by government regulations is a constant source of complaint by many owner-managers[7]. Unfortunately, these complaints often overlook the real benefits which can result from the use of information in all areas of small business management.

4. People

Small firms employing up to 200 people now account for probably 50% or more of all UK private sector employment[8]. The small business sector became an increasingly important employer in the 1980s (see also Unit 1 "Small Business and the National Economy" for a more detailed discussion).

In most small firms, people will be the key resource. The management of other people is often the most important role played by the owner-manager. Like all other functional areas in a new start-up, the owner-manager will tend to take control of the personnel function. It is also the function which the owner-manager is least likely to give up as the firm grows. Rarely is a trained human resources manager appointed from outside, as even high growth small firms tend to 'make do' in this area. It is also the function in which owner-managers assess themselves as having the lowest level of expertise[9]. It would seem that one half of private sector employees are being managed by self-confessed amateurs!

4.1 Employment law

One reason for the low level of confidence of owner-managers in their personnel role is the complexity of employment law. An employee gains rights according to the length of time they are employed by a firm. Figure 13.3 summarises some of the main obligations of the owner-manager as an employer. Although at first sight, these legal rights may seem weighted towards the employee, in practice, owner-managers can employ who they want, and remove those they do not want, provided they behave 'reasonably'. This involves abiding by the regulations, and giving employees the opportunity to explain themselves in the event of a problem[10].

Figure 13.3: Employment obligations

Length of employment	Legal obligation of employer
RECRUITMENT	❑ no discrimination because of:
	– race
	– sex
	– marriage
	– union membership
▼	❑ collect income tax and national insurance for the Inland Revenue (Collect P45 or P46)
	❑ written statement on health and safety (5+ employees)
	❑ Employer's liability insurance
1 MONTH PLUS	❑ minimum notice period 1 week (2 weeks after 2 years, and 1 week for each additional year, to 12 weeks maximum, unless contract states more)
▼	❑ pay guarantee payments if no work available
13 WEEKS	❑ provide employee with a written statement of the main terms and conditions of employment, i.e. job title, pay, hours, holiday, sick pay, notice, pension (within 13 weeks, if employee works 16 hours + per week)
▼	
2 YEARS PLUS	❑ do not dismiss unfairly and give written reasons, which can be: incapability of doing job, misconduct, illegality of employment, redundancy or other substantial reason
	❑ do not dismiss because of pregnancy
▼	❑ pay statutory maternity pay
	❑ give job back to employee returning from maternity leave
	❑ give redundancy pay to redundant employees working 16 hours + (0.5 to 1.5 weeks pay per year of employment, depending on age and length of employment)
5 YEARS PLUS	❑ accord part time staff working 8–16 hours per week the same rights as full time staff

4.2   Harmony versus conflict

The case for harmony

A widely held view is that the small firm provides a more motivational and happier working environment than the larger firm. This was certainly endorsed by the Bolton Report, which stated:

"In many aspects, the small firm provides a better working environment for the employee than is possible in most large firms. Although physical working conditions may sometimes be inferior in small firms, most people prefer to work in a small group where communications present fewer problems; the employees in the small firm can easily see the relation between what they are doing and the objectives and performance of the firm as a whole."[11]

This opinion was based largely on earlier work, which had suggested that better personal relationships between employer and employee was made possible by the low level of bureaucracy in the small firm[12].

This picture of harmony within a small enterprise was contrasted to the confrontational industrial relations in larger firms - the 'all one happy family' environment of the small firm, versus the 'them and us' attitudes in larger companies.

Some evidence does seem to support this view. There are lower levels of unionisation and industrial action in smaller firms. One survey found that a large organisation (1000+ employees) is 40 times more likely to experience industrial action than a small one (less than 10 employees), and that trade union recognition was much lower in smaller enterprises[13].

Less idealistic views

However there are several important challenges to this representation of harmonious working relations in the small firm.

The lack of unionisation and strike activity cannot be taken as synonymous with lack of conflict. There is considerable evidence that conflict expresses itself in different ways within the smaller firm[14].

Employees in small firms are difficult to organise into unions, because of the fragmentation of their work places, the larger numbers of part-time employees and higher labour turnover rates.

Unions, therefore, find it difficult to establish communications to encourage membership in the first place, especially as this is often hindered by owner-manager antipathy to unions. Where they are successful, unions then find that maintenance of membership is expensive. Conspicuous disputes and strikes may be relatively rare because of this lack of organisation of labour in small firms, but it does not mean that the incidence of grievances is any less. Research has confirmed that not only do small business employees feel as much discontent as those in larger organisations, but that employers also have high levels of dissatisfaction. Owner-managers frequently complain of the difficulties of finding and retaining staff with the 'right' attitudes, behaviour and skills[14].

Other research has noted that working relationships are as much dependent on the type of industry and individual circumstances of a firm as they are on its size[15]. In this, as in other aspects, generalisation is difficult because of the huge variety of contexts in which small firms exist. Employment conditions in a high technology service firm (for example, a small firm dependent on individual expertise such as a design consultancy), are likely to be very different to those in a more traditional manufacturing company (for example, a small firm dependent on its production line, such as a bottling plant).

At the extreme, the small firm can be reduced to a 'sweatshop' working environment with employees suffering low pay, autocratic management and poor conditions. Some research has concluded that market forces largely determine the likelihood of adverse working conditions. Rainnie[16], for example, studied small firms in the clothing industry, and observed the dependence of small garment manufacturers on large high street retailers. The buying power of large retailing chains, combined with intense rivalry amongst suppliers, who tended to be small firms because of the low barriers of into a fragmented industry, creates intense cost cutting pressures on the owner managers. They in turn tend to use autocratic methods, exploiting a captive labo market to keep down their employment costs and maximise their output.

Other circumstances also influence behaviour. Friendly relationships can be destroyed by external pressures exerting stress on employers and employees. A cash crisis can ruin the good intentions of all parties to enjoy their work. Partners often know each other socially before joining forces in a small business, and they believe their excellent relationship will continue to the benefit of the enterprise. Whilst this may be true in good times, the stress of less successful periods of trading can ruin relationships (including marriages) to the detriment of partners, managers and employees alike.

Expressions of conflict in small firms are more likely to take the form of employees leaving a firm, or a partnership breaking up, than the conventional form of disputes in larger firms. The higher than average level of labour instability in small firms, which experience higher employee turn over rates than larger firms, bears witness to the less than ideal working situation which often exists beneath the surface in a small firm.

Despite the possibility of problems, lower than average pay and less than ideal working conditions, many employees do still prefer to work in small rather than large organisations. Their experience will undoubtedly be conditioned by the type of management control exercised by the owner-manager.

4.3   Types of management control

The way in which an owner-manager exercises control over their work force will depend not just on the personality of the manager, but also the disposition of power in the employer – employee relationship. Some circumstances will give the owner-manager, as the employer, relatively high levels of control over employees; in other situations, employees may be able to call more of the tune. For example, the owner-manager of a small firm requiring unskilled labour in an area of high unemployment is in a much more dominant position than the manager of a small enterprise, reliant on employees with specialist skills which are in short supply.

To illustrate this relationship Goss[17] identified four types of management control in small firms, which are shown in figure 13.4.

Figure 13.4: Types of management control in small firms

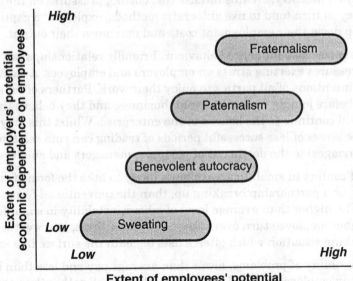

Fraternalism

This describes a situation where the owner-manager is heavily dependent on the skills of the employee(s) to get the job done. They in turn are relatively independent of the small firm because their expertise is in demand elsewhere. Employer and employee work along side each other, with decisions made from a position of mutual respect. This is common in the construction and building industry and craft-based companies. For example, the owner-manager and the craftsman who work in a small joinery, specialising in the restoration of old window frames and doors, were so dependent on each other that a harmonious working relationship evolved with no formal hierarchy for decision making.

This management style is also common in some professional and high technology small businesses. For example, a private physiotherapy practice, a training company or a software development business will be dependent on the skills of individuals, who can only be managed by mutual consent.

Paternalism

Where the alternatives for employees are more limited, and the employer is less dependent on them, then a paternalist management style may emerge. A clear distinction between employer and employee exists, but owner-managers are still sufficiently aware of the importance of their workforce to encourage common ties and personal relations. Farming[18] has been typified as paternalistic because of the economic situation of small farms and the traditional role of the landowner in society. Farm workers often have little choice of alternative employment, and are poorly paid. Yet the farmer is dependent on their commitment and experience, as they will be working for long hours with little supervision. Whilst maintaining a clear social and economic distance the small farmer will encourage mutual identification of aims among their farm labourers by gifts and wider community involvement.

Benevolent autocracy

This is the most common situation for a small firm; the owner-manager is less dependent on the employee, and able to exercise their influence from a position of power as an employer. However, employees are not so economically dependent on the small firm that they become totally subservient. Close links exist between employer and employee, and friendly relations exist, often on a first name basis, but this rarely extends beyond the work place (except for an annual outing or Christmas festivity). The founder of a small electronics company, for example, chose the location of the factory to ensure a ready supply of skilled and semi-skilled labour. Although able to hire and fire more or less at will, the owner-manager was anxious to keep employee turnover to a minimum because the selection and training of new staff was expensive and time consuming. The firm developed a name in the area as a good employer, a reputation the owner was anxious to preserve by acting fairly, paying the market rate and providing reasonable working conditions.

Sweating

There are some circumstances which conspire to give the employer all the power, and the employee virtually none. We have already described the environment of parts of the clothing industry, in which fragmented suppliers, dependent on powerful buyers, exploit their labour force in order to provide a low cost, flexible service. The 'sweat shop' emerges in conditions such as these. Some workers, especially immigrant female labour, are particularly vulnerable to exploitation because they lack relevant skills in an area of high unemployment. They have little alternative but to accept low pay, and erratic employment dependent on the work load of the small firm. Their employers trade in marginal, highly competitive industries, subject to sudden rushes of orders, and then gluts of production. They survive by keeping overheads down, using poorly equipped premises and hiring and firing workers at the first indication of growth or contraction of the business.

These four examples of the types of management control are not meant to be exhaustive; there are many variations on the theme. Nor are the types mutually exclusive. In some small firms two different modes of relationship can exist side by side. An electronics design and manufacturing company, for example, employs highly skilled technicians, who enjoy an egalitarian, 'fraternal', relationship with the owner-manager, who is very dependent on their design expertise. The semi-skilled production operators also employed are more easily replaced, and treated in a more autocratic, although still benevolent, fashion.

What does emerge from looking at these types is that there is a highly varied pattern of management of people in the small firm. Central to them all is the owner-manager whose personal style will be conditioned by the external forces prevalent in the industry.

4.4 Personnel practices

'Good practice' human relations management in larger firms relies on formalised, written procedures and longer term planning.

Small firms tend to manage people through informal, unwritten and ad hoc practices. Much will depend on the management qualities of the owner-manager to make them work effectively.

❑ *Recruitment*

Recruitment theory advocates several formal stages to ensure the selection of the right person for the job:

❏ A job description, which carefully analyses the work to be done and details the responsibilities and levels of authority of the job.

❏ A person specification which attempts to match the ideal candidate to the job, reflecting essential and desirable qualifications, experience, skills and characteristics.

❏ A promotional campaign advertising the vacancy to attract the best possible candidates, using advertisements and possibly recruitment agencies.

❏ A short listing and interviewing process, which is designed to find out as much as possible about the applicant, and also allows them the opportunity to find out as much as possible about the employer.

In practice the small firm tends to follow a much less structured approach.

Job descriptions and person specifications are unlikely to exist, except for management positions.

Several studies have concluded that 'word of mouth' is the most commonly used advertising medium for job vacancies in small businesses[14]. Agencies and advertising are regarded as expenses to be avoided if at all possible, particularly as small firms are big employers of part-time staff. Interviews tend to be with owner-managers, who will be more concerned to see how well the person fits into the team than with their formal qualifications and experience.

There is evidence of some sectoral differences in this general pattern, with high technology firms, for example, more likely to follow more formal procedures[14].

❑ *Training*

Small firms have a much lower incidence of formal training, relying mainly on training on-the-job[19]. Owner-managers are reluctant to pay the price of external training, particularly the cost of loosing staff for the time needed.

Although owner-managers tend to retain control over personnel matters, they also complain that people management is one of their biggest problems. Some avoid the issue altogether by remaining a one person business, often by sub contracting work to other self-employed people. This has the added attraction of only incurring costs when necessary. In other cases, small enterprises grow by using labour within the family rather than employing others.

4.5 The non-owner-manager

If a small firm is pursuing a strategy of growth, it needs to develop a management team. The owner-manager cannot maintain personal control over every aspect of an enterprise once it has grown to a certain size. The size at which a management structure is required will vary; some commentators have suggested that once a firm reaches 20 employees, it should begin to employ managers.

We have already examined some of the implications of this. (see Unit 12 "Successful and Unsuccessful Small Business Strategies"). The failure of the owner-manager to build a management team and carefully define their own role within it, can seriously threaten the growth and even the survival of a small firm. Despite this the role of the non-owner-manager has been largely neglected by researchers. A review by Curran[20] of small business research in the fifteen years after the Bolton Report failed to reveal a single reference to the non-owner-manager. Yet the managerial team of a small firm will be crucial to its success once it has achieved initial viability. More recent research has suggested that managers with larger company experience are more likely to help a small firm grow than those with more limited experience[21].

Not bosses but leaders

Despite the lack of detailed investigation, the management message is clear. The functions of leadership are as relevant in the small firm environment as the large. Leaders[22] are concerned with three primary functions:

- ☐ The achievement of the task
- ☐ The building and maintenance of the team.
- ☐ The support and development of the individual.

Our earlier portrayal of management in the small firm, using the analogy of the entertainer balancing plates on the ends of poles, seems to imply concentration on the achievement of the task, if the plates are to be kept up. Because the owner-manager takes on all the key roles in a small firm, the management style can become very task-oriented. There seems little time for the team, or the individuals within it, who are supporting the small enterprise. The 'team' may not all be employed by the small firm. Financial supporters, bankers, key suppliers and customers all form part of an extended team which the owner-manager leads. People within a small firm may also be neglected, particularly as relationships tend to rely on informal structures. The owner-manager can become so engrossed in managing the impersonal resources that they neglect the people resources. They can become pre-occupied and distant, appearing as more of a 'boss' than a leader. The appointment of managers at an early stage may be expensive (and therefore risky) but it may also represent the only way an owner-manager can fulfil the functions of leadership, and provide support for the team, as well as achieving the task.

5. References and further reading

5.1 References and further information

1. By Stan Mendham of the 'Forum of Private Business'

2. See also Stanworth, J and Gray, C (eds), *Bolton 20 Years On: The Small Firm in the 1990s,* Appendix A, PCP. 1991.

3. Enterprise Zones were established mainly between 1981–1984 for a period of 10 years. 25 zones have been defined within inner cities or other neglected areas, such as the Isle of Dogs, N W Kent, Trafford, Tyneside, and Workington in England, Clydebank and Invergordon in Scotland, Lower Swansea Valley in Wales, and Belfast in Northern Ireland.

   Further information is given in a Department of Environment booklet available from DoE, 2 Marsham Street, London SW1P 3EB tel. 071 2123434.

4. See Falk, N, "Premises and the development of Small Firms" in Watkins, D et al (eds), *Stimulating Small Firms,* Gower, 1982.

5. Falk, N, "Small Firms in the Inner City", in *Policy Issues in Small Business Research,* Cribbs, A and Webb, T (eds), Saxon House, 1980

6. Coopers and Lybrand, *The Provision of Premises for Small Firms,* Department of Industry, 1980.

7. See for example, the Small Business Research Trust's *Quarterly Survey of Small Business in Britain,* which records significant levels of problems with government regulations and paperwork (see also Unit 6, "The Small Business Environment.)

8. Stanworth, J and Gray, C, (eds), *Bolton 20 Years On: The Small Firm in the 1990s,* Chapter 9. PCP, 1991.

9. Stanworth, J, (see ref 8) Chapter 10.

10. For advice on good practice in employment, contact ACAS (Advisory, Conciliation and Arbitration Service, 27 Wilton Street, London SW1X 2AZ) who offer information and free booklets on many areas.

    See also Henderson, J, *The Law on Unfair Dismissal, Guidance for Small Firms,* Department of Employment (free from Job Centres.)

11. Bolton Report, *Committee of Inquiry on Small Firms,* page 21, HMSO Cmnd. 4811, 1971.

12. Most notably that of Ingham, G, *Size of Industrial Organisation and Worker Behaviour,* Cambridge University Press, 1970.

13. Daniel, W and Millward, W, *Workplace Industrial Relations in Britain,* Heinemann, 1983.

14. See Scott, M, Roberts, I, Holroyd G, and Sawbridge D, *Management and Industrial Relations in Small Firms,* Department of Employment, Research Paper No. 70, 1989.

15. See a series of articles by Curran J, and Stanworth, J, including "Some reasons why small is not beautiful", *New Society,* 14 December 1978 and "Size of workplace and attitudes to industrial relations", *British Journal of Industrial Relations,* X1X, 1981.

16. Rainnie, A, "Combined and uneven development in the clothing industry", in *Capital and Class* 22, 1984.

17. Goss D, *Small Business and Society,* page 73, Routledge, 1991.

18. See Newby H., "The Deferential Worker", Penguin, 1977.

19. Blackburn, R, "Job Quality in Small Businesses: Electrical and Electronic Engineering Firms in Dorset", in *Environment and Planning* 22, 1990.

20. Curran, J, *Bolton Fifteen Years On: A Review and Analysis of Small Business Research in Britain 1971–1986,* Small Business Research Trust, 1986.

21. Stanworth, J, and Gray, C (eds), *Bolton 20 Years On: The Small Firm in the 1990s,* PCP, 1991 See Chapter 11 'Managers and Management within Small Firms'.

22. See for example Adair, J, *Not Bosses But Leaders,* Talbot Adair Press 1987.

5.2 Recommended further reading

Stanworth, J and Gray, C (eds), *Bolton 20 Years On: The Small Firm in the 1990s,* PCP, 1991, Chapter 9 "Employment and Employment Relations in the Small Enterprise", and Chapter 10 "Managers and Management within Small Firms".

Goss, D, *Small Business and Society,* Routledge, 1991, Chapter 4 "Employment relations in Small Firms".

Barrow, C, *The New Small Business Guide,* BBC Books, 1989, Section 7 "Premises", "Employing People" and "Insurance".

Clayton, P, *Law for the Small Business,* Kogan Page, 1991. Chapter 8 "Employment Law".

Unit 14: Marketing

This unit looks at the theory and practice of marketing in the small firm and at marketing strategy and tactics. The reasons for a limited approach to marketing in many small firms are explored. The framework for a marketing plan is identified and marketing methods as practised in the small firm are considered.

1. Marketing strategy – implementation of concepts

This unit considers marketing in the small enterprise at both the strategic and tactical level. Marketing strategy is often indistinguishable in a small firm from its overall business strategy; considerations of how a small business relates to the market place, and the customer, are important themes in any business plan. Some of these aspects have already been discussed in earlier units; the need for market focus, analysis of market segments and niches, and customer buying habits have been looked at as an essential part of the development of the business concept. This unit looks at some of the issues in the implementation of marketing strategies, and at the marketing methods available to the small business.

1.1 Strategic or tactical?

In larger organisations the difference between strategy and tactics can become a question of level within the structures[1]. What seems a 'tactic' to the managing director, may be a 'strategy' to the sales manager (the size of the salesforce, for example). In a small enterprise, the differences all but disappear (the size of the salesforce is likely to be a strategic decision at all levels). Strategies are differentiated from tactics in the small firm according to the scope and term of their influence.

❑ *Marketing strategies* will define a continuing basis for determining how an enterprise interacts with the market place to achieve its broad objectives.

❑ *Marketing tactics* are short duration actions, adapted to specific situations to achieve limited objectives.

For example, the marketing *strategy* of a small firm may be to use agents on commission to penetrate a particular market. In order to promote one product which is overstocked, the firm makes a *tactical* marketing decision to increase the commission applicable to the product for one month.

1.2 Tactics become strategies

The importance of the distinction is that whilst a small firm's tactics are usually very evident, its strategy is sometimes less obvious. The tactical decisions - in terms of pricing and promotion for example – are very visible, but the strategy behind them may not be deliberately conceived, and only emerges as a pattern (as covered in Unit 12, "Successful and Unsuccessful Small Business Strategies"). The small business owner-manager may not believe they *have* a marketing strategy at all. They may be aware only of a series of tactical decisions in reaction to market forces (for example, a decision to raise prices because of increases in costs of goods supplied, an effort to find new clients because of the loss of an important customer, a mail shot to stimulate interest as enquiry rates are low). However, any pattern which emerges from these tactical activities can be seen as a strategy, especially from the perception of the customer. For example, if the methods which a small business uses to communicate with its customers have a pattern of low quality (for example, badly set out or even mis-spelt letters, frequent, low grade mail shots, inefficient telephone answering systems), then customers may well assume that the strategy of the firm is also to produce low quality goods and services. Likewise if a small firm makes a series of 'expensive' tactical decisions, then a customer may assume that it is part of a pattern which adds up to a high price strategy (for example, glossy brochures, elaborate logos and signage, plush furniture in reception areas).

In implementing an intended strategy, an important emphasis for a small firm lies in making sure that all its tactical activities are consistent with the strategy it wishes to pursue. If it believes it's competitive edge lies, for instance, in a very high standard of professional service, then it will need to make sure all its tactical activities reflect professionalism and service.

For a small firm with few intentional marketing strategies, tactical actions effectively form an 'emergent' strategy for the business, as customers perceive the patterns which emerge from the activities and draw their own conclusions. In this sense a marketing strategy is not an 'optional extra'.

The complaint of a small business owner that they have no time to consider marketing strategy because of the pressure of day to day work means they will be adopting a strategy by default, not that they will have no strategy at all.

2. The marketing plan

An intended marketing strategy for a small firm can be summarised as a marketing plan. A possible marketing planning process for a small firm is illustrated in figure 14.1. This involves looking at three areas:

1. The marketing environment
2. The marketing objectives
3. The marketing methods.

Figure 14.1: Marketing planning in the small firm

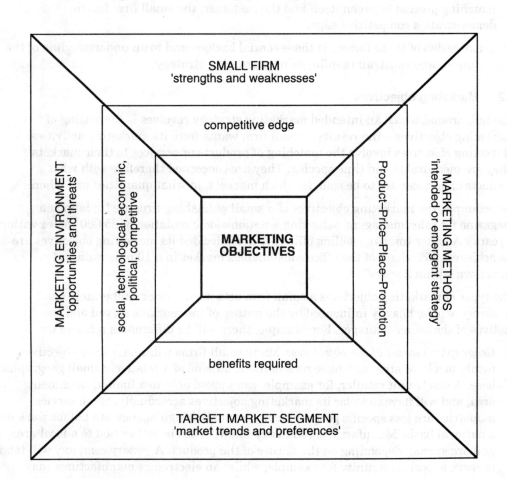

SMALL FIRM
'strengths and weaknesses'

competitive edge

MARKETING ENVIRONMENT
'opportunities and threats'

social, technological, economic,
political, competitive

MARKETING OBJECTIVES

Product–Price–Place–Promotion

MARKETING METHODS
'intended or emergent strategy'

benefits required

TARGET MARKET SEGMENT
'market trends and preferences'

2.1 The marketing environment

Earlier Units have considered the major variables in the marketing environment of a small firm. These include:

❏ *The customer.* Who precisely is the customer? (See Unit 4, "The Customer", 2.1 'Market Segments and Niches'.) The target customer group for a small firm have characteristics and buying behaviours which can be defined.

❏ *The market.* How big is it and what are the trends? (See Unit 5, "Market Research".) The chosen market may be large or small, growing or declining, showing favourable, or unfavourable trends.

❏ *The competition.* Who is serving the target customer group at present? (See Unit 4, "The Customer", 3.3 'Competition and Substitutes' and Unit 5, "Market Research", 5.2 'Competitor Sources'.) Competition may be direct, whether active or passive, or indirect, offering substitute products or services.

❏ *The outside world.* How will other trends affect the chosen market, customers and competition? (See Unit 6, "The Small Business Environment".) Social, technological, economic and political factors will continue to play an important role.

❏ *The competitive edge.* Why will the customer buy from the small firm? (See Unit 4, "The Customer", 3.1 'The Matching Process'.) The small firm will have strengths and

341

weaknesses in relation to the opportunities and threats facing it. To complete the matching process between itself and the customer, the small firm has to demonstrate a competitive edge.

An examination of these factors is the essential background to an understanding of the opportunities and constraints influencing marketing strategy.

2.2 Marketing objectives

The hub around which an intended marketing strategy revolves is the setting of marketing objectives – the results a small firm wants from its marketing activities. Marketing objectives involve the matching of products or services to their markets. They are measurable and time specific. They are concerned therefore with what products or services are to be sold, in which markets, in what quantities and when.

For example, the marketing objectives of a small publishing firm are "to launch a magazine for sales managers, achieving a nationwide circulation of 25,000 copies within 3 years". Another company selling office products decided its marketing objectives are "to achieve a 25% share of the office consumables market in a 10 mile radius of Dunstown within 2 years".

The types of marketing objectives a small firm sets itself, either deliberately or passively, will be heavily influenced by the nature of the markets served and the motives of the owner-manager. For example, there will be differences relating to:

❒ *Geographic market of the objectives:* Many small firms will relate their objectives firmly to a local area, and have no ambitions outside of a relatively small geographic base. A single unit retailer, for example, can appeal only to a limited catchment area, and will have to tailor its marketing objectives accordingly. Some service industries are less specific geographically; a small design agency can bid for work on a national basis. Manufacturing industry likewise can be either tied to a local area, or more spread, depending on the nature of the product. A joinery company will tend to serve a local community for example, whilst an electronics manufacturer may envisage a much wider customer base.

❒ *Growth ambitions of the owners:* Small business owners have different attitudes to growth (as covered in Unit 12, "Successful and Unsuccessful Small Business Strategies"). As their own personal motives will largely determine the objectives of the enterprise, small firms can have marketing objectives between the extremes of rapid penetration of a given market, to no further expansion at all, or even withdrawal. The consensus will of course be somewhere in between with most small firms desiring some growth, but at a modest rate.

2.3 Marketing methods

The specific instruments of marketing available to the manager in small and large firms alike are often referred to as the "4 Ps" of the marketing mix – Product, Price, Place and Promotion. Optimisation of the marketing mix means having the right Product available at the right Price, in the right Place, supported by the right Promotion. Each of these variables will be considered separately, but first it is important to consider the reality of their use in the small firm environment.

3. Application of marketing by small firms

3.1 Marketing methods in practice

The marketing methods available to a small firm are no different to the marketing methods used by larger firms. Texts on marketing in the small business generally confirm this by reviewing the elements of marketing in much the same way as more generalised marketing books[2]. Yet they frequently overlook the reality of the methods used by small firms.

Small business marketing does differ in practice. There is evidence that small firms only use a small range of marketing methods, with limited expenditures. For example, research involving small electronics and printing companies[3] revealed that respondents put little effort into marketing their businesses at all unless they lost custom; otherwise they were content to allow 'word of mouth' to do their marketing for them. Figure 14.2 illustrates the degree to which the small businesses were content to use 'passive' methods, such as word of mouth and Yellow Pages, compared to more active promotional methods, such as cold calls, salesmen and direct mail.

Figure 14.2: Small business methods of finding customers

Method	% used
Word of mouth	73
Cold Calls	29
Press Advertising	22
Shop Advertising	17
Exhibitions	10
Salesmen	7
Direct Mail	5
Yellow Pages	15

(NB As more than one method could have been used, the percentages add up to more than 100.

Respondents were electronic and printing firms in Kingston and Sheffield).

Reproduced from *"Small Firms and Local Economic Networks. A report to the Midland Bank."* by James Curran and Robert Blackburn December 1991[3].

In addition to restricted use of marketing communications and promotional methods, there is also evidence that small firms tend to underprice themselves - particularly their own labour. A report[4] on self-employed people in Britain showed that they paid themselves less on average than the comparable employed person's pay; the self-employed person earned £6.67 per hour compared with the average wage of £7.30.

Whilst firms in manufacturing industries may have product development records comparable to their larger company counterparts, service sector small firms (the vast majority of all small businesses), have poorer records for innovation.

Small firms tend to restrict the place in which they do business. Although some distribute products nationally, most small firms do not make use of extensive distribution networks, especially as most are in the service sector. Distribution through international markets is particularly rare; a survey of small firms in all sectors of the economy revealed that 94% did not export at all[5].

It would seem that in practice small firms do not use the '4 Ps' of the marketing mix in quite the way that some theorists would advocate.

Many small firms maintain a paradoxical attitude to marketing. On the one hand it is regarded as 'something for the larger company' and of little practical use to the small business. On the other hand small enterprises show themselves to be the personification of the marketing concept. The customer orientation practices of small business, which respond flexibly and fast to the demands of the consumer, have been held up as a model to larger organisations, private and public alike. Undoubtedly, the proximity of the owner-manager to the market place helps them appreciate the needs of the customer, and therefore respond to changes in demand. The same owner-manager however may have a healthy disdain for using the tools of marketing to attract more custom. Some reasons for this limited application of marketing methods amongst small business owners are:

❏ *Diseconomies of scale:* Small firms are unable to commit the same pro-rata level of marketing expenditure as larger firms because of diseconomies of scale. A small firm, which does not enjoy the scale or experience economies of a larger company, will have less, as a percentage of its sales revenue, to spend on sales related activities; other expenses will account for a higher proportion of its revenue.

❏ *Lack of specialised knowledge and skills:* Small firms often do not optimise their marketing approach because the owner-manager does not have experience of specialised aspects of marketing. Promotional or distribution routes may therefore be overlooked, pricing or product development opportunities missed.

❏ *Distrust or lack of interest:* Some owner-managers have a distrust of marketing which they view as inappropriate to small firms. Others may not take any overt interest, as they are caught up with day to day operational details; marketing strategies emerge and limited tactics are employed, but they are not deliberately conceived as long term activities.

Again the motives of the owner-manager, and their attitude to growth will be important ingredients here.

3.2 Distinctive marketing style

It has been suggested that all of these influences[5] add up to a distinctive marketing style which typifies the small business sector. Carson[6] has proposed that this style has a number of characteristics:

❏ *Lack of formalised planning of marketing strategies:* Small firms rely more on informal procedures, often in reaction to activity in the market place.

☐ *Restricted scope and activity:* Small business shies away from wide ranging and expensive marketing campaigns.

☐ *Simplistic and haphazard:* Owner-managers rarely indulge in sophisticated, integrated marketing approaches, relying instead on rather random and basic marketing efforts.

☐ *Product and price orientation:* The marketing mix tends to over rely on developing products at competitive prices, and be less adventurous in promotional activities, and in seeking different channels of distribution, or potential new markets.

☐ *Owner-manager involvement:* The marketing strategy of small firms tends, like all aspects in the early days, to be driven by the owner-manager. The influence of their personal skills, experience and motives will be paramount in determining the nature and complexity of marketing methods used.

Whilst all of this may sound rather critical of the marketing processes adopted by small firms, the same commentator warns that marketing theorists should not be too hasty in their judgements, just because small firm marketing approaches do not conform to standard theoretical models. Marketing has to fit around the capabilities of the practitioner to be effective; if an owner-manager's background precludes sophisticated marketing techniques, then more basic practices can still be effective.

Evolution of marketing

Marketing cannot be regarded as a static discipline in the small firm. Practices will change as the firm develops, and particularly if it grows. Carson[7] has suggested there are four stages in the evolution of marketing in the small firm:

1. *Initial marketing activity:* there is usually considerable marketing activity in the set up stages of a new business, based mainly on the products, and their pricing and delivery.

2. *Reactive selling:* as demand grows, activities are usually in response to enquiries from potential customers.

3. *D.I.Y marketing approach:* as the firm develops the need for a more positive marketing approach is seen. Owner-managers rely on their own capabilities to implement any marketing campaigns, which tend to be disjointed and sporadic as a result.

4. *Integrated, pro-active marketing:* in the final stage the small firm emerges with more sophisticated marketing planning. The various elements of the marketing mix are coordinated into longer term strategies, aimed at controlling market forces rather than being controlled by them. This usually implies the recruitment of specialist marketing management.

Whilst this is an oversimple model, which does not take account of the full variety of business types, owner-manager personalities and skills or market conditions, it does illustrate that small firms can be expected to travel along an experience curve in their marketing activities, which is likely to improve their capabilities in this area.

4. Product

4.1 The extended product

'Product' is a very wide term, meaning basically anything that is offered to the market place; it can be a physical item, or an intangible service. Some small firms sell only one standard product; many offer a service which is tailor made to the customer. More often than not, a small firm and its products are indistinguishable by the customer; their perceptions of the firm will equate to their perceptions of the products it offers.

A product is more than it seems at first sight. It exists on several levels. It extends inward to represent a simple benefit to the purchaser and outwards to include a whole range of added features.

This concept of the 'extended product' is illustrated in figure 14.3, using the example of a small firm which designs, produces and installs signs.

Figure 14.3: The extended product concept for a small firm

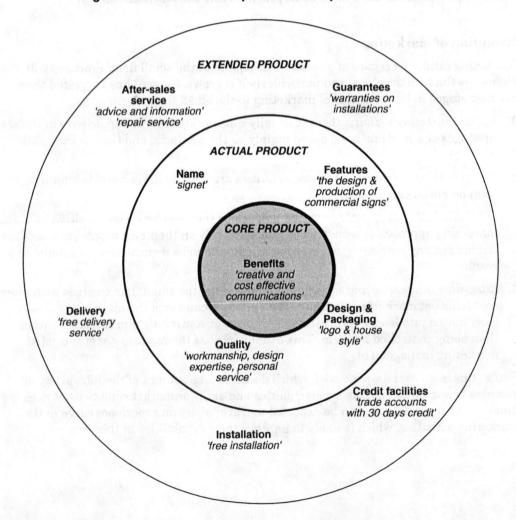

❏ the ***core product*** is the benefit which the customer purchases. It represents the motivation for the buyer to buy.

The sign company's product offers the benefit of creative communication in a cost effective way for its commercial customers.

❏ the ***actual product*** is the essential characteristics of what is on offer. It includes:

– the *features* of the product, that is a description of what it is, and does.

The sign company's product is the planning, design, production and installation of commercial signs.

– the *name* of the product or service. This is the proprietary name of the product or service, which may or may not be the same as the small firm.

In our example, the firm is a partnership, Smith and Jones, who trade as "Signet", which is the name of the service they offer.

– *quality* is an important attribute reflecting how well a product is made or a service delivered.

Signet's quality will be a function of not only their workmanship in producing the signs, but also the expertise of their design and the helpfulness of their personal service.

– *design and packaging* is normally associated with tangible items. In some products, such as perfumes, it is more important than what is actually of use.

In our example, each product is individually designed and although there is no conventional packaging, the trading name has a logo and a house style is used on all literature which forms a recognisable themed package to the customer.

❏ the ***extended product*** includes additional benefits and services offered to the customer, which add value to the basic product.

Signet do not only design and produce signs; they deliver and install them, offer advice and a repair service, give guarantees on their performance, and credit on their payment.

All this adds up to a package of features and benefits described as a 'product'.

4.2   The differentiated product

Small firms are continually advised to be different – to 'differentiate' themselves from the competition. In practice, they cannot avoid being different; the issue is being different in a positive way. The concept of the extended product implies that no small firm can offer exactly the same as another. Even if the tangible product is identical, other aspects of what is offered in terms of service, credit terms, brand name, advice and information will be different. The problem for small firms is first understanding how they are different, and secondly finding out what differences are most appreciated by the customer.

The owners of 'Signet', for example, believed their personal design service represented the difference between what they had to offer and the competition; but in fact most of their customers recommended them for the quality of their workmanship. Their design service was different, but the personality of the partner in charge of this activity made a negative impact on many customers.

4.3   Product mix

Most small firms offer more than one product or service. Whilst this may lend longer term stability, it can cause shorter term problems in determining the most favourable product mix. Some products may sell high volumes, but at small profit margins; other more specialised lines have limited demand but at very attractive margins. Achieving a balance between the necessary volume to cover overheads and the high margin to make attractive profits can be a difficult juggling act for a small business with limited resources.

A wine bar, for example, can sell large quantities of wine at small margins, but has the opportunity to make high profits from food sales. The owner manager has to decide how much space they can devote to the tables, chairs and the service area needed to promote food sales, without risking the regular trade of his customers who only want to drink and socialise.

'Signet' can offer standard products of ready made sign units. As they are adding less value to this range, they will make less margin than from their own fully designed service. However, to compete they need to have this lower priced alternative available. The partners in Signet find it difficult to keep the balance between sufficient higher margin work, and sales of the standard product which are easier to find, but produce less profit.

4.4   Names, products and the law

The new small business will need to decide if their business and product should share the same name. Practically, a small firm usually has only the resources to promote one name, and it could be confusing to try and create two or more images.

The Law

The law both restricts the use of certain names, and gives protection to the value built up by names, products and processes.

❏ *Company names:* The name of a limited company can be registered provided it is not identical to an existing company, nor can be considered offensive or illegal. Certain words, about eighty in total, such as Royal, Windsor, National, British, University, Chemist, Trust, can only be used with the approval of the Secretary of State[8].

   Sole traders and partnerships can use their own names without consent. If they choose, however, to operate under a name, other than their own, they are legally required to disclose their names on business letters, invoices, receipts and other stationery.

❏ *Trademarks:* Brand names, or a distinctive mark associated with a product, can be registered with the Trade Mark Registry. Imitation of registered trade marks is a criminal offence[9]. Even where names are not registered, attempts to 'pass-off' other goods for the real thing are also illegal.

❏ *Service Marks:* Registration of Service Marks, which are used to identify services as opposed to products, can also be made with the Trade Marks Registry, affording them similar protection.

☐ *Copyright:* Where the 'product' is a literary, artistic or musical creation, it can be protected by copyright, which under the 1988 Copyright, Designs and Patent Act[9] also covers computer software.

☐ *Design right:* Designs for products, either initial drawings or a prototype, are also protected by 'design right', a new concept introduced by the 1988 Act.

☐ *Patents:* Inventions of products or processes, accepted as superior to what went before, can be given temporary protection by patents. The owner of a patent can give rights to others to manufacture or sell the patented product, or use the patented process, usually granted through a license.

4.5   Product development

Not surprisingly, the product idea selected by the new owner of a small business is most likely to be determined by their previous experience. According to one survey[10], 78% of new owners chose a product which was the same or similar to their previous employment. This leaves most small firms with a narrow base for future product development.

We have already discussed the relationship between the small firm and innovation (see Unit 3 "Small Business and Innovation"). In terms of new product development the record is highly variable. In some sectors, the small firm is responsible for a high percentage of new products introduced. For example 58% of innovations in the scientific instruments industry, between 1945 and 1983, are calculated to have come from SME's [Small and Medium-sized Enterprises, defined as having fewer than 500 employees]. This compares to only 14% for SME's in the pharmaceuticals industry[11]. There are barriers to introducing new products, just as there are barriers to entry for small firms, which vary by industry.

Another theme, previously emphasised, is the variability of motives among owner managers, which will affect their product development policy. Although some will show highly innovative tendencies, many others will not have the desire or capability to introduce new products.

The problems in new product development for a small firm are considerable. The rate of failure of new products is high; the resources for new product research and development will be limited, coming in most cases from internal sources[12].

Failure of new products can easily cause the failure of the small firm if the stakes are high. For this reason, many small businesses adopt a cautious approach.

☐ *Incremental innovations:*[13] By developing new products within the existing framework of knowledge and experience, a small firm can more safely predict the outcome of any innovative move. The development may be of new markets, and different customer groups rather than new products.

☐ *Radical innovation:* This increases the risk significantly by taking the small firm into new technology, process and markets, where there is little in-house information and experience. Whilst this route may produce substantial profits and growth, it also represents high risk with the future of the whole enterprise often dependent on the success of the new product.

☐ *Licensing:* A way of remaining innovative but reducing the risk is to license proven products or processes, from other companies. For a small firm, unable to invest in their own R & D, this may be an attractive option.

Licenses to manufacture, or distribute new products are becoming increasingly available. The Technology Exchange[14], set up as a non profit making company in 1985 to assist small and medium sized enterprises to locate opportunities through licensed manufacture, now has a computer index of some 20,000 licence offers.

❏ *Collaborative ventures:* The traditional British inventiveness still evident in scientific establishments, Universities, Polytechnics and colleges has too often stopped short of the application of new products in the market place.

Many observers have compared Britain's innovation record to Japan's as there is evidence that, whilst the UK scores heavily in terms of pure inventiveness and research skills, Japanese industry has excelled at product development[15]. The opportunism of smaller firms has been seen as a potential positive influence in the UK to overcome this reluctance to bring new ideas into the market. The government has therefore set up schemes such as LINC, which aims at bringing commerce and research institutions together with the government funding up to 50% of project costs, and SPUR which makes grants of up to £150,000 to help small firms develop technologically advanced products.

There are mixed reports of the success of these initiatives. "Partners in Innovation", a report[16] by the McKinsey group criticised academia and business alike (including small firms) for not making more of technological opportunities. However, it would appear that some sectors are doing better than others. The LINC initiative has been particularly well supported, for example, in the development of scientific instruments, with smaller firms playing a prominent role[17].

Product considerations in a small firm's marketing strategy often point to a dilemma. Without new products, small firms cannot survive in most competitive markets. Yet the costs of product development, and the risks of failure, are often too high for the limited resources of a small firm to accept. The way out of the dilemma will probably involve closer co-operation and teamwork in new product development between small and large organisations, in the private and public sector alike.

5. Price

5.1 Pricing - the weak link?

Much over-simplified advice has been offered on the subject of pricing for the small business. Low price, we are told, is not a sustainable competitive advantage for small firms, as they do not have the necessary economies of scale to support long term price cutting. Price is described as the weak link in the marketing mix of a small firm because lower prices can easily be copied and beaten by competitors, particularly larger companies. Yet many small firms survive, and thrive, on prices substantially lower than their larger competitors. If you want your car serviced cheaply, or a domestic appliance mended inexpensively, you will expect the lowest price from a local trader, not a national company. On the other hand, there are circumstances where the local small firm cannot compete on price alone. Food prices will always be higher in the village general store than in the out of town supermarket. A craftsman-joiner cannot supply windows and doors at anything like the price of the national D.I.Y chain.

In practice, pricing as a competitive instrument in the marketing mix depends on the industry and the market. Some markets, especially those involving a customised product or service, suffer diseconomies of scale which a small firm can exploit to produce a price advantage. A small garage or appliance repair firm do not carry the overheads, particularly in people and premises, of larger operations. The service offered by both has to be individual to the customer and cannot therefore be made more efficient by mass production techniques. In circumstances like these the small firm can establish a lasting competitive edge using price.

In other industries, especially where standard products or services can be produced, economies of scale will operate, and the small firm cannot seek a competitive advantage in pricing. Food and D.I.Y. chains can use production efficiencies, and their buying power to reduce prices to levels which the local trader cannot hope to match, let alone beat. Pricing decisions may be crude processes in most small firms, but in the right circumstances low price can still be an effective strategy.

5.2 "What the market will bear"

Small firms are often exhorted to price according to 'what the market will bear', by always asking the question: "What is the maximum price that a customer is prepared to pay for this?" Market pricing makes sense in theory, but there are some practical problems.

❑ In some markets prices are fixed – sometimes to the advantage of the small firm. Small enterprises are a strong force in retailing generally, accounting for about 28% of all retail businesses. However they are more numerous in the book trade, and particularly as outlets selling newspapers and magazines[18]. In these cases, national agreements preventing price cutting has effectively protected small firms who can compete in other ways. Other retailers do have price discretion, but of a limited range, as manufacturers often 'recommend' an end-user price, and sometimes advertise it in their own promotional campaigns.

❑ Consistency of prices is often necessary. Many small firms sell standard products from a price list. Even though some customers may be willing to pay more, pricing to what an individual will pay is clearly impractical in these circumstances.

A hairdresser could probably charge some clients more than others for the same service, and the customers would still be happy – until they talked to each other that is. In practice, a compromise is struck which may push some customers to the limit, but leaves others short of the full price they will bear.

❑ Competitors condition the market's reaction to what is an acceptable price. Where there is established competition which has pitched its prices low – below what in theory the market would bear – then it will be very difficult to persuade a customer to accept a higher price, without some other incentive. If there is no competitor setting a market price, then it will be hard for a small firm to find out the maximum price the customer will pay. Market research or test marketing will help, but a thorough evaluation may be beyond the resources of a new small enterprise. If a small firm is first into a specific market, then premium prices may be good for short term profits, but not for long term growth, as competitors are attracted in by the high prices which they can easily undercut. For example, in one small town there were two video hire firms, which had to compete aggressively to survive. As their services were not differentiated in other respects, their prices become more and more competitive until finally, during a period of poor trading, one was forced out of business by the inadequate margins. With no other local competition, the surviving firm put up their prices, without any adverse reaction from customers. The higher profitability of this market did not go unnoticed, however, and soon another competitor had set up, offering lower prices to establish themselves. Prices soon fell to their previous levels.

This is more in keeping with the economists view of the operation of a competitive market. The market price will often have more to do with competitor's pricing than any notion of the maximum a customer is prepared to pay.

5.3   Cost plus pricing

Deciding prices by calculating costs and adding what is judged to be an adequate element of profit, is probably the most common method in use in small firms. Marketing theorists frown upon this approach, as it does not always maximise the price that could be charged. Costs, they say, should not be directly linked to price, which should be determined by market forces; costs help to determine how well a business has done in terms of the profit generated by its pricing decisions but this should be the extent of the relationship between the two. In practice, however, most small firms will use certain costs as an important element in their pricing decision. Pricing in small firms is more likely to be based on a compromise between an estimate of what the business needs to cover its costs and a view on what the customer expects and competitors are charging.

A common issue for small firms is to understand the costs it incurs – not just their extent – but different types:

❑ Fixed costs refer to business expenses which do not vary with the level of trading. They are the overheads of a small firm, such as rent, rates, insurances, heating, lighting and most salaries. A small manufacturer, or retailer will have the same costs to pay for premises and full time staff whether they have sales of £500 or £5,000 per week. As all fixed costs have to be recovered eventually from sales, a crucial element in the pricing decision is the volume of sales that can be allocated to cover these overheads.

   If a small manufacturer or retailer has fixed overheads of £2,000 per week, and sales estimates vary from 1000 to 5000 units per week, the allocation of fixed costs will range from £2 to 40p per unit.

❑ Variable costs are expenses which do change in direct proportion to the level of trading. They are the costs of raw materials for manufacturing, or the costs of stock that a retailer will sell, and are sometimes referred to as the 'cost of sales' or 'cost of goods sold' (COGS). Most small firms that use stock in significant quantity will have a clearer idea of what these costs are in terms of a mark-up or a gross margin (although the two terms are sometimes confused).

❑ 'Mark-up' relates the selling price of an item to its variable costs. It takes the costs of the unit as the starting point, and represents how much is added to reach the selling price. It is often expressed as a percentage of the variable costs. If a retailer buys from a supplier for £20 + VAT and sells to the customer for £50 + VAT then the mark-up is £30, or 150% (on top of the costs of £20). If the price is increased to £60 + VAT, the mark-up is £40 or 200%.

   This can be expressed mathematically as:

$$\% \text{ Mark-up} = \frac{\text{sales price} - \text{variable cost}}{\text{variable cost}} \times 100\%$$

Mark-ups are used particularly in the retail trade, where variable costs are usually a very significant but known factor in the price of an item. To ensure that its prices reflect up to date suppliers prices, a small retailer may, for example, operate a standard minimum mark-up, which it simply adds on to suppliers invoices as a first step in a pricing decision.

❏ 'Gross margin' also relates the sales price of an item to the variable costs, representing the difference between the sales price and the variable costs. However, it takes the sales price as its starting point, and expresses how much of the sales price is left after deducting variable costs; it is often expressed as a percentage of the sales price. In our previous example, a small retailer selling an item for £50, which had been purchased for £20, would have a gross margin of £30 or 60% of the sales price. If the sales price is increased to £60, the gross margin of £40 is 66% or two-thirds of the sales price.

This can be expressed mathematically as:

$$\text{Gross margin} = \frac{\text{sales price - variable costs}}{\text{sales price}} \times 100\%$$

Gross margins are particularly useful where the variable costs of an item may be difficult to precisely allocate, but an average overall margin is targeted. For example, a small manufacturer, or retailer, selling several products, budgets for a gross margin of 50%. Each month, their management accounts report total sales and variable costs and therefore a gross margin. This will be an average of the margin of all products, which gives a first indication whether prices are in line with costs.

5.4 Pricing in practice

There are a number of tools and methods which small firms use to assist them in their pricing decisions.

Break even analysis

A useful concept for the small firm which relates costs, prices and volumes is a break even analysis. This begins with an analysis of the fixed and variable costs which can be illustrated graphically as in figure 14.4.

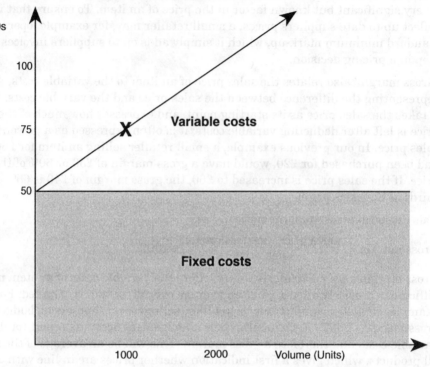

Figure 14.4: Fixed and variable costs

In this example, the fixed costs of overheads and salaries are £50,000p.a. and variable costs are £25 per unit.

If **1,000** units are produced, the costs will be:

Fixed costs	£50,000
Variable costs (£25 x 1,000)	£25,000
Total costs	£75,000

Therefore total costs per unit   **£75**

If 2000 units are produced, the costs will be:

Fixed costs	£50,000
Variable costs (£25 x 2000)	£50,000
Total costs	£100,000

Therefore total costs per unit: **£50**

This information can be used in a number of ways:

1. A manufacturer, with the cost profile just described, looks at market prices and decides that £50 per unit is the maximum price obtainable.

   A revenue line can now be added to the graph, as in figure 14.5, to form a break even analysis.

Figure 14.5: Break even analysis

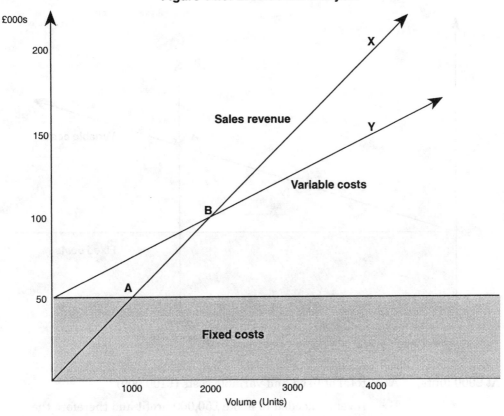

This shows that, at a price of £50 per unit:

A = volume where fixed costs covered (1,000 units)

B = Break even volume (2,000 units)

X = Sales target for the product (£200,000 or 4,000 units)

XY = Profits (After deducting the fixed and variable costs, this equates to £50,000. After deducting only variable costs this is £100,000 or a 50% gross margin)

A break even point can be calculated by using the following formula:

Break even volume = $\dfrac{\text{Fixed costs}}{\text{Gross margin per unit}}$

In our example, break even = $\dfrac{£50,000}{£25}$ = 2,000 units

2. Another small firm with the same cost profile is operating in a less competitive situation where there are no firm market prices. The firm believes it can make 2,000 units a year and would like to make a £50,000 profit on those sales. It can now plot what price to charge, as in figure 14.6.

Figure 14.6: Price setting analysis

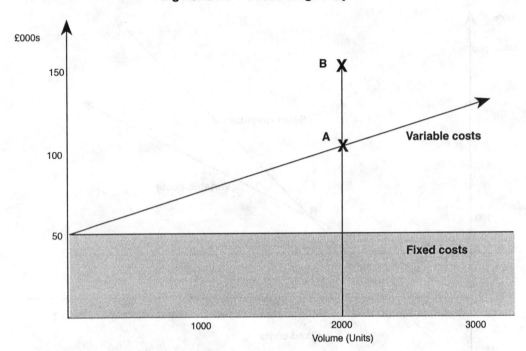

At 2000 units,   A =   total of fixed and variable costs (£100,000)

                    B =   revenue needed to make £50,000 profit and therefore the price per unit. (£75 per unit or £150,000 divided by 2000 units.)

3. A retailer is planning to open a new shop unit. Because they buy their products from suppliers with known prices, they can predict a gross margin of 50% on their current pricing policies. They also know that the fixed costs of the new shop in rent, wages etc will be £50,000p.a. They therefore have a break even point of sales of £100,000 if they continue their existing prices. If they believe this to be unlikely to be achieved, they have the choice of increasing their prices, to achieve a better gross margin and therefore lower break even point, or of dropping the venture altogether.

Customised pricing

Another variation of cost plus pricing is customised pricing. In this method, the customer effectively dictates the price, and the producer then works out what can be supplied for that price.

For example, a large supermarket chain is looking to buy a product which it will sell as an 'own-brand' (i.e. under its own name). The end user price has to be just lower than the brand leaders (say £2) and the supermarket has strict gross margin targets for this category of products, (say a minimum of 40%). The supermarket buyer will be sourcing a product at a known price therefore (no more than £1.20p in our example). A small firm wishing to bid for this business will attempt to tailor a product and a minimum order volume to match this price requirement.

Time and materials

Many small businesses are in a service sector business, where the key cost element will be the time spent on the job. These include domestic services such as plumbing, building and repair work, landscape gardening, tree felling and many more. Garages, secretarial services, free lance trainers, business consultants, solicitors and accountants also base their charges on time spent, plus any additional expenses incurred. The problems for a small firm in calculating time and materials include:

❒ *Hourly rate:* Surprise is sometimes expressed by customers at the hourly rate charged by a service organisation. Plumbers and mechanics charging £20 per hour, and partners in accountants and solicitors charging themselves at £80 per hour, all cause eyebrows to be raised. In fact small firms often undercharge for their services, forgetting the hours of travelling, selling, administration or preparation that they will need to spend, which are unpaid and bring down their average hourly rate. Evidence that small firms under price their labour has already been quoted with the average self-employed hourly rate below the employed national average (£6.67p vs £7.30p).

❒ *Time:* Where a fixed price is required for a quotation then an estimate of the total time necessary for the job becomes a key pricing decision. This would be typical of a builder quoting a fixed price for a specified job.

❒ *Materials:* Materials are expected to be invoiced at cost in most service situations, but this can overlook some of the hidden costs in obtaining the materials, such as the time taken to source and buy the materials, and the travelling costs involved in picking them up. To overcome this, materials are often charged at a full retail price, although discounts or wholesale prices were obtained.

Discounting

Discounts are a commonly used pricing mechanism by small firms. The use of discounts include selling off old or damaged stock, rewarding customer loyalty, launching a new product or service, and matching a competitor's price. These are often valid reasons for giving a discount which are to the benefit of the business.

However discounts, special offers and sales to help improve demand and cash flow are also misused by small firms, who overlook the real increase in volume that is required to make up for discounted prices.

For example a retailer, averaging a 50% gross margin on sales, offers a 20% discount off all stock for a limited period. Sales volume jump by 50% from the normal level of 10,000 units for the month to 15,000 units; but the owner-manager would be mistaken to believe this has been a successful promotion, as the following calculation reveals:

Normal Trading		'Special Offer'	Offer Break Even
10,000	sales units	15,000	16,666
£1	av. price per unit	80p	80p
£10,000	total sales	£12,000	£13,333
50p	cost per unit	50p	50p
£5,000	total cost	£7,500	£8,333
£5,000	gross margin	£4,500	£5,000

Although sales volume has increased considerably and sales revenue is also up by 20%, the effect of the discount more than takes away this advantage, and less gross margin is made during the period. In fact, for the offer to break even at the gross margin, sales volume would need to increase by 66.6%, or two-thirds up on normal trading. If small retailers calculated the real increase in volume they needed to recover the discounts they gave, then there would almost certainly be a drop in the number of 'Special Sales' that we see in our high streets today.

The corollary of this is that price increases can support relatively higher drops in sales volume before they have a negative effect on the gross margin. A small firm operating on a 40% gross margin, can support a 20% loss of volume for a 10% increase in prices before its realised gross margin is affected. It is more profitable to sell fewer items at a higher price.

In practice, then, pricing in the small firm is subject to a variety of influences. External factors relating to the specific industry and market situation, as well as internal variables of costs, and management policies, will be taken into account. Whilst pricing theory might indicate that small firms would benefit from more market pricing strategies, there are practical problems which have led many small enterprises to lean more towards a cost plus approach.

6. Promotion

6.1 Promotional inadequacies in small firms

Commentators on the performance of small firms have been more critical of their approach to promotion than perhaps any other aspect of marketing[6]. The consensus of opinion is that small firms do not do nearly enough to promote themselves. Considering that lack of sufficient custom is a frequent cause of small business failure, this seems an incongruous omission by small firm managers. There is certainly no shortage of texts giving advice on what to do to promote a small business.

Some of the reasons for this cautious approach to promotion are probably misplaced, and include issues that small firms have with marketing in general, such as:

❑ a suspicion of marketing and advertising;

❑ a reactive mentality which copes only with immediate problems, and does not look ahead to what is required to find tomorrow's customers;

❏ a perception of advertising and other forms of promotion as a cost, which, like other overheads has to be kept to a minimum;

❏ a belief that good products and services will find the customers they deserve;

❏ a vagueness about where customers come from in the first place, and therefore inadequate knowledge on which to base promotions;

However there are also some reasons for this apparent inactivity which are more rational. For example:

❏ *lack of resources:* advertising and other promotional forms can be expensive, especially for newly established firms which have not yet developed a positive cash flow.

❏ *limited impact:* promotions may have a very limited impact, and produce poor returns for a small firm. It may be that repeat promotions are required before significant benefits are seen; or it may be that several different approaches have to be tried before a winner is found. Either way, the small firm is likely to give up before achieving any real results because they simply cannot justify the risk of continuing.

❏ *difficult to target markets:* for some new businesses, there is no established promotional vehicle that can cost effectively deliver the message. The chosen market may be a niche, so specialised that no media is sufficiently targeted, and there are no other appropriate channels of communication. This could apply to some craft products; for example, a small firm hand producing specialised doll's houses had a limited output which ruled out the need for widespread promotions, but the only alternative was found to be word of mouth recommendations from customers.

❏ *lack of specialist expertise:* the previous experience of many owner-managers is based in the technology, or production aspects of their chosen product or service. They therefore recognise their limitations in marketing, particularly in the promotional field. Lack of sales experience increases the natural fear of rejection that even hardened sales people feel before visiting a prospect, and deters an inexperienced owner-manager from even making the appointment.

Although local promotional agencies do exist, it is often a fragmented service which relies on the owner-manager to coordinate the activity. A small firm wishing to undertake a direct mail shot, for example, may not find one local agency to handle all aspects; the owner-manager ends up commissioning a creative agency to write the letter and leaflet, finding a printer, sourcing an appropriate list from a list broker, and then ensuring all the materials and names are put together by a fulfilment house to complete the mailing. This is not only time consuming, but also off putting to the owner-manager with no real experience of these activities.

❏ *Lack of advice on implementation:* although much generalised advice exists on what can be done to promote a small business, there is much less information on how to use marketing communications more effectively within the internal and external constraints of a small firm's specific industry or market.

For example, a restaurant owner wishes to promote their business to the local community. Although they easily obtain general guidance on advertising, leaflets and personal selling, they find it harder to obtain knowledgeable advice on what is the most cost effective method for a restaurant, and how to implement a promotion for their new menu. One of the advantages of franchising is that the franchisor finds out, often by trial and error, the most effective promotional methods for their franchisees, and gives them clear guidelines on how to implement the strategy.

❏ *Lack of growth motive:* the small firm owner may not have an objective to increase sales much above present levels, and therefore sees little need to promote the business other than replace lost customers. This perfectly valid approach is sometimes misunderstood by observers who assume that, just because increased sales can be achieved, they necessarily ought to be achieved. Some owner-managers feel that they would not necessarily benefit from increased business; their personal satisfaction would not be better met by having extra sales. They are therefore happy to forgo promotional opportunities.

❏ *Use of personal communication channels:* Many owner-managers dislike impersonal sales approaches such as advertising and direct mail. They prefer personal communication channels which build a business by the sales activities of the owner-manager, and by the use of formal and informal networks, such as the chamber of commerce, professional advisors, trade associations, existing customers and friends who recommend their business. 'Word of mouth' becomes the most important method of promotion. Research already quoted earlier in this unit (see figure 14.2 'Small Business Methods of Finding Customers') illustrated that 73% of the promotional activity of a sample of printers and electronic manufacturers was based on word of mouth. For many small firms which do not need large numbers of customers, and who offer a personalised service, this is the most valid and cost effective promotional activity. However, some commentators on small business have failed sometimes to include the cost of the owner-manager's time in generating these recommendations as a promotional expense. If the cost of this time was included, then the promotional expenditure levels of many small firms would look very different indeed.

6.2 Options for marketing communications

The options for promoting the small firm are very wide. 'Promotion' is being used in its general sense of any form of marketing communication, which has the objective of either finding a new customer, or selling more to existing customers. There are personal, impersonal and implied methods of communicating with the market place.

6.3 Personal methods

Personal methods of promotion involve direct contact between the customer, or prospective customer, and a representative of the small firm. This contact can take the form of:

❏ direct selling;

❏ telephone selling;

❏ retail selling;

❏ exhibitions or trade shows.

The selection of the specific option will depend on the personal motivations of the owner- manager, as well as the business environment. As we have seen small firms seem to have a general preference for personal communication with the customer, rather than more impersonal methods, such as advertising. The reasons for this are often twofold:

❑ *A desire by the owner-manager to stay in touch with the market.* The competitive edge of some small enterprises is their rapid response to individual customer needs which is facilitated by the owner-manager's regular contact with the customer base. As many small firms are in service industries, where a more flexible response is possible, this can be an important competitive consideration over larger organisations, whose reaction time is often longer.

❑ *A belief that personal contact is the most cost effective method of promotion.* This may or may not be valid, but because owner-managers frequently do not cost their own time into the equation, this can often appear to be the case. However, as cash flow is usually the most important financial consideration of a young business, and the owner-manager's costs represent a fixed overhead, then personal selling by the owner-manager is often the only available option in the start up phase.

Whilst personal promotional methods may be the preferred route, there is a common danger in this approach if the responsibility is always left with the owner-manager. Other pressures on the owner-manager's time may make this strategy into a purely reactive one; the internal management requirements of the small firm can leave insufficient time for long term, planned sales approaches, and personal methods are resorted to when business looks slack.

For example, the owner-manager of a company, set up to provide commercial slide presentations, generated all the early business by personal selling. The demands of those early customers and the management of the production process soon took up all the manager's time. The business remained 'trapped' into this narrow base, until a key account was lost to a competitor, and the owner-manager was forced out selling once again. This cycle repeated itself several times until the small firm took the decision to employ a full time sales person. Even a retail business can develop problems when the owner-manager is serving in the shop; attention to customers can suffer because there is an urgent phone call, or an important supplier makes a visit.

Each personal promotional method involves skills and techniques which can enhance performance. These are not peculiar to small enterprises, but generic in the activity, and therefore it is not appropriate to develop these in great depth here.

However each activity does have advantages and pitfalls which may have more emphasis in the small firm.

Direct selling

It is difficult to think of a small business owner-manager who does not have some involvement in selling, even though they may not recognise it as such. Even the self-employed plumber or builder makes a sales call when asked in for an estimate. Some owners may have a background in sales; those in distributive industries such as office equipment, cars and engineering components will probably have had prior experience in the industry which involved some sales training. Most owners however, will have had no formal training in personal selling. Yet the owner-manager is most likely to be the front line sales person for the small firm.

Direct selling means face to face interviews with customers, usually on their premises with the objective of taking an order. It is most common in firms which sell to other businesses - manufacturers, distributors, or services. It can also be used for selling direct to consumers and is widely used by financial services and some home products, such as window and security systems, for instance.

The advantages for a small firm often lie in the visibility of results. Direct selling is a very measurable activity where, over an appropriate period of time, results can be judged against the effort expended. Direct customer contact also emphasises the need for small firms to build good relationships with existing customers. The goodwill generated from continuous personal contact of the owner-manager with clients can represent a key competitive advantage for a small firm over a larger firm relying on high turnover sales people with little decision making power. Direct contact with the market place will also have the spin off benefit of providing ongoing market research, often the only information of this kind that a small firm will obtain.

The pitfalls: Most experienced sales people will testify to the fact that the sales interview, or the actual moment of contact with the customer, is not the difficult part of selling; the problem is getting to see the customer in the first place. Typically a salesperson will spend less than 20% of their time face to face with a customer. The other 80% is spent trying to arrange appointments, travelling to them, and on administration. Selling is more about rejection than acceptance, and rejection comes at each stage in the process. It may take 10 phone calls to make 1 appointment, and 5 appointments to make 1 sale; that represents 50 phone calls per sale. These ratios often make selling more of a number's game than a sophisticated technique. The most successful sales people are those who persist, and make the 50 calls to obtain one sale, rather than give up after 10 calls and 1 disappointing appointment. Successful sales people are not necessarily those with the best presentation and sales technique before the customer[19].

The implications for the small business owner-manager who begins selling with little prior experience is that, like most novice sales people, they give up too soon. However, unlike most new sales people in larger companies, they have three further problems:

1. They do not have a sales manager to chase and support them. Therefore their lapses can be more permanent, as the owner-manager feels isolated by customer rejection, with no internal company support to fall back on.

2. Their lack of sales training may further decrease self confidence, and sales approaches become even more tentative.

3. Their wide ranging responsibilities produce a host of other 'more urgent' things to do, as replacement activities for the lonely job of selling.

This can result in a downward spiral, as the effort required to generate the number of sales leads to produce the final sale becomes sporadic and insufficient.

Alternatives: There are alternatives to owner-managers performing the sales function directly themselves.

❏   *A sales person(s)* can be employed by the small firm. The major barrier to this is cost, which is unlikely to be less than £30,000 per annum including travel and other overhead costs. For a small firm operating on a 50% gross margin this implies that sales of £60,000 will be needed to cover just the marginal costs of employing a sales person before any contribution to general overheads or additional profit is made.

❏   *Agents-on-commission* represent a way of overcoming this high fixed cost for a small firm. An agent will represent several manufacturers or distributors in a given trade, and sell their products to the relevant outlets in return for a commission (usually in the region of 10-15%) on sales made. This is often an appropriate method for a new firm in a market where typically high volumes of relatively low priced units are sold through a fragmented distribution. For example, a manufacturer of gift products might appoint four or five regional agents to sell their products to gift shops, stationers and other specialist outlets.

The advantage of this method is the rapid coverage of a large number of potential customers, at no risk to the manufacturer. The disadvantage is that there is no control over the effort in terms of amount or kind, and there is a loss of margin.

Telephone selling

The telephone can be used as part of the process of making a sale by direct customer contact – by making an appointment or answering an enquiry, for example. 'Telesales' can complete the whole process by taking the order on the phone.

For a small firm with limited resources, the telephone has become an indispensable part of selling. The problems start when the objective of the call is not clear. Use of the telephone to make a sales appointment is sometimes confused with making a sale, as the caller attempts to persuade the listener of all the benefits of the product or service during the call. This is a particular temptation for enthusiastic small business owners, who feel short of time to fully present their case at a later date. The result is often confusion of the listener, and a reluctance to take the approach further. Larger firms sometimes employ telephone sales personnel to fix appointments for other sales people to fulfil. They are trained to offer short clear reasons for an appointment which refrain from over elaboration, a technique which would benefit many small business owner-managers[20].

Taking telephone orders is used particularly to contact existing customers, who regularly place orders. For example, a health food wholesaler first developed outlets for its products by direct sales visits. It is not economic to make further regular visits, so customers are telephoned once a week and asked if they need to order further items. The phone call reminds retailers of the need to restock, and keeps out competitive products as the shelves are kept full.

Retail selling

Small independent or franchised shops can be classified into two main types in relation to retail selling: convenience outlets, such as newsagents and confectioners, and specialist shops, varying from fashion wear boutiques to art galleries. In both, there is a form of customer contact. In the convenience store, it will probably be no more than order taking after customers have served themselves. In the specialist outlet, the contact is more likely to involve some selling.

The advantage of a retail outlet is that it represents a (hopefully) convenient, permanent place of contact between buyer and seller. The difficulty for the specialist retailer is in recognising the line between the need to help the buyer make a decision, and maintaining a comfortable environment, in which the customer does not feel threatened or pressured.

The shop window is a key sales aid. It is often the method by which the retailer achieves contact with the customer, by tempting them inside in the first place. Larger firms, employing professional window dressers, know the importance of a regularly changed, attractive display, which is sometimes overlooked by smaller firms.

Independent retailers are a declining, but still significant part, of our high streets; the total number of independent stores declined from 450,000 shops in 1950, to 220,000 in

1980, and the proportion of retail sales from 64% to 34%[21]. Most new entrants to small business retailing have no experience of retail selling, and so learn through practice[22]. The variability of sales skills encountered in small shops testifies to the patchiness of that learning.

Exhibitions and trade shows

National trade shows and exhibitions cover every significant trade or industry, from lingerie and corsetry (at LACE in Harrogate) to electronic equipment (at INTERNEPCON in Birmingham).

There are also regional 'business-to-business' exhibitions serving more varied industries on a local basis. These can represent a concentrated meeting place for a small business, and therefore an efficient way of seeing customers and competitors alike.

Exhibitions are expensive in stand costs and the time involved in preparation and attendance. They are essentially points of contact, and although orders are sometimes written during the exhibition, the key to productive use of this resource is usually in the follow up to the introductions made. Exhibition catalogues can also provide useful further information for market research, or the basis of a mailing list. Exhibition organisers usually compile a list of visitors, made available to participating firms, which can form useful data for future promotions.

A problem for small firms is often in the small size, poor presentation and out-of-the-way position of their stand, which can combine to significantly reduce the number and quality of contacts made.

6.4   Impersonal methods

Impersonal methods of promoting a small firm include:

❑ Advertisements in various media

❑ Direct Mail

❑ Press releases

❑ Leaflets and brochures

Media advertisements

In practice there are two distinct types of media advertising for the small enterprise:

1. *Directories and trade listings.* These are permanent references, outlining the products or services offered by a small firm which can be consulted by potential buyers. This form of advertising is widely used by owner-managers, who see the benefit of a permanent indication of their business in popular directories, such as 'Yellow Pages' and 'Business Pages'. One disadvantage is that it is quite expensive, with a display advertisement costing several hundreds of pounds for one area listing in a national directory. Judgement of which category or service, and which geographic region to enter, is sometimes a further complication and expense. For example, a commercial catering company with a private functions room, whose target market overlapped two geographic areas of a national directory, couldn't decide whether 'Banqueting Rooms', 'Conference Facilities' or 'Catering' would be their best category, and were faced with an invoice for six insertions if they wished to cover all options in both geographic regions.

2. *Press, radio or television advertising:* There is a wide choice of media for a small firm to use on a more irregular basis, in the hope of creating or reinforcing awareness and demand for products or services.

   Small enterprises are reluctant to commit expenditure on this kind of advertising. The link between advertising and sales is difficult to establish, and often requires a long term investment to be cost effective. Small firms often therefore consider substantial expenditure on this type of promotion as a luxury they cannot afford. Detailed planning of an advertising campaign and a creative and media strategy with clear objectives, over an adequate time period, helps achieve the desired results from promotional expenditure, but it is generally rare in the small business sector.

   Instead, typical small firm advertising practices seem haphazard, restricted and reactive. Often the stimulus for advertising lies with media sales people who persuade small firms to take space in an appropriate "Special Feature" of their publication. At other times, advertising is in response to a direct competitive threat. Planned advertising may be generated to support a particular special offer, or sales drive, but opportunities for a sustained campaign, which build and reinforce awareness and interest are often missed.

Direct mail

Direct mail has become an increasingly popular form of advertising over the last two decades; it is third in the national advertising expenditure league table, after Press and TV[23]. The reasons for this increased popularity are particularly relevant to small business:

1. *Direct mail is targeted.* Small firms often trade in very narrow or fragmented markets, which traditional media over-hit or miss altogether. Direct mail has been likened to using the rifle, rather than a blunderbus, as promotional messages can be directed very specifically.

2. *Direct mail results can be quantified.* Unlike other forms of advertising, the results of a direct mail campaign, in terms of response back from the recipients, can be measured and valued. A small firm can decide from the results whether the campaign justifies its costs.

3. *Direct mail can be tested.* Although the set up costs of producing letters and leaflets are fixed, other costs of a mailing campaign vary with the quantity posted. It is possible to test the response from direct mail on a limited basis, before extending the mailing to the full list. A small firm can thus reduce the risks involved in this type of promotional expenditure.

   For example, a picture framing business found that advertising in the local press was either ineffective or swamped the workshop with too many orders in a short space of time. Instead the owner-manager tried direct mail to a list of existing customers and local residents on a progressive basis, to both test the response and stagger the resulting workload.

The problems associated with direct mail are:

1. *The quality of the mailing list is crucial;* the best designed mail shot sent to the wrong people will not produce results. Finding an appropriate list can be a problem. There are a number of sources for the small firm.

First, the best list is usually of existing customers; they are after all known buyers of the product or service on offer, and up to date details should be obtainable. Although small firms are becoming more aware of the importance of building a customer list, and computer databases can provide an easy storage facility (note the Data Protection Act[24]), many owner-managers still overlook this opportunity, and have no systematic system for recording customer information.

Secondly, lists can be compiled from a number of sources, including local or trade directories, electoral registration rolls, or other official listings. An office stationery suppliers, for example, decided to target professional categories such as accountants and solicitors, which are listed in local business directories. The disadvantage was that this did not include names of partners, so that the mailing could not be personalised.

Thirdly, lists can be purchased, or rented, from list brokers who have compiled or acquired lists of many different classifications, from sales managers to sports players. Such lists are normally rented on a cost per 1,000 basis, with a minimum charge. A potential problem for a small business is that, although lists can be localised, by breaking them down into postcodes, the result is often a small list which incurs the fixed minimum charge.

Lastly, lists can be geographically designated simply by the hand delivery of mail shots to specified streets or business areas. Although response from this is generally low, as the mailings are not personalised and rather random, it can be cost effective as delivery expenses are low.

2. *Direct mail can be a fragmented and time consuming promotional method.* An owner-manager may find it necessary to become personally involved in the various stages of a direct mail campaign, from the creation and production of letters and leaflets, to the researching of lists and appropriate delivery methods. This not only effectively increases the cost of the promotion, but also puts off some owner-managers who feel they do not have either the time or expertise to manager these functions.

3. *Response rates from direct mail are usually very low,* often less than two or three percent. Whilst such responses may still meet the costs of the campaign, they limit the scope of the effort. For example, the office stationery supplier mailing to professional lists received seven inquiries from the 200 names mailed, which converted into four orders, the value of which more than justified the expense of the mailing. However, the firm soon ran out of lists to mail, and the total volume of business generated was small.

Press releases

Larger companies have long recognised the importance of good public relations, and the value that can be obtained by working with the media. P.R. departments and agencies can point to 'free advertising' on TV or in the Press to justify their costs to large corporations. Small firms can similarly benefit, but few make full use of the possibilities.

Local media and the trade press consume large quantities of news, and small firm activities are often newsworthy, but unnoticed. The problems are familiar: owner-managers with no time, or expertise to put together press releases, or make the necessary media contact.

Leaflets and brochures

Most small firms produce a leaflet or brochure describing their product or service. Desk top publishing has encouraged many small firms to produce more literature about themselves which, at a relatively modest cost, can now be made to look professional and business like. Small firms used to suffer considerable diseconomies of scale because of the short run nature of their publicity material. Computer graphics and laser printing technology have changed all that to the benefit of small enterprises, which now have no excuse for poorly produced literature. Whilst their general standard of graphic reproduction has undoubtedly improved, small firms still have problems with the distribution and contents of leaflets and brochures. Common problems include:

- ❑ *Unclear objectives:* A small firm's leaflet will typically try to be all things to all people. Whilst this is an understandable reaction to the need for economies in producing publicity material, the impact of what is produced can be considerably reduced by confusion or profusion of objectives. Brochures may be distributed by a variety of methods, and to different customer groups. For example, an upholsterers, selling their services mainly to hotels, decided to also target the domestic market of local householders. As they had a good stock of existing leaflets, they offered these to potential customers from this new segment. Unfortunately, householders were confused by the technical specifications in the leaflet, particularly those referring to 'flame-retardent materials', and 'British Standard Specifications.'

- ❑ *Product, not customer, centred:* Small firms often describe what they have to offer in terms of the technical specifications of their product or service, rather than by reference to what use this will be to a potential customer. Whilst there is a place for detailed product descriptions, and technical data (usually the back page) the first consideration to a reader will be the benefits they can perceive for themselves. Owner-managers, who probably have the greatest input into the contents of a small firm's leaflet, may be involved with the technology or production aspect of a small business, and therefore write literature about it from this, and not the customer's, perspective.

- ❑ *Wasteful quantities:* Small firms typically seem to have a large pile of outdated brochures gathering dust in a corner of the office. Whilst some waste is inevitable, more attention to leaflet composition and content can keep this to a minimum. Many expensive brochures contain details and prices which are bound to date rapidly. The conflict for a small firm is usually between printing enough to represent an economic order quantity, and maintaining flexibility in the content of the literature as information changes. The permutations of graphic production are now so great that it is often possible to resolve this conflict. For example, one small enterprise, a primary school, needed a brochure every year, for the new intake of parents and prospective parents. The head teacher felt that presentation was important in the changed environment of primary schools, which had become more competitive. The annual requirement was for only 200 brochures, and some details, such as the names of teachers and governors, could change every year. This seemed to preclude the preferred four colour cover on cost grounds. A solution was found by producing a more expensive outer folder, which could be printed in larger quantities to be used over several years, into which loose sheets containing the information likely to change were inserted.

6.5   Implied communications

We have already seen that marketing strategies can emerge from a pattern of a small firm's activities as perceived by customers. The image portrayed by marketing communications adds to this pattern of perceptions. An impression of a small enterprise, and its products or services, is given by its letterhead, the signage on a shop or delivery van, the answering of the telephone, the style of leaflets and advertisements, the tone of its letters, the decor of its premises as well as the way a customer is served. These impressions form implied communications from the business which promote it either positively or negatively.

The issue for any business, small or large, is to ensure that all forms of communication are consistent with the objectives of the enterprise and the needs of its customers. In this the small firm should have advantages, because of its shorter, less complicated internal lines of communication. The owner-manager of a small business should be in a better position than the chief executive of a large organisation to ensure that all messages from the company to customers are consistent and in line with company policy. In practice, larger companies probably work harder at their image than smaller ones, as a reaction to the possibility of inconsistent communications. Successful small firms project an image which matches the aspirations of the target customer group by reflecting what they are looking for. The important questions for a small firm to ask is, 'what kind of messages would target customers like to receive from this kind of enterprise?' and 'what messages are we actually sending them?' Too often, the answers are different.

7. Place

7.1   Distribution channels

The final element in the marketing mix – place – refers to how goods reach the market place. As it is describing the methods by which products or services move from supplier to user, a more appropriate title is perhaps distribution (except that it doesn't begin with 'P'!)

For any firm, there is a fundamental choice in deciding its channels of distribution: to distribute direct to end-users or through intermediaries. From this basic choice, other options then emerge as illustrated in figure 14.7.

Figure 14.7: Distribution channels

Direct to end-users	Through intermediaries
❏ Direct sales	❏ Agents/distributors
❏ Retail and specialist outlets	❏ Wholesalers
❏ Mail order	❏ Mail order companies
❏ Direct marketing	❏ Retailers and specialist outlets

7.2 Direct to end users

Where products or services are sold by a small firm direct to the final user this can be done by:

❐ *Direct sales:* Small firms frequently sell directly to the customer through the personal representation of the owner-manager, employed sales people, or agents on commission visiting customers. This is most frequent in the 'business to business' service sector covering a whole range of professional services, and supplies. Some small firms in this category are themselves acting as intermediaries for other producers; for example a distributor of office products, or a wholesaler of wine.

❐ *Retail and specialist outlets:* Many small firms operate either a shop, or other form of outlet, such as a public house, wine bar or restaurant, which is visited by the customer. The consumer visits the supplier on their premises because of convenience, or the nature of the service. As such outlets often need to be near consumers, and therefore decentralised and fragmented. This is a popular form of small business, which has also lent itself particularly to franchising.

❐ *Mail order:* Customers can be sold goods directly via a catalogue, or a newspaper advertisement, which are then shipped through the mail. Small firms sell a variety of goods via mail order, from philatelic items to specialist publications. The high entry barriers to the mail order catalogue business have prevented much small firm participation, but many individual items are offered via mail order by small enterprises. The value-weight ratio of the product will be the key determinant of the suitability of this channel, as marketing costs are usually high, and delivery costs are based on weight and bulk.

❐ *Multi-level marketing:* This rather confusing term has been used to describe a variety of ways of reaching consumers, by a chain of direct selling agents. At one extreme this includes 'Pyramid selling' which is now legally regulated, as many self employed people were duped into buying a stock of product which was being sold only to fill up the distribution pipe-line and rarely to end-users. However it does have its more legitimate forms. 'Party plan', for example, is a method of distributing a variety of products, including plastic containers, books and cosmetics by encouraging household gatherings at which the products are sold. This approach involves sales agents, usually operating on a part-time self-employed basis, who organise the gatherings and earn commission on the sales.

In the USA, an increasingly used distribution system is sometimes referred to as 'multi-level' or 'network marketing'. It does involve setting up a pyramid structure of sales agents, who earn commission both on their sales to consumers and to other agents, but there is a crucial difference to the discredited pyramid selling. The agent does not need to buy stock in order to make a sale, other than for demonstration purposes; thus if final users are not buying the product the system breaks down. The promoters of this system make extravagant claims about the level of sales now being achieved in the UK, and the growth they expect. It is certainly attracting more participation from self-employed business people, selling such products as water softeners and household cleaning materials[25].

7.3   Through intermediaries

When the title to products or services passes from one organisation to another, before reaching the final consumer, then distribution is being carried out through intermediaries. These can be:

❏ *Agent or distributors:*

Agents or distributors represent the supplier in a given territory or market, by buying stock and selling it either direct to the end user or on down the distribution channel to wholesalers or retailers.

Agents are particularly useful for small firms, where the potential market is large, and the resources of the small business limited. It is for this reason that most small firms export through agents and distributors.

Many agents and distributors are themselves small firms, as the entry barriers to this type of business are low, and the local knowledge and contacts of the owner-manager give benefits to a supplier, unable to set up a directly controlled distribution system.

Agents and distributors have evolved into licensed dealerships in certain trades, for example motor cars and drinks, where distributors are controlled by strict agreements.

This system also provided the basis from which format franchising has grown; a franchisee is effectively an agent for the franchisor in a given territory.

❏ *Wholesalers*

The proliferation of products or retailers in some trades makes it necessary for a further link in the distribution chain. For example a small publisher of specialist magazines could not possibly distribute directly to all the newsagents and other possible outlets for their publications, so they sell through wholesalers. Some major retail chains have established their own wholesaling divisions to break bulk before passing goods onto the stores; W.H.Smith and food chains such as Sainsburys or Tescos are examples. A small firm wishing to sell to these large companies will have to distribute via the wholesale company.

Some wholesalers are also small firms operating on a regional basis, for example in the cards and stationery markets.

❏ *Retailers and specialist outlets*

Many small firms sell to retailers, and specialist outlets, such as public houses, restaurants and wine bars. These are often themselves small businesses. As the retailer is providing the interface with the final user, there is normally competition for shelf space and positions which favour sales.

❏ *Mail order companies*

A small firm can sell to specialist mail order companies, who offer a variety of goods to consumers usually via a catalogue. Obtaining a listing in a catalogue is not easy, as there is limited space which the buyer in the mail order company will want to fill only with strong selling lines.

7.4   For and against intermediaries

Advantages

Small firms, with limited resources and expertise, can particularly benefit from using intermediaries. Specific advantages are:

1. *Local knowledge and contacts of the intermediary:* Small firms often base their business on the owner-managers local know-how. Expanding into territories where it no longer applies can be risky without an intermediary to supply specific knowledge of the environment.

2. *Reduced distribution costs:* A small manufacturer can considerably reduce their distribution costs by using an agent or wholesaler, thereby eliminating the need for a large number of small deliveries direct to retailers.

3. *Reduced stock holding:* By shifting the responsibility for stockholding down the distribution chain, a small manufacturer can reduce their own stock holding requirements and the associated financial and space considerations.

Disadvantages

There are of course disadvantages:

1. *Loss of contact with the market place:* A small firm relying on intermediaries for their distribution and selling will be one or more steps removed from the consumer they are seeking to serve. Their customer becomes the distributor, wholesaler, or retailer, and they must rely on them for information about customers down the chain, including the final consumer.

2. *Less control over how the product is presented to the final customer:* As we have already seen, products extend beyond the physical attributes of an item. By using intermediaries, the original manufacturer is handing over control of some aspects of the extended product to somebody else. An intermediary may be providing the after sales service and certainly the information and advice; packaging can be changed by distributors, and the presentation of the benefits of the product to the consumer is out of the control of the originator.

3. *Less influence over the levels of marketing effort:* Most intermediaries represent more than one supplier. They therefore exercise choice over which products receive the most effort in terms of display, promotional effort and selling time. One of the strengths of the franchise system is that it avoids this issue, by insisting on the exclusivity for a franchisor's products or services with the franchisee.

4. *Less revenue per item sold:* Last but not least, intermediaries cost money; although this is not a fixed cost, but a variable depending on the level of sales, loss of revenue can be substantial – commonly at least one third of the final selling price if distributed direct to retail or up to two thirds where agents and wholesalers are used.

All these disadvantages multiply as the distribution chain becomes longer.

7.5   Choosing a distribution channel

For a small firm the choice of distribution channel will be conditioned by a number of factors:

☐ *The customer:* The existing buying pattern of the target end use group will not be easy to change. A small firm will normally wish to follow traditional distribution routes for their product or services, leaving major innovations in this area to better resourced companies. However, it may be appropriate to try different channels to reach a wider audience. For example, a small manufacturer of soft toys followed the customary wholesale/retail channels for its regular production. But for special occasions, an inexpensive addition to the product could temporarily extend the market potential, which warranted innovative distribution methods. For example, on Valentine's Day, the simple addition of a message to a soft teddy bear created a new product, whose market would not be reached by traditional methods. The company found that press advertising reached a new audience for their product, which was physically distributed to respondents by mail order.

☐ *The product:* Distribution channels need to match the needs of the product that is on offer. An electronics manufacturer, designing highly technical products, customised to client requirements, probably has no choice but to sell and distribute directly themselves. A publisher of greetings cards, sold through a multiplicity of independent retailers, probably has no option but to use a wholesaler.

Most small firms offer a service rather than manufacture a tangible product. In some cases this precludes any form of intermediary distribution. A training consultant can only really deliver their product directly themselves (although they might franchise the format). In other cases, as we have seen, the service offered is part of the distribution chain anyway. For example, a small health food wholesaler is a service company as they manufacture nothing themselves.

☐ *Finance:* There is usually a financial trade off for a small firm in the use of intermediaries. A small business's cash flow benefits from selling large amounts of stock to distributors and wholesalers. Profitability suffers, however, because of the need to give up margin. The financial circumstances of a small firm will determine which factor predominates.

☐ *Objectives:* The marketing strategy of a small firm will indicate objectives somewhere between the extremes of high volume to wide markets, or lower volume to a select niche. The more the strategy leans towards the former, the more intermediaries will be appropriate; the more it looks like the latter, the more direct distribution will be considered.

7.6   Distribution practices in small firms

The evidence points towards unadventurous distribution practices in small firms. As has been emphasised before, however, the heterogeneous nature of the small firm sector makes this a far from universal rule.

Many small firms are restricted by their product or service to a local market, and traditional distribution methods. An independent retailer or a small hotel will have little option for example; for them 'place' is the key decision, as location will largely determine the market they can serve. Once that decision is made, it cannot be easily varied; the other 3 'P's will then become the active elements in the marketing mix.

Other, less restricted business types, are heavily influenced by the attitude of the owner-manager. A strong desire to retain control may steer the small firm away from more enterprising distribution possibilities.

International distribution

International markets are typically ignored by small firms. Surveys of small businesses in all sectors of the economy suggest that a mere 6% sell any of their output outside of the UK[5]. This is despite considerable effort that has been put into providing help[26] and assistance for would be exporters from such areas as:

❑ Department of Trade and Industry 'country desks', which provide information on trade with all foreign countries.

❑ British Chambers of Commerce, which issue export documentation, and may offer advice.

❑ Export Credits Guarantee Department, which arranges insurance against the possibility of non-payment.

❑ Central Office of Information offering export publicity services.

In anticipation of the open European market from 1992 onwards, small firms were encouraged to look more at export opportunities. So far though, there is little evidence that there has been a change in the attitude which has regarded exports as something to explore once all home market possibilities are exhausted.

8. References and further reading

8.1 References and further information

1. For further discussion of strategies versus tactics see for example Quinn, J, *Strategies for Change: Logical Incrementalism,* Irwin Inc, 1980.

2. See for example: Waterworth, D, *Marketing for the Small Business,* MacMillan Education 1987 (in the MacMillan Small Business series); Brown, R, *Marketing for the Small Firm,* Holt, Rhinehart & Winston, 1985; Fowler, D, *Selling and Marketing for the Small Business,* Sphere Study Aids, 1984.

    One book which concentrates on the practical aspects of what is used by small businesses is Hingston, P, *The Greatest Sales & Marketing Book,* Hingston, 1989.

3. Curran, J Blackburn R, *Small Firms and Local Economic Network,s* A report to the Midland Bank, December 1991.

4. *Starting-Up: A Barclays Report on Britain's Small Business Men and Women,* Barclays Bank, 1992.

5. See Storey, D and Johnson, S, *Job Generation and Labour Market Change,* MacMillan Press, 1987.

6. See Carson, D, "Some Exploratory Models of Assessing Small Firms Marketing Performance", *European Journal of Marketing,* Vol 24, No 11, 1990.

7. Carson, D, "The Evolution of Marketing in Small Firms", in Marketing and Small Business (Special Issue), *European Journal of Marketing,* Vol 19, No 5, 1985.

8.   Free advice on business names can be obtained from Companies House, Crown Way, Cardiff CF4 3U2 telephone no. 0222-388588. The D.T.I. produce two helpful leaflets, *Control of Business Names,* and *Disclosure of Business Ownership,* obtainable from the same address.

9.   The recent 1988 Copyright, Designs and Patents Act reformed much of British law in this respect, but laws protecting intellectual property rights in the EC are to be harmonised, so further changes are inevitable. There are proposals for an EC wide trademark which would overcome the present need to apply for registration in each member state by setting up a Community Trade Marks Office.

10. Binks, M and Jennings, A, "New Firms as a Source of Industrial Regeneration." in Scott, M et al (eds), *Small Firms Growth and Development,* Gower, 1986.

11. Rothwell, R, 'The Role of Small Firms in Technological Innovation' in Curran, J (eds) *The Survival of the Small Firm,* 1986 Gower.

12. See Adams, A. and Wallbank W. *The Introduction of New Products by Smaller Manufacturing Firms,* SRC Final Report GR/A 71072, UMIST, 1981.

13. See Adams, A and Wallbank, M, "The Evaluation of New Product Ventures in Small Firms," in Scott, M et al (eds), *Small Firms Growth and Development,* Gower 1986.

14. The Technology Exchange Ltd, Wrest Park, Silsoe, Bedford MK45 4HS.

15. See for example Stanworth, J and Stanworth, C, *Work 2000 - the Future for Industry, Employment and Society*, Chapman, 1991.

16. *Partners in Innovation: Business and Academia,* McKinsey and Co. Inc. Innovation Project.

17. *The Guardian* reported on September 23rd 1991 (Page 12 New Business) that 14 of the 24 companies, working on projects in Link programmes developing analytical and measurement technology, were small to medium sized companies.

18. See *Retailing* SDA 25 H.M.S.O.

19. There are many books on selling, many of which concentrate only on sales technique in front of the customer. One that gives practical tips on the other 80% of a sales person's efforts is Bettger, F, *How I Multiplied my Income and Happiness in Selling,* Prentice Hall, 1954.

     Some of the self-motivational aspects of selling are dealt with in Forbes Ley D, *The Best Seller,* Kogan Page, 1989.

20. See Tack, A., *How to Increase Sales by Telephone,* Heinemann, 1978.

21. For a survey of the problems of small retailers see Kirby, D A, "The Small Retailer" in *The Survival of the Small Firm,* Vol 1., Curran, J. et al (eds), Gower, 1986.

22. Kirby, D A and Law, D C, *The Birth and Death of Small Retail Units in Britain: A Preliminary Study, Retail and Distribution Management,* Vol. 9 No.1. 1981.

23. See Andrew, L (ed), *The Royal Mail Direct Mail Handbook,* Exley Publications, 1984. This is an excellent guide to direct mail with relevant advice on all aspects.

24. If information on individuals is stored on computer, then registration under the Data Protection Act is normally required, which currently costs £56. Further information can be obtained from the Registrar's Enquiry Service, telephone 0625 535777.

25. For the background information on Multilevel marketing (although not totally objective) see Clothier, P, *Multilevel Marketing,* XXX, 1990

26. For a detailed listing of help that is available from the D.T.I., Chambers of Commerce, and other sources, see Wilson, J, *The Barclays Guide to International Trade for the Small Business,* Blackwell, 1990.

8.2   Recommended further reading

Barrow, C, *The New Small Business Guide,* BBC, 1989 section 5, 'Finding out about your market'. (This has a good list of marketing organisations and their services).

Higston, P, *The Greatest Sales and Marketing Book,* Higston 1989.

Carson, D J "Some Exploratory Models of Assessing Small Firms Marketing Performance", *European Journal of Marketing,* Vol 24 No 11 1990.

Unit 15: Money

This Unit is about another of the three major strategic influences on a small business – money. The Unit considers the financial needs of small firms, the sources of funds available to them, and the appropriate control of those funds.

1. Financial requirements

Small firms need money to finance a host of different requirements. In looking at the types and adequacy of funds available, it is important to match the use of the funds with appropriate funding methods. Figure 15.1 illustrates the principle capital needs of a small firm.

Figure 15.1: The uses and sources of funds for a small business

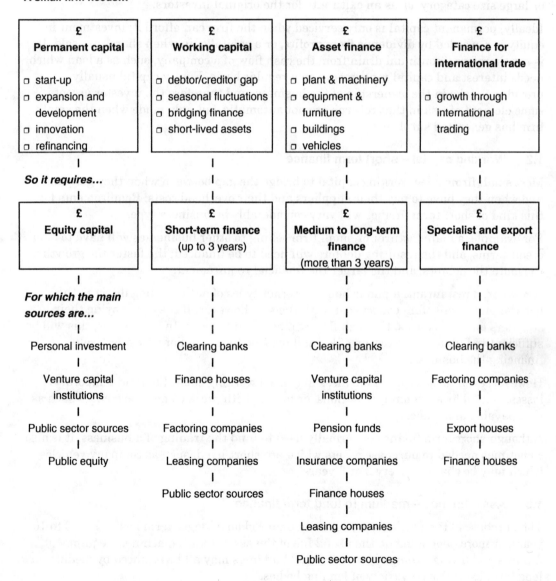

A small firm needs...

£ **Permanent capital**	£ **Working capital**	£ **Asset finance**	£ **Finance for international trade**
□ start-up □ expansion and development □ innovation □ refinancing	□ debtor/creditor gap □ seasonal fluctuations □ bridging finance □ short-lived assets	□ plant & machinery □ equipment & furniture □ buildings □ vehicles	□ growth through international trading

So it requires...

£ **Equity capital**	£ **Short-term finance** (up to 3 years)	£ **Medium to long-term finance** (more than 3 years)	£ **Specialist and export finance**

For which the main sources are...

Personal investment	Clearing banks	Clearing banks	Clearing banks
Venture capital institutions	Finance houses	Venture capital institutions	Factoring companies
Public sector sources	Factoring companies	Pension funds	Export houses
Public equity	Leasing companies	Insurance companies	Finance houses
	Public sector sources	Finance houses	
		Leasing companies	
		Public sector sources	

1.1 Permanent capital – equity capital

The permanent capital base of a small firm usually comes from some form of equity investment in shares in a limited company, or personal loans to or from partners or sole traders. It is used to finance the one-off start-up costs of an enterprise, or major developments and expansions in its life-cycle. It may be required for a significant innovation, such as a new product development. In some cases, it is required to refinance a firm that has acquired borrowings which are inappropriate to its current situation; short term borrowings, in the form of loans or overdrafts, may need to be converted into more permanent capital as a small firm grows, or runs into problems. Equity from private investors may also be sought to take a small firm into the medium or large size category, or as an exit route for the original investors.

Ideally, permanent capital is only serviced when the firm can afford it; investment in equity is rewarded by dividends from profits, or a capital gain when shares are sold. It is not therefore a continual drain from the cash flow of a company, such as a loan which needs interest and capital repayments on a regular basis. Equity capital usually provides a stake in the ownership of the business, and therefore the investor accepts some element of risk in that returns are not automatic, but only made when the small firm has generated surpluses.

1.2 Working capital – short term finance

Most small firms need working capital to bridge the gap between when they get paid, and when they have to pay their suppliers and their overhead costs. Requirements for this kind of short term finance will vary considerably by business type.

For example, a manufacturer or small firm selling to other businesses will have to offer credit terms, and the resulting debtors will need to be financed; the faster the growth, the more the debtors, and the larger the financial requirement.

A retailer, a restaurant, a public house, or other types of outlet selling direct to the general public will often collect cash with the sale however. If they are paying their suppliers on credit terms, the cash flow will be advantageous. In some cases, this will be sufficient to finance the start-up of a small firm, so that suppliers are effectively financing the business.

However, even these types of business may need working capital to fund temporary losses, caused by seasonal fluctuations, or to cope with prepayment of expenses such as rent payable in advance.

Although short term finance is normally used to fund the trading of a business, it is also sometimes needed to purchase assets which are short-lived, such as company vehicles which may be changed every 2 or 3 years.

1.3 Asset finance – medium to long term finance

The purchase of tangible assets is usually financed on a longer term basis, from 3 to 10 years, or more depending on the useful life of the asset. Plant, machinery, equipment, fixtures and fittings, company vehicles and buildings may all be financed by medium or long term loans from a variety of lending bodies.

1.4 International trade finance

Exporting brings its own set of money problems. Currency fluctuations, lengthy payment terms and security of payment all give rise to the need for some kind of specialist or export finance.

2. Sources of finance

To meet these differing types of funding requirement, the owner-manager has a number of options to obtain finance.

2.1 Personal investment by owner-managers

Several studies have confirmed that the most important source of start-up capital comes from owner-managers themselves. There is evidence of regional differences, however. For example, Mason and Lloyd's study of new manufacturing firms in South Hampshire[1] revealed that 66% used personal savings, and 42% obtained bank loans or overdrafts as launch capital. Other studies, in less prosperous regions of the UK, have shown that a higher percentage of start-ups (usually over 80%) have used personal funds from the owners.

It would seem that the level of owner investment is conditioned by two main factors:

❑ *Creditworthiness of the owner:* As homes are the major source of guarantee on borrowings, the higher value of property, and higher rates of home ownership in more prosperous regions, will allow owners to borrow relatively more money as mortgages or second mortgages to finance their business.

❑ *Experience and awareness of sources of funds:* In regions where redundancy from traditional industry sectors is a key source of new business formation, those people 'pushed' into new ventures as the only realistic alternative employment, tend to have limited experience of financial management, and restricted awareness of the possible sources of funds. In the 1980s large companies in the UK economy shed an estimated 3.5 million jobs, and small businesses and self-employment created an estimated 3 million jobs. Redundancy payments and personal savings formed a major source of start-up capital for those moving from the large to the small firm sector.

2.2 The Business Expansion Scheme

The need for the investment of permanent capital as equity in small businesses from private sources prompted the government to introduce the Business Expansion Scheme (BES) in 1983. This was not targeted at investment by the owner-manager; the scheme specifically precluded investors from being directors or employees of the business. The objective of the scheme was to encourage outside investment in small firms, by individuals who would remain as investors, not as managers. The incentive for this investment was generous tax relief to help compensate for the higher risks involved (for fuller details of the scheme see Information Bank, Unit 6, 'The Small Business Environment', 2.2 "UK government policy").

Between 1983/84 and 1987/88, the BES attracted over £750 million of new investment, in nearly 4000 small and medium-sized enterprises. Not much of this reached the truly small firm, however. Over half of the amount invested was raised by a few companies (less then 4% of the total), which each raised over £1 million. Moreover in 1988, the scheme was extended to include residential property, let under an assured tenancy agreement. This asset-backed investment proved so attractive that it siphoned off over 90% of BES funds invested in 1988/9 and 1989/90[2]. In short, BES was no longer a significant source of equity investment for small firms. It was therefore no great surprise when Chancellor Norman Lamont announced that the scheme would be scrapped in 1993 (in the 1992 Budget).

2.3   Venture capital

Venture capital funds in the UK provide finance for growing businesses, usually through equity capital with some loan element. There are over 100 Venture Capital companies in the UK, who obtain investment funds from a variety of sources, including pension funds, insurance companies, investment trusts, regional development agencies, and private individuals through the BES. The best known is probably 3i (Investors in Industry), established by the Bank of England and the clearing banks in 1945 to provide finance to growing firms.

The venture capitalist provides risk finance, which will come after banks and other preferential lenders in terms of security. The returns sought from the investment will therefore be high; the internal 'rate of return' targets of most venture capitalists are between 25–60% depending on the risk involved.

The structure of any particular investment will vary, but usually involves any combination of three types of capital: equity shares, preference shares and loans. The level of share ownership required is normally less than 50%, with a typical stake between 30–40%; a seat on the board of directors is also common.

The venture capital fund will wish to see ways of cashing in their investment by selling their shares in the future. These so-called 'exit routes' include:

❏ a public listing on the stock exchange, usually the Unlisted Securities Market (see below);

❏ a sale of the company to another interested business;

❏ the company may wish to repurchase the shares of the venture capitalist.

The need for clearly visible exit routes restricts the types of company in which the venture capitalist is interested. Whilst they do invest in start-ups, this is not particularly favoured, unless it is already a substantial looking business in its early days, capable of generating profits over £250,000 within 4–5 years; this often implies involvement in a new, high technology industry. More commonly, Venture Capital Funds are used for the expansion of already established, successful firms capable of sustained growth, or for 'Management Buy-Outs', or 'Management Buy-Ins', (as covered in Unit 9, "Buying an Existing Business").

According to the British Venture Capital Association (BVCA)[3] UK venture capitalists invested £1.4 billion in 1990 in 1559 companies (compared to £20 million in 1979). The breakdown of these investments was:

❏ Start-ups 12% (26% of companies)

❏ Expansion investment 31% (41% of companies)

❏ 'Buy-outs' and 'buy-ins' 52% (26% of companies)

The most popular industry sector was consumer related businesses (35% of total invested), followed by technology related businesses (14% of total invested).

The South East and Greater London continued to be the most important investment regions, accounting for 61% of the amount invested.

2.4 The 'Equity gap' and LINC

Venture capitalists have substantial funds under management, which, together with the relatively fixed costs of investigating and setting up investments, has pushed them into seeking investments above significant threshold amounts. For example, the British Venture Capital Association (BVCA) lists 115 full members in the 1992 directory[3]; 79 of these state their minimum investment levels to be £200,000 or above. 12 state their minimum to be £100,000 or above. Of the 24 who will look at investments below £100,000, 12 are government bodies such as Development Boards or Enterprise Agencies. As other common sources of funds from banks and other lenders tend to be for amounts up to only £100,000, this has lead to the so-called 'equity-gap', for investment amounts from £100,000 to £250,000.

LINC

The Local Investment Networking Company – LINC – was formed to try and bridge this equity gap. As a business introduction service run by Local Enterprise Agencies, it attempts to match small businesses seeking funds, with potential investors, who have from £10,000 to £250,000 available for investment. Investors receive a monthly bulletin of opportunities available, submitted to LINC as business plans from small firms seeking finance.

2.5 Public equity – the USM

One source of capital for the developed small or medium sized firm is via a listing on a securities market, which allows shares in the company to be bought and sold by individuals and institutions. The Unlisted Securities Market was launched in 1980 to give smaller companies, with a minimum three year trading record, access to a stock market. This was followed in 1987 by the Third Market, aimed at regulating the existing 'over-the-counter' market, trading in higher risk shares of smaller or younger companies with a minimum of only one year's trading record.

The USM has proven to be a qualified success, with over 400 companies listed at the end of 1990. However its initial popularity is now waning; a listing is very expensive, with a minimum of around £100,000 costs for the simplest introduction method, and the market has not performed well for investors, ending its first decade of operation below its opening index of 100.

The Third Market did not last long, closing in 1990 when it was combined with the USM. This increased concerns that the Stock Market does not have a vehicle which closely meets the need of small firms, to raise new equity finance, or for owner-managers to realise some of the fruits of their labours by selling shares[4].

2.6 Clearing banks

After investment by owner-managers or private individuals, overdrafts and loans from a clearing bank are the next most popular form of small business finance.

Banks and the small firm

Until the end of the 1970s the major banks did not differentiate small businesses as a customer group, offering them two very basic products: standard overdrafts and loans.

The dramatic increase in the numbers of small businesses and the self-employed during the 1980s, stimulated the main banks to develop services specifically targeted at small firms. Barclays, Lloyds, Midland, National Westminster and other clearing banks have all now developed a range of products, and advisory services to more closely meet the varying needs of small business.

For example, National Westminster Bank offers free banking for the first year and a range of borrowing options: a Business Start-up Loan, with a fixed rate of interest and a possible capital repayment holiday for the first 6 months; a Business Development Loan for the growing business, with a capital repayment holiday for up to 2 years; or a more simple and flexible overdraft. In addition, they have an extensive network of small business advisory centres, offering personal advice and written information, and the bank is also a significant contributor of finance for research into the small firms sector.

More recently, the relationship between the major Banks and small firms has been given much attention by newspapers and politicians[5]. Small businesses have complained that banks have responded to the particular problems and stresses of the recession and high interest rates by using high-handed and unfair practices in their dealings with small firms. Complaints have focused on a number of issues including:

❐ *Bank charges and interest:* Small businesses are charged rates of interest on their borrowings, which vary widely from 3% to 10% over base rate, depending on the deal negotiated. A bank will also levy charges on a business account in line with the activity on the account. Associations of small firms, such as the Forum of Private Business, have complained that these charges are both unpredictable and often unjustifiably high.

❐ *Lack of support in problem times:* Small firms have also complained that banks tend to withdraw their support when it is most needed. Heavy handed attitudes towards small firms during times of difficulty have been contrasted to national advertising slogans implying a high level of understanding by banks towards their customers. The harsh reality is that overdrafts have been reduced or removed at the moment when a business needs them most. Whilst banks would justify their actions in minimising their exposure at times when the risk of maintaining a facility are increased, the problems encountered have lead to calls for a code of conduct between banks and small firms. The Forum of Private Business have gone further, calling for a written contract between banks and small business customers, which would operate on the same principle as points on a driving licence, making sure that overdrafts could not be removed without a recognised cause[5].

❐ *Advice and information:* Support given by banks has been criticised for its variable quality. There have been complaints that borrowing was encouraged when the 'enterprise culture' really got going in the mid-1980s, only to be unexpectedly curtailed in the more difficult 1990s. Problems have also surfaced over specific advice given by banks which has proven to be misleading, for instance over the credit ratings of customers.

Whilst many of these issues have been magnified by the particular strains of a recessionary economy, they do point to an underlying shift in the relationships between banks and small business. This has evolved from disinterested detachment prior to the

1970s, through an over-enthusiastic honeymoon in the 1980s, to a slightly disenchanted, uneasy alliance in the 1990s.

The Loan Guarantee Scheme (LGS)

For those small businesses not able to arrange a bank loan under normal policies, the government's Loan Guarantee Scheme can provide a guarantee of up to 80% of loans under £100,000 (as covered in Unit 6 'The Small Business Environment', 2.2 "Government Policy").

2.7 Public sector sources

There are a number of central and local government sources of finance for the small business which represent both equity and short and long term loan capital.

☐ *The Enterprise Allowance Scheme (EAS)*, operated by the Department of Employment pays an unemployed person £40 a week for a year if they become self-employed in their own business (as covered in Unit 6, 'The Small Business Environment', 2.2, "Government Policy").

☐ *British Technology Group (BTG)*[6] provides finance for innovative small firms requiring funds to develop new or existing products and ideas.

☐ *Development Agencies and Boards* have been set up to co-ordinate new and small business support in their areas. Agencies such as the Scottish Development Agency and the Welsh Development Agency have become significant sources of finance.

☐ *Local Enterprise Agencies* are co-ordinated under the 'Business in the Community' umbrella, to provide advice and funds for small enterprises, including equity finance.

☐ *EC funds* are also available in certain areas affected by the decline of a particular industry, such as coal mining and shipbuilding.

☐ *The Rural Development Commission* have limited funds available to promote small rural firms with specific projects or grants to convert premises.

☐ *Tourist Boards* encourage the growth of the tourist business, partly by offering loans and grants for specific projects likely to enhance the tourist trade in the UK.

☐ *The Prince's Youth Business Trust* is a charity which provides finance (as well as advice and training) to young people to set up and develop their own business. It is supported by funds from the EC, national and local government, as well as companies, and private individuals. The Trust has helped over 7000 businesses through a combination of loans and bursaries to unemployed people aged 18–25, or up to the age of 30 if they are disabled. In 1991/92, the Trust provided 2000 bursaries totalling £2.8 million, and 1500 low interest loans costing £3.8 million.

☐ *SMART, the Small firms Merit Award for Research and Technology*, offered under the Enterprise Initiative, is a package of advice and help for smaller businesses from the Department of Trade and Industry (see Unit 6 'The Small Business Environment', 4. 'Government Policy'). 180 awards, of up to £105,000 each, are offered through an annual competition. The object is to "inject financial assistance into viable ideas from small firms at just the critical point – when the idea is still at its embryonic stage and not yet mature enough to interest financiers".

2.8   Finance houses and leasing companies

An important source of either short or medium term asset finance is in the form of leasing and hire purchase. Both involve regular payments for the use of an asset, but with different ownership implications.

❏ *Leasing* allows a small firm to obtain the use of equipment, machinery or vehicles without owning them. Ownership is retained by the leasing company, although in many cases there is a purchase option at the end of the lease period.

❏ *Hire purchase* provides the immediate use of the asset and also ownership of it, provided that payments according to the agreement are made.

Finance houses are the main providers of hire purchase funds. They date back to the last century, when they were set up principally to provide finance for the purchase of railway wagons by colliery owners and coal merchants.

2.9   Factoring

Factoring is a specialist form of finance to provide working capital to young, under-capitalised businesses. A small firm, which grants credit terms to its customers, can soon have considerable sums of money tied up in unpaid invoices. Factoring is a method of releasing these funds; the factoring company takes responsibility for collection of debts and pays a percentage (usually up to 80%) of the value of the invoices to the issuing company. The company thus has immediate payment once an invoice is issued, although it pays for this service by not receiving the full value of the invoices.

The service is designed for firms up to seven years old, with an established turnover (over £250,000) and reliable debtors.

2.10   Export finance

The most important step in financing international trade is in ensuring full and prompt payment.

❏ *The Export Credits Guarantee Department (ECGD)* of the DTI provides credit insurance that gives cover in the event of non payment by an overseas customer. The ECGD offer a variety of insurance schemes, which a small firm can assign to a bank, or other lending body, in order to obtain export finance.

❏ *Export Houses* offer a wide range of services to exporters including finance.

3.   Control of financial resources

3.1   Financial problems

If the first hurdle for a small firm is to ensure the availability of the appropriate amount and type of funds, the next step is to optimise the use of those financial resources by effective planning and control.

The Bolton Committee were critical of many aspects of the financial management of small firms, reporting that information was "often so poor that management frequently learns of an impending crisis only with the appearance of the annual accounts, or following an urgent call from the bank manager"[7].

Fast growing small businesses have particular problems in controlling their finances. Growth brings frequent changes to the internal structures and external environment of a small firm. It is often difficult to ensure that financial control systems keep pace with the changing circumstances. For example, a small firm, which historically traded directly with consumer markets, expanded by setting up distributors both in the UK and overseas. This lead to the development of debtors, as the distributors were given credit, and a rapid increase in stocks which were needed to service the new outlets. The small firm did not have control systems in place to cope with these new demands and soon ran into liquidity problems.

The small business is likely to be confronted by a variety of financial problems as it advances through its life cycle. Figure 15.2 illustrates some of the potential issues in each stage:

Figure 15.2: The financial life cycle of a small firm

Stage	Likely sources of finance	Financial issues
Conception	Personal investment	Under capitalisation, because of inability to raise finance
Introduction	Bank loans, overdrafts	Control of costs and lack of information
Development	Hire purchase, leasing	'Overtrading', liquidity crisis
Growth	Venture capital	'Equity gap', appropriate information systems
Maturity	All sources	Weakening return on investment
Decline	Sale of business/ liquidation	Finance withdrawn. Tax issues if business is sold

In the early stages, the lack of track record can hinder raising the required money, and lead to an under capitalised business.

As the business begins to trade, it will have little experience on which to base forecasts for planning purposes, and vital information may therefore be lacking. Costs will be incurred as the company finds its feet, for which there may be inadequate control systems at this stage.

Once full development gets underway and sales grow, over trading can result, with debtors and stocks increasing rapidly as the negative cash flow builds up into a liquidity crisis.

If growth continues, and requires further funding through investment in equity, it may be difficult to raise the required amount if less than £250,000 because venture capitalists shy away from these 'small' investments.

Finally the business matures and although cash flow at this stage is positive, profitability levels off, and return on investment may worsen. As maturity turns to decline, the business may be sold, or go into liquidation; new partners may buy into the business in an attempt to kick it back into growth. Overdraft facilities and other renewable finance, may be withdrawn at this stage as confidence wanes. If the business is sold, taxation of any capital gain requires careful consideration by the vendor.

Is there any relief from this rather gloomy picture of a small firm staggering from one financial crisis to another? It would be easy to say that adequate forecasting and the appropriate control systems can minimise the problems. The reality is that most small firms do experience financial stress at various moments in their history. It is also true, however, that these problems are often exacerbated by inadequate planning and control.

3.2 Cash flow – debtors and stocks

Financial management in a small firm starts with the management of the cash flow. Cash is critical to survival, representing the lifeblood which enables all the activities of a firm to be undertaken.

It is easy for the fragile cash resources of a small business to become 'locked up' in unproductive areas, such as debtors, work in progress and finished stocks. Any areas where funds can become locked-up require effective management to minimise the extent of the 'lock-up'.

Debtors' control

Debtors can hurt a small business in two major ways. Firstly, they absorb cash and effectively increase the funding requirement of a small firm. Secondly, the longer a debt is alive, the greater the risk of a bad debt. Particularly in recessionary times, the risks of having invoices which go unpaid are high. The impact on a small firm can be disastrous, even causing the failure of the business in a domino effect as one firm falls after another.

These problems are not unique to small firms, but they can be accentuated by the smallness of an operating unit in any of the following ways:

❑ The costs of chasing slow payers or bad debts may be greater than the amount of money being pursued. This is a particular problem for companies with a large number of small customers.

For example, a small mail order firm sells products priced under £50 on a 30 day trial basis, as part of its marketing approach. It quickly generated over one thousand customers in this way, and found that considerable time and money had to be spent to control a sales ledger with this profile.

❑ The time taken to establish the credit worthiness of a potential customer may be longer than the sales process. Keenness to win an order, and not to jeopardise it by lengthy credit checks, may cause an owner-manager to accept imprudent credit risks.

For example, the owner-manager of a small manufacturing firm was short of custom and loosing money as production operatives and expensive equipment stood idle. A large order from a company not previously known to the owner-manager looked like their saviour: it returned the factory back to full capacity following a hasty negotiation. Unfortunately the order increased the firm's cash problems, as the customer had liquidity difficulties of their own and proved to be an extremely reluctant payer.

❑ A small firm may not have the control systems to identify individual debtor problems before they become critical. An essential part of any management accounting system is an analysis of debtors by their age, as well as their amount, so that appropriate action can be triggered to chase up slow payers. This rigorous pursuit of payment, which gradually escalates the tone of requests from polite reminder to threat of legal action is an unfortunate but essential element in small business management today. To be done effectively, accurate information on customer's indebtedness is required on a very regular basis.

For example, a small business set up a debtor control system using a series of standard letters which were sent to customers once the age of their debt passed a certain number of days. These letters were triggered by information from the computerised accounting system which produced an aged debtor-analysis. The firm was not large enough to employ full time accounting staff, and therefore used an external book keeper who came in near the end of each month to process invoices and payments. Unfortunately this system generated considerable confusion and aggravation, as the information on customer payments was invariably out of date. Customers became irritated by threatening letters after they had actually paid. Also, so much time was wasted chasing payments received but not entered into the system, that serious problems were not attended to as they developed.

Management of stock

Stock represents a poor investment for a small firm's financial resources. Stock surpluses earn no money, and risk deterioration if not used quickly. However the consequences of running short of stock can be even more punitive; if orders go unfulfilled, or are even lost because of stock shortages, the effect on the cash flow can be disastrous. Stock management is therefore about balance, and the *optimisation* of resources; weighing up the risk of running out versus the costs of playing it too safe. Stocks need controlling in three areas:

❑ *Raw material stocks* represent what a manufacturer needs to produce its own products and services.

❑ *Work-in-progress (WIP)* is stock which is currently being worked on, but is not yet saleable as finished items.

❑ *Finished stock* is ready for sale, but either awaiting shipment to a customer, or unsold.

Keeping all these types of stock to an optimum level is a difficult balancing act, particularly in industries where demand is unpredictable, and often short lived. The fashion and toy industries, for example, are notorious for developing severe cash problems because of the difficulties of stock management. Fast moving clothes can suddenly become virtually unsaleable as fashions change. Toy products still on the shelf after the Christmas rush may have to wait until the following Christmas season to be sold.

Liquid assets and current liabilities

A good measure of the health of a small firm's cash position comes from an estimate of its liquid assets and current liabilities: its assets which can quickly be turned into, or are already represented by, cash, and liabilities which should be paid in the short term (12 months). Figure 15.3 illustrates the items normally found in such an estimate.

Figure 15.3: Liquid assets and current liabilities

	Current period	Prior period
Assets:		
STOCK plus WIP	_____	_____
DEBTORS	_____	_____
CASH IN BANK	_____	_____
TOTAL LIQUID ASSETS **(A)**	_____	_____
Liabilities:		
CREDITORS - trade suppliers	_____	_____
- VAT/PAYE/NIC	_____	_____
SHORT TERM BORROWINGS		
- overdraft	_____	_____
TOTAL CURRENT LIABILITIES **(B)**	_____	_____

If a small business's Current Liabilities (B in figure 15.3) exceed the total of Liquid Assets (A in figure 15.3), then problems may be just around the corner.

3.3   Costs and profits

Profitability and cash flow are sometimes confused by owner-managers ,struggling to come to grips with the financial management of their business.

Profits and losses are theoretical figures representing the difference between the total earnings (whether received, or not), and the total expenditure (whether paid for, or not), incurred by a small firm in achieving those earnings. Profits or losses should, of course, be translated into cash surpluses or deficits, but this may take some time.

Profitability can be improved in a large variety of ways, but they can be classified under three headings:

❐ reduction of costs;

❐ increase of sales prices; and

❐ increase of sales volume.

Costs

Costs are further classified as fixed or variable.

❐ *Fixed costs* remain unchanged in the short term, however much is sold by a business. They are fixed in the sense of not varying with the volume of goods or services sold. Fixed costs are the overheads of a business, comprising such expenses as management and administrative salaries and wages, premises costs, and the costs of finance and depreciation of assets.

In the longer term, fixed costs do of course vary. The resources represented by the overheads of a business can only cope with so much before they need to be increased. People and premises, for instance, can only manage up to a certain capacity before new resources have to be added.

☐ *Variable costs* do change directly in line with how much is sold. They are variable in the sense of varying according to the volume of goods or services sold. Variable costs include the raw materials used in production by a manufacturer, or the costs of stock sold by a retailer.

☐ *The gross margin* of a business represents its sales revenue less any variable costs. A careful identification of the gross margin by significant product lines is an important cost control and pricing tool. It is also used to estimate the break-even point of a business, as this is reached when the gross margin generated by sales is sufficient to cover the fixed costs of the business. (See Information Bank Unit 14, "Marketing", 5, 'Price' for more detailed explanation of break-even calculations. This was also covered in Assignment 1, Task 1.6 Assessing the Risk.)

Managing the cost base of a small firm involves the identification of the types of costs, setting budgets for them and monitoring the results compared to the forecasts. The Bolton Committee were not impressed by the practices they observed in small firms, commenting that "lack of costing data may make it impossible to gauge the effects on profits of different levels or courses of action, especially where there is a variable product mix"[7]. In other words, basic data on the profitability of one product or service, compared to another, may not be available, which causes planning problems. For example, a small firm with limited resources will wish to put its marketing effort behind its most profitable product or service first. If it has no information on the gross margin of its different products, then a decision cannot be made in this way.

Prices and volume

Profitability is also influenced by prices charged and sales volumes achieved. These also benefit from budgetary control and monitoring. They are however most influenced by marketing decisions, and have been considered in Unit 14 "Marketing".

4. Financial analysis

4.1 Management accounts and forecasting:

Small firms differ greatly in their approach to the provision of accounting information, and the use of forecasts and budgets for planning and control of the business. Some studies suggest that there is a considerable gulf between small 'entrepreneurial' companies aiming for high growth, and 'firms' who have no great ambitions to grow other than that required to survive[8]. Whilst there are less differences between the provision of historical accounting information, the 'entrepreneurial' small firms make much greater use of forecasted financial information than the 'passive' firms. This illustrates the greater perceived need for forecasting during times of change, than during periods of relatively stable sales.

The three most widely used financial summaries are the profit and loss account, the cash flow, and the balance sheet.

❑ *The profit and loss account* shows how a business is doing in terms of sales and costs - and the difference between them of profit or losses. It is a moving picture and can be used to forecast, and monitor, results on a monthly basis or for a longer period.

❑ *The cash flow* is perhaps the most important summary for a young firm as it indicates the movement of cash into and out of the business. Similar to the profit and loss account, it differs in the important respect of reflecting credit given to customers and received from suppliers, as well as the amount of money invested in a business, or borrowed by it. Because of their importance, cash flows are used on a very regular weekly or monthly basis.

❑ *The balance sheet* is a snapshot, rather than a moving picture, as it represents a summary of what money has been spent by a business, and what it has been spent on. It is usually an annual summary of the use and sources of funds in a company.

4.2 The 21 steps to profit/loss, cash flow and balance sheet forecasts

Although they are different forms of financial analysis, a series of steps can be used to build up a set of forecasts of profit and loss, cash flow, and the balance sheet. This can be done manually, but a computer spread sheet is a highly useful tool, as it allows for regular modifications and sensitivity analysis (for example to project the effect of a drop in sales or a rise in costs).

The following 21 steps are explained and a worked example of a fictional company, Kal Kulate Ltd, given.

Note: Each *step* (on the following pages) can be related to the Profit and Loss, Cash Flow and Balance Sheets of Kal Kulate Ltd on pages 400, 401 and 402.

Profit and loss

STEP 1

Estimate likely sales turnover for the forecast period, based on historical precedent and research in the market place. Also work out any *VAT element* on those sales. (Output VAT.)

For Kal Kulate Ltd., this was estimated as follows:

Example: Kal Kulate Ltd – Step 1			
Month	*Net Sales*	*Output VAT*	*Gross Sales*
	£	£	£
1	19000	3325	22325
2	13000	2275	15275
3	14000	2450	16450
4	20500	3588	24088
5	15500	2713	18213
6	20000	3500	23500
7	15500	2713	18213
8	17500	3063	20563
9	17000	2975	19975
10	18000	3150	21150
11	21000	3675	24675
12	20500	3588	24088
TOTAL	211500	37015	248515

STEP 2

Work out what *materials* will be used to make the goods needed to achieve the sales estimated in step 1. This can only be accurately calculated by taking the opening stock, adding all the purchases in the period, and deducting the closing stock (see step 14). Although this is done on a regular basis to verify actual profits, forecasts usually assume a percentage usage based on historical data.

Example: Kal Kulate Ltd – Step 2
For example, Kal Kulate had an established pattern of materials costing 50% of the net sales value. So sales of £19000 in January would require £9500 (50%) worth of materials to make them.

STEP 3

Work out the *wages* and other employment costs of those involved directly in production. This should include gross wages, plus employer's national insurance.

Example: Kal Kulate Ltd – Step 3

Kal Kulate employed 3 Full time and 2 part time operatives who together were estimated to cost as follows:

	£
Gross wages	33000
Employers national insurance	3000
Total (12 months)	36000
Total (1 month)	3000

STEP 4

Work out the *overheads* of running the business. These will normally be the fixed costs and include:

❐ the *salaries* of directors and non-production staff

❐ rent, rates, insurance and other *premises* costs

❐ telephone, postage, printing, stationery, accounting and other office costs

❐ advertising, exhibitions, selling, commissions and other *publicity* costs.

Note: Some of these costs will attract VAT which needs to be added to the cash flow, but excluded in the profit and loss account.

For ease of calculation later on, it is wise to group costs where possible into those which do, and those which do not, attract VAT.

It is also easier to identify significant costs at this stage which may be on a different payments cycle to other costs, as this will make transference of those items to the cash flow simpler. (For example rent, which has no VAT, and which is often paid quarterly, can be identified separately from other premises costs, some of which include VAT, and are paid on a monthly basis.)

Example: Kal Kulate Ltd – Step 4

Kal Kulate grouped their fixed costs as follows:

	£
Salaries of director and office manager	24000
Rent	12000
Rates and insurance	6000
Other costs including energy, stationery, postage, accounting and sundry costs	12000
Publicity costs including advertising and exhibitions	6000
Total (12 months)	60000
Total (1 month)	5000

(Salaries, rent, rates and insurance do not attract VAT for cash flow purposes.)

STEP 5

Calculate interest on borrowings and other bank charges.

Interest and bank charges will clearly vary with borrowing levels, usage of the bank account and national interest rates which will not be known at this stage. An estimate based on the likely average level of borrowing and known interest rates can be made, which should be kept pessimistic as change in this area can be swift.

Example: Kal Kulate Ltd – Step 5

Kal Kulate's overdraft was thought to average up to £15000 with 15% p.a. interest so that the following allowance was made:

	£
Interest	2250
Bank charges	750
Total (12 months)	3000
Total (1 month)	250

STEP 6

Depreciation is calculated by taking the expected life of the fixed assets of the business and 'writing them off' progressively over that period, by making a charge to the profit and loss account.

Example: Kal Kulate Ltd – Step 6

Depreciation was based on new assets of £18000 (plus VAT at 17.5% of £3150)

These were depreciated over 3 years, giving an annual depreciation charge of £6000, or £500 per month.

Cash flow

STEP 7

Work out how quickly sales will be turned into cash, that is when debtors are going to pay their invoices. Receipts from customers include any VAT which has been invoiced to them.

Example: Kal Kulate Ltd – Step 7

Kal Kulate's customers were invoiced on 30 days credit. In practice most took longer than this, and 60 days were allowed for payment in the cash flow. In other words, it was assumed that January's gross sales would be paid for in March, February's in April and so on. The receipts at the beginning of the year in January and February were November and December's sales of the previous year which were both £20000 + VAT. (£23500.)

STEP 8

Work out when overhead costs and interest will actually have to be paid for. Some costs are paid for in the same month, for example salaries and wages. Others are paid on a regular credit basis, for example materials used, and other overhead costs. Some important overheads are paid quarterly, for example rent.

Example: Kal Kulate Ltd – Step 8

The pattern of Kal Kulate's payments were as follows:

Materials purchased, publicity and other costs – 60 days

Salaries and wages – same month

Rent – quarterly (March, June, Oct, Dec)

Rates and insurance – same month by monthly standing order

Interest and bank charges – quarterly (March, June, Oct, Dec)

For example:

In January and February, purchases of materials used in November and December of the previous year are paid for. In March, purchases of materials used in January are paid for and so on.

Publicity and other costs are ongoing costs, estimated to be the same each month. In January, the costs incurred in November of the previous year are paid for; in February, the costs from December are paid for and so on.

STEP 9

Work our the VAT paid on invoices for overhead costs. Some purchases attract VAT, which has to be added to the amount when it is paid. Although salaries, wages rent, rates and insurance do not attract VAT, most other costs do.

Example: Kal Kulate Ltd – Step 9

Kal Kulate paid VAT on their purchases of materials and on their publicity and other costs. VAT paid on these purchases was therefore worked out at 17.5% and included as a separate item.

For example in January £10000 of materials and £1500 of publicity and other costs were paid for. As the invoices would have had VAT added, the payments must include this amount (£11500 x 17.5% = £2013)

(It can be added to the individual amounts, or, as in Kal Kulate's cash flow, noted as a separate line.)

STEP 10

Work out how much VAT is due to be paid to H M Customs and Excise on the quarterly returns. This is calculated by totalling the *output* vat added to sales invoiced in the quarter and totalling all the *input* vat added to purchases invoiced to you in the same quarter. the difference between the total Output VAT and the Input VAT is paid to the government in the month following the end of the quarter.

Example: Kal Kulate Ltd – Step 10

Kal Kulate's VAT calculation looked like this:

	Jan–March	*April–June*	*July–Sept*	*Oct–Dec*
	£	£	£	£
VAT – outputs	8050	9801	8751	10413
VAT – inputs				
Materials used	4025	4900	4375	5206
Publicity & other costs	788	788	788	788
Capital equipment (VAT element)	3150			
Total inputs	7963	5688	5163	5994
VAT due	87	4113	3588	4419
	(Due April)	(Due July)	(Due Oct.)	(Due Jan of following year)

Example: Kal Kulate Ltd – Step 10 continued

Output VAT represents the VAT element on the sales invoiced in the period. (For example see Step 1 VAT: Jan = £3325, Feb = £2275, March = £2450, so the total Jan–March = £8050)

Input VAT represents 17.5% on the costs of materials, publicity and other costs, on receipt of invoices not when they are paid. (For example see step 2: Materials used in Jan. = £9500, Feb. = £6500, March = £7000. Total for the period Jan–March = £23000 x 17.5% VAT = £4025.)

VAT Due represents the difference between output and input VAT. It is payable one month after the quarter end, which in Kal Kulate's case was April, July, October and January (following year).

(No VAT was payable in January of this year, as Kal Kulate only registered for VAT at this time).

STEP 11

Add in any capital purchases, including VAT, which are to be paid. If they are to be financed by hire purchase, then put the deposit and the repayments in the cash flow.

Example: Kal Kulate Ltd – Step 11

Kal Kulate purchased £18000 plus £3150 VAT worth of equipment from its working capital, so this appears as a lump sum of £21150 in the month of January.

STEP 12

Calculate the monthly cash flow by subtracting total payments from total receipts for the month.

Then work out an opening and closing balance for each month which represents the cumulative cash position of the business.

Example: Kal Kulate Ltd – Step 12

Kal Kulate starts with a clean sheet as it is a new limited company formed from the on going trading of a sole trader. The opening balance is nil, as no cash is transferred, but during the first month (January) receipts from debtors total £23500. The total of payments out, including £21150 on capital equipment, is £40163. So the cash flow for the month is negative (–£16663). The closing balance of January is the opening balance for February. There is a positive cash flow of £4487 during the month of February, so that February's closing balance is –£12176 (–£16663 – £4487 = –£12176). This negative position is effectively Kal Kulate's overdraft at the bank.

The balance sheet – end of year

STEP 13

Work out the end of year value of fixed assets by taking away the depreciation charge from the total fixed asset costs.

Example: Kal Kulate Ltd – Step 13	
	£
Fixed assets costs, excluding VAT	18000
Depreciation during year	6000
	———
Net balance sheet value	12000

STEP 14

Stocks are entered into the balance sheet at cost, less any provisions for damaged, or slow moving and obsolete stock.

Example: Kal Kulate Ltd – Step 14			
Kal Kulate valued their stocks at the beginning and end of the year to verify not only the closing value of stocks, but also the materials used during the year (in Step 2). The company's policy was to hold approximately one month's usage of stocks, and the forecast position was as follows:			
Opening stock(Jan)	Purchases	Closing Stock(Dec)	Materials used
£10000	£106000	£10250	£105750

STEP 15

Estimate the total amount, including VAT, owed to you by customers at the end of the period. These debtors should be reduced by any debts where there is a good chance they will not be paid.

Example: Kal Kulate Ltd – Step 15	
Kal Kulate assumed they would have 2 months of debtors at the year end; i.e. sales for November and December would not be paid so that debtors would be:	
	£
November sales	24675
December sales	24088
	———
Total	48763

STEP 16

Estimate the total amount owing to trade suppliers, including VAT. This liability is entered as trade creditors.

Example: Kal Kulate Ltd – Step 16

Kal Kulate assumed they would pay for materials purchased 2 months after purchase; i.e. at the end of December, they would owe for materials used in November and December + VAT, so that trade creditors would be

	£
November	9000 + VAT
December	8500 + VAT
Total	17500 + VAT = £20563

STEP 17

Estimate how much money is owed to other creditors for other supplies, for example telephone, electricity, office supplies. Also include any tax collected but not yet paid, for example VAT, PAYE and NIC.

Example: Kal Kulate Ltd – Step 17

At the end of December, Kal Kulate estimated they would still owe for November and December purchases and the October – December VAT quarter.

	£	
Other costs November	1500	+ VAT
December	1500	+ VAT
	3000	+ VAT = 3525
VAT – Oct - Dec		
(see step 10)		= 4419
Total		7944

STEP 18

Estimate any borrowings from banks and other sources such as overdrafts or loans. For an overdraft, this should be the figure shown as the cash flow projection.

Example: Kal Kulate Ltd – Step 18

Kal Kulate's cash flow showed a negative cash position of £7714 at the end of December which effectively represented their overdraft.

STEP 19

Calculate 'Net Current Assets' of the business by deducting current liabilities from current assets.

Current assets (Step 14 + Step 15) represent the assets of a business which can be realised in the short term – normally within 12 months.

Current liabilities (Step 16 + Step 17 + Step 18) represent what the business owes, and can be made to pay for, in the short term – normally the amounts due within 12 months.

> **Example: Kal Kulate Ltd – Step 19**
>
> Kal Kulate's current assets of £59013 (stock of £10250 and debtors of £48763), less their current liabilities of £36220 (trade creditors of £20562, other creditors of £7944, and a bank overdraft of £7714) gave net current assets of £22793.

STEP 20

Calculate 'Net Assets' by adding Fixed Assets to Net Current Assets. This represents one measure of the worth of a business.

> **Example: Kal Kulate Ltd – Step 20**
>
> Kal Kulate's fixed assets totalled £12000 (£18000 less £6000 depreciation) which when added to their net current assets (£22793) gave a net asset position of £34793.

STEP 21

Add in share capital – the amount paid for the shares of the company. Add in 'reserves' of profits (or losses) retained in the company. (This figure should balance with the net assets when added to the share capital.)

Together these make up the 'Capital and Reserves' of the company, which represents what would theoretically be left to distribute to shareholders should the company be wound up at the balance sheet date (it is therefore sometimes referred to as 'Shareholders Funds'.)

> **Example: Kal Kulate Ltd – Step 21**
>
> Kal Kulate was set up with £5000 capital subscribed for shares. This does not appear in the cash flow forecast, as it was put into the company before the beginning of the forecast period.
>
> The reserves carried forward represent this year's profit, plus profits retained in the business since it was started. In this forecast balance sheet, it is a balancing figure which, when added to the share capital, equals the total net assets of £34793.

Example: Kal Kulate Ltd: Profit and Loss and Cash Flow

Step number		Jan	Feb	March	April	May	June
	PROFIT AND LOSS						
1	**Sales:**						
1	Gross	22,325	15,275	16,450	24,088	18,213	23,500
1	VAT	3,325	2,275	2,450	3,588	2,713	3,500
1	Net	19,000	13,000	14,000	20,500	15,500	20,000
2	**Materials used: (50%)**	9,500	6,500	7,000	10,250	7,750	10,000
3	Production wages	3,000	3,000	3,000	3,000	3,000	3,000
	Gross profit	6,500	3,500	4,000	7,250	4,750	7,000
4	**OVERHEADS:**						
4	Salaries	2,000	2,000	2,000	2,000	2,000	2,000
4	Rent	1,000	1,000	1,000	1,000	1,000	1,000
4	Rates & insurance	500	500	500	500	500	500
4	Other costs	1,000	1,000	1,000	1,000	1,000	1,000
4	Publicity	500	500	500	500	500	500
	TOTAL OVERHEADS	5,000	5,000	5,000	5,000	5,000	5,000
5	Bank charges and interest	250	250	250	250	250	250
6	Depreciation	500	500	500	500	500	500
	PROFIT/–LOSS	750	–2,250	–1,750	1,500	–1,000	1,250
	CASH FLOW						
7	RECEIPTS^A	23,500	23,500	22,325	15,275	16,450	24,088
8	**PAYMENTS:**						
8	Purchase of materials	10,000	10,000	9,500	6,500	7,000	10,250
8	Salaries and wages	5,000	5,000	5,000	5,000	5,000	5,000
8	Rent	—	—	3,000	—	—	3,000
8	Rates and insurance	500	500	500	500	500	500
8	Publicity and other costs	1,500	1,500	1,500	1,500	1,500	1,500
8	Interest	—	—	750	—	—	750
9	VAT PAID	2,013	2,013	1,925	1,400	1,488	2,056
10	VAT DUE	—	—	—	3,287	—	—
11	CAPITAL	21,150					
	TOTAL REPAYMENTS^B	40,163	19,013	22,175	14,987	15,488	23,056
12	CASH FLOW (A–B)	–16,663	4,487	150	288	962	1,032
12	OPENING BALANCE	—	–16,663	–12,176	–12,026	–11,738	–10,766
12	CLOSING BALANCE	–16,663	–12,176	–12,026	–11,738	–10,776	–9,744

July	Aug	Sept	Oct	Nov	Dec	Total (12 months)
18,213	20,563	19,975	21,150	24,675	24,088	248,515
2,713	3,063	2,975	3,150	3,675	3,588	37,015
15,500	17,500	17,000	18,000	21,000	20,500	211,500
7,750	8,750	8,500	9,000	10,500	10,250	105,750
3,000	3,000	3,000	3,000	3,000	3,000	36,00
4,750	5,750	5,500	6,000	7,500	7,250	69,750
2,000	2,000	2,000	2,000	2,000	2,000	24,000
1,000	1,000	1,000	1,000	1,000	1,000	12,000
500	500	500	500	500	500	6,000
1,000	1,000	1,000	1,000	1,000	1,000	12,000
500	500	500	500	500	500	6,000
5,000	5,000	5,000	5,000	5,000	5,000	60,000
250	250	250	250	250	250	3,000
500	500	500	500	500	500	6,000
−1000	—	−250	250	1,750	1,500	750
18,213	23,500	18,213	20,563	19,975	21,150	
7,750	10,000	7,750	8,750	8,500	9,000	
5,000	5,000	5,000	5,000	5,000	5,000	
—	—	3,000	—	—	3,000	
500	500	500	500	500	500	
1,500	1,500	1,500	1,500	1,500	1,500	
—	—	750	—	—	750	
1,619	2,013	1,619	1,794	1,750	1,838	
4,113	—	—	3,588	—	—	
20,482	19,013	20,119	21,132	17,250	21,588	
−2,269	4,487	−1,906	−569	2,725	−438	
−9,744	−12,013	−7,526	−9,432	−10,001	−7,276	
−12,013	−7,526	−9,432	−10,001	−7,276	−7,714	

EXAMPLE: KAL KULATE LTD.
FORECAST BALANCE SHEET

	Step no		£	£
FIXED ASSETS		cost	18000	
		depreciation	−6000	
	13	book value		12000
CURRENT ASSETS	14	stocks	10250	
	15	debtors	48763	
			59013	
CURRENT LIABILITIES	16	trade creditors	20562	
	17	other creditors	7944	
	18	bank overdraft	7714	
			36220	
NET CURRENT ASSETS	19		22793	
NET ASSETS	20		34793	
CAPITAL AND RESERVES				
	21	share capital	5000	
	21	reserves	29793	
	21		34793	

5. References and suggested reading

5.1 References and further information

1. Mason, C and Lloyd, P, "New Manufacturing Firms In A Prosperous UK Sub-Region: The Case Of South Hampshire," in Scott, M et al (eds), *Small Firms Growth and Development,* Gower, 1986. Page 26 draws some interesting comparisons with other studies.

2. For a summary of the effects of BES investment see Stanworth, J and Gray, C, *Bolton 20 Years On: The Small Firm in the 1990s,* PCP Ltd, 1991, Chapter 6 pages 129–134.

3. British Venture Capital Association (BVCA) *Directory 1992.* The BVCA Directory is available (free of charge) from The British Venture Capital Association. (Telephone number 071-233-5212) 3 Catherine Place, London SW1E 6DX.

4. See Stanworth, J and Gray, C, '*Bolton 20 Years On: The Small Firm in the 1990s,* PCP, 1991, Chapter 6.

5. This and other aspects of the relationship between banks and small firms was reported in *The Guardian,* Monday September 16th, 1991, page 12.

6. For further information contact, BTG, 101 Newington Causeway, London SE1 6BU. (Telephone 071-403-6666)

7. Bolton Report, *Committee of Inquiry on Small Firms,* HMSO, Cmnd. 4811, 1971.

8. See Hutchinson, P and Ray, G, "Surviving the Financial Stress of Small Enterprise Growth", in Curran, J et al (eds.) *The Survival of the Small Firm,* Vol 1, Gower, 1986.

5.2   Recommended further reading

Barrow, C and Barrow, P, *The Business Plan Workbook,* Kogan Page, 1988. especially Phase 5: "Forecasting Results" and Phase 6: "Business Controls".

Stanworth, J and Gray, C, *Bolton 20 Years On: The Small Firm in the 1990s,* PCP, 1991 Chapters 4 "Banks and the Provision of Finance to Small Firms" Chapter 6 "The Small Firm Equity Gap Since Bolton".

Barrow, C, *The New Small Business Guide,* BBC Banks, 1989. Section 6 "Raising the Money".

Index